new interchange

English for international communication

Jack C. Richards
Tay Lesley

INTRO

teacher's edition

PUBLISHED BY THE PRESS SYNDICATE OF THE UNIVERSITY OF CAMBRIDGE
The Pitt Building, Trumpington Street, Cambridge, United Kingdom

CAMBRIDGE UNIVERSITY PRESS
The Edinburgh Building, Cambridge CB2 2RU, UK
40 West 20th Street, New York, NY 10011–4211, USA
10 Stamford Road, Oakleigh, VIC 3166, Australia
Ruiz de Alarcón 13, 28014 Madrid, Spain
Dock House, The Waterfront, Cape Town 8001, South Africa

http://www.cambridge.org

First published 2000
2nd printing 2001

New Interchange Intro Teacher's Edition has been developed from *Interchange* Intro Teacher's Manual, first published by Cambridge University Press in 1995.

Printed in the United States of America

Typeface New Century Schoolbook *System* QuarkXPress® [AH]

A catalog record for this book is available from the British Library

ISBN 0 521 77399 7 Intro Student's Book
ISBN 0 521 77398 9 Intro Student's Book A
ISBN 0 521 77397 0 Intro Student's Book B
ISBN 0 521 77390 3 Intro Workbook
ISBN 0 521 77389 X Intro Workbook A
ISBN 0 521 77388 1 Intro Workbook B
ISBN 0 521 77391 1 Intro Teacher's Edition
ISBN 0 521 77387 3 Intro Teacher's Manual
ISBN 0 521 77386 5 Intro Class Audio Cassettes
ISBN 0 521 77385 7 Intro Student's Audio Cassette A
ISBN 0 521 77384 9 Intro Student's Audio Cassette B
ISBN 0 521 77375 X Intro Class Audio CDs
ISBN 0 521 77374 1 Intro Student's Audio CD A
ISBN 0 521 77373 3 Intro Student's Audio CD B
ISBN 0 521 96802 X Intro Audio Sampler

Also available
ISBN 0 521 55574 4 Intro Video (NTSC)
ISBN 0 521 62964 0 Intro Video (PAL)
ISBN 0 521 62965 9 Intro Video (SECAM)
ISBN 0 521 55573 6 Intro Video Activity Book
ISBN 0 521 55572 8 Intro Video Teacher's Guide
ISBN 0 521 95017 1 Intro Video Sampler
ISBN 0 521 00008 4 CD ROM (PC & MAC format)
ISBN 0 521 77383 0 Intro Lab Guide
ISBN 0 521 77382 2 Intro Lab Cassettes
ISBN 0 521 46759 4 Placement Test (valid for New Interchange and Interchange)
ISBN 0 521 80575 9 Teacher-Training Video with Video Manual

Forthcoming
ISBN 0 521 62882 2 New Interchange/Passages Placement and Evaluation Package

Book design, art direction, and layout services: Adventure House, NYC
Illustrators: Adventure House, Daisy de Puthod, Randy Jones, Wally Neibart, Roger Roth, Bill Thomson, Daniel Vasconcellos, Sam Viviano; Adam Hurwitz *(Tests)*
Photo researchers: Sylvia P. Bloch, Adventure House

Contents

Introduction

THE NEW EDITION

New Interchange is the second edition of *Interchange*, one of the world's most successful and popular English courses. *New Interchange* incorporates suggestions from around the world, offered by students and teachers using the first edition. Some major changes include many new Conversations, Snapshots, and Readings; more extensive Grammar Focus models and activities; a greater variety and amount of listening materials; and extensive changes to the **Teacher's Edition** and **Workbook**. The Student's Book includes fresh new content, more visuals to introduce vocabulary, more opportunities to build fluency, and up-to-date art and design.

New Interchange is a multi-level course in English as a second or foreign language for young adults and adults. The course covers the four skills of listening, speaking, reading, and writing, as well as improving pronunciation and building vocabulary. Particular emphasis is placed on listening and speaking. The primary goal of the course is to teach the ability to communicate according to the situation, purpose, and roles of the participants. The language used in *New Interchange* is American English; however, the course reflects the fact that English is the major language of international communication and is not limited to any one country, region, or culture. The first level is designed for beginners and for learners needing a thorough review of basic structures and vocabulary. It provides a smooth transition to the remaining levels in the series.

COURSE LENGTH

Each full level of *New Interchange* contains between 70 and 120 hours of class instruction time. For classes where more time is available, the Teacher's Edition gives detailed suggestions for Optional Activities to extend each unit. Where less time is available, the amount of time spent on Interchange Activities, Readings, Optional Activities, and the Workbook can be reduced.

Each split edition contains approximately 35 to 60 hours of classroom material. The Student's Book, Workbook, and Student's Audio Cassettes or CDs are available in split editions.

COURSE COMPONENTS

The **Student's Book** contains 16 six-page units, each divided into two topical/functional "cycles," as well as four review units. At the back of the book are 16 communication tasks, called "Interchange Activities," and summaries of grammar and vocabulary taught in each unit.

The full-color **Teacher's Edition** features detailed teaching instructions directly across from the Student's Book pages, along with audio scripts, cultural notes, answer keys, and optional activities. At the back of the Teacher's Edition are instructions for Interchange Activities, an Optional Activities Index, a Workbook Answer Key, and four photocopiable Achievement Tests with audio scripts and answer keys.

The **Workbook** provides a variety of reading, writing, and spelling exercises to reinforce the grammar and vocabulary taught in the Student's Book. Each six-page unit follows the same teaching sequence as the Student's Book; some exercises recycle teaching points from previous units in the context of the new topic. The Workbook can be used for classwork or homework.

The **Class Audio Program**, available on cassette or CD, is intended for classroom use. The Conversations, Grammar Focus models, Pronunciation exercises, and Listening activities in the Student's Book are all recorded naturally with a variety of native and some nonnative accents. The Class Audio Program for this level of *New Interchange* also provides recordings of all Readings and of many Snapshots and Word Power sections. Recorded exercises are indicated with the symbol .

The **Student's Audio Program** provides opportunities for self-study. It contains recordings of all Student's Book exercises marked with the symbol , except for the Listening tasks, which are intended only for classroom use. These appear exclusively on the Class Audio Program and are indicated by the symbol CLASS AUDIO ONLY.

The **Video** offers entertaining dramatic or documentary sequences that review and extend language learned in each unit of the Student's Book. The **Video Activity Book** contains comprehension, conversation, and language practice activities, and the **Video Teacher's Guide** provides instructional support, answer keys, and photocopiable transcripts of the video sequences.

The **CD-ROM**, appropriate for home or laboratory use, offers a wealth of additional practice. Each of the 16 units is based on a sequence from the Video. Four tests help students monitor their progress.

The **Placement Test** helps determine the most appropriate level of *New Interchange* for incoming students. A booklet contains the four-skills test on photocopiable pages, as well as instructions for test administration and scoring. A cassette accompanies the listening section of the test.

The **Lab Cassettes** provide self-study activities in the areas of grammar, vocabulary, pronunciation, listening, and functional use of English. The **Lab Guide** contains photocopiable pages that guide students through the activities.

The **Teacher-Training Video** offers clear guidance for teaching each section of the Student's Book and professional development activities appropriate for individual or group use.

APPROACH AND METHODOLOGY

New Interchange teaches students how to use English for everyday situations and purposes related to school, social life, work, and leisure. The underlying philosophy is that learning a second or foreign language is more rewarding, meaningful, and effective when the language is used for authentic communication. Throughout *New Interchange,* students are presented with natural and useful language. In addition, students have the opportunity to personalize the language they learn, make use of their own knowledge and experiences, and express their ideas and opinions.

Adult and International Content

New Interchange deals with contemporary topics that are of high interest and relevance to both students and teachers. The topics have been selected for their interest to both homogeneous and heterogeneous classes.

Integrated Syllabus

New Interchange has an integrated, multi-skills syllabus that links topics, communicative functions, and grammar. Grammar – seen as an essential component of second and foreign language proficiency and competence – is always presented communicatively, with controlled accuracy-based activities leading to fluency-based communicative practice. In this way, there is a link between grammatical form and communicative function. The syllabus is carefully graded, with a gradual progression of teaching items.

Enjoyable and Useful Learning Activities

A variety of interesting and enjoyable activities provide thorough individual student practice and enable learners to apply the language they learn. The course also makes extensive use of information-gap tasks; role plays; and pair, group, and whole class activities. Task-based and information-sharing activities provide a maximum amount of student-generated communication. These variations in learning activities allow for a change of pace within lessons while also making the course ideal for both large and small classes, as *New Interchange* gives students a greater amount of individual practice and interaction with others in the classroom.

Focus on Productive and Receptive Skills

In *New Interchange*, both production and comprehension form the basis of language learning. Students' productive skills are developed through speaking and writing tasks, and their receptive skills are developed through listening and reading. The course recognizes that students can understand language that is at a higher level than they can produce, and this prepares them to make the transition from the classroom to the real world.

Teacher's and Learners' Roles

The teacher's role in *New Interchange* is to present and model new learning items; however, during pair work, group work, and role play activities, the teacher's role is that of a facilitator. Here the teacher's primary function is to prepare students for an activity and then let them complete it using their own language resources. During this phase, the teacher gives minimum informal feedback to students but also encourages maximum student participation.

The learners' role in *New Interchange* is to participate actively and creatively in learning, using both the materials they study in the course and their own knowledge and language resources. Students are treated as intelligent adults with ideas and opinions of their own. Students learn through interacting with others in pair, group, or whole class activities and draw on previous learning as well as their own communicative skills.

Teacher-friendly and Student-friendly Presentation

New Interchange is easy to follow, with clearly identified teaching points, carefully organized and sequenced units, comfortable pacing, and a variety of stimulating and enjoyable learning tasks.

SYLLABUS

Grammar The course has a graded grammar syllabus that contains the essential grammar, tenses, and structures needed for a basic level of language proficiency. The grammar points are introduced in communicative contexts (in each Conversation, in Grammar Focus exercises, and in example dialogs included in activities throughout the rest of a cycle) and through grammar summaries (the Grammar Focus models, which are presented in easy-to-read boxes) that illustrate the meaning and usage of each item.

Functions A functional syllabus parallels the grammar syllabus in the course. Each unit presents several key functions (e.g., introducing oneself, exchanging personal information, talking about oneself) that are linked to the grammar points and topics of the two cycles in each unit. The *Intro* Student's Book presents about 50 essential functions, which develop the students' communicative skills and enable them to participate in simple communication on a wide variety of topics.

Topics The course deals with topics that are of interest to learners of various ethnic and cultural backgrounds. Information is presented that can serve as a basis for cross-cultural comparison and that both students and the teacher will find stimulating and enjoyable. The topics have been selected for their interest to students of both genders in homogeneous and heterogeneous classes.

Listening The course reflects current understanding of the nature of listening comprehension in second and foreign language learning. Two kinds of listening skills are taught: *Top-down processing skills* require students to use background knowledge, the situation, context, and topic to arrive at comprehension through using key words and predicting; *bottom-up processing skills* require students to decode individual words in the message to derive meaning. Both of these skills are used in listening for gist, listening for details, and inferring meaning from context.

Speaking Speaking skills are a central focus of *New Interchange.* Many elements in the syllabus (grammar, functions, topics, listening, pronunciation, vocabulary) provide solid support for oral communication. Speaking activities in the course focus on conversational fluency, such as the ability to open and close conversations in English, introduce and develop conversational topics, take turns in conversations, use communication strategies and clarification requests, and understand and use a variety of idiomatic expressions. In addition, a range of useful conversational expressions is taught and practiced.

Reading The course treats reading as an important way of developing receptive language and vocabulary. At the same time, the reading passages provide stimulating adult content that both students and the teacher will enjoy. The *Intro* readings, which begin in Unit 5, include personal accounts of people's everyday lives, informative articles on a variety of interesting topics, advertisements, and extracts from travel guides. The reading exercises develop the skills of guessing words from context, skimming, scanning, and making inferences, as well as reading for pleasure and for information. This approach also develops both top-down and bottom-up processing skills in reading.

Writing Writing activities in *New Interchange* focus on various forms of writing such as descriptions, instructions, narratives, and reviews. *Intro* writing exercises generally ask students to compose several sentences on a topic of personal interest. Writing is often used as a basis for other activities such as grammar practice, games, and information-sharing.

Pronunciation The *Intro* level treats pronunciation as an integral part of oral proficiency. Pronunciation exercises focus on important features of spoken English, including stress, rhythm, intonation, reductions, and blending.

Vocabulary Vocabulary plays a key role in *New Interchange.* The *Intro* Student's Book teaches a productive vocabulary of about 1,000 words. Vocabulary is introduced in two main ways: Productive vocabulary is presented through a wide variety of vocabulary exercises and through speaking and grammar activities; receptive vocabulary is introduced through reading and listening exercises.

UNIT STRUCTURE AND ORGANIZATION

Although the sequencing of exercise types varies throughout *New Interchange,* a typical unit presents two main topics and functions with related exercises. The exercises in each unit are grouped into two sections; these are referred to as "Cycle 1" and "Cycle 2" in the teaching notes.

A cycle is a self-contained sequence of exercises that usually consists of the introduction of a new topic through a Snapshot or Word Power exercise; a Conversation that introduces the new grammar structure; a Grammar Focus that provides controlled practice, which is usually followed by freer communicative grammar practice; Pair Work, Group Work, Role Play exercises, or Class Activities that provide fluency practice on a specific teaching point; and a Listening exercise.

Also, in each unit there are a Pronunciation exercise, a Writing activity, and an Interchange Activity note. (This note refers students to the unit's communicative activity, which is presented at the back of the Student's Book.) Finally, there is an interesting Reading exercise that ends Cycle 2. In *Intro,* Readings begin in Unit 5.

The exercise types listed in the chart below are used throughout the course.

EXERCISE TITLE	PURPOSE
Snapshot	These exercises contain interesting, real-world information that introduces the topic of a unit or cycle. They also build receptive and productive vocabulary. The information in the Snapshot is presented in a graphic form, which makes it easy to read. Follow-up questions encourage discussion of the Snapshot material and personalize the topic.
Word Power	Word Power activities develop students' vocabulary as related to the unit or cycle topic through a variety of interesting tasks, such as word maps and collocation exercises. These activities are usually followed by oral or written practice that helps students understand how to use the vocabulary in context.
Conversation	Conversation exercises introduce new grammar points and functions in each cycle. They present the grammar in a situational and communicative context and also serve as models for conversational expressions and for speaking tasks.
Grammar Focus	These exercises present summaries of new grammar items followed by controlled and freer communicative practice of the grammar. These freer activities often have students use the grammar in a personal context.
Pair Work **Role Play** **Group Work** **Class Activity**	These oral fluency exercises provide more personalized practice of the new teaching points and increase the opportunity for meaningful individual student practice.
Pronunciation	These exercises practice important pronunciation features – such as stress, rhythm, intonation, reductions, and blending – that are usually found in the Conversation or Grammar Focus exercises.
Listening	The listening activities develop receptive skills, including listening for gist, listening for details, and inferring meaning from context. Charts or graphics often accompany these task-based exercises to lend support to students.
Writing	The Writing exercises include practical writing tasks that extend and reinforce the topic and grammar of the unit or cycle and help develop students' compositional skills. These exercises are often task-based.
Reading	Reading exercises develop reading skills as well as receptive language and vocabulary. The reading passages use various types of texts adapted from authentic sources. Pre-reading and post-reading questions use the topic of the reading as a springboard to discussion.
Interchange Activities	These information-sharing and role-playing activities provide a communicative extension to the unit. These exercises are a central part of the course and allow students to extend and personalize what they have practiced and learned in each unit.

REVIEW UNITS, UNIT SUMMARIES, AND TESTS

Review Units These occur after every four units and contain exercises that review the teaching points from the four preceding units. They are mainly speaking exercises, including one listening activity, that review grammar, vocabulary, conversational functions and expressions, and listening. They can also be used as informal criterion reference tests of students' oral production and listening skills.

Unit Summaries These are at the end of the Student's Book and contain a summary of the key productive vocabulary used in each unit, together with functional expressions and grammar extensions. The Key Vocabulary lists the productive vocabulary used in the Conversations, Word Power, pair, group, whole class, and role play activities.

Tests There are four tests, one for use after every four units of the Student's Book. The tests enable the teacher to evaluate students' progress in the course and to decide if any areas of the course need further review. The tests are on pages T-158–T-170 in this Teacher's Edition; all tests may be photocopied for class use. Complete information on administering and scoring the tests, and test answer keys, are located at the back of this book.

GENERAL GUIDELINES FOR TEACHING *NEW INTERCHANGE*

New Interchange follows a multi-skills syllabus in which each component of the course is linked. For example, a vocabulary-building exercise can serve as the basis for a speaking task; a role play activity may lead into a listening task or vice versa; or a grammar exercise prepares students for a functional activity.

The following general guidelines can be used when teaching the course.

Teaching Vocabulary

Vocabulary is a key element in *New Interchange* because a wide productive vocabulary is essential in learning a second or foreign language. Before presenting any exercise, it is helpful to determine which words are needed in order to complete the task and which are not essential – not all new vocabulary needs presentation in advance. Students should recognize that in most language-learning situations, they will encounter vocabulary they do not know; however, they do not need to understand every word. In addition, students need to understand that when they encounter an unknown word, they can often guess its meaning from the situation or context.

Where it is necessary to pre-teach new vocabulary, the following strategies may be helpful:

- Ask students to look at the context in which a word is used and to try to find any clues to its meaning. Encourage students to guess the meaning of a new word by first looking at all the other words surrounding it and then considering the general meaning of the phrase or sentence in which it is located. Encourage students to ask themselves: How does this new word fit into this general idea or the context here?
- Where necessary, provide the meanings of words through definitions, mime, synonyms, antonyms, examples, or translation. It is not necessary to give long explanations as the majority of adult students will already understand the concept of the new word (or know the equivalent word) in their native language.
- In general, discourage the use of dictionaries during class time, except where it is suggested in the teacher's notes within an exercise.
- After teaching a unit, ask students to review the Unit Summary (at the back of the Student's Book) to check how many of the words and their meanings they can remember.
- Encourage students to keep a vocabulary notebook (or a special section of their English class notebook) and to write down new words as they learn them.

Teaching Grammar

Correct use of grammar is an essential aspect of communicative competence. In *New Interchange,* grammatical accuracy is an integral part of proficiency, but it is always a means to an end rather than an end in itself. It is important to remember that second language learners do not usually develop grammatical proficiency by studying rules. They generally acquire new grammar by using the language in situations where it is needed. This means that grammar should always be practiced communicatively. However, language learning also involves testing out hypotheses about how the language works. In developing these hypotheses, some students will rely more on grammatical explanations than others.

In the Grammar Focus exercises, the information in the boxes should be used to explain new grammar points. Give additional examples and explanations, if necessary, to clarify the grammar, but avoid turning any lesson into a grammar class. Lead students into the practice activities for the new grammar points as quickly as possible. Then use the students' performance on these activities to decide if further clarification or grammar work is needed. Whenever this is the case, remember that there are additional grammar exercises in the Workbook that can be used as a follow-up.

Teaching Listening Skills

The Listening exercises are designed to bridge the gap between the classroom and the real world. While most of these exercises have the heading "Listening," there are also some that act as an extension in the Conversations, the Word Power activities, or fluency activities.

When teaching listening, it is important to remind students that in most listening situations the aim is *not* to remember the specific words or phrases used but to extract the main ideas or information. To help students do this, the Listening exercises usually contain a task that enables students to identify a purpose for listening which, in turn, encourages them to ignore language that is not related to that purpose. When presenting an exercise, it is also important to prepare students for the task through pre-listening activities. These include asking questions about the topic, asking students to make predictions, and making use of the context provided by the pictures and the situation.

Teaching Speaking Skills

A number of different kinds of activities focus on speaking skills in the course: Conversations, pair work, role plays, group work, whole class activities, and Interchange Activities. Each of these activities involves different learning arrangements in the class.

In doing these types of speaking activities, the following guidelines are important:

- Set up pairs or groups so that students of different ability levels and different native languages can work together. This arrangement will encourage students to help and learn from one another.
- Vary the pair or group arrangements so that students do not always work with the same classmates.
- Discourage use of the students' native languages when doing an activity by continually encouraging students to use as much English as possible in class.

Giving Feedback It is important to give clear feedback on students' performances, but feedback should not inhibit students' attempts to communicate with one another. Accuracy in speaking a new language takes a long time to accomplish, and both student and teacher need to realize this fact. Also, some aspects of language will be more difficult than others – depending on the students' levels of proficiency and/or first languages. Immediate results are not always apparent. Assess which aspects of the students' performances are worth drawing attention to at any particular time in their language development.

It is better to give occasional but focused feedback on one thing at a time than to overwhelm a student with too much information. There will be many opportunities to give individual feedback when students are working in pairs or groups. During these activities, walk around the class and discreetly listen in to what the students are doing and how they are getting along with the task. Then either take notes on any problems the students seem to be having in order to share them later with the whole class, or decide to give immediate feedback to the pair or group on any difficulties they might be experiencing with grammar, pronunciation, and vocabulary. Students often prefer this type of "private" or personalized feedback to feedback given in front of the whole class. This is also an opportunity to determine if additional practice work is needed before the class goes on to the next exercise.

Conversations These exercises can be used for both listening and speaking practice. They usually require students to work with a partner. Since the Conversation exercises model conversational expressions and pronunciation, and present new teaching items, accurate repetition of the Conversations on the audio program is important. However, students should not be asked to memorize these conversations verbatim.

When students practice Conversations, teach them to use the "Look Up and Say" technique: A student looks at the line of the dialog that he or she needs to say next, and then looks up and says the line while maintaining eye contact with a partner. This encourages students to avoid a "readinglike" pronunciation and intonation when practicing Conversation exercises together.

Pair Work The course makes extensive use of pair work activities. These give students a chance for individual practice and maximize the amount of speaking practice they get in each class. However, some students may be unfamiliar with pair work tasks and may not think that they can learn from their classmates. If so, remind students that practicing with a partner is a useful way of improving their fluency in English because it gives them more opportunities to speak English in class.

Role Plays These exercises are important for developing fluency and are also fun. They focus on the creative use of language and require students to draw on their own personal language resources to complete a task or to improvise and keep a conversation going.

Role plays are not used in the Intro *level as students do not yet have sufficient personal language resources to exploit role play situations. Role plays begin with Level 1.*

Group Work and Class Activities The course also makes frequent use of group work and whole class activities. In the group work activities, students usually work in groups of three to six. Often one student is the group secretary and takes notes to report back to the class later. In the class activities, however, the whole class is involved (e.g., completing a survey, gathering information, sharing facts or ideas previously learned in a group work activity).

Teaching Reading Skills

The approach for teaching reading in *New Interchange* is similar to that used for teaching listening. The purpose for reading determines the strategy the students should use, such as reading the passage for main ideas (skimming), looking quickly for specific information in the passage (scanning), reading more slowly for detailed understanding, reading for the author's attitude or tone, or reading to identify a sequence of events. It is important not to present each reading exercise as if it always requires the same approach (e.g., 100 percent comprehension of the passage). When students are doing a reading exercise, check that they are using appropriate reading strategies. For example:

- Students should read silently and not subvocalize (pronounce words or move their lips while reading).
- Students should read only with their eyes and not use a pencil or finger to follow each sentence they are reading.
- Students should not use their dictionaries to look up every new word they encounter in a reading passage.

To encourage student interaction in the class, many reading passages can be done as pair work, group work, or whole class activities. In addition, reading activities can be assigned for homework if class time is short.

Strategies for teaching reading are somewhat different for the Intro *level. See the Reading section of* How to Teach a Typical Unit of New Interchange Intro *on page xi.*

Teaching Writing Skills

The Writing exercises present models of different kinds of writing, but it is important to use these models simply as a springboard for the students' writing rather than as a basis for copying. Most of the writing tasks can be completed by a sequence of activities that focus on the writing process.

Pre-writing Phase Through discussion of the topic, reading of the model composition or the example of the beginning of one, brainstorming on the topic, or interviews, students generate ideas and collect information related to the topic, and then make notes.

Free Writing Students use their ideas, information, and notes to plan their compositions. During this phase, students write freely on the topic. The focus here is on organizing their ideas – not yet on having to worry about perfecting grammar and spelling.

Drafting Students now write a first complete draft in sentence and paragraph form, but again without worrying too much about spelling, grammar, or punctuation.

Revising In pair or small group feedback sessions, students read their own or a classmate's composition. Then they ask questions for clarification, or they can give suggestions for what additional information might be included. After this type of feedback session, each student works alone again to reorganize, revise, and rewrite his or her draft.

Editing Students, working alone or in pairs, check their second drafts for accuracy. This time, they concentrate first on checking that their ideas are clearly organized and that they have included enough details. When content and organization seem fine to them, students then focus their attention on correcting grammar, spelling, and punctuation.

Final phase Students write, word process, or type a clean third (and final) draft to hand in for comments, or they can put their compositions up on a classroom bulletin board for others to read.

At the Intro *level, writing tasks are integrated into other activities. These writing tasks include making lists, completing sentences, writing questions and writing several sentences on a topic. Students are provided with a variety of writing tasks, but as the* Intro *level requires these tasks to be short the typical writing procedures explained above do not apply to this level. Writing as a separate exercise begins with Level 1.*

TESTING STUDENTS' PROGRESS

The following testing procedures are suggested for use with *New Interchange.*

Using the Tests in the Teacher's Edition

Four tests are contained in the Teacher's Edition (see pages T-158–T-170) to assess students' learning. There is one test to be used after every four units. These are progress tests (also known as criterion reference tests, which only test what students have actually studied, learned, and practiced in a unit or in a set of units). These tests assess students' learning of grammar, conversational expressions, productive vocabulary, and listening skills. (For testing students' oral performance, see the following section – "Using Tests Prepared by the Teacher.") The tests draw on each set of four units as a whole. Only items actively presented and practiced in the Student's Book are tested. Each test takes approximately 45–60 minutes to complete in class; this includes one listening test item that has been included in the audio program. A satisfactory rate of learning should lead to accuracy of 80 percent and above. If students score lower than this, the teacher may wish to reteach some sections of the units, give additional supplementary exercises, or assign extra homework exercises. In addition to using these tests, the teacher can also informally check students' oral and written progress at the end of each unit.

Using Tests Prepared by the Teacher

It is also possible to check students' progress at the end of each unit using teacher-prepared tests. When developing such tests, it is important to keep the following principles in mind.

- The main goal of *New Interchange* is communicative competence. Therefore, test items should reflect use of language in communicative contexts rather than in isolation.

- Test items should closely mirror the kind of practice activities used within a unit, i.e., test only what has been taught and test it in a format similar to that in which it was originally presented.
- Distinguish items that were presented receptively (i.e., listening and reading activities) from those that were presented productively (i.e., speaking and writing activities) in the class. Then focus on testing productively only the language that students have practiced productively.

Here are some examples of acceptable types of test items for any unit in *New Interchange.*

1. Asking follow-up questions on a particular topic to keep the conversation going or to get more information.
2. Completing missing parts of a conversation while focusing on the grammar, vocabulary, or expressions in the unit.
3. Providing suitable conversational expressions for various purposes or functions (e.g., opening a conversation, expressing apologies).
4. Selecting an item from two or three choices (e.g., choosing an appropriate pronoun or adverb in a sentence).
5. Completing a sentence with the suitable grammatical form or the correct word.
6. Reordering scrambled sentences using the correct word order.
7. Choosing the correct word or phrase to complete a sentence.
8. Supplying missing words in a passage either by selecting from choices given in a list or in parentheses, or by using the cloze technique (the random removal of words from a text, such as every verb or every tenth word).
9. Completing a short writing task similar to one presented in the unit.
10. Answering questions or supplying information following a model provided in the unit.
11. Reading a sentence aloud with correct pronunciation.
12. Reading a passage similar to one in the unit and completing questions or a simple task based on it.

Other useful information on oral testing techniques can be found in *Testing Spoken Language* by Nic Underhill (Cambridge University Press, 1987).

HOW TO TEACH A TYPICAL UNIT OF *NEW INTERCHANGE INTRO*

The procedures outlined below are basic, generic ways to teach each of the recurring types of exercise in the *Intro* Student's Book. (For detailed and varied suggestions for each exercise in each unit, see the teaching notes, which begin on page 1.)

The basic procedures for *Intro* differ from those for Levels 1–3 in some respects. For example, *Intro* exercises often begin with books open so that the students can see the pictures and charts, and tasks are demonstrated rather than explained. In addition, more *Intro* material is included in the audio program. The basic procedures include use of the audio program for the Reading exercises, and most Snapshots and Word Powers, as well as for Conversation, Grammar Focus, Listening, and Pronunciation exercises.

Teaching the Exercises in a Unit

Snapshot

- With books open, use the audio program and the illustrations to present the information. Go over any problems of comprehension as they arise. Have students repeat any new words that they will be using in the unit.
- At this level, it is usually best to make the questions a class activity. Alternatively, students can answer the questions in pairs or groups. In this case, write a model conversation or useful expressions on the board for students to use if they need them.
- If the questions were not a class activity, elicit a few answers to each question to share with the class.

Word Power

- With books open, use the illustrations and the audio program to present the new words. Have students repeat them.
- Demonstrate the task. Provide extra examples if necessary.
- Students complete the task individually or in pairs.
- Students compare answers. At this time, allow students to check their dictionaries if necessary.
- Check students' answers.

Conversation

- With books open, use the picture to set the scene.
- Play the audio program while students listen.
- Clarify any new vocabulary or idiomatic expressions. Encourage students to guess words before explaining them. Use the illustrations and context clues as much as possible. Paraphrase and mime can also be used if necessary.
- Play the conversation again line by line so that students can repeat it. Focus their attention on pronunciation, intonation, and stress.
- Students practice the conversation together using the "Look Up and Say" technique described on page ix of this Teacher's Edition.
- **Optional:** Ask for volunteers to act out the conversation in front of the class.

Grammar Focus

- Use the audio program to present the grammar examples in the boxes and have students repeat them.
- If necessary, provide additional examples. If appropriate, practice the language in the boxes by conducting a drill.

- Use the example to demonstrate the first task. Provide additional examples on the board if necessary. If appropriate, elicit useful vocabulary from the students and make a list on the board.
- Students complete written exercises individually or in pairs. A written exercise can also be done orally as a whole class activity before students do it individually.
- Students compare written answers in pairs or groups.
- Check written answers and write the correct answers on the board.
- If an exercise involves a conversation, model it for the students line by line and have them repeat. If written work precedes spoken work, separate the two tasks.
- Students complete oral exercises in pairs or groups. While they work, move around the class and give help as needed.
- Proceed with subsequent exercises in the same way.
- **Optional:** If appropriate, choose one or two pairs or groups to role play their conversation for the class.

Pair Work

- Model the example conversation, if there is one, line by line, and have students repeat.
- Demonstrate the task with one or two students. Call on another pair to do the task as an additional example if necessary.
- If appropriate, elicit useful vocabulary from the students and make a list on the board.
- **Optional:** Set a time limit and write it on the board, like this:

  5 minutes

  or

  9:20–9:25
- Divide the class into pairs. If there is an odd number of students, form one group of three.
- Students practice in pairs, changing roles so that both students practice both roles. While they practice, move around the class and give help as needed.
- **Optional:** Students change partners and do the activity again.
- **Optional:** Call on one or two pairs you identified while they were practicing. Have them do the activity in front of the class. Give or elicit one or two helpful points as feedback on their performance.

Group Work

- Model the example conversation, if there is one, line by line, and have students repeat.
- Demonstrate the task with some students. Take the most challenging role yourself.
- If appropriate, elicit useful vocabulary from the students and make a list on the board.
- **Optional:** Set a time limit.
- Divide the class into groups. Students practice in groups, changing roles to try different parts. While they practice, move around the class and give help as needed.
- **Optional:** Students form new groups and do the activity again.
- **Optional:** Call on one or two groups you identified while they were practicing. Have them do the activity in front of the class. Give or elicit one or two helpful points as feedback on their performance.

Pronunciation

- Use the audio program to introduce the pronunciation point.
- Play the audio program again. Students practice by repeating the words or sentences.
- If helpful, give additional examples for students to practice by writing them on the board and then modeling each one.
- When doing other tasks in the unit (e.g., during the Conversation, Pair Work, Group Work, or Interchange Activity), remind students of the pronunciation point.

Listening

- Books open. Use the picture, if there is one, to set the scene.
- If necessary, pre-teach any vocabulary students will need for a general understanding of the listening passage or passages.
- Remind students that they don't have to understand everything they hear. Play the audio program. Students listen for general comprehension.
- Demonstrate the task. Use the board if that is helpful.
- Play the audio program as many times as necessary for students to complete the task.
- Students compare answers in pairs or groups.
- Elicit answers from the students and write the correct answers on the board.
- **Optional:** Play the audio program once more while students verify the answers.

Reading

At the *Intro* level, typical reading strategies such as skimming, scanning, reading for details, reading for tone, or reading to identify a sequence of events are not specifically identified in the reading task instructions. The simple tasks themselves provide a focus for students and are sufficiently varied from unit to unit so that students get practice in reading for different purposes.

A note on the vocabulary: Most reading passages include unfamiliar vocabulary. New vocabulary in reading passages is receptive vocabulary, that is, students are not required to produce it. Some of the new vocabulary may be needed for completing the comprehension task. Usually, these words are illustrated or can be guessed from the context. Occasionally, it may be useful to pre-teach a few key words or expressions before doing the comprehension task. Other new vocabulary can be left untaught, or some of it can be clarified after students have done the comprehension task.

A note on the audio program: In *Intro,* reading passages are recorded in the audio program. Students can listen to the passage at different points in a reading lesson, with different benefits. As a basic teaching procedure, use the audio program at one of these points:

1. Before the first reading, with books closed – to preview the passage.
2. During the first reading – to help students read at a steady pace and to aid comprehension.
3. After doing the comprehension exercise, while students read the passage again – to improve overall understanding and to let students check their answers.

Varying the point at which students hear the audio program from unit to unit will make the Readings more interesting and challenging for them.

- With books open, use the pictures to introduce the topic.
- Demonstrate the pre-reading task and do it as a whole class activity. The pre-reading task helps establish the students' background knowlege.
- **Optional:** Demonstrate the comprehension task before students read the passage. This will give students a purpose for reading.
- Students read the passage and complete the comprehension task.
- Check the answers and write them on the board.
- **Optional:** Let students ask questions about vocabulary. Get the answers from other students if possible. Encourage students to use the pictures and the context to guess words.
- Demonstrate the group work task. This task lets students give their own reactions to the topic of the reading.
- If appropriate, provide a model conversation or some useful expressions for group work.
- Students do the task in groups and report back to the class. Alternatively, if students need more support, do the task as a whole class activity.

Interchange Activities

- Where necessary and appropriate for the task, divide the class into pairs or groups and assign the students their roles (A, B, C, etc.) and their corresponding page numbers.
- Model the activity with one or more students. Encourage students to be creative and to have fun. They should focus on communication, not on grammar. Also, they should not refer back to the unit once they have begun the activity.
- Students do the task. Go around the class and give help as needed.
- Where appropriate, call on pairs or groups to do the activity in front of the class. As usual, elicit and give some helpful feedback on each performance.
- **Optional:** Use an audio tape recorder or a video camera to record the students' performances. Then play them back to the class and discuss their merits.

Unit Summaries

The Unit Summaries are a practice and study resource.

- After finishing a unit, students can plan and perform role plays using some of the Expressions listed in the Unit Summary. They can use the Key Vocabulary list to prepare for a vocabulary or spelling quiz on the unit.
- After finishing four units, the Unit Summaries are a useful word bank and vocabulary review when doing the corresponding review unit. The four Unit Summaries can also help students prepare for the test supplied in the Teacher's Edition.

Using the Workbook

Preview each unit of the Workbook exercises before introducing a unit, or part of a unit, in class. Note that the Workbook exercises present teaching points in the same sequence as the exercises in a unit in the Student's Book, but the Workbook exercises are more integrative, often combining vocabulary and teaching points from two or more exercises in the Student's Book into one activity. In addition, most units contain "review exercises" that recycle teaching points from earlier units in the context of the new topic. The Workbook can be used in a number of ways:

- After students complete a Student's Book exercise, assign a Workbook exercise that has the same teaching point. Students can complete it in class individually, in pairs, or in groups, or as a homework assignment.
- After several Student's Book exercises have been completed, assign appropriate Workbook exercises to be done as homework.
- After completing one cycle of a unit in the Student's Book (see how each unit is divided by checking the teacher's notes), assign the designated Workbook exercises included in the teacher's notes at the end of each cycle.
- At the end of a unit, have students do the entire Workbook unit as an in-class review or for homework.

FROM THE AUTHORS

We hope you enjoy teaching *New Interchange* and using the exercises and activities in it. We have confidence that this course will be interesting, innovative, and useful to you, the teacher, and to your students who want to learn English as a second or foreign language. We would be most happy to receive any comments that you or your students might like to share with us.

Best wishes,

Jack C. Richards
Tay Lesley

Spelling Differences Between American and British English

Words in Intro that have a different spelling in British English:

American spelling	*British spelling*
center	centre
check	cheque
color	colour
favorite	favourite
gray	grey
kilometer	kilometre
mom	mum
neighbor	neighbour
practice	practise
theater	theatre
tire	tyre
yogurt	yoghourt

Phonetic Symbols

iy	(sh**ee**p)	ʊ	(b**oo**k)	k	(**k**ey)	w	(**w**indow)
ɪ	(sh**i**p)	uw	(b**oo**t)	g	(**g**irl)	y	(**y**ellow)
ɛ	(y**e**s)	ay	(f**i**ne)	s	(**s**un)	h	(**h**ow)
ey	(tr**ai**n)	ɔy	(b**oy**)	z	(**z**oo)	θ	(**th**ink)
æ	(h**a**t)	aw	(h**ou**se)	ʃ	(**sh**oe)	ð	(**th**e fea**th**er)
ʌ	(c**u**p)	ɜr	(w**or**d)	ʒ	(televi**si**on)	m	(**m**outh)
ə	(**a** b**a**nan**a**)	p	(**p**en)	tʃ	(**ch**air)	n	(**n**ose)
ər	(lett**er**)	b	(**b**a**b**y)	dʒ	(**j**oke)	ŋ	(ri**ng**)
ɑ	(f**a**ther)	t	(**t**ie)	f	(**f**an)	l	(**l**etter)
ɔ	(b**a**ll)	d	(**d**oor)	v	(**v**an)	r	(**r**ain)
ow	(n**o**)						

Authors' Acknowledgments

A great number of people contributed to the development of *New Interchange*. Particular thanks are owed to the following:

The **reviewers** using the first edition of *Interchange* in the following schools and institutes – the insights and suggestions of these teachers and their students have helped define the content and format of the new edition:

Laura Renart, **TS Eliot Bilingual Studies,** Buenos Aires, Argentina; Blanca Arazi and the teachers at **Instituto Cultural Argentino Norteamericano (ICANA),** Buenos Aires, Argentina; Alda Lafeta Toledo, Márcia Soares Guimarães, and the teachers at **ICBEU Belo Horizonte,** Brazil; Jorge Haber Resque, **Centro Cultural Brasil-Estados Unidos (CCBEU),** Belém, Brazil; Mary Oliveira and Montserrat M. Djmal, **Instituto Brasil-Estados Unidos (IBEU),** Rio de Janeiro, Brazil; Maria Emilia Rey Silva, **UCBEU,** São Paulo, Brazil; Carmen Moreno, **IMPACT Institute,** Las Condes, Chile; Liliana Baltra, **Instituto Chileno Norteamericano,** Santiago de Chile; Amnerys Barrientos Usman, **Corporación Universitaria Tecnológica de Bolívar,** Cartagena, Colombia; Paul Dean Warman, **Tokyo Air Travel College,** Tokyo, Japan; Claude Arnaud and Paul Chris McVay, **Toyo Women's College,** Tokyo, Japan; Michael Barnes, **Tokyu Be Seminar,** Japan; Valerie Benson, **Suzugamine Women's College,** Hiroshima, Japan; Eric Bray, **Kyoto YMCA English School,** Kyoto, Japan; James Hale, **Sundai ELS,** Japan; Christopher Lynch, **Sunshine College,** Tokyo, Japan; Mike Millin and Kelley Seymour, **James English School,** Japan; John Pak, **Yokohama YMCA English School,** Yokohama, Japan; Lynne Roecklein, **Gifu University,** Japan; Hae-Kyong Park, **Handong University,** Pohang, Korea; Mae-Ran Park, **Pukyong National University,** Pusan, Korea; Luís Hernández Acosta, **Instituto Mexicano Norteamericano de Relaciones Culturales (IMARC),** Saltillo, Mexico; Matilde Legorreta and Manuel Hidalgo, **Kratos, S.A. de C.V.,** Mexico D.F.; Lilia Ortega Sepúlveda, **Unidad Lomoa Hermosa,** Mexico D.F.; Elizabeth Restivo, **St. Augustine College,** Chicago, Illinois, USA; Kim Sanabria, **Columbia University,** New York, New York, USA; Peg Donner, Ricia Doren, and Andrew Sachar, **Rancho Santiago College Centennial Education Center,** Santa Ana, California, USA; and the many teachers around the world who responded to the *Interchange* questionnaire.

The **editorial** and **production** team: Sylvia P. Bloch, John Borrelli, Karen Brock, Liane Carita, Mary Carson, Karen Davy, Andrew Gitzy, Christa Hansen, Pauline Ireland, Stephanie Karras, Penny Laporte, Sharon Lee, José Antonio Mendez, James R. Morgan, Kathy Niemczyk, Linda Olle, Kathleen O'Reilly, Howard Siegelman, Rosie Stamp, Jane Sturtevant, and Mary Vaughn.

And Cambridge University Press **staff** and **advisors**: Carlos Barbisan, Natalia Bochorishvili, Kathleen Corley, Kate Cory-Wright, Riitta da Costa, Peter Davison, Peter Donovan, Robert Gallo, Cecilia Gómez, Bob Hands, Colin Hayes, Catherine Higham, James Hursthouse, Koen Van Landeghem, Alejandro Martínez, Nigel McQuitty, Carine Mitchell, Lu-Ann Ong, Chuanpit Phalavadhana, Andrew Robinson, Dan Schulte, Cathy Smith, Ian Sutherland, Janaka Williams, and Ellen Zlotnick.

Plan of the Book

Title/Topics	Functions	Grammar
UNIT 1 PAGES 2–7		
It's nice to meet you. Alphabet; greetings and leave-takings; names and titles of address; numbers 1–10 and telephone numbers	Introducing yourself and friends; saying hello and good-bye; asking for names and phone numbers	Possessive adjectives *my, your, his, her*; the verb *be*: affirmative statements and contractions
UNIT 2 PAGES 8–13		
What's this? Possessions, classroom objects, personal items, and locations in a room	Naming objects; asking for and giving the location of an object	Articles *a, an,* and *the*; *this/it* and *these/they*; plurals; yes/no and *where* questions with *be*; prepositions of place
UNIT 3 PAGES 14–19		
Where are you from? Cities, countries, and regions; adjectives of personality; numbers to 100 and age	Talking about geographical locations; asking for and giving information about places of origin, nationality, native language, and age; describing people	The verb *be*: affirmative and negative statements, yes/no questions, short answers, and Wh-questions
UNIT 4 PAGES 20–25		
I'm not wearing boots! Clothing; colors; seasons of the year; weather	Asking about and describing clothing; talking about the weather; finding the owner of an item	Possessive adjectives *our, their,* and possessives of names; present continuous affirmative and negative statements; *isn't* and *aren't*; conjunctions *and* and *but*; color adjectives before nouns
REVIEW OF UNITS 1–4 PAGES 26–27		
UNIT 5 PAGES 28–33		
What are you doing? Times of the day, clock time; daily activities, Saturday activities	Asking for and telling time; asking about and describing current activities	Questions with *what time*; *what + doing* and Wh-questions with the present continuous; conjunction *so*
UNIT 6 PAGES 34–39		
We live in the suburbs. Places and transportation; family relationships; daily routines; days of the week	Asking for and giving information about where people live and how they go to work or school; talking about family members; talking about daily routines	Simple present statements with regular and irregular verbs; simple present yes/no and Wh-questions; time expressions
UNIT 7 PAGES 40–45		
Does the apartment have a view? Houses and apartments; rooms; furniture	Asking about and describing homes; saying what furniture is in a room	Simple present short answers; *how many*; *there is, there are*; *there's no, there isn't a, there are no, there aren't any*
UNIT 8 PAGES 46–51		
What do you do? Occupations and workplaces	Asking for and giving information about work; giving opinions about jobs	Simple present Wh-questions with *do*; placement of adjectives before nouns; descriptive adjectives for occupations
REVIEW OF UNITS 5–8 PAGES 52–53		

Listening/Pronunciation	Writing/Reading	Interchange Activity
		PAGES IC-2 AND IC-4 UNIT 1
Listening for the spelling of names; listening for telephone numbers Pronunciation of the alphabet and numbers 1–10	Writing a list of telephone numbers	"Directory assistance": Calling the operator to find out phone numbers
		PAGE IC-3 UNIT 2
Listening to find the location of an item Pronunciation of plural *s*	Writing the location of objects	"Find the differences": Comparing two rooms
		PAGE IC-5 UNIT 3
Listening for countries and languages; listening to descriptions of people Syllabic stress of numbers; blending with *is* and *are*	Writing questions requesting personal information	"Class personalities": Identifying classmates' personality traits
		PAGES IC-6 AND IC-7 UNIT 4
Listening for descriptions of clothing Sentence stress and rhythm	Writing questions about what people are wearing	"Celebrity fashions": Describing celebrities' clothing
		REVIEW OF UNITS 1–4
		PAGE IC-8 UNIT 5
Listening for the time; listening to identify what people are doing Question intonation	Writing about what people are doing "It's Saturday! What Are You Doing?": Reading about Saturday activities	"Time zones": Talking about what people are doing in different cities around the world
		PAGE IC-9 UNIT 6
Listening to people describe how they go to work or school; listening for days of the week Pronunciation of third-person singular *s*	Writing about daily schedules and habits "What's Your Schedule Like?": Reading about daily schedules	"Class survey": Finding out more about classmates' daily schedules and habits
		PAGE IC-10 UNIT 7
Listening to descriptions of houses and apartments; listening to people shop for furniture Pronunciation of *th*	Writing about a dream house "Two Special Houses in the American Southwest": Reading about unique houses	"Find the differences": Comparing two apartments
		PAGE IC-11 UNIT 8
Listening to people describe their jobs Reduction of *do* and *does*	Writing about jobs "What Do You Do, Exactly?": Reading about people's occupations	"The perfect job": Figuring out what job is right for you
		REVIEW OF UNITS 5–8

Title/Topics	Functions/Vocabulary	Grammar
UNIT 9 PAGES 54–59		
Broccoli is good for you. Food Pyramid: basic foods; desserts; meals	Talking about foods that are good or bad for you, food likes and dislikes, and eating habits; talking about food items you need	Countable and uncountable nouns; *some* and *any*; adverbs of frequency: *always, usually, often, sometimes, seldom, never*
UNIT 10 PAGES 60–65		
You can play baseball really well. Sports; talents and abilities	Talking about sports you like and dislike; talking about talents and abilities	Simple present Wh-questions; *can* for ability
UNIT 11 PAGES 66–71		
What are you going to do? Months and dates; birthdays, holidays, and celebrations	Saying dates; asking about birthdays; asking for and giving information about future plans, holidays, and celebrations	The future with *be going to*: Wh-questions with *be going to*; future time expressions
UNIT 12 PAGES 72–77		
What's the matter? Parts of the body; health problems and advice; medications	Talking about illnesses and health problems; giving advice; giving instructions	*Have* + noun; *feel* + adjective; affirmative and negative imperatives
REVIEW OF UNITS 9–12 PAGES 78–79		
UNIT 13 PAGES 80–85		
You can't miss it. Stores and things you can buy; locations in a city; tourist attractions	Talking about shopping; asking for and giving locations and directions	Prepositions of place: *on, on the corner of, across from, next to, between*; giving directions with imperatives
UNIT 14 PAGES 86–91		
Did you have a good weekend? Weekends: household chores and leisure activities	Asking for and giving information about activities in the recent past	Simple past statements with regular and irregular verbs; simple past yes/no questions and short answers
UNIT 15 PAGES 92–97		
Where were you born? Biographical information; years; school subjects	Asking for and giving information about date and place of birth, school experiences, and the recent past	Statements and questions with the past of *be*; Wh-questions with *did, was,* and *were*
UNIT 16 PAGES 98–103		
Please leave us a message. Telephone calls and invitations; going out with friends	Making phone calls; leaving phone messages; inviting people and accepting and declining invitations; making excuses	Object pronouns; verb + *to* + verb; *would*
REVIEW OF UNITS 13–16 PAGES 104–105		
UNIT SUMMARIES PAGES S-2–S-17		
APPENDIX		

Listening/Pronunciation	Writing/Reading	Interchange Activity
Listening for people's food preferences Sentence stress	Writing questions about personal eating habits "Eating for Good Luck": Reading about foods that people eat for good luck	PAGE IC-12 UNIT 9 "Eating habits": Taking a survey about foods you eat
Listening for people's favorite sports; listening to people describe their talents Pronunciation of *can* and *can't*	Writing Wh-questions about sports "Race the U.S.!": Reading about unusual races in the U.S.	PAGE IC-13 UNIT 10 "Hidden talents": Learning about your classmates' special talents
Listening to people talk about evening plans Pronunciation of *going to*	Writing about weekend plans "What Are You Going to Do on Your Birthday?": Reading about birthday customs in different places	PAGE IC-14 UNIT 11 "Celebrations": Talking about how people celebrate special events
Listening to people talk about health problems; listening for medications and instructions Sentence stress	Writing advice for improving your health "10 Simple Ways to Improve Your Health": Reading about healthy habits	PAGE IC-15 UNIT 12 "Helpful advice": Giving advice for some common problems
		REVIEW OF UNITS 9–12
Listening to people talk about shopping; listening to directions Intonation for checking information	Writing directions "A Walk up Fifth Avenue": Reading about New York City landmarks	PAGES IC-16 AND IC-18 UNIT 13 "Directions": Finding your way around a neighborhood
Listening to people talk about their past weekend activities Pronunciation of regular simple past verb endings: /t/, /d/, /ɪd/	Writing about weekend activities in the recent past "The Changing Weekend": Reading a short history of the U.S. weekend	PAGE IC-17 UNIT 14 "Past and present": Comparing your classmates' present lives with their childhoods
Listening for place and date of birth Pronunciation of negative contractions	Writing Wh-questions about artists' lives "Three Famous Artists": Reading about Hiroshige, Frida Kahlo, and Alexander Calder	PAGE IC-20 UNIT 15 "Time line": Mapping out important events in your life
Listening to people make phone calls; listening for information in telephone messages Pronunciation of *want to* and *have to*	Writing about things you want to do "Free Activities This Weekend": Reading notices about events	PAGES IC-19 AND IC-21 UNIT 16 "Let's make a date!": Making a date
		REVIEW OF UNITS 13–16
		UNIT SUMMARIES
		APPENDIX

1 It's nice to meet you.

1 CONVERSATION

A Listen and practice.

Michael: Hi. My name is Michael Parker.
Jennifer: I'm Jennifer Yang.
Michael: It's nice to meet you, Jennifer.
Jennifer: Nice to meet you, too.
Michael: I'm sorry. What's your last name again?
Jennifer: It's Yang.

B ***Pair work*** Introduce yourself to your partner.

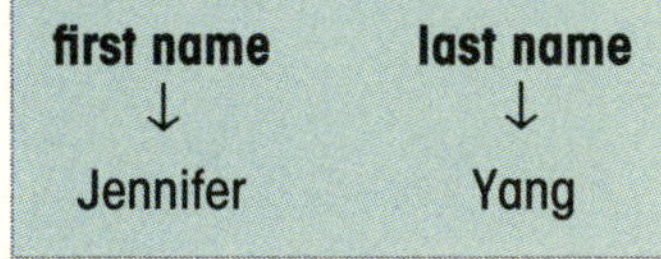

2 SNAPSHOT

 Listen and practice.

Popular First Names in the United States

for males		for females	
Christopher	Joshua	Ashley	Lisa
David	Matthew	Jennifer	Michelle
James	Michael	Jessica	Nicole
Jason	Robert	Katherine	Sarah
John	Steven	Kimberly	Stephanie

Source: *The Cambridge Encyclopedia,* Third Edition

What is another first name for a male in English?
for a female?
What is your favorite first name in English?
List some popular names in your country.

1 It's nice to meet you.

This unit presents expressions for making introductions, saying hello and good-bye, and asking for names and telephone numbers. It introduces subject pronouns, possessive adjectives, and affirmative statements and contractions with the verb be.

Cycle 1, Exercises 1–6

1 CONVERSATION

A 

This exercise presents expressions used for introducing yourself.

- Books closed. Introduce yourself. Shake hands with a S and say, "Hi. My name is . . . ." or "I'm . . . ." Encourage Ss to respond using their own names ("My name is . . . ." or "I'm . . . ."). When Ss respond, say, "It's nice to meet you."
- Books open. Have Ss look at the illustration and the names in the conversation.
- Play the audio program. Ss read and listen.
- Write these sentences on the board:

  I'm Jennifer Yang.
  My name is Michael Parker.

  Show Ss that "I'm . . ." and "My name is . . ." mean the same. Change *Jennifer Yang* to *Michael Parker* (and vice versa) in the sentences on the board.
- Play the audio program again. Ss read and listen. If necessary, answer questions about vocabulary. Explain that *Nice to meet you* means *It's nice to meet you* and *I'm sorry. What's your last name again?* means *Please repeat your last name.*
- To clarify *too,* write "It's nice to meet you" on the board. Get a S to say the sentence to you. Respond, "It's nice to meet you, too." Then draw two female stick figures on the board and label each figure *Jennifer.* Point to one and say, "My name is Jennifer." Point to the other and say, "My name is Jennifer, too."
- Teach Ss how to use the Look Up and Say technique described here and on page ix in the Introduction: Ss read a sentence silently. Then they look up at their partners and say the sentence from memory.
- Practice the Look Up and Say technique with the whole class. Play the audio program again or read the conversation, line by line. Ss listen and read, then look up and repeat.

B *Pair work*

- Point to *first name* and *last name* in the box. Clarify the expressions by using your own names. Say, "My first name is . . . . My last name is . . . ." Then ask several Ss "What's your first name?" and "What's your last name?" until Ss understand the terms.
- Ss practice in pairs, using their own names and the conversation as a model. Encourage Ss to use gestures and to show appropriate emotions. In this conversation, have Ss shake hands and smile while introducing themselves. Have Ss change roles and partners at least once. Walk around the class and give help as needed.
- **Optional:** Have a few Ss act out the conversation for the class.

2 SNAPSHOT Popular First Names in the United States

This graphic presents information about names in the United States. The questions help Ss understand the information and relate it to themselves.

- Books open. Give Ss a few seconds to look at the graphic. Then play the audio program. Ss listen and repeat.
- Check Ss' understanding of *male* and *female.* Write the two words on the board. Say the name of a S in the class. Have Ss tell you where to write the name – under *male* or under *female.* Continue with other names until it's clear that Ss understand the words.
- Ask the questions one by one. Give several answers of your own to each question so that Ss understand what is expected. Elicit more answers from Ss, and write them on the board.

  For the last question, if Ss are from several different countries, write the names of their countries on the board along with the name of your country. List some popular names from your country under the name of your country. Then elicit names from Ss for their countries and list them under their respective countries.

Optional activity: *Comparing names*

- See page T-147.

3 GRAMMAR FOCUS My, your, his, her

This grammar focus presents the possessive adjectives *my, your, his,* and *her*. It also presents the question "What's . . . name?"

- Books closed. Ask a male and a female S to stand next to you. Use this conversation to demonstrate the meanings of *my, your, his,* and *her*.

  T: My name is (your name). What's your name?
  S1: My name is (Keiko).
  T: *(to class)* Her name is (Keiko).
  T: What's your name?
  S2: My name is (Juan).
  T: *(to class)* His name is (Juan).
- Books open. Play the audio program. Ss listen and read.
- Point to Ss and elicit *his* or *her* from the class. Then elicit a complete sentence from a volunteer: "His name is . . . ." or "Her name is . . . ." The other Ss repeat.
- Play the audio program again or model the sentences. Ss listen and repeat.

Group work

- Books open. Demonstrate "The Name Game."
- Make groups of five to ten Ss, and have each group stand in a circle. Help the Ss get started playing the game.
- After Ss have learned the names of the people in their groups, make new groups and play again.

Optional activity: *Classmate's names*

- See page T-147.

4 WORD POWER The alphabet

This exercise presents the alphabet and practices spelling.

A

- Books open. Play the audio program. Ss listen and read.
- Play the audio program again or read the alphabet letter by letter. Ss listen and repeat. Give extra practice with any letters that are especially difficult for your Ss.
- **Optional:** In pairs, Ss say the alphabet twice, taking turns saying alternate letters.

B Group work

- Books open. Show Ss the conversation. (The illustration at the right shows what Student A writes.)
- Play the audio program line by line. Ss listen and read, then look up and repeat.
- Demonstrate the task with a S. For example:

  T: What's your name?
  S: I'm Akira Sato.
  T: *(writing the name on the board)* Is that A-K-I-D-A?
  S: No, it's A-K-I-R-A.
  T: *(corrects the name)* How do you spell your last name? *(writing the name on the board)* S-A-T-O?
  S: Yes, that's right.
- Ss practice in groups of four or five, writing the names of the Ss in their group.

Optional activity: *Game – Letter bingo*

- See page T-147.

5 LISTENING Spelling names

This exercise practices listening for the correct spelling of names.

- Books open. Have Ss look at the double list of names. Read the five pairs of names aloud. Ss should understand that each pair is pronounced the same.
- Play the first item on the audio program and use the example to demonstrate the task.

Audio script

1. SALES REPRESENTATIVE: Your name is Jon Lee?
   JON: That's right.
   SALES REPRESENTATIVE: And how do you spell your first name, Mr. Lee?
   JON: It's J-O-N.
   SALES REPRESENTATIVE: OK. Thank you.
2. SALES REPRESENTATIVE: Sara Brown. Your first name is spelled S-A-R-A-H?
   SARA: No. My name is spelled S-A-R-A.
   SALES Representative: I'm sorry. Could you repeat that?
   SARA: Yes. It's S-A-R-A.
   SALES REPRESENTATIVE: Got it. Thanks.

3 GRAMMAR FOCUS

My, your, his, her

What's your name?
My name is Jennifer.
What's his name?
His name is Michael.
What's her name?
Her name is Nicole.

What's = What is

Group work Play "The Name Game." Make a circle. Learn the names of your classmates.

A: My name is Keiko.
B: Her name is Keiko. I'm Akira.
C: Her name is Keiko. His name is Akira. And I'm Kumiko.

4 WORD POWER *The alphabet*

A Listen and practice.

A B C D E F G H I J K L M N O P Q R S T U V W X Y Z
a b c d e f g h i j k l m n o p q r s t u v w x y z

B **Group work** Listen. Then practice using your own information. Write down your classmates' names.

A: What's your name?
B: I'm Sarah Conner.
A: Is that S-A-R-A-H?
B: Yes, that's right.
A: How do you spell your last name? C-O-N-N-O-R?
B: No, it's C-O-N-N-E-R.

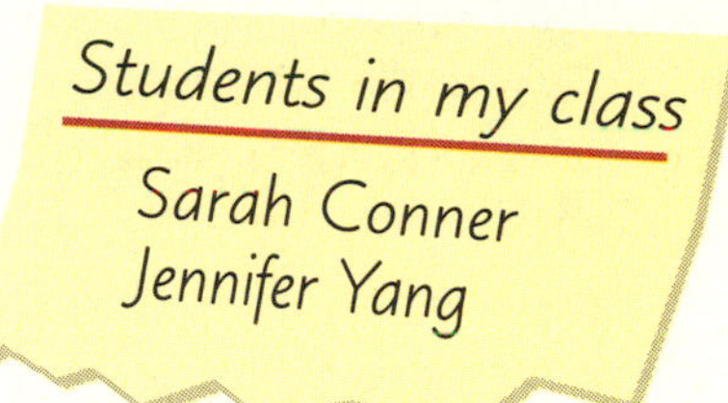

Students in my class
Sarah Conner
Jennifer Yang

5 LISTENING *Spelling names*

How do you spell the names? Listen and check (✓) the correct answers.

1. ☑ Jon ☐ John
2. ☐ Sara ☐ Sarah
3. ☐ Steven ☐ Stephen
4. ☐ Katherine ☐ Kathryn
5. ☐ Kris ☐ Chris

6 SAYING HELLO

A Listen and practice.

1
Hi, Matthew.
How are you?
Great!
How about you, Lisa?

2
Good morning, Mr. Duran.
How are you?
I'm just fine, Alex.
Thank you.

3
Good afternoon, Brad.
How are you?
Not bad, thanks.
How are you?

4
Good evening,
Mrs. Morgan.
Hello, Ms. Chen.
How are you?
I'm OK, thank you.

TITLES		
For males: Mr.	**For females:** Ms. Miss Mrs.	**Use titles with older people:** *Good morning, Mr. Duran.* **Use titles to show respect:** *Good evening, Mrs. Morgan.*

B ***Class activity*** Go around the class. Practice greeting your classmates formally (with titles) and informally (without titles).

3. STEPHEN: My name is Stephen Jones.
SALES REPRESENTATIVE: Thank you. Steven . . . that's S-T-E-V . . .
STEPHEN: No. It's spelled S-T-E-P-H-E-N.
SALES REPRESENTATIVE: Oh, excuse me. S-T-E-P-H-E-N.
STEPHEN: That's right.
4. SALES REPRESENTATIVE: Your name, please?
KATHRYN: It's Kathryn Simpson.
SALES REPRESENTATIVE: Is that K-A-T-H-E-R-I-N-E?
KATHRYN: No, it's K-AT-H-R-Y-N.
SALES REPRESENTATIVE: Oh, so it's K-A-T-H-R-Y-N. Thank you, Ms. Simpson.
5. SALES REPRESENTATIVE: And what's your first name, please?
KRIS: It's Kris.
SALES REPRESENTATIVE: Is your name spelled C-H-R-I-S?
KRIS: No, it's spelled K-R-I-S. Kris with a "K."
SALES REPRESENTATIVE: Kris with a "K." Thanks.

- Play the audio program as many times as necessary. Ss listen and check the correct boxes. Ss compare their answers in pairs.
- Play the audio program again, and write answers on the board.

Answers

1. Jon 2. Sara 3. Stephen 4. Kathryn 5. Kris

6 SAYING HELLO

This exercise presents and practices greetings and responses. It also introduces the titles *Ms., Miss, Mrs.,* and *Mr.*

A

- Give Ss time to look at the pictures.
- Play the audio program twice. Ss read and listen.
- With the Ss' help, list the words and expressions that mean *hello: Hi, Good morning, Good afternoon, Good evening, Hello.* Encourage Ss to use the pictures to guess the meanings of *morning, afternoon,* and *evening.*
- Point out the box with information about titles. Remind Ss of the meanings of *male* and *female.* Read each title aloud and have Ss repeat. (*Note:* We do not usually use titles with first names in English.)
- Check Ss' understanding of when to use titles. Point to picture 2 and invent full names for the boy (e.g., Alex *Conner*) and the man (*John* Duran). Write the names on the board.

  T: *(pointing to the boy's speech bubble)* Good morning, John. How are you? *(then asking Ss)* OK?
  Ss: No!
  T: *(pointing to the man's speech bubble)* I'm just fine, Mr. Conner. Thank you. *(then asking Ss)* OK?
  Ss: No!
- Play the audio program again or model the conversations line by line. Ss read and listen, then look up and repeat.

B *Class activity*

- Books closed. Demonstrate the first task. Greet several Ss using their titles. For example:

  T: Good evening, (Mr. Chen).
  S1: Good evening, (your title and last name).
  T: Hello, (Ms. Ramirez).
  S2: Hello, (your title and last name).
- **Optional:** If Ss are not familiar with each other, make name tags before beginning the activity.
- Have all the Ss stand and move around the room greeting each other. Make sure they use titles and last names only.
- When each S has greeted four or five others, stop the activity.
- Introduce the second task. Lead two Ss through greeting each other using first names only:

  S1: Hi, (Alicia).
  S2: Hi, (Maria).
- Have Ss continue to greet each other, now using first names only.

Workbook

Workbook Exercises 1–7 on pages 1–4 correspond to Cycle 1, Exercises 1–6 of the Student's Book. Answers to the Workbook exercises begin on page T-182 of this Teacher's Edition.

Cycle 2, Exercises 7–11

CONVERSATION

This conversation introduces the singular subject pronouns *I, you, she, he,* and *it* and expressions for introducing others.

A

- Have Ss look at the pictures. Remind them that the woman is Jennifer Yang (from Exercises 1 and 3).
- Play the audio program. Ss listen and read.
- Play the audio program again. Clarify key vocabulary if necessary. For *excuse me,* tap someone on the shoulder and say, "Excuse me," to get their attention. For *over there,* put a S's book on the other side of the classroom. Return to the S, point to the book, and say, "Your book is over there."
- Play the audio program again or read the conversation line by line. Ss listen and read, then look up and repeat.
- Ss practice the conversation in groups of three using the Look Up and Say technique. Have them change roles and practice all three parts.
- **Optional:** Have one or two groups of volunteers act out the conversation for the class. They all smile and use appropriate gestures. Encourage the volunteers to avoid looking at their books.

B ***Group work***

- Books closed. Demonstrate the task with three Ss. Lead them through a conversation like this one:

S1: Hi, (Luis).
S2: Hi, (Sun-hee).
S1: Luis, this is (Akira).
S2: Hi, Akira.
S3: Hi, Luis. Nice to meet you.

- Ss form groups of three. Do not let them look at their books. If necessary, write the model conversation on the board for Ss to refer to. Ss greet and introduce each other using their own names.
- Have Ss change roles so that they practice all the parts. If time permits, have them form new groups and practice again.

8 GRAMMAR FOCUS The verb be

This grammar focus presents and practices the singular subject pronouns *I, you, she, he,* and *it* and their contractions with *am, are,* and *is.*

- Books open. Give Ss a little time to look at the grammar box.
- Use the audio program to present the information. Ss listen and read.
- Contrast the pronunciation of *I am* and *I'm, you are* and *you're,* and so on. (*Note:* Contractions of *be* are in statements, not in questions.)
- Play the program again or model the sentences. Ss listen and repeat.
- **Optional:** Have Ss name the missing letter in each contraction.

A

- Books closed. Demonstrate the task. Write the first two lines of the exercise on the board. Do not fill in the example.
- Read the first line aloud, and show Ss the two choices in parentheses. Elicit the correct answer from the Ss, and fill it in on the board. Do the same with the second line.
- Books open. Ss read the conversation silently. They write the answers in their books or on a separate piece of paper.
- While Ss are working, copy the rest of the conversation on the board. Then walk around to look at Ss' answers. When you see a correct answer, send the S to write it on the board.

Answers

DAVID: Hello, Jennifer. How **are** you?
JENNIFER: **I'm** fine, thanks. **I'm** sorry – what's your name again?
DAVID: **It's** David – David Medina.
JENNIFER: That's right! David, this **is** Sarah Conner. **She's** in our math class.
DAVID: Hi, Sarah. **It's** nice to meet you.
SARAH: Hi, David. I think **you're** in my English class, too.
DAVID: Oh, right! Yes, I **am.**

- Have Ss check their answers with those on the board.
- Read the conversation line by line. Ss read and listen, then look up and repeat.
- Ss practice the conversation in pairs using the Look Up and Say technique.

7 CONVERSATION

A Listen and practice.

Jennifer: Excuse me. Are you Steven Carson?
David: No, I'm not. He's over there.
Jennifer: Oh, I'm sorry.

Jennifer: Steven? This is your book.
Steven: Oh, it's my math book! Thanks. You're in my class, right?
Jennifer: Yes, I am. I'm Jennifer Yang.
Steven: It's nice to meet you.

Steven: David, this is Jennifer. She's in our math class.
David: Hi, Jennifer.
Jennifer: Hi, David. Nice to meet you.

B ***Group work*** Greet a classmate. Then introduce him or her to another classmate.

8 GRAMMAR FOCUS

The verb *be*

I'm Jennifer Yang.	**Are you** Steven Carson?	**I'm** = **I am**
You're in my class.	Yes, **I am**.	**You're** = **You are**
She's in our math class. (**Jennifer is** in our math class.)	No, **I'm not**.	**He's** = **He is**
He's over there. (**Steven is** over there.)		**She's** = **She is**
It's my math book.	How **are you**?	**It's** = **It is**
It's Yang. (**My last name is** Yang.)	**I'm** fine.	

A Complete the conversation with the correct words in parentheses. Then practice with a partner.

David: Hello, Jennifer. How ....*are*.... you? (is/are)
Jennifer: .... fine, thanks. (She's/I'm)
.... sorry – what's your name again? (I'm/It's)
David: .... David – David Medina. (He's/It's)
Jennifer: That's right! David, this .... Sarah Conner. (is/am)
.... in our math class. (She's/He's)
David: Hi, Sarah. .... nice to meet you. (I'm/It's)
Sarah: Hi, David. I think .... in my English class, too. (you're/I'm)
David: Oh, right! Yes, I .... (are/am)

B Complete the conversation. Then practice in groups.

Nicole: Excuse me. ....*Are*.... you Steven Carson?
David: No, ... not. My name .... David Medina. Steven .... over there.
Nicole: Oh, sorry.

Nicole: .... you Steven Carson?
Steven: Yes, I ....
Nicole: Hi. .... Nicole Johnson.
Steven: Oh, ... in my math class, right?
Nicole: Yes, I ....
Steven: .... nice to meet you.

C ***Class activity*** Write your name on a piece of paper. Put the papers in a pile. Take a paper from the pile. Find the other student.

A: Excuse me. Are you Sonia Gomes?
B: No, I'm not.

A: Hi. Are you Sonia Gomes?
C: Yes, I am.

9 *NUMBERS*

A Listen and practice.

0	1	2	3	4	5	6	7	8	9	10
zero (oh)	one	two	three	four	five	six	seven	eight	nine	ten

B Say these numbers.

C ***Group work*** Listen. Then make a list of names and phone numbers for people in your group.

A: What's your name?
B: I'm Michelle Jenkins.
A: And what's your phone number?
B: It's 555-2491.

B

- Show Ss that this time there are no choices in parentheses. They can refer to the grammar box on page 5 for help. Demonstrate the task as in part A.
- Ss read the conversations silently and fill in the answers. Then they compare their answers in pairs.
- To check, elicit answers from the Ss. Write them on the board just as the Ss give them – correct or not.
- Have the class participate in verifying and correcting the answers on the board. Then Ss correct their own papers while referring to the board.

Answers

NICOLE: Excuse me. **Are** you Steven Carson?
DAVID: No, **I'm** not. My name **is** David Medina. Steven **is** over there.
NICOLE: Oh, sorry.
NICOLE: **Are** you Steven Carson?
STEVEN: Yes, I **am.**
NICOLE: Hi. **I'm** Nicole Johnson.
STEVEN: Oh, **you're** in my math class, right?
NICOLE: Yes, I **am.**
STEVEN: **It's** nice to meet you.

- Read the conversation aloud line by line. Ss read and listen, then look up and repeat.
- Ss practice the conversation in groups of three using the Look Up and Say technique.

C *Class activity*

- Books open. To prepare for the task, each S writes his or her name on a piece of paper and puts it in a pile. You can pile the pieces of paper on a desk or collect them in a bag or other container.
- Demonstrate the task. Take a piece of paper from the pile. Speak to the nearest S (not the S whose name is on the paper).

  T: Excuse me. Are you (name on paper)?
  S1: No, I'm not.

  Ask one or two more Ss, then ask the S whose name *is* on the paper.
- Each S takes a name (but not his or her own name). Then everyone stands up and finds the person whose name is on their paper by asking questions. If Ss know the people in their class well, you may ask them to imagine that they are just meeting each other for the first time.

9 *NUMBERS*

This exercise introduces the numbers from zero to ten. In part C, Ss write a list of telephone numbers.

(*Note:* When used with other numbers, *0* is pronounced either "zero" or "oh" (*505* is "five-zero-five" or "five-oh-five"). When the number *0* is alone, it is always pronounced "zero.")

A

- Books open. Play the audio program. Ss listen and read.
- Play the audio program again or model the numbers one at a time. Ss listen and repeat.

B

- Demonstrate the task. On the board, write a long number similar to the ones on the cards. Say each digit of the number, pointing to each digit as you say it. Ss repeat. Have a volunteer read the complete number.
- In pairs, Ss take turns reading the numbers on the illustrations.
- **Optional:** Each S writes a long number on a piece of paper. With new partners, Ss read their numbers aloud, and the partners write them. Ss compare their papers.

C *Group work*

- Books open. Play the audio program once. Ss read and listen. Play it again or model the conversation line by line. Ss read and listen, then look up and repeat.
- Ss work in groups of four or five. They take turns asking each others' names and phone numbers. Each S makes a list. If Ss prefer not to give their actual phone numbers, they can invent numbers.
- **Optional:** Collect the group lists, and ask a volunteer to make a telephone list for the whole class. Make copies for the Ss, or post the list in the classroom.

Optional Activities

1. ***Game – Number bingo***

- See page T-147.

2. ***Number rhythm***

- See page T-147.

10 LISTENING

This exercise practices listening for and writing down names and telephone numbers.

- Refer to the pictures in Exercises 1 and 7. Remind Ss that Michael and Jennifer are in the same English class.
- Write the beginning of the list on the board.

Name	*Telephone number*
David Medina	____________

- Demonstrate the task. Play the first item on the audio program. When you hear David Medina's telephone number, write it on the board.

Audio script

JENNIFER: What's David Medina's telephone number, Michael?
MICHAEL: It's five-five-five, one-nine-three-seven.
JENNIFER: Five-five-five, one-nine-three-seven?
MICHAEL: Yes, that's it.
MICHAEL: OK. Sarah Conner. What's her telephone number?
JENNIFER: Hmm. Sarah. Her number is five-five-five, seven-six-four-five.
MICHAEL: Five-five-five, seven-six-four-five.
JENNIFER: That's right.
JENNIFER: And what's James's phone number?
MICHAEL: It's five-five-five, eight-four-one-two.
JENNIFER: OK. Five-five-five, eight-four-one-two.
MICHAEL: Let's see. How about Anna Silva? Is her number five-five-five, two-nine-four-seven?
JENNIFER: No, it's not. It's five-five-five, two-*five*-four-seven.
MICHAEL: I'm sorry. Could you repeat that?
JENNIFER: Sure. Five-five-five, two-five, four-seven.
JENNIFER: Now, let's see. Steven Carson. His phone number is five-five-five, three-six-four-eight. Right?
MICHAEL: Yes, that's right. Five-five-five, three-six-four-eight.
MICHAEL: And Nicole Johnson's number?
JENNIFER: Oh, Nicole is my roommate. Our number is five-five-five, three-eight-oh-six.
MICHAEL: So, Nicole is five-five-five, three-eight-oh-six, and Jennifer is five-five-five, three-eight-oh-six. It's the same number.
JENNIFER: Right.
JENNIFER: What's *your* phone number, Michael?
MICHAEL: It's five-five-five, nine-nine-six-oh.
JENNIFER: OK. Great!

- Write the other names on the board. Ask for a volunteer to work at the board.
- Play the audio program as many times as necessary. Ss listen and fill in the telephone numbers.
- To check, correct the phone numbers on the board as a class. In case of disagreement, read that part of the audio script. Ss then check their own answers against those on the board.

Answers

David Medina	555-1937	Steven Carson	555-3648
Sarah Conner	555-7645	Nicole Johnson	555-3806
James Sato	555-8412	Jennifer Yang	555-3806
Anna Silva	555-2547	Michael Parker	555-9960

INTERCHANGE 1 Directory assistance

See page T-106 in this Teacher's Edition for notes.

11 SAYING GOOD-BYE

This exercise presents and practices expressions for saying good-bye.

A

- Refer Ss to the pictures in Exercise 6. The people who were saying "hello" are now saying "good-bye."
- Play the audio program twice. Ss read and listen.
- With the Ss' help, list the words and expressions that mean *good-bye: See you later, Bye-bye, Good-bye, See you tomorrow, Bye, Good night.* Point out that *good morning, good afternoon,* and *good evening* mean *hello* (Exercise 6), but *good night* means *good-bye.*
- Play the audio program again or model the conversations line by line. Ss read and listen, then look up and repeat.

B *Class activity*

- Books closed. Demonstrate the activity. Say good-bye to several Ss in different ways. For example, "Good night, Juan. Have a good evening, Kumiko. See you later, Nadia."
- Have Ss stand and move around the room saying good-bye to each other and to you. Encourage them to use different expressions. If necessary, write the different expressions on the board for Ss to refer to.

Optional activities

1. *Scrambled letters*

- See page T-147.

2. *Spelling contest*

- See page T-148.

Workbook

Workbook Exercises 8–10 on pages 5–6 correspond to Cycle 2, Exercises 7–11 of the Student's Book. Answers to the Workbook exercises begin on page T-182 of this Teacher's Edition.

10 LISTENING

Jennifer and Michael are making a list of telephone numbers of classmates. Listen and complete the information.

Name	Telephone number
David Medina	555-1937
Sarah Conner	
James Sato	
Anna Silva	
Steven Carson	
Nicole Johnson	
Jennifer Yang	
Michael Parker	

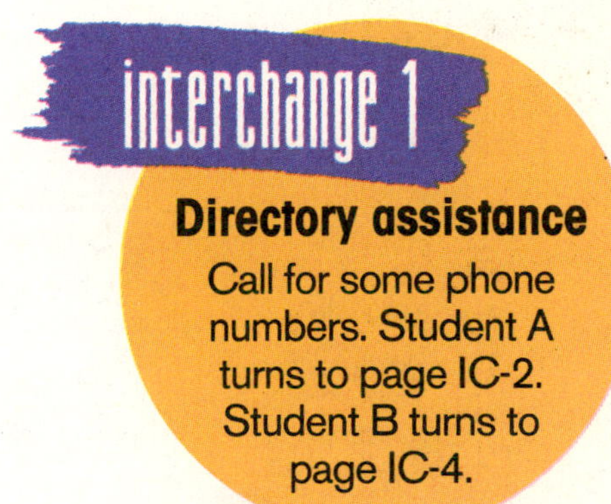

interchange 1
Directory assistance
Call for some phone numbers. Student A turns to page IC-2. Student B turns to page IC-4.

11 SAYING GOOD-BYE

A Listen and practice.

Bye-bye, Lisa.

Thanks, Kim. You, too.

Good-bye, Ms. Chen.

B ***Class activity*** Go around the room. Practice saying good-bye to your classmates and to your teacher.

2 What's this?

1 SNAPSHOT

Listen and practice.

Check (✓) the things you have.
Choose two things you want.

2 ARTICLES *Classroom objects*

Articles
an + vowel sound
a + consonant sound

A Listen. Complete these sentences with **a** or **an**.

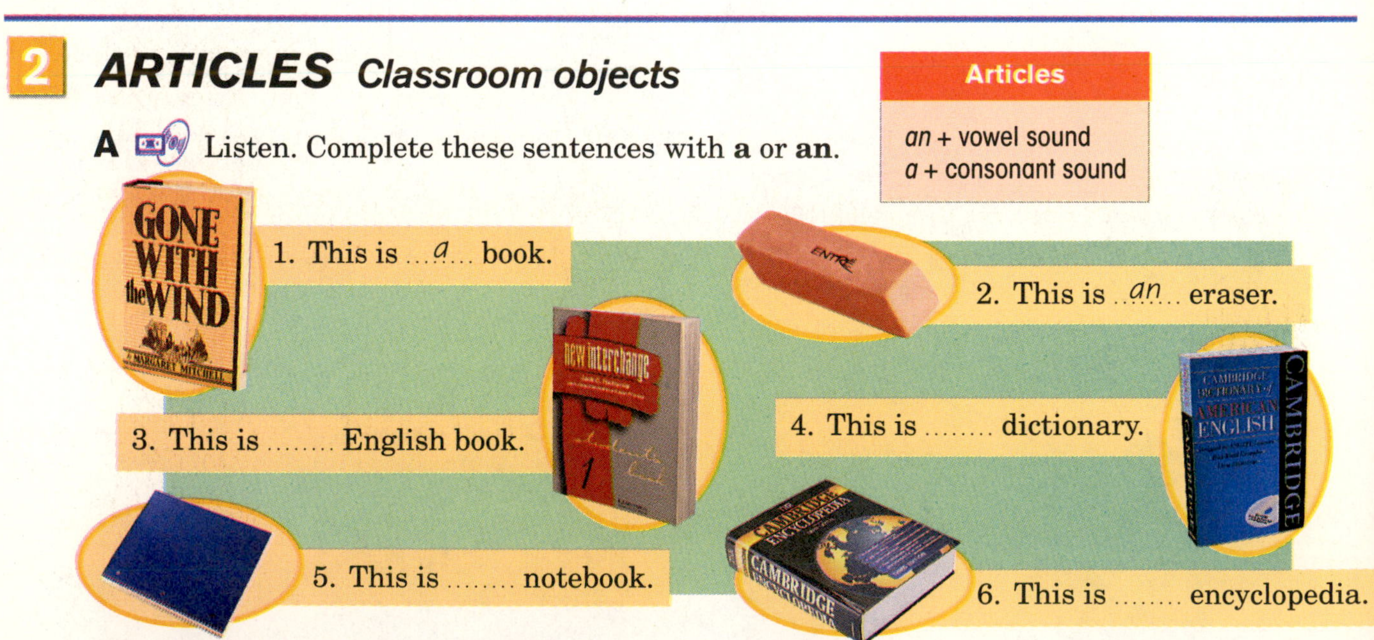

B ***Pair work*** Find these things in your classroom.

wastebasket	pen	desk	map	table
English dictionary	pencil	book bag	board	window
cassette player	clock	chair	wall	door

A: This is a wastebasket.
B: How do you spell *wastebasket*?
A: W-A-S-T-E-B-A-S-K-E-T.

2 What's this?

This unit presents language for personal possessions and common classroom objects. It introduces articles a, an, and the; this/it and these/they; regular noun plurals; yes/no questions and short answers with be; questions with where; and some prepositions of place.

Cycle 1, Exercises 1–6

1 SNAPSHOT On-Line Shopping

This exercise illustrates some things that people might buy on the Internet (*on-line* means *connected to the Internet*). It introduces the topic of personal possessions.

(*Note:* This presentation does not ask Ss to produce sentences with *a/an, have,* or *want.* Instead, they raise their hands. If your Ss can produce these structures, let them say their answers to the questions.)

- Books open. Give Ss time to look at the illustration. Then play the audio program. Ss listen and read.
- Play the audio program again or model the words one by one. Ss listen and repeat.
- Write the names of the eight things in a list on the board. Clarify the meaning of *have*. Show Ss your own watch or a S's watch. Say, "I have a watch." Make a check mark next to *watch* on the board.
- Ss check the items they have in their books or write the words on a separate piece of paper.
- Ask Ss about each of the items illustrated, for example, "Who has a pager?" Ss respond by raising their hands. On the board, check the items that Ss have.
- Clarify the meaning of *want*. Use gestures and emphasis to help convey the meaning. Say, for example, "I don't have a camera. I *want* a camera." Then say, "I want a camera and a cell phone." Hold up two fingers to show you want two things.
- Say, "*You* want two things." Ask, "Who wants a pager?" Ss raise their hands. Write the number of people next to *pager* on the board. Continue with the other seven items.

2 ARTICLES Classroom objects

This activity introduces the names of objects commonly found in classrooms and presents the indefinite articles *a* and *an*.

A

- Books open. Go over the task. Point out the information about articles in the box.
- Play the audio program. Ss fill in the articles they hear. If necessary, play the audio program again.
- Elicit answers from Ss, and write them on the board.
- Ss check their answers with those on the board. Then they read the sentences to each other in pairs.

Answers

1. This is **a** book.
2. This is **an** eraser.
3. This is **an** English book.
4. This is **a** dictionary.
5. This is **a** notebook.
6. This is **an** encyclopedia.

B *Pair work*

- Give Ss time to read the words in the box and find as many objects as possible in the classroom.
- Say the words one by one. Ss listen and repeat.
- Let Ss ask about words they don't know. Let other Ss identify the objects by pointing to them, or do it yourself.
- Read the conversation aloud. Then model the conversation line by line. Ss repeat. When you say, "This is a wastebasket," go over to the wastebasket and touch it or point down at it.
- Ask two or three pairs to act out the conversation with some of the other objects. For the first line, the S goes to the object and touches it or picks it up.
- In pairs, Ss walk around the classroom identifying and spelling objects for each other.
- **Optional:** If there are other objects in the classroom that Ss can name, write the names on the board, and go over pronunciation. Then continue practicing with the new objects.

3 CONVERSATION

This conversation introduces expressions for talking about gifts both enthusiastically and politely. It introduces the questions *What's this?* and *What are these?* and answers with *it* and *they*.

- Books open. Give Ss a few seconds to study the picture. Play the audio program. Ss listen and read.
- Check Ss' understanding of the situation. Elicit the names of the people in the picture (from left to right: Rex, Wendy, and Helen).
- Play the audio program again. If necessary, clarify vocabulary. Communicate the meanings of *Wow!* and *Oh, cool!* with your tone and facial expression. Use *Thank you* (from Unit 1) to clarify *You're welcome*. Contrast *interesting* and *very nice* with *Wow!* and *Oh, cool!* to show that the first two words are less enthusiastic.
- Play the audio program again or model the conversation line by line. Ss listen and read, then look up and repeat.
- Ss practice the conversation in groups of three using the Look Up and Say technique. Walk around the classroom while they practice. Encourage them to use appropriate emphasis, gestures, and facial expressions.
- **Optional:** Choose some of the more expressive Ss to act out the conversation for the class. Encourage them to use their books as little as possible.

4 PRONUNCIATION Plural s

This exercise practices the pronunciation of plural *s*. (*Note:* For a key to phonetic symbols, see page xiv of this Teacher's Edition.)

Pronunciation rules:

1. When nouns end in the sibilant sounds /s/, /z/, /ʃ/, /tʃ/, /ʒ/, or /dʒ/, the plural takes an extra syllable /ɪz/ (e.g., watch – watches).
2. When nouns end in a vowel sound after other voiced consonants /b/, /d/, /g/, /l/, /m/, /n/, /ɲ/, /r/, /ð/, or /v/, *s* is pronounced /z/ (e.g., camera – cameras).
3. After other unvoiced final consonants /p/, /t/, /k/, /f/, or /θ/, *s* is pronounced /s/ (e.g., map – maps).

A

- Books closed. Write these words on the board, and underline the endings. Say each word aloud slowly so that Ss can hear the endings.

  days   *nights*   *classes*

- Write the corresponding phonetic symbol above each word. Pronounce each symbol, then the word. Again, speak slowly so that Ss can hear the differences.

/z/	/s/	/ɪz/
days	*nights*	*classes*

- Books open. Give Ss time to look at part A. Then play the audio program. Ss listen and read.
- Play the audio program again or model the words one at a time. Ss listen and repeat.

B

- Pronounce the (singular) words one by one. Ss repeat.
- Quickly copy the chart on the board. Use the example to demonstrate the task.
- Ss fill in the chart in their books or on a separate piece of paper. Have one S work at the board.

Answers and Audio Script

/z/	/s/	/ɪz/
newspapers	clocks	addresses
keys	stamps	briefcases
televisions	wallets	purses

C

- Play the audio program while you correct the answers on the board with the whole class. Ss correct their own answers from the chart on the board.

3 CONVERSATION

Listen and practice.

Wendy: Wow! What's this?
Helen: It's a camera.
Wendy: Oh, cool! Thank you, Helen. It's great!
Helen: You're welcome.
Rex: Now open this box!
Wendy: OK. Uh, what are these?
Rex: They're earrings.
Wendy: Oh. They're . . . interesting. Thank you, Rex. They're very nice.

4 PRONUNCIATION *Plural s*

A Listen and practice. Notice the pronunciation of the plural **s** endings.

s = /z/		*s* = /s/		*(e)s* = /ɪz/	
telephone	telephone**s**	desk	desk**s**	sentence	sentence**s**
camera	camera**s**	map	map**s**	exercise	exercise**s**
book bag	book bag**s**	wastebasket	wastebasket**s**	watch	watch**es**

B Say the plural forms of these nouns. Then complete the chart.

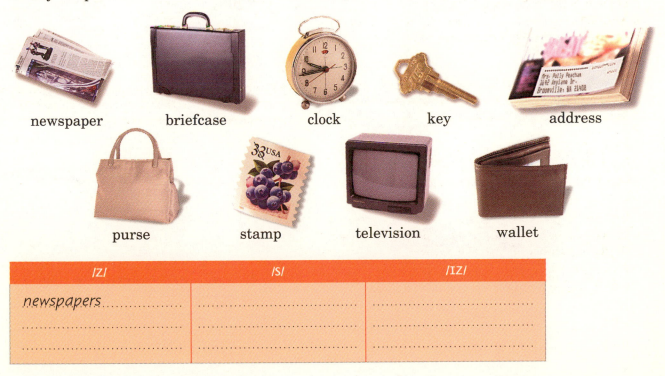

/z/	/s/	/ɪz/
newspapers		

C Listen and check your answers.

5 GRAMMAR FOCUS

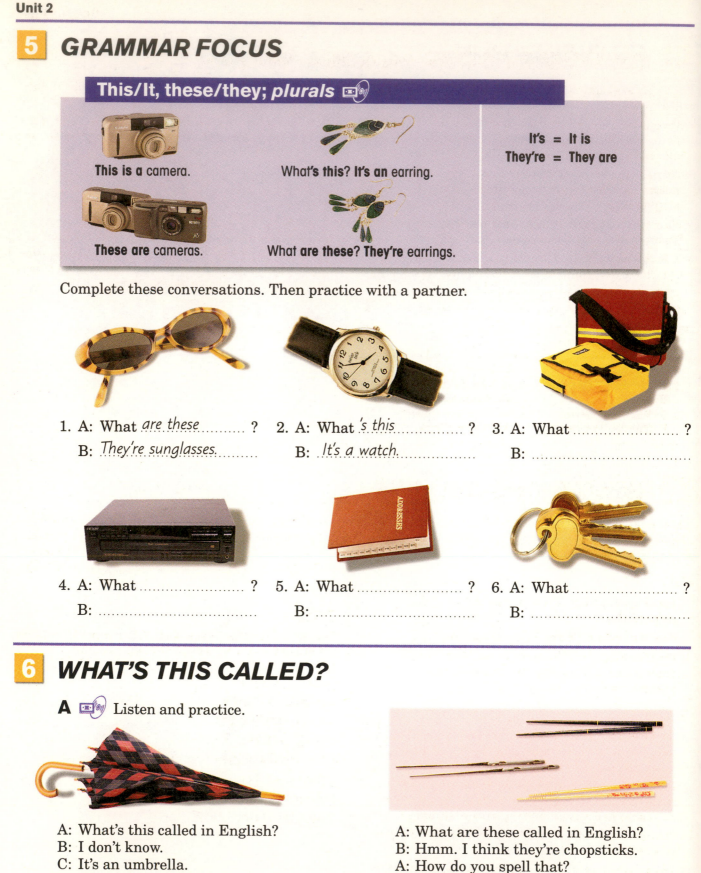

This/It, these/they; *plurals*

This is a camera.	What's **this**? **It's an** earring.	**It's** = **It is**
These are cameras.	What **are these**? **They're** earrings.	**They're** = **They are**

Complete these conversations. Then practice with a partner.

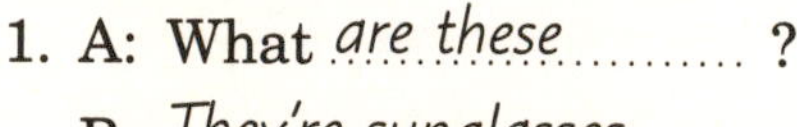

1. A: What *are these* ?
   B: *They're sunglasses.*

2. A: What *'s this* ?
   B: *It's a watch.*

3. A: What .... ?
   B: ....

4. A: What .... ?
   B: ....

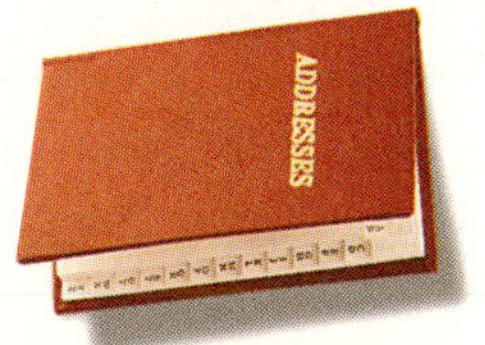

5. A: What .... ?
   B: ....

6. A: What .... ?
   B: ....

6 WHAT'S THIS CALLED?

A Listen and practice.

A: What's this called in English?
B: I don't know.
C: It's an umbrella.
A: How do you spell that?
C: U-M-B-R-E-L-L-A.

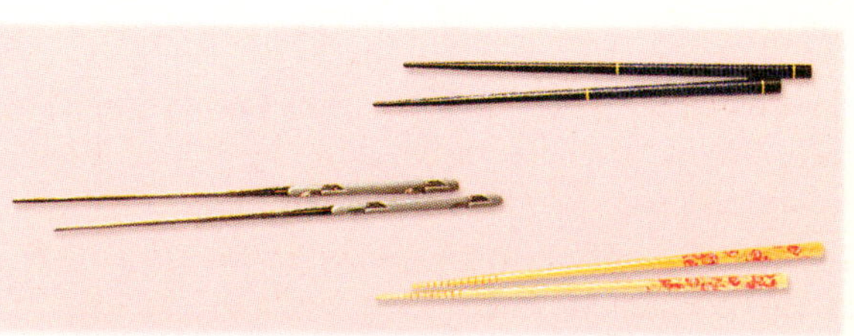

A: What are these called in English?
B: Hmm. I think they're chopsticks.
A: How do you spell that?
B: C-H-O-P-S-T-I-C-K-S.

B ***Group work*** Choose four things. Put them in the center of the group. Take turns asking about the name and spelling of each thing.

5 GRAMMAR FOCUS This/It, these/they; *plurals*

This exercise presents questions with *this* and *these* and answers with *it* and *they*.

- Books open. Give Ss time to look at the information in the box. Play the audio program to present the information. Ss listen and read.
- Contrast the pronunciation of *this* and *these*. Elicit the information that *this* and *it* are singular; *these* and *they* are plural.
- Play the audio program again or model the sentences line by line. Ss listen and repeat.
- Use the examples to demonstrate the task. Ss look at the photos and complete the conversations.
- While Ss are working, copy conversations 3–6 on the board. Fill in the answers, making a few "mistakes."

Answers

1. A: What are these? B: **They're sunglasses.**	4. A: What**'s this**? B: **It's a CD player.**
2. A: What**'s this**? B: **It's a watch.**	5. A: What**'s this**? B: **It's an address book.**
3. A: What **are these**? B: **They're book bags.**	6. A: What **are these**? B: **They're keys.**

- When Ss have finished, invite volunteers to correct the answers on the board.
- When the answers are correct, Ss check one anothers' work in pairs. Then they practice the six conversations with their partners.
- **Optional:** Books closed. For additional practice, write this on the board:

  What's ____________? *It's* ____________.
  What are ____________? *They're* ____________.

  Model questions and answers about objects in the classroom. Ss repeat. Then have Ss practice asking and answering the questions. If necessary, correct their use of *a/an* and the pronunciation of plurals.

6 WHAT'S THIS CALLED?

This exercise teaches the question *What's this called in English?* and reviews identifying and spelling the names of objects.

A

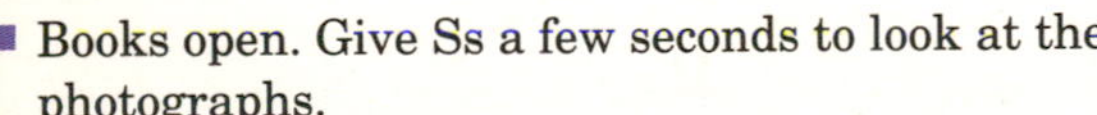

- Books open. Give Ss a few seconds to look at the photographs.
- Play the audio program. Ss listen and read.
- Play the audio program again or model the conversations line by line. Ss listen and read, then look up and repeat.

B *Group work*

- Demonstrate the task. Put four objects on your desk, including at least one unfamiliar object. Call four volunteers to the front of the room.
- Lead the four Ss through the conversation. If no S can name an object in English, get them to ask you, "What's this called in English?" and then answer them.
- Put Ss in small groups. Each S puts at least one object on a desk in the center of the group.
- Taking turns, each S picks up an object and asks its name and how to spell it. The other Ss answer the questions.
- **Optional:** If no one in the group knows the name of an object or how to spell it, one S takes the object to other groups to ask them about it. That S's group continues without him or her until the S returns with an answer.

Workbook

Workbook Exercises 1–5 on pages 7–9 correspond to Cycle 1, Exercises 1–6 of the Student's Book. Answers to the Workbook exercises begin on page T-182 of this Teacher's Edition.

Optional Activities

1. *Game – Hangman*
- See page T-148.

2. *Crossword puzzle*
- See page T-148.

3. *Scrambled letters*
- See page T-147.

CONVERSATION

This conversation introduces expressions for asking about ownership. It also introduces the possessives *my* and *your*, yes/no questions, and *where* questions with *be*.

- Books open. Give Ss time to look at the illustration.
- Play the audio program. Ss listen and read. Check Ss' understanding of the situation. Elicit the names of the people in the picture (from left to right, the waiter, Kate, and Joe).
- Play the audio program again. Ss listen and read. If necessary, clarify key vocabulary. Use mime to demonstrate *They're gone! I bet* means *I think. (Note:* Ss do not need to understand *still* to understand the conversation.)
- Play the audio program again or model the conversation line by line. Ss listen and read, then look up and repeat.
- Ss practice the conversation in groups of three using the Look Up and Say technique. Have groups say the conversation three times, with Ss changing roles each time. Walk around and give help as needed.
- **Optional:** If one or two groups are especially good at saying the conversation expressively, have them act it out for the class. Encourage them not to use their books if possible.

8 GRAMMAR FOCUS *Yes/No and* where *questions with* be

This grammar focus presents the verb *be* in yes/no questions and short answers, and questions with *where*.

- Give Ss time to look at the information in the box. Play the audio program to present the information. Ss listen and read.
- Point out that there is no contraction in short answers with *yes*.
- Play the audio program again or model the sentences line by line.

A

- Use the example to demonstrate the task.
- Ss complete the two conversations.
- To check answers, have volunteers spell the answers as you write them on the board. Write exactly what they say. For example, if Ss say "e" for "i," write "e." Do not write apostrophes or capital letters unless Ss say them. If necessary, demonstrate how to do this.
- Have Ss tell you how to correct any mistakes. Ss must use only English to get you to erase and write letters. Allow imperfect English if you can understand it.

Answers

1. A: Where **are** my glasses?
   B: Are **they** in your bag?
   A: No, they're **not**.
   B: Wait! **Are** they in your pocket?
   A: Yes, **they** are. Thanks!
2. A: **Is** this my pen?
   B: No, **it's** not. It's *my* pen.
   A: Sorry. **Where** is my pen?
   B: **It's** on your desk.
   A: Yes, it **is**. You're right!

- Model the conversations line by line. Ss repeat. Then Ss practice the conversations in pairs.

B *Group work*

- Books open. Model the conversation line by line. Ss repeat.
- Use mime to demonstrate the meaning of *Let me see*. Reach for someone's pen saying, "Let me see." Examine the pen, then say, "No, it's not my pen."
- Collect an object from each of three Ss, getting a pen from one of them.
- In front of the class, lead the three Ss through a demonstration of the task. Have the group try the conversation using their own names and an object. The conversation may not follow the example exactly, depending on whose object is chosen. Help them if necessary.
- Divide the class into groups of four or five. In each group, each S puts three objects in front of them. They practice with all their objects, taking different roles.

7 CONVERSATION

Listen and practice.

Kate: Oh, no! Where are my car keys?
Joe: Relax, Kate. Are they in your purse?
Kate: No, they're not. They're gone!
Joe: I bet they're still on the table in the restaurant.
Waiter: Excuse me. Are these your keys?
Kate: Yes, they are. Thank you!
Joe: See? No problem.
Waiter: And is this your wallet?
Kate: Hmm. No, it's not. Where is your wallet, Joe?
Joe: In my pocket. . . . Wait a minute! That's my wallet!

8 GRAMMAR FOCUS

Yes/No and *where* questions with *be*

Is this your wallet?	**Are your keys** in your purse?
Yes, **it is.**	Yes, **they are.**
No, **it's not.**	No, **they're not.**
Where is your wallet?	**Where are my keys?**
It's in my pocket.	They're in the restaurant.

A Complete these conversations. Then practice them.

1. A: Where ....*are*.... my glasses?
   B: Are .... in your bag?
   A: No, they're ....
   B: Wait! .... they in your pocket?
   A: Yes, ... are. Thanks!

2. A: .... this my pen?
   B: No, ... not. It's *my* pen.
   A: Sorry. .... is my pen?
   B: .... on your desk.
   A: Yes, it .... You're right!

B ***Group work*** Put three things from the classroom, your pocket, or your bag in a box. Find the owner of each item.

A: Is this your pen, Young-ho?
B: No, it's not.

A: Is this your pen, Sun-hee?
C: Let me see. Yes, it is.

9 WORD POWER *Prepositions; article* the

A Listen and practice.

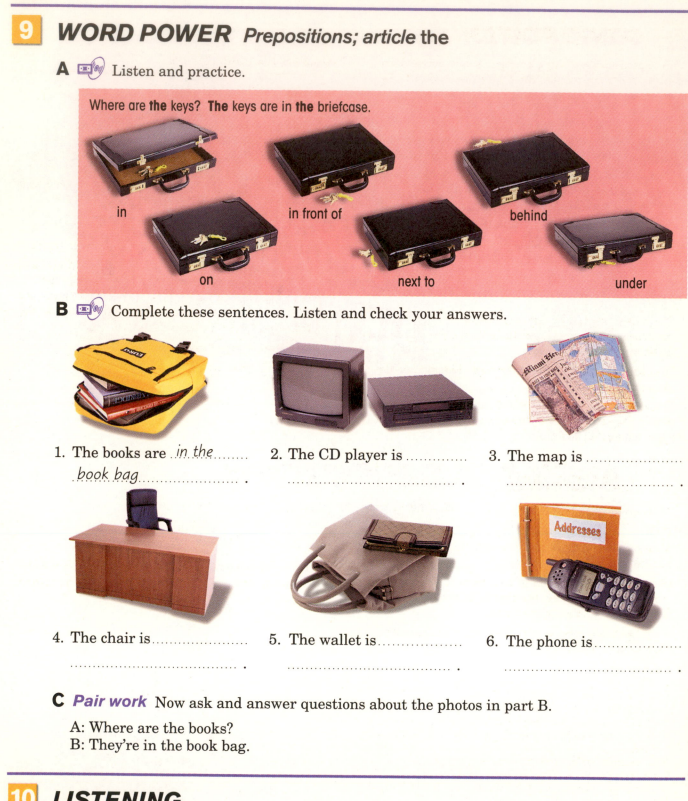

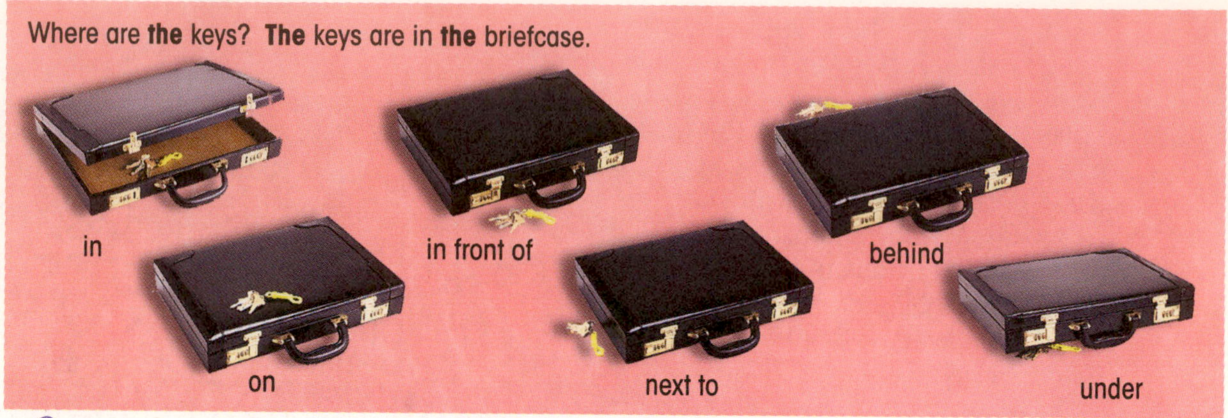

B Complete these sentences. Listen and check your answers.

1. The books are *in the book bag*.

2. The CD player is ....

3. The map is ....

4. The chair is ....

5. The wallet is ....

6. The phone is ....

C ***Pair work*** Now ask and answer questions about the photos in part B.

A: Where are the books?
B: They're in the book bag.

10 LISTENING

Kate is looking for some things in her house.
Where are they? Listen and match each thing to its location.

1. earrings	a. under the table
2. watch	b. on the chair
3. sunglasses	c. in front of the television
4. address book	d. in her purse

9 WORD POWER Prepositions; article the

This exercise presents and practices some prepositions of place. It also introduces the article *the*. In part B, Ss practice writing about the locations of objects.

A

- Books open. Give Ss time to look at the photographs and captions. Play the audio program. Ss listen and read.
- Play the audio program again or model the sentences and words one by one.
- Check Ss' understanding of the prepositions. Use an actual briefcase or a book bag and someone's keys. Demonstrate the different prepositions in random order. Call on Ss to ask the question, "Where are the keys?" Other Ss answer, "They're . . ."

B

- Have Ss study the pictures and the beginnings of the sentences. Have Ss tell you the name of the other object in each photograph.
- Use the example to explain the task. Ss complete the exercise individually.
- Have five Ss write answers 2–6 on the board. Play the audio program. Ss listen and correct the answers on the board and their own answers.

Answers and Audio Script

1. The books are **in the book bag**.
2. The CD player is **next to the television**.
3. The map is **under the newspaper**.
4. The chair is **behind the desk**.
5. The wallet is **on the purse**.
6. The phone is **in front of the address book**.

- **Optional:** Have Ss make a clean copy of the sentences for homework.

C *Pair work*

- Use the example conversation to demonstrate the task.
- In pairs, Ss ask and answer questions about the objects. Encourage them to ask two questions about a photo when possible. This is not possible with the first photo, but with the second photo, they can ask, "Where is the CD player?" and "Where is the television?"

Optional Activity: *True or false?*

- See page T-148.

10 LISTENING

This exercise practices listening for locations of objects.

- Books open. If necessary, review the list of objects and the list of locations.
- Demonstrate the matching task. Show Ss that they should draw lines from the objects in the left column to the locations in the right column.
- Play the audio program as many times as necessary. Ss complete the exercise.

Audio script

KATE: Where are my earrings?
JOE: Are they on the table?
KATE: No. . . . Oh, here they are–in my purse. Now, where's my watch? Hmmm . . . It's not in my purse. Where–
JOE: There it is! In front of the television!
KATE: Oh, of course! Thanks, Joe. Let's see. My sunglasses. Where are they? Next to my watch? No,–
JOE: Are they behind your purse?
KATE: No, they aren't. Oh, they're on the chair. Great! Now, I just need one more thing: my address book. . . . It's probably on the table.
JOE: No, it's not. . . . It's *under* the table.

- Ss check their answers by looking at the illustration on page 13.

Answers

1. d 2. c 3. b 4. a

- Have volunteers make statements about each of Kate's things. For example, "Kate's earrings are in her purse."

 WHERE ARE MY THINGS?

This activity provides further practice with questions and answers about the location of things.

Pair work

- Use the illustration and the example conversation to clarify the task.
- If necessary, have two Ss do another example with another object.
- In pairs, Ss take turns asking and answering questions about the eight things on the list. Walk around to give help as needed.
- **Optional:** Choose an item from Exercise 10, and ask where it is. Elicit an answer with the possessive *her* (e.g., "Where are Kate's sunglasses?" "Her sunglasses are on the chair"). Then, choose an item from Exercise 11, and ask where it is. Elicit an answer with the possessive *his* (e.g., "Where is Joe's wallet?" "His wallet is under the chair").
- **Optional:** Have a S (Student A) choose an item from Exercise 10 or 11 and ask about its location. Student A calls on a second S (Student B) to respond. After Student B responds, he or she asks a question about another item and calls on a third S to respond. Continue until all items in both Exercise 10 and Exercise 11 have been discussed.

INTERCHANGE 2 Find the differences

See page T-108 of this Teacher's Edition for notes.

Workbook

Workbook Exercises 6–9 on pages 10–12 correspond to Cycle 2, Exercises 7–11 of the Student's Book. Answers to the Workbook exercises begin on page T-182 of this Teacher's Edition.

Optional Activity: *Spelling contest*

- See page T-148. Use this activity to review the names of objects from the unit.

11 WHERE ARE MY THINGS?

Pair work Joe is looking for these things. Ask and answer questions.

pager	glasses
briefcase	umbrella
keys	cell phone
wallet	notebook

A: Where is his pager?
B: It's in front of the television.

interchange 2

Find the differences

Compare two pictures of a room. Turn to page IC-3.

3 Where are you from?

1 SNAPSHOT

 Listen and practice.

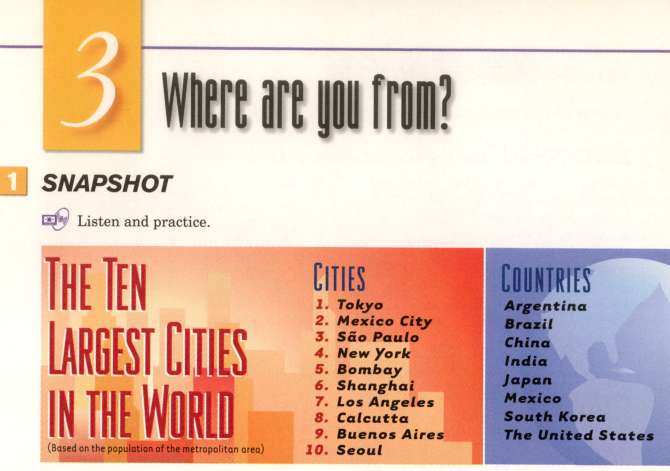

THE TEN LARGEST CITIES IN THE WORLD
(Based on the population of the metropolitan area)

CITIES	COUNTRIES
1. Tokyo	Argentina
2. Mexico City	Brazil
3. São Paulo	China
4. New York	India
5. Bombay	Japan
6. Shanghai	Mexico
7. Los Angeles	South Korea
8. Calcutta	The United States
9. Buenos Aires	
10. Seoul	

Source: http://www.infoplease.com

Where are these cities? Match the cities to the countries. Check your answers in the appendix. What are some large cities in your country?

2 CONVERSATION

A Listen and practice.

Tim: Where are you from, Jessica?
Jessica: Well, my family is here in the United States, but we're from Korea originally.
Tim: Oh, my mother is Korean – from Seoul! Are you from Seoul?
Jessica: No, we're not from Seoul. We're from Pusan.
Tim: So is your first language Korean?
Jessica: Yes, it is.

B Listen to Jessica and Tim talk to Tony, Natasha, and Monique. Check (✓) **True** or **False**.

	True	False
1. Tony is from Italy.	☐	☐
2. Natasha is from New York.	☐	☐
3. Monique's first language is English.	☐	☐

3 Where are you from?

This unit introduces the names of cities, countries, and regions of the world. It practices giving personal information and describing people. It presents the verb be in negative statements, yes/no questions, short answers, and Wh-questions.

Cycle 1, Exercises 1–4

1 SNAPSHOT The Ten Largest Cities in the World

This exercise introduces the topic of international cities. The questions relate to the Ss' own experiences.

- Give Ss time to look at the chart. Then play the audio program once while Ss listen and read.
- Play the audio program again or read the cities and countries one by one. Ss repeat.
- Demonstrate the matching task. Ss match the cities and countries. (*Note:* There are ten cities but only eight countries.)
- Ss compare to check their answers. Then they look at the answers in the appendix.

Answers

Answers are in the appendix at the back of the Student's Book.

- Ask the discussion question, "What are some large cities in your country?" or "What are some large cities in this/our country?"

  (*Note:* Help Ss identify city or country names that may be different in their language.)

2 CONVERSATION

This exercise introduces negative statements with *be* and expands yes/no questions. It also introduces the question "Where are you from?" and the pronoun *we*.

A

- Books open. Have Ss look at the illustration. The people in front are Tim and Jessica. Play the audio program. Ss read and listen.
- Play the audio program again. Ss listen and read. Give Ss a chance to guess the meaning of new vocabulary. For example, they may ask about *originally,* but they should be able to guess that it means *first* (approximately).
- It would be good to teach *family* and *mother* plus *brother, sister,* and *parents.* The five words appear in this unit. Make a family tree diagram with stick figures on the board to teach or review the words. (*Note:* Words explaining family relationships are specifically taught in Unit 6, Exercise 3.)
- Play the audio program again or model the conversation line by line. Ss listen and read, then look up and repeat.
- Ss practice the conversation in pairs using the Look Up and Say technique.
- **Optional:** Have a few pairs of Ss act out the conversation for the class.

B

- Books open. Use the illustration to set the scene. Tony, Natasha, and Monique are behind Tim and Jessica. They are all talking together.
- Go over the statements in the box. Clarify *True* and *False* if necessary:

  T: My name is (your name). Yes?
  Ss: Yes.
  T: Yes, true! My name is (another name). True?
  Ss: No.
  T: No, false!

- Books closed. Play the audio program. Ss listen only.
- Books open. Play the audio program as many times as necessary. Ss check *True* or *False* in the box.

Audio script

1. JESSICA: So where are you from, Tony?
   TONY: I'm Brazilian.
   JESSICA: Oh, what part of Brazil are you from?
   TONY: I'm from Rio.
2. TIM: Is your name Russian, Natasha?
   NATASHA: Yes, it is. But I'm from the United States – from New York.
   TIM: So you're American.
   NATASHA: Yes, I am. But my parents are from Russia originally.
3. TONY: By the way, Jessica, this is Monique.
   JESSICA: Nice to meet you, Monique. Are you from Brazil, too?
   MONIQUE: No, I'm from Montreal.
   JESSICA: So you're Canadian. Is your first language English?
   MONIQUE: No, it's not. My first language is French.

- Elicit answers from the Ss. Write their answers on the board, and correct them if necessary.

Answers

1. False (He's from Brazil.)
2. True
3. False (Her first language is French.)

3 GRAMMAR FOCUS Statements and yes/no questions with be

This grammar focus brings together previously presented information about *be*. It adds more affirmative and negative statements and the pronoun *we*.

(*Note:* For simplicity, only one negative form of *be* has been presented so far: *I'm not, he's not,* and so forth. The form *she isn't, we aren't, . . .* is presented for the first time in Unit 4, with the present continuous.)

- Books open. Use the audio program to present the information in the box. Students listen and read.
- Draw Ss' attention to the new pronoun *we*.
- Play the audio program again or model the sentences line by line. Ss listen and repeat.

A

- Use the example to demonstrate the task. Show Ss that they can refer to the grammar box while they complete the conversations. Ss complete the conversations individually.
- While Ss are working, put answer blanks like these on the board for all three conversations:

  1. *A:* _______
  B: _______
  A: _______
  B: _______ _______

- Walk around the classroom to give help. When you see a correct answer, send the S to write it on the board.
- Correct the answers on the board with the whole class. Then have Ss correct their papers in pairs.

Answers

1. A: Hiroshi, **are** you and Maiko from Japan?
   B: Yes, we **are**.
   A: **Are** you from Tokyo?
   B: No, **we're** not. **We're** from Kyoto.
2. A: **Is** Laura from the U.S.?
   B: No, **she's** not. She's from the U.K.
   A: **Is** she from London?
   B: Yes, she **is**. But her parents **are** from Italy originally.
   A: **Is** Italian her first language?
   B: No, **it's** not. **It's** English.
3. A: **Are** Elena and Carlos from Mexico?
   B: No, **they're** not. **They're** from Peru.
   A: What about you? Where **are** you from?
   B: **I'm** from São Paulo.
   A: So your first language **is** Portuguese.
   B: Yes, it **is.**

- Model the completed conversations line by line. Ss listen and repeat.
- Ss practice the conversations in pairs using the Look Up and Say technique. While they work, circulate to give help with pronunciation.

B

- Use the example to demonstrate the task on the board. In this matching exercise, Ss write the letter of the answer next to the question.
- Ss work individually to match the questions and answers.
- Ss compare answers in pairs and correct their work if they wish. Then pairs read the questions and answers aloud for the class. If there is a mistake, invite the class to correct it.

Answers

1. d	2. c	3. e	4. a	5. b

- Ss practice the questions and answers in pairs.

C *Pair work*

- Explain or demonstrate the task. Ss work individually to write five questions. They use the questions in part B as models.
- As they write, circulate to check their work.
- Elicit questions from several Ss, and have volunteers answer them.
- In pairs, Ss ask each other their questions. Then they change partners and ask their questions again. Encourage Ss to give as much information as possible when answering.

Optional Activity: *Yes or no?*

- See page T-149.

3 GRAMMAR FOCUS

Statements and yes/no questions with be

Are you from Seoul?	**I'm not** from Seoul.	**I'm** from Pusan.
Is Tony from Italy?	**He's not** from Italy.	**He's** from Brazil.
Is your first language French?	**It's not** French.	**It's** English.
Are you and Maria from Chile?	**We're not** from Chile.	**We're** from Argentina.
Are your parents in the U.S.?	**They're not** in the U.S.	**They're** in Europe.

Are your parents in the U.S.?
Yes, they are.
No, they're not.

Are you and your family from Asia?
Yes, we are.
No, we're not.

we're = we are

For a list of countries, nationalities, and languages, see the appendix.

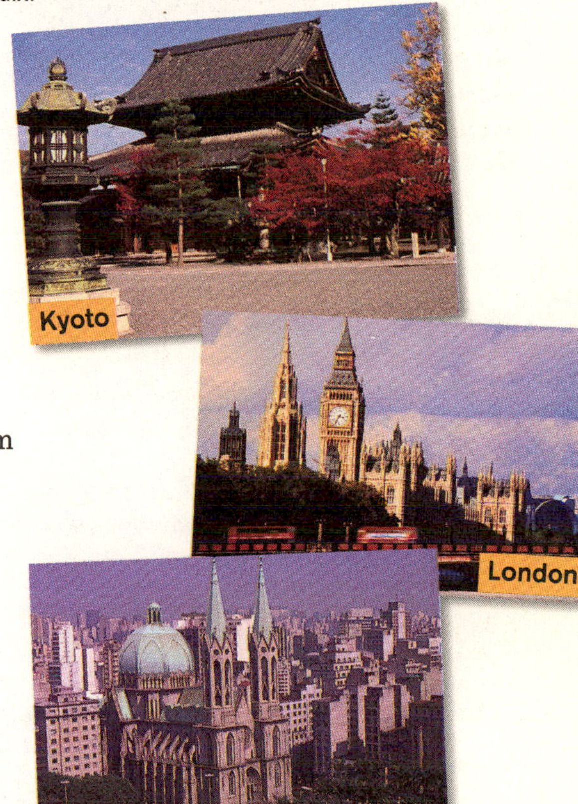

A Complete the conversations. Then practice with a partner.

1. A: Hiroshi, ...*are*.... you and Maiko from Japan?
   B: Yes, we ....
   A: .... you from Tokyo?
   B: No, ... not. .... from Kyoto.
2. A: .... Laura from the U.S.?
   B: No, ... not. She's from the U.K.
   A: .... she from London?
   B: Yes, she .... But her parents .... from Italy originally.
   A: .... Italian her first language?
   B: No, ... not. .... English.
3. A: .... Elena and Carlos from Mexico?
   B: No, ... not. .... from Peru.
   A: What about you? Where .... you from?
   B: .... from São Paulo.
   A: So your first language .... Portuguese.
   B: Yes, it ....

B Match the questions with the answers. Then practice with a partner.

1. Are you and your family from Canada? ..*d*..
2. Is your first language English? ......
3. Are you Brazilian? ......
4. Is Mr. Ho from Hong Kong? ......
5. Is your mother from the United States? ......

a. No, he's not. He's from Singapore.
b. Yes, she is. She's from California.
c. No, it's not. My first language is Japanese.
d. No, we're not. We're from Australia.
e. Yes, we are. We're from São Paulo.

C ***Pair work*** Write five questions like the ones in part B. Ask and answer your questions with a partner.

4 REGIONS OF THE WORLD

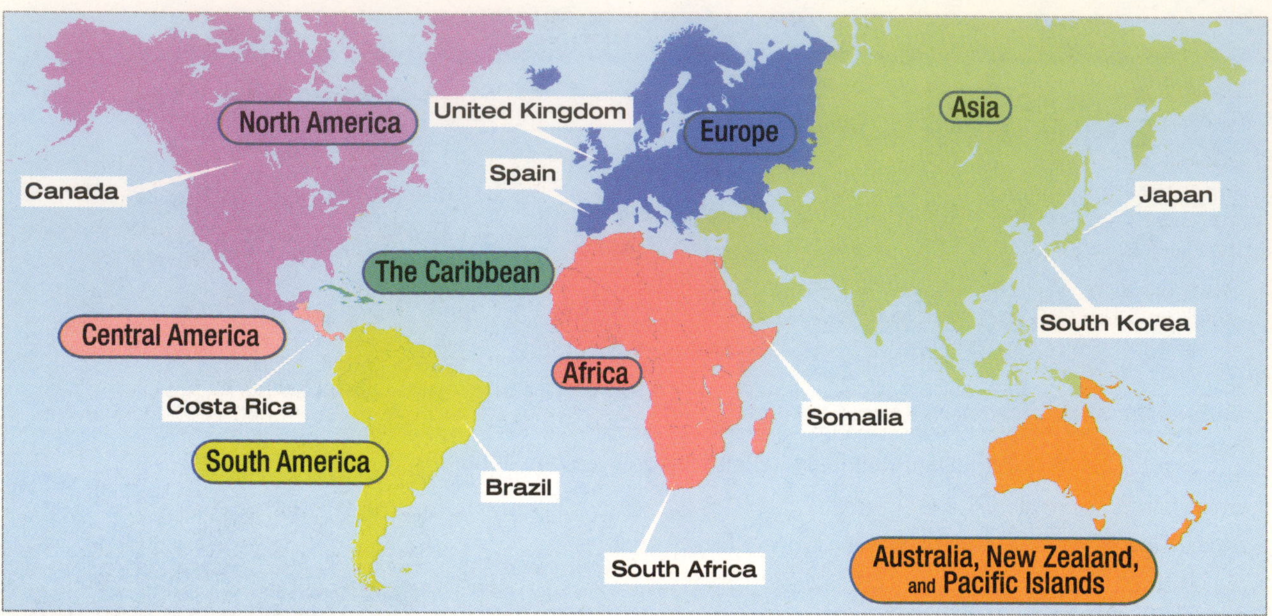

See the appendix for a list of countries and nationalities.

A ***Group work*** Name two more countries in each of these regions. Compare your charts.

Europe	Africa	Asia	South America	North America
....	....	....	....	....
....	....	....	....	....

A: France is in Europe.
B: Greece is in Europe, too.

B ***Pair work*** Where are these people from?

Student A: Guess where these people are from. Ask Student B questions.

Student B: Turn to the appendix. Use the map to answer Student A's questions.

A: Is Antonio Banderas from Puerto Rico?
B: No, he's not.
A: Is he from Spain?
B: Yes, he is. That's right.

4 REGIONS OF THE WORLD

This exercise presents and practices names of countries and regions.

- Books open. Give Ss time to look at the map and read the captions.
- Hold up your book or use a large world map. Read the captions aloud. Read the name of a region first, then the countries that are in it. Point to each area as you say the names. Ss repeat.
- Say a sentence about each region, for example, "South Africa and Somalia are in Africa." Ss repeat.

A *Group work*

- Explain the task. Ss work together in groups to name two more countries for each region (*not* the countries already shown on the map). They can use the list of countries in the appendix at the back of the book.
- Model the two example statements. Ss repeat.
- Ss work on the task in groups of three to five Ss. Walk around to give help.
- To check answers, write the five regions on the board. Ss from different groups call out their group's countries under the regions. Except for Russia and Turkey, each country is in only one region.
- Correct the answers on the board. Check spelling and go over pronunciation.

Possible answers (based on the list of countries in the appendix)

Europe: Austria, England, France, Germany, Greece, Ireland, Italy, the Netherlands, Poland, Portugal, Russia, Sweden, Switzerland, Turkey, the United Kingdom (England, Scotland, Wales, and Northern Ireland)
Africa: Egypt, Ghana, Morocco, Nigeria, Sudan, Tanzania
Asia: Cambodia, China, India, Indonesia, Israel, Jordan, Laos, Lebanon, Malaysia, Nepal, the Philippines, Russia, Saudi Arabia, Singapore, Thailand, Turkey, Vietnam
South America: Argentina, Bolivia, Chile, Colombia, Ecuador, Paraguay, Peru, Uruguay, Venezuela
North America: Mexico, the United States

B *Pair work*

- Books open. Have Ss study the pictures and read the names. Model the conversation line by line. Ss listen and repeat.
- Put Ss in pairs. Student A looks at page 16. Student B turns to the map in the appendix.
- Explain the task. Student A asks the questions. Student B looks at the map and answers the questions.
- Ss complete the task in pairs.

Answers

Answers are in the appendix at the back of the Student's Book.

- **Optional:** Have a class discussion about where other international celebrities are from.

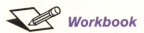

Workbook

Workbook Exercises 1–3 on pages 13–15 correspond to Cycle 1, Exercises 1–4 of the Student's Book. Answers to the Workbook exercises begin on page T-182 of this Teacher's Edition.

Optional Activities

1. *Game – Hangman*

- See page T-148. Use the names of countries and/or regions of the world.

2. *Scrambled letters*

- See page T-147. Scramble the names of ten countries and/or regions of the world.

3. *That's wrong!*

- See page T-149.

Cycle 2, Exercises 5–10

5 CONVERSATION

This exercise introduces Wh-questions with *who, what,* and *where* and the verb *be.* It also introduces expressions for asking about and describing people.

- Books open. Use the illustration to set the scene. Emma is looking at a photograph in Jill's wallet. Ask, "Who is in the photograph?" Tell Ss to listen for the answer.
- Play the audio program. Ss read and listen for the answer. Elicit the answer (James, Jim, or Jill's brother).
- Play the audio again. Ss listen and read. If necessary, answer questions about key vocabulary. Encourage Ss to guess and to be satisfied with approximate meanings.

  Cute means *good-looking* or *attractive. College* means *university. Vancouver* is a city in Canada. To explain *funny,* laugh. *What's he like?* is usually a question more about personality than appearance.
- Play the audio program again or read the conversation line by line. Ss listen and read, then look up and repeat.
- Ss practice the conversation in pairs using the Look Up and Say technique. Walk around while they practice. Encourage them to use appropriate gestures, facial expressions, and emphasis.
- **Optional:** Have a few of the more expressive Ss act out the conversation for the class. Encourage them to refer to their books as little as possible.

6 NUMBERS AND AGES

This exercise presents the numbers from 11 to 102. It also practices some pronunciation contrasts and expressions for talking about people's ages.

A

- Books open. Play the audio program. Students listen and read.
- Play the audio program again or read the numbers one by one. Give extra practice with any numbers that are particularly difficult for your students to pronounce.

B

- Books open. Play the audio program while Ss listen and read. Draw Ss' attention to the differences in pronunciation. "Teens" have two long syllables: **thir-teen**. "Tens" have one long syllable and one short: **thir**-ty.
- Play the audio program again or read the pairs of numbers one by one. Ss listen and repeat.
- **Optional:** Write these number sequences on the board:

  20–29 30–39 40–49 50–59
  60–69 70–79 80–89 90–99

  Point to sequences at random, and call on Ss to say the nine numbers.

C *Group work*

- Demonstrate the task using the model conversation. Tell Ss to look at page 16. Point to the photographs there. Ask, "How old is Antonio Banderas?" Elicit guesses from Ss.
- Show Ss that they must write down their guesses for each person.
- Ss do the exercise in groups of three to five. When most of the groups have finished, stop the activity.
- Ss turn to page S-4 to check their answers.

Optional Activity: ***Game – Higher, lower***

- See page T-149.

5 CONVERSATION

Listen and practice.

Emma: Who's that?
Jill: He's my brother.
Emma: Wow! He's cute. What's his name?
Jill: James. We call him Jim. He's in college here in Vancouver.
Emma: Oh, how old is he?
Jill: He's twenty-one years old.
Emma: What's he like? I bet he's nice.
Jill: Yes, he is – and he's very funny, too!

6 NUMBERS AND AGES

A Listen and practice.

11 eleven	**21** twenty-one	**40** forty
12 twelve	**22** twenty-two	**50** fifty
13 thirteen	**23** twenty-three	**60** sixty
14 fourteen	**24** twenty-four	**70** seventy
15 fifteen	**25** twenty-five	**80** eighty
16 sixteen	**26** twenty-six	**90** ninety
17 seventeen	**27** twenty-seven	**100** one hundred
18 eighteen	**28** twenty-eight	**101** one hundred and one
19 nineteen	**29** twenty-nine	**102** one hundred and two
20 twenty	**30** thirty	

B Listen and practice. Notice the pronunciation.

thirtéen – thírty   fourtéen – fórty   fiftéen – fífty   sixtéen – síxty

C ***Group work*** How old are the people on page 16? Write down your guesses and then compare. (Check your answers on page S-4 in the Unit Summaries.)

A: How old is Antonio Banderas?
B: I think he's twenty-nine (years old).
C: I think he's thirty-five. . . .

7 WORD POWER Descriptions

A Listen and practice.

She's pretty.
He's serious.
She's smart.
He's handsome.
She's shy.
They're very good-looking.
He's very funny.
She's really friendly.
They're nice.
He's really tall.
He's thin.
He's short.
He's a little heavy.

B Complete the chart with words from part A. Add two more words to each list.

Appearance		Personality	
heavy	....	*friendly*	....
....	....	....	....
....	....	....	....

8 LISTENING

CLASS AUDIO ONLY

Listen to descriptions of four people. Check (✓) the correct words.

Descriptions			
1. Karen	☑ friendly	☑ short	☐ tall
2. James	☐ funny	☐ nice	☐ thin
3. Stephanie	☐ cute	☐ shy	☐ smart
4. Andrew	☐ a little heavy	☐ handsome	☐ funny

interchange 3

Class personalities

What are people in your class like? Turn to page IC-5.

7 WORD POWER Descriptions

This exercise introduces adjectives for describing people's appearance and personality. It also introduces the adverbs *a little* and *really*. (*Very* was introduced in Unit 2, Exercise 3.)

A

(*Note: Heavy, thin, tall,* and *short* can be positive or negative, depending on the person and the culture. *Funny* has various meanings in English. Throughout the *Intro* level, *funny* is used in a positive way to describe someone who makes jokes or acts humorously so that others laugh with enjoyment.)

- Books open. Tell Ss to look at the pictures and to study the new vocabulary for a minute.
- Play the audio program. Ss listen and read.
- If necessary, clarify key vocabulary. *Good-looking, handsome,* and *pretty* mean about the same thing. Use the illustration to show that *pretty* is generally used for women and *handsome* is used for men. The other adjectives are used for both men and women.

  Really and *very* mean about the same thing. If necessary, use gestures or quick sketches on the board to illustrate *thin* versus *really thin* or *very thin.*
- Play the audio program again or model the sentences one by one. Ss repeat.
- **Optional:** Ask Ss if they know other adjectives to describe people. Write them on the board, and clarify what they mean.

B

- Demonstrate and explain the task using the example.
- Ss work individually to complete the chart. Walk around to give help as needed.
- Ss check their answers in pairs. Have one or two Ss write their answers in a chart on the board. Correct them with the whole class.

Answers

Appearance		*Personality*	
good-looking	short	friendly	serious
handsome	tall	funny	shy
heavy	thin	nice	smart
pretty			

8 LISTENING

This exercise practices listening for details in descriptions of people.

- Explain the task. Ss will hear four short conversations about Karen, James, Stephanie, and Andrew.
- Go over the adjectives in the chart. (*Note: Cute* was introduced in Exercise 5.)
- Use the first part of the audio program and the examples in the chart to demonstrate the task. If necessary, copy the first line of the chart onto the board.
- Play the rest of the program as many times as necessary. Ss listen and check off their answers in the chart.

Audio script

1. MAN 1: What's your friend Karen like?
   WOMAN 1: She's great. She's really friendly.
   MAN 1: Is she very tall?
   WOMAN 1: No. No, she's not. She's short.
2. WOMAN 2: *(laughs)* James, you're very funny!
   MAN 2: Thanks.
   WOMAN 2: And you're really nice.
   MAN 2: *(laughs)* Thanks. You're nice, too.
3. MAN 1: Wow! Who's that? She's really cute.
   MAN 2: Oh, that's my girlfriend, Stephanie.
   MAN 1: Really? What's she like?
   MAN 2: Well, . . . she's cute. And she's really smart!
4. WOMAN 1: What's Andrew like?
   WOMAN 2: Hmm. . . . He's a little heavy, but he's very handsome.
   WOMAN 1: Is he funny?
   WOMAN 2: Funny? Uh, well, no. He's not funny, but he's . . . very handsome.

- Ss compare their answers in pairs, making corrections if they wish.
- Call on Ss to give their answers in sentences, for example, "Karen is friendly and short." Let the other Ss correct any mistakes.

Answers

1. Karen: friendly, short
2. James: funny, nice
3. Stephanie: cute, smart
4. Andrew: a little heavy, handsome

INTERCHANGE 3 Class personalities

See page T-109 of this Teacher's Edition for notes.

9 PRONUNCIATION Blending with *is* and *are*

This exercise practices the blended forms of *is* and *are* in Wh-questions.

- Books open. Play the audio program several times. Ss listen and read. Then listen and repeat.
- Provide more examples of blending. Write on the board:

  Where's she from?
  Where are they from?

Model the first question. Ss repeat. (In the written example, the contraction shows the blending of *is* with *where.*) Model the second question without blending, and then with blending, with the vowel of *are* reduced: Whe**re're** they from? (*Are* is not usually contracted in writing, but it is often blended in speaking.) Model the blended form several times. Ss repeat.

10 GRAMMAR FOCUS Wh-questions with *be*

This grammar focus brings together all of the Wh-questions with *be* taught so far. In part B, Ss write questions requesting personal information.

- Books closed. Write these examples on the board. Use the answers to review the meanings of the Wh-words.

  What's this? It's my briefcase.
  Where are you from? I'm from Brazil.
  Who's that? That's Bill.
  How old is he? He's 17.

- Books open. Use the audio program to present the information in the box. Ss listen and read.
- Play the audio program again. Ss listen and repeat. Remind Ss to blend *is* and *are* with Wh-words. (*Note:* We do not write *is* as a contraction after *How* questions, but we often blend *is* and *are* with *How* in speaking.)

A

- Books open. Show Ss that the photographs illustrate the three conversations.
- Copy the first three or four lines of the exercise on the board, and fill in the first answer. Tell students to refer to the questions in the grammar box for help. Call on volunteers to do the other items. Write their answers on the board.
- Ss complete the exercise individually.
- To check answers, elicit responses from around the class. Write the correct answers on the board.

Answers

1. A: Look! **Who's that**?
   B: Oh – he's a new student.
   A: **What's his name**?
   B: I think his name is Chien Kuo.
   A: Chien Kuo? **Where is he from**?
   B: He's from China.
2. A: Keiko, **where are you from**?
   B: I'm from Japan – from Kyoto.
   A: **What's Kyoto like**?
   B: Kyoto is very old and beautiful.
   A: By the way, **what's your last name**?
   B: It's Noguchi. N-O-G-U-C-H-I.
3. A: Hi, John. **How are you**?
   B: I'm just fine. My friend Carolina is here this week – from Argentina.
   A: Carolina? I don't know her. **What's she like**?
   B: She's really pretty and very smart.
   A: **How old is she**?
   B: She's eighteen years old.

- Model the first conversation line by line. Ss listen and repeat. Then Ss practice it in pairs.
- Do the same with the second and third conversations.

B *Pair work*

- Use the example to demonstrate the task. If necessary, explain *best friend*. Draw stick figures on the board to represent some of your friends. Circle one figure and put stars around it to show Ss that this is your *best* friend. If necessary, elicit one or two more questions from Ss.
- Have Ss write their questions individually while you go around the class to check their work. If you see a mistake, mark an *X* next to the question on the S's paper, but do not correct the mistake. The S must identify and correct the mistake. Let them ask other Ss for help if they wish.
- **Optional:** If there is time, go back and check their corrections while they are working in pairs.
- Ask several Ss to read their questions aloud. Pay attention to the blending of *is* and *are*.
- In pairs, Ss take turns asking each other their questions.

Workbook

Workbook Exercises 4–8 on pages 16–18 correspond to Cycle 2, Exercises 5–10 of the Student's Book. Answers to the Workbook exercises begin on page T-182 of this Teacher's Edition.

Optional activity: *Game — What's the question?*

- See page T-149.

9 PRONUNCIATION *Blending with* is *and* are

Listen and practice. Notice how **is** and **are** blend with Wh-question words.

Who's that? **What's** he like? **Who are** they? **What are** they like?

10 GRAMMAR FOCUS

Wh-questions with be

What's your name?	**Who's that?**	**Who are they?**	**Who's = Who is**
My name is Jill.	He's my brother.	They're my classmates.	
Where are you from?	**How old is he?**	**Where are they from?**	
I'm from Canada.	He's twenty-one.	They're from Rio de Janeiro.	
How are you today?	**What's he like?**	**What's Rio like?**	
I'm just fine.	He's very funny.	It's very beautiful.	

A Complete the conversations with Wh-questions. Then practice with a partner.

1. A: Look! ....*Who's that*.......... ?
   B: Oh – he's a new student.
   A: .... ?
   B: I think his name is Chien Kuo.
   A: Chien Kuo? .... ?
   B: He's from China.

2. A: Keiko, ... ?
   B: I'm from Japan – from Kyoto.
   A: .... ?
   B: Kyoto is very old and beautiful.
   A: By the way, ... ?
   B: It's Noguchi. N-O-G-U-C-H-I.

3. A: Hi, John. .... ?
   B: I'm just fine. My friend Carolina is here this week – from Argentina.
   A: Carolina? I don't know her.
   .... ?
   B: She's really pretty and very smart.
   A: .... ?
   B: She's eighteen years old.

B ***Pair work*** Write five Wh-questions about your partner and five questions about your partner's best friend. Take turns asking and answering questions.

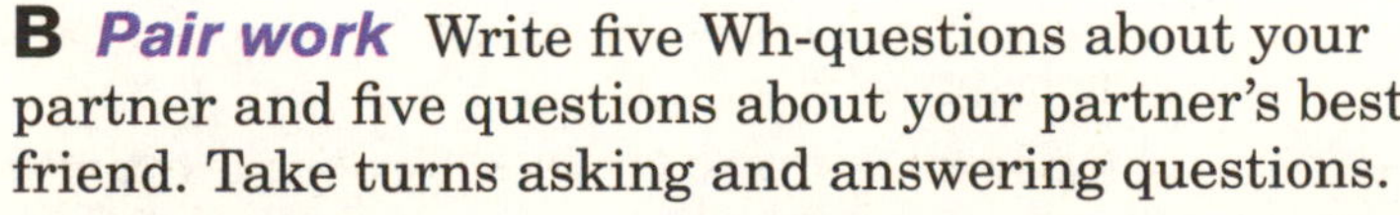

Your partner
Your partner's best friend
Where are you from?
Who's your best friend?

4 I'm not wearing boots!

1 WORD POWER *Clothes*

A Listen and practice.

B ***Pair work*** Fill in the chart with words from part A. Add two more words to each list. Then compare answers with your partner.

Clothes for warm weather	Clothes for cold weather
....	....
....	....
....	....
....	....
....	....

4 I'm not wearing boots!

This unit provides language for talking about clothing and the weather, including colors and seasons. It presents statements in the present continuous, some additional possessive forms, and the conjunctions and *and* but.

Cycle 1, Exercises 1–6

1 WORD POWER Clothes

This exercise introduces the names of articles of clothing.

(*Note:* In this illustration, many words are presented only for one gender or another. However, many of the words can be used to describe clothing worn by a man or a woman. Words that are usually only used for women are: *blouse*, *skirt*, *heels*, and *dress*. *Tie* is usually only used for men.

There are many styles of athletic shoes today. This exercise illustrates *sneakers,* but Ss may also be familiar with *running shoes, tennis shoes, aerobic shoes,* and so on.)

A

- Books open. Have Ss study the pictures.
- Play the audio program. Ss listen and read. If necessary, help Ss use the illustrations to guess the meanings of *clothes, work*, and *leisure*.
- Play the program again or model the words one by one. Ss listen and repeat.
- **Optional:** Let Ss add other words they may know. Write the Ss' words on the board and have them demonstrate the meanings if necessary. Model pronunciation and have Ss repeat.

B *Pair work*

- Use the illustrations in the chart to demonstrate the task. Elicit the names of one or two articles of clothing from each side of the chart.
- Ss work individually to complete the chart.
- To check, elicit answers from the Ss. Write their answers on the board, or have a S write them. Ss' answers may vary. Accept any reasonable answers.

Possible answers

Clothes for warm weather:	*Clothes for cold weather:*
cap	hat
T-shirt	scarf
shorts	sweater
sneakers	coat
swimsuit	gloves
	boots

2 COLORS

This vocabulary exercise introduces and practices the names of colors.

A

- Books open. Ss study the colors. Play the audio program. Ss listen and read.
- Play the audio program again or model the colors one by one. Ss listen and repeat.
- Check comprehension. Look for colored objects in the classroom, including clothes. Look at an object, and name its color. Ss name the object or point to it. Then name colored objects in the room. Ss name the colors.

B *Group work*

- Model the question and answer. Ss listen and repeat.
- Call on one or two pairs of Ss to demonstrate the conversation.
- Ss work in groups to ask and answer the question.

C *Group work*

- Use the model conversation to demonstrate the task. Hold up your book and point to the suit and the T-shirt in Exercise 1 as you model the statements.
- Read the statements again. Ss listen and repeat.
- If necessary, have one or two pairs of Ss demonstrate the task for the class. Help them as needed.
- Ss work in groups to make statements about the clothes in Exercise 1.
- **Optional:** Have groups also talk about the clothing of people in the class.

Optional Activity: *Game – Treasure hunt*

- See page T-149.

3 CONVERSATION

This conversation introduces questions with *what color* for talking about clothing. It recycles possessives and introduces some new forms. It also introduces expressions for apologizing and accepting an apology.

- Books open. Use the picture to set the scene: Pat and Julie are in a laundromat. Play the audio program while Ss listen and read.
- Play the audio program again. If necessary, explain *dry* by pointing to the dryer in the picture. Say, "This is a dryer. The clothes are dry now." Encourage Ss to try to guess the meanings of other words, including *probably, ruined,* and *problem*.
- Play the audio program again or model the conversation line by line. Ss listen and read, then look up and repeat.
- Ss practice the conversation in pairs using the Look Up and Say technique. As you walk around the room, encourage them to speak with expression.
- **Optional:** Ask volunteers to act out the conversation in front of the class.

4 PRONUNCIATION *Sentence stress and rhythm*

This exercise introduces the idea of sentence stress, which gives a natural rhythm to spoken English.

(*Note:* Stressed syllables occur at more or less equal intervals in English, regardless of how many syllables there are between stresses. The other syllables are reduced or blended if necessary to fit between the stressed syllables. This is different from many other languages. Ss should aim for an English stress-timed rhythm rather than a syllable-timed rhythm as in French, Spanish, and Japanese.)

- Books open. Play the audio program. Ss read and listen.
- Copy the first two sentences on the board. Underline the syllables that are in boldface in the book. Point to the words and say, "These words are different. How are they different?" Tell them to listen again.
- Play the audio program again. Elicit answers to your question. (The syllables are louder; they are stressed.) Accept partial, ungrammatical, or native-language answers.
- Model the sentences with exaggerated stress so that Ss understand the point.
- Play the audio program again, or model the sentences one by one with natural stress. Ss listen and repeat.

2 COLORS

A Listen and practice.

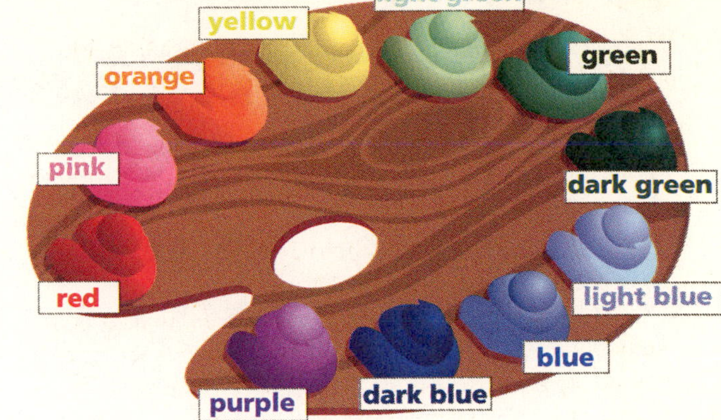

B ***Group work*** Ask about favorite colors.

A: What are your favorite colors?
B: My favorite colors are red and purple.

C ***Group work*** Describe the clothes in Exercise 1.

A: The suit is blue.
B: The T-shirt is light green.

3 CONVERSATION

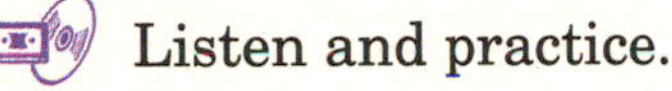

Listen and practice.

Pat: Are our clothes dry?
Julie: Yes, they are.
Pat: Where are my favorite socks?
Julie: What color are they?
Pat: They're white.
Julie: Are these your socks? They're blue and white.
Pat: No, they're probably Liz's socks. Wait! They *are* my socks! They're ruined!
Julie: Yeah. The problem is this T-shirt. It's dark blue.
Pat: Is it Liz's?
Julie: Actually, it's *my* T-shirt. I'm sorry.
Pat: That's OK. It's not important.

4 PRONUNCIATION *Sentence stress and rhythm*

Listen and practice. Notice the stress in these sentences.

A: What **cólor** is Julie's **T́-shirt**?
B: It's **dárk blúe**.

A: What **cólor** are Pat's **sócks**?
B: They're **blúe** and **whíte**.

5 GRAMMAR FOCUS

Possessives

			Pronunciation
Are **our** clothes dry?	Are **Julie's** and **Pat's** clothes OK?	I → my	**Pat's** /s/
Where are **my** socks?	No, **their** clothes aren't OK.	you → your	**Julie's** /z/
Are these **your** socks?	What's **Josh's** favorite color?	he → his	**Liz's** /ɪz/
Is this **Liz's** T-shirt?	**His** favorite color is blue.	she → her	
No, it's not **her** T-shirt.		we → our	
		they → their	

A Write a question for each sentence. Compare with a partner. Then ask and answer the questions.

1. Liz's jeans are black. — What color *are Liz's jeans* ?
2. Dan's favorite color is green. — What .... ?
3. James's shoes are on the table! — Where .... ?
4. Julie's T-shirt is dark blue. — What color .... ?
5. Debbie and Jeff's house is white. — What color .... ?
6. My favorite color is purple. — What .... ?
7. Our classroom is light yellow. — What color .... ?

A: What color are Liz's jeans?
B: Her jeans are black.

B ***Group work*** Write five questions about your classmates. Ask and answer your questions.

A: What color is Maria's skirt?
B: Her skirt is . . . .

B: What color are Victor's shoes?
C: His shoes are . . . .

6 LISTENING

A Listen to these people describe their clothes. Number the pictures from 1 to 4.

B ***Pair work*** Now talk about these people. What colors are their clothes?

A: What color is Peter's T-shirt?
B: His T-shirt is yellow.

5 GRAMMAR FOCUS Possessives

This grammar focus reviews possessive adjectives, adding *our* and *their*, and presents the possessive form of names.

- Books closed. Go over the pronunciation of the possessive *'s* in *Liz's, Julie's,* and *Pat's*. Possessive *'s* follows exactly the same pronunciation rules as plural *s* (Liz'*s* = /ɪz/; Julie'*s* = /z/; Pat'*s* = /s/). See page 8, Exercise 4, for an explanation of these rules.
- Ask Ss to predict the pronunciation of *Josh's*. Have Ss listen for it when you play the audio program.
- Play the audio program to present the information in the grammar box.
- Check with Ss about the pronunciation of *Josh's* that they heard in the audio program. (The possessive is pronounced /ɪz/.)
- Draw Ss' attention to the new possessive adjectives *our* and *their*. Point out that *their* has the same pronunciation as *there* and *they're; are* and *our* have different pronunciations, but often sound the same when people are speaking quickly.

A

- Use the example to demonstrate the task. Ss work individually to complete the questions. In pairs, Ss compare their answers and make corrections if they wish.
- Write the correct answers on the board or have a S write them. Ss check their answers with those on the board.

Answers

1. What color **are Liz's jeans**?
2. What **is Dan's favorite color**?
3. Where **are James's shoes**?
4. What color **is Julie's T-shirt**?
5. What color **is Debbie and Jeff's house**?
6. What **is your favorite color**?
7. What color **is our classroom**?

- Go over the model conversation. Make sure Ss understand that they should use *my, your, his, her, our,* and *their* in their answers. For example, the first answer is not *Liz's jeans are black*. The answer is *Her jeans are black* because Liz's name is in the question.

Answers

1. Her jeans are black.
2. His favorite color is green.
3. His shoes are on the table!
4. Her T-shirt is dark blue.
5. Their house is white.
6. My favorite color is purple.
7. Our classroom is light yellow.

- In pairs, Ss ask and answer the questions using the Look Up and Say technique.

B Group work

- Working individually, Ss write at least five questions about their classmates' clothing, using their classmates' names.
- Use the model conversation to demonstrate the task.
- In groups of three to five, Ss take turns answering and asking questions.

Optional activities

1. *Spelling contest*

- See page T-148.

2. *Crossword puzzle*

- See page T-148.

6 LISTENING

This exercise practices listening for details about clothing and colors.

A

- Books open. Use the first item on the audio program and the example to demonstrate the task.

Audio script

1. MAN 1: My T-shirt is yellow, my jeans are blue, and my boots are black.
2. WOMAN 1: My skirt is green, my sweater is dark gray, and my scarf is red.
3. MAN 2: My pants are dark green, my jacket is beige, and my tie is gray and blue.
4. WOMAN 2: My T-shirt is yellow, my shorts are beige, and my sneakers are white.

- Play the audio program as many times as necessary. Ss number the box as they listen to each description.
- Ss compare answers in pairs. Play the audio program again so they can check answers they're unsure of. Go over the answers with the class.

Answers

Bob: 3	Elizabeth: 2	Diane: 4	Peter: 1

B Pair work

- Use the model conversation to demonstrate the task.
- In pairs, Ss take turns asking and answering questions about the clothes in the pictures.

Workbook

Workbook Exercises 1–4 on pages 19–21 correspond to Cycle 1, Exercises 1–6 of the Student's Book. Answers to the Workbook exercises begin on page T-182 of this Teacher's Edition.

Cycle 2, Exercises 7–10

7 SNAPSHOT Weather in the United States and Canada

This activity introduces the topic of weather. It presents some basic information about weather and seasons in much of the United States and Canada.

(*Note:* The present continuous appears twice in this snapshot. Ss should be able to understand the sentences without difficulty. There is no need to explain the grammar at this point.)

- Give Ss a little time to study the pictures. Play the audio program while Ss listen and read.
- Play the audio program again or model the sentences aloud, line by line. Ss repeat.
- Ask the questions one by one. For the second question, write *seasons* on the board. Underneath, write all four seasons. Count the number of seasons out loud and write *United States and Canada = four seasons.*

  Elicit from Ss the seasons of their country. If Ss come from several countries, write the names of the countries on the board and the names of the appropriate seasons under each one. If the seasons don't exactly correspond to winter, spring, summer, or fall, help students choose words that accurately reflect the seasons of their countries.

8 CONVERSATION

This conversation introduces the present continuous.

- Turn back to the illustration on page 21. Remind Ss of Pat and Julie's conversation in the laundromat. Set the scene: they are going home.
- Books open. Play the audio program. Ss listen and read.
- Play the audio program again. Ss listen and read. There is little new vocabulary in this conversation. Encourage Ss to guess it.
- Play the program again or model the conversation line by line. Ss listen and read, then look up and repeat.
- Ss practice the conversation in pairs using the Look Up and Say technique. Encourage them to speak with expression.
- **Optional:** Have a few Ss act out the conversation for the class.

7 SNAPSHOT

Listen and practice.

Weather in the United States and Canada
IT'S WINTER. . . .
It's snowing. It's very cold.
IT'S SPRING. . . .
It's raining. It's warm.
IT'S SUMMER. . . .
It's very sunny, hot, and humid.
IT'S FALL. . . .
It's cool. It's cloudy and windy.

What's the weather like in your city today?
What are the seasons in your country? Are they the same as in the U.S. and Canada?
What season is it now?
What's your favorite season?

8 CONVERSATION

 Listen and practice.

Pat: Uh-oh!
Julie: What's the matter?
Pat: It's snowing, and it's very cold!
Julie: Are you wearing a scarf?
Pat: No, I'm not.
Julie: Well, you're wearing a coat.
Pat: But I'm not wearing boots!
Julie: OK. Let's take a taxi.
Pat: Thanks, Julie.

9 GRAMMAR FOCUS

Present continuous statements; isn't *and* aren't

		OR:	*Conjunctions*
I'**m**	I'**m not**		It's snowing,
You'**re**	You **aren't**	You'**re not**	**and** it's very cold.
She'**s** **wearing** shoes.	She **isn't** **wearing** boots.	She'**s not**	I'm wearing a coat,
We'**re**	We **aren't**	We'**re not**	**but** I'm not wearing boots.
They'**re**	They **aren't**	They'**re not**	
It'**s snowing**.	It **isn't raining**.	It'**s not**	

A Complete these sentences. Then compare with a partner.

1. My name's Claire. I *'m wearing* a black suit today. I .... high heels, too. It's raining, but I .... a raincoat.

2. It's hot today. Dan and Sally .... shorts and T-shirts. It's very sunny, but they .... sunglasses.

3. Phil .... a suit today – he .... pants and a jacket. He .... a white shirt, but he .... a tie.

4. It's cold today, but Kathy .... a coat. She .... a sweatshirt, gloves, and a hat. She .... boots. She .... running shoes.

9 GRAMMAR FOCUS *Present continuous statements;* isn't *and* aren't

This first grammar box presents the conjunctions *and* and *but* and statements with the present continuous. Two negative forms are given: *'s not/'re not* and *isn't/aren't*. There is a second grammar box on page 25.

1. The present continuous is used to talk about actions in progress (what is happening now). For example:

   She's wearing jeans today. (She wears jeans is the simple present.*)*

2. *And* and *but* connect two sentences. *And* shows addition. *But* shows a difference or contrast. For example:

   She's wearing a suit, and she's wearing high heels, too.
   He's wearing a shirt, but he's not wearing a tie.

- Play the audio program to present the information in the box. Point out that *be* in present continuous statements is blended in speech and contracted in writing in the same ways as *be* in the simple present.

A

- Play the audio program again or model the statements one by one. Ss listen and repeat.
- Write the example on the board to demonstrate the task. If necessary, tell Ss that the verb for all of the answers is *wear*.
- Ss complete the sentences individually. Circulate to help and to check their work.
- Have Ss compare their sentences with a partner, making corrections if they wish. Have volunteers write the sentences on the board. Correct the sentences with the whole class.
- **Optional:** Have a S read the first negative answer aloud and ask another S to give the alternate way of saying it. Continue until all negative answers have been given in both ways.

Answers

1. My name's Claire. **I'm wearing** a black suit today. **I'm wearing** high heels, too. It's raining, but **I'm not wearing** a raincoat.
2. It's hot today. Dan and Sally **are wearing** shorts and T-shirts. It's very sunny, but they **aren't wearing/'re not wearing** sunglasses.
3. Phil **isn't wearing/'s not wearing** a suit today – he**'s wearing** pants and a jacket. He**'s wearing** a white shirt, but he **isn't wearing/'s not wearing** a tie.
4. It's cold today, but Kathy **isn't wearing/'s not wearing** a coat. She's **wearing** a sweatshirt, gloves, and a hat. She **isn't wearing/'s not wearing** boots. She**'s wearing** running shoes.

- **Optional:** In pairs, Ss take turns reading about the people (one reads about Claire, the other reads about Dan and Sally, and so on). Circulate to encourage them to use the Look Up and Say technique on these longer texts.

Present continuous yes/no questions

This second grammar box presents yes/no questions and short answers in the present continuous. It also presents the new pattern *adjective* + *noun*.

- Play the audio program to present the information in the box. Ss listen and read.
- Point out the new pattern *adjective* + *noun* (a black suit, gray pants).
- Play the audio program again or model the statements one by one. Ss listen and repeat.

B *Pair work*

- Use the model conversation to introduce the task. Read it line by line. Ss repeat. Point out that both forms are correct for negative short answers. Ss can decide which form to use.
- In pairs, Ss ask the questions and answer them using the pictures. Each S asks half the questions and answers the other half.

C *Pair work*

- Ss work individually to write four new questions about the same pictures. Then they ask their partners the questions. While they are working, walk around the room looking at their questions. Have Ss write all the different questions they think of on the board. When Ss have finished asking and answering their four questions, they continue practicing with the new ones they see on the board.

Optional activity: *True or false?*

- See page T-148. Ss write statements about what they're wearing.

10 *LISTENING*

This exercise practices listening for names and for details about clothing. In the exercises, Ss talk about and then write questions about what people are wearing.

A

- Use the picture to set the scene: Beth and Bruce are at a party. They are talking about the people.
- Use the instructions and the example to demonstrate the task. Show Ss the boxes at the top of the illustration. One answer is filled in. They fill in the other four names.
- Play the audio program while Ss listen and fill in the names. Play it as many times as necessary.

Audio script

BETH: Hi, Bruce! You look great.
BRUCE: Hi, Beth!
BETH: That's a beautiful jacket. Light brown is my favorite color.
BRUCE: Thanks. You look great, too. Your green pantsuit is really cool.
BETH: Thank *you*. So, who's here?
BRUCE: Hmm. Let's see. Well, there's Jon. He's really nice.
BETH: Where's Jon?
BRUCE: He's over there. He's wearing blue pants and a white T-shirt.
BETH: Who's Jon with?
BRUCE: The woman in the purple skirt and blouse? That's Anita.
BETH: Anita?
BRUCE: Yeah. She's very funny.
BETH: Oh, no. Look at Nick! He's wearing shorts and a cap! He's wearing a T-shirt, too!
BRUCE: But Jon is wearing a T-shirt.
BETH: Yes, he is. But Jon's wearing a nice, white T-shirt . . . and he's not wearing a cap and shorts.
BRUCE: You're right, Beth. Well, Nick's clothes are . . . um . . . interesting.

Answers

Beth	Bruce	Anita	Jon	Nick

- To check, play the audio program again. While the program is playing, write the correct answers on the board.

B *Pair work*

- Use the model conversation to demonstrate the task.
- In pairs, Ss describe what the people in the picture are wearing.

C *Group work*

- Use the example to explain the writing task. Require three questions with *are* and three with *is*.
- Go around while Ss work to check their questions. Mark incorrect sentences with an X. Ss must identify the errors and correct them. Let them consult with other Ss if they wish. Do not let Ss erase errors. Have them write the correction next to the mistake. This is much easier to check.
- Make groups of three to five Ss. Ss take turns answering and asking their questions.

See page T-110 of this Teacher's Edition for notes.

Optional activity: *Sentence-making contest*

- See page T-150.

Present continuous yes/no questions

Are you **wearing** a black suit?	Yes, I **am**.	No, I**'m not**.
Is she **wearing** boots?	Yes, she **is**.	No, she**'s not**. No, she **isn't**.
Are they **wearing** sunglasses?	Yes, they **are**.	No, they**'re not**. No, they **aren't**.

adjective + noun

My suit is black.
I'm wearing **a black suit**.

B ***Pair work*** Ask and answer the questions about the pictures in part A.

1. Is Claire wearing a black suit?
2. Is she wearing a raincoat?
3. Is she wearing high heels?
4. Is Phil wearing gray pants?
5. Is he wearing a white shirt?
6. Is he wearing a tie?
7. Are Dan and Sally wearing swimsuits?
8. Are they wearing shorts?
9. Are they wearing sunglasses?
10. Is Kathy wearing boots?
11. Is she wearing a coat?
12. Is she wearing a hat and gloves?

A: Is Claire wearing a black suit?
B: Yes, she is.
A: Is she wearing a raincoat?
B: No, she isn't. (No, she's not.)

C ***Pair work*** Write four more questions about the pictures in part A. Ask and answer questions with your partner.

10 LISTENING

A Listen. Write the names **Bruce**, **Beth**, **Jon**, **Anita**, and **Nick** in the correct boxes.

B ***Pair work*** Talk about the people in the picture.

A: Jon is wearing a white T-shirt.
B: And he's wearing blue pants.

C ***Group work*** Write questions about six people in your class. Then take turns asking and answering the questions.

Are Sonia and Paulo wearing jeans?
Is Paulo wearing a red shirt?

interchange 4

Celebrity fashions

What are your favorite celebrities wearing? Turn to pages IC-6 and IC-7.

Review of Units 1–4

1 WHAT'S THE QUESTION?

Pair work Match the questions with the answers and practice with a partner. Then take turns asking the questions. Answer with your own information.

1. What's your name? ..d.....
2. Where are you and your family from? ....
3. How are you today? ....
4. What color are your shoes? ....
5. What's your favorite color? ....
6. What's your telephone number? ....
7. Who is your best friend? ....
8. What's your best friend like? ....
9. How old is he? ....
10. Where's my English book? ....
11. What's our teacher wearing today? ....
12. How do you spell *calculator*? ....

a. My best friend is Ken.
b. It's 555-3493.
c. We're from Thailand.
d. My name is Sarah Smith.
e. It's under your chair.
f. They're black.
g. He's wearing a suit and tie.
h. It's purple.
i. It's C-A-L-C-U-L-A-T-O-R.
j. He's funny and very smart.
k. I'm just great!
l. He's sixteen years old.

2 LISTENING

A Listen to the conversations. Complete the chart.

Who are they?	Where are they from?
1. Ryan	
2.	
3.	
4.	

B ***Pair work*** Write five questions about these people. Then take turns asking and answering your questions.

A: Is Ryan very tall?
B: No, he's not. . . .

Review of Units 1–4

This unit reviews the present tense of be, the present continuous, Wh-questions, and prepositions of location. It focuses on vocabulary and functions related to exchanging personal information, describing people, and giving locations.

1 WHAT'S THE QUESTION?

This exercise reviews Wh-questions with vocabulary from Units 1–4.

Pair work

- Use the example to demonstrate the matching exercise. Ss work individually to match the answers with the questions.
- To check answers, have Ss raise their hands when they finish the exercise. Go to the Ss one by one. Make an *X* next to wrong answers. Ss raise their hands again when they have corrected the wrong answers.

When a S's answers are all correct, the S stands up and walks around to check other Ss' papers. Like you, they do not explain anything – they just make *X*s.

Answers

1. d	2. c	3. k	4. f	5. h	6. b
7. a	8. j	9. l	10. e	11. g	12. i

- When everyone has the correct answers, demonstrate the pair work with a S. Ask the first question. The S reads the answer silently, then looks at you and says it.
- In pairs, Ss take turns asking and answering the questions using the Look Up and Say technique.

2 LISTENING

A This exercise practices listening for the names of people and places and the spelling of names. Ss also practice describing people.

(*Note:* The name Min Ho in this exercise is Korean. There are several styles of writing Korean names in English. Frequently, the hyphenated style is used in the Student's Book. What is important is that Ss understand what the audio program explains about the name – that it consists of two words. You can point out that each word begins with a capital letter.)

- Have Ss study the illustrations. Point to the first picture and ask, "Who is he?" Elicit "Ryan," the example in the chart.
- Show Ss that they fill in a name for each person and also a country or a city.
- Books closed. Play the audio program once while Ss listen. Explain that one place for each person is OK.

Audio script

1. RYAN: Hi. My name's Ryan.
LAURA: Ryan. That's an interesting name. How do you spell it?
RYAN: R-Y-A-N.
LAURA: I see. It's nice to meet you, Ryan. I'm Laura Morgan.
RYAN: I think you're in my math class.
LAURA: Yeah, you're right. So where are you from, Ryan?
RYAN: I'm from New York.

2. ROBERT: Hi, I'm Robert.
ELENA: Hello, Robert. I'm Elena.
ROBERT: Helena? H-E-L-E-N-A?
ELENA: No, *Elena*. E-L-E-N-A.
ROBERT: That's a beautiful name. Where are you from?
ELENA: I'm from Mexico.
ROBERT: Really? Where in Mexico?
ELENA: Mexico City.

3. WOMAN 1: John, this is Stephanie King.
JUAN: Hi. How are you?
STEPHANIE: Fine, thanks. It's nice to meet you.
JUAN: Nice to meet you, too. Your first name is Stephanie?
STEPHANIE: Yes, it is.
JUAN: And how do you spell that, Stephanie?
STEPHANIE: It's S-T-E-P-H-A-N-I-E.
JUAN: I see. Thank you.
WOMAN 1: Stephanie is from Los Angeles.
JUAN: Oh, Los Angeles! I have lots of friends there.

4. WOMAN 2: Is your name Chinese, Min Ho?
MIN HO: No, it's not, Min Ho is a Korean name.
WOMAN 2: How do you spell it?
MIN HO: It's two words: M-I-N H-O.
WOMAN 2: So are you from Korea?
MIN HO: Yes, I am – from Seoul.

- Books open. Play the audio program again, as many times as necessary. Ss fill in the chart.
- Ss compare answers in pairs and make corrections. Invite volunteers to come to the board and write their answers.
- Play the audio program again. Ss check the answers on the board and their own answers.

Answers

1. Ryan	New York
2. Elena	Mexico City, Mexico
3. Stephanie	Los Angeles
4. Min Ho	Seoul, Korea

B *Pair work*

- Ss work individually to write five questions. Then they ask their partners the questions.
- Ss change partners and practice again.

3 WHAT'S WRONG?

This exercise reviews prepositions of location and the names of common objects in a room.

- Books open. Have Ss study the picture. Use the example to explain the task.
- Ss write five sentences. As Ss work, walk around to give help if necessary.
- Send Ss to the board to write the different problems.
- Correct the list on the board with the whole class. Ss then correct their own papers.

Possible answers

The umbrella is behind the picture.
The clock is in front of the TV.
The clock and the TV are in front of the window.
The newspaper is on the wall.
The CD player is in the wastebasket.
The telephone is under the desk.
The chair is on the desk.
The desk and chair are in front of the door.
The chairs are under the table.

4 SAME OR DIFFERENT?

This exercise reviews the present continuous, the names of clothing and colors, and the conjunction *but*.

Pair work

- **Optional:** To re-introduce the topic of clothing, have students describe what the people are wearing in the illustrations in Exercise 2.
- Have Ss look at the picture and read the two examples. Use the illustrations to explain the meaning of *same, different,* and *both.*
- Check comprehension.

  T: What is Jun wearing?
  S1: He's wearing blue jeans and boots.
  T: What else is he wearing?
  Ss: A yellow T-shirt.
- Demonstrate the task. Look for two Ss who are wearing something "the same." Ask them to stand so the Ss can see their clothes. Ask, "What's the same?" and elicit the answer (e.g., "Gabriela and Alfredo are both wearing red sweaters.") Then ask, "What's different?" and elicit an answer.
- Ss choose two classmates and write their names at the top of a piece of paper.
- Ss write five sentences comparing the clothes of the Ss they chose. Walk around to check their work. Make sure they write sentences using *both* and *but.*
- In pairs, S read and check each other's answers.
- If a pair of Ss has a question or disagreement about one of their sentences, ask them to write the sentence on the board. Let the other Ss comment or try to correct it. Make sure the final result is correct.

Test 1

See page T-158 of this Teacher's Edition for general instructions on using the tests. Test 1 covers Units 1–4. Photocopy the test (pages T-159–T-162) and give a copy to each S. Allow 45–60 minutes for the test. Listening material for the tests is at the end of the class audio program. The Test Audio Scripts and Answer Key start on page T-175 of this book.

Optional activity: *Game – Word bingo*

- See page T-150.

3 WHAT'S WRONG?

What's wrong with this room?
Write down five problems.
Then compare with a partner.

> *The umbrella is behind the picture.*

4 SAME OR DIFFERENT?

Pair work Choose two classmates. Are their clothes the same or different? Write five sentences. Then compare with a partner.

> **Same**
> *Jun and Akira are both wearing blue jeans.*
> **Different**
> *Jun is wearing boots, but Akira is wearing shoes.*

5 What are you doing?

1 CONVERSATION

Listen and practice.

Debbie: Hello?
John: Hi, Debbie. This is John. I'm calling from Australia.
Debbie: Australia?
John: I'm at a conference in Sydney. Remember?
Debbie: Oh, right. What time is it there?
John: It's 10:00 P.M. And it's four o'clock there in Los Angeles. Right?
Debbie: Yes – four o'clock in the morning.
John: 4:00 A.M.? Oh, I'm really sorry.
Debbie: That's OK. I'm awake . . . now.

2 TELLING TIME (1)

A  Listen and practice.

It's five o'clock **in the morning**.
It's 5:00 **A.M.**

It's seven o'clock **in the morning**.
It's 7:00 **A.M.**

It's twelve o'clock.
It's **noon**.

It's four **in the afternoon**.
It's 4:00 **P.M.**

It's seven **in the evening**.
It's 7:00 **P.M.**

It's twelve o'clock **at night**.
It's **midnight**.

B ***Pair work*** Say each time another way.

1. It's eight o'clock in the evening. *"It's 8:00 P.M."*
2. It's twelve o'clock at night.
3. It's three in the afternoon.
4. It's 3:00 A.M.
5. It's 6:00 P.M.
6. It's 4:00 P.M.

5 What are you doing?

This unit presents expressions for talking about time and daily activities, including the question "What time is it?" The unit also introduces present continuous Wh-questions, including what + doing *questions, and the conjunction* so.

Cycle 1, Exercises 1–5

1 CONVERSATION

This conversation introduces expressions for talking about clock time and time of day.

- Books open. Have Ss look at the illustration and the names in the conversation. Write this question on the board:
  Where are John and Debbie?
  (John is in Sydney. Debbie is in Los Angeles.)
- Play the audio program while Ss read and listen for the answers. Elicit the answers. Point out the map on page 29. Ask Ss to find Sydney and Los Angeles.
- Play the audio program again. Ss read and listen. Try to elicit the meanings of *conference, remember,* and *awake.* Encourage guessing.
- Play the audio program again, or model the conversation line by line. Ss listen and read, then look up and repeat.
- Ss practice the conversation in pairs using the Look Up and Say technique.
- **Optional:** Have a few students act out the conversation for the class.

2 TELLING TIME (1)

This exercise presents and practices expressions for giving the hour of the day and the part of the day.

(*Note:* Use of these expressions is generally as follows:
in the morning = 1:00 A.M. until noon
in the afternoon = noon until around 5:00 P.M.
in the evening = 5:00 P.M. until around 9:00 P.M.
at night = can be used from 7:00 P.M. and continues until just before 1:00 A.M.
Noon is 12:00 P.M.; *Midnight* is 12:00 A.M.)

A

- Books open. Ss study the illustrations. Play the audio program. Ss read and listen.
- Remind Ss that *afternoon* is stressed on the last syllable: after**noon**. Point out that *morning* and *evening* both have two syllables: **mor**-ning and **eve**-ning.
- Play the audio program again, or model the sentences line by line. Ss repeat.
- **Optional:** Point to pictures in the book at random and use this conversation for practice. Ss answer chorally:

  T: *(pointing at the second picture)* What time is it?
  Ss: It's seven o'clock in the morning.
  T: I'm sorry. What time is it?
  Ss: It's seven A.M.

B *Pair work*

- Use the example to demonstrate the task with a S:

  S: It's eight o'clock in the evening.
  T: It's 8:00 P.M.
- If necessary, lead two Ss through another example.
- Ss work in pairs to say each time another way. Walk around the class, and give help as needed.
- **Optional:** Check answers as a class.

Answers

1. It's 8:00 P.M.
2. It's 12:00 A.M./It's midnight.
3. It's 3:00 P.M.
4. It's three in the morning.
5. It's six in the evening.
6. It's four in the afternoon.

- **Optional:** Write additional statements of time on the board. Ss change partners and continue practicing.

Optional activity: *Telling time*

- See page T-150.

3 SNAPSHOT Time Zones

This map gives information about international time zones. The questions relate the information to Ss' own lives.

(*Note:* A *solar day* is the time it takes for Earth to circle the Sun once. The length of a *solar day* varies. It is therefore easier to define time in terms of *mean time* or *average solar time. Greenwich* (pronounced /grɛnitʃ/) *mean time* is the local time at the former site of the Royal Observatory in Greenwich England, located on Earth's prime meridian (0° longitude). Other time zones add or subtract time from the time in Greenwich.)

- Books open. Play the audio program. Ss listen and repeat.
- Ask the questions one by one. **Important: For purposes of the exercise, have Ss round the time to the nearest hour when answering these questions.** If your Ss are not studying in their hometowns, first ask, "What time is it here?" Elicit answers from the Ss.

  To figure out the current time in the cities on the map, add or subtract hours from your local time according to the key at the bottom of the map.

4 LISTENING

In this exercise, Ss listen for specific information: the time of day in various cities.

- Books open. Have Ss look at the illustration. Explain the task: Ss listen to a conversation between Tracy and Eric, who are calling friends in different cities around the world. Ss listen for the time in the cities. Play the first part of the audio program, and use the example to demonstrate the task.
- Check Ss' comprehension:

  T: Where are Tracy and Eric?
  Ss: Vancouver.
  T: And what time is it in Vancouver?
  Ss: 4:00 P.M.
- Play the audio program once or twice. Ss fill in the times in each city on the chart.

Audio script

TRACY: What time is it now?
ERIC: It's four o'clock.
TRACY: OK. It's 4 P.M. here in Vancouver, so it's 7 A.M. in Bangkok. I'm calling Permsak right now.
ERIC: Permsak? At 7 A.M.? Permsak is sleeping now.
TRACY: You're right. What time is it in Tokyo?
ERIC: It's 9 A.M.
TRACY: Great. *(picks up phone)*
ERIC: Wait a minute. Are you calling Kyoko in Tokyo?
TRACY: Yeah. She's not sleeping at 9 A.M.
ERIC: But Kyoko is in Brazil this week. Remember?
TRACY: Oh, right.
TRACY: But I have her telephone number at the hotel in São Paulo.
ERIC: Uh, what time is it there?
TRACY: Um . . . it's nine o'clock in the evening. Hmm . . . nine o'clock. Kyoko is probably watching television right now. *(picks up phone)*
ERIC: So are you calling her?
TRACY: Yeah. We have to tell someone that we're getting married!

- Ss compare answers in pairs, changing them if they wish.
- Play the audio program again so that Ss can verify their answers. While the program is playing, write the correct answers on the board.

Answers

Vancouver	4:00 P.M.
Bangkok	7:00 A.M.
Tokyo	9:00 A.M.
São Paulo	9:00 P.M.

- **Optional:** Write these comprehension questions on the board:

  What are their friends' names?
  (Permsak and Kyoko.)
  Where are they?
  (Permsak is in Bangkok. Kyoko is in Brazil.)
  Why are Tracy and Eric calling their friends?
  (Tracy and Eric are getting married.)

  Elicit answers. Then play the audio program so that Ss can verify them.

3 SNAPSHOT

Listen and practice.

What time is it right now in your hometown?
What time is it in the cities on the map?

4 LISTENING

LASS UDIO ONLY

Tracy and Eric are calling friends in different parts of the world. Listen. What time is it in these cities?

City	Time
Vancouver	4:00 P.M.
Bangkok	....
Tokyo	....
São Paulo	....

5 TELLING TIME (2)

A Listen and practice.

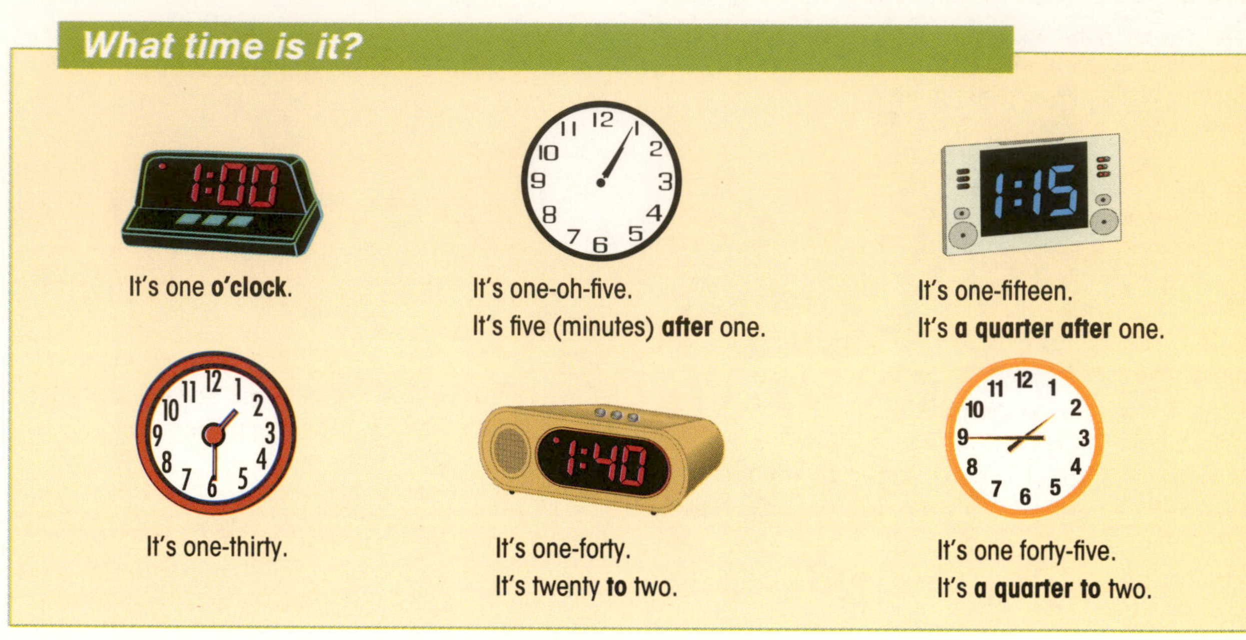

What time is it?

It's one **o'clock**.

It's one-oh-five.
It's five (minutes) **after** one.

It's one-fifteen.
It's **a quarter after** one.

It's one-thirty.

It's one-forty.
It's twenty **to** two.

It's one forty-five.
It's **a quarter to** two.

B ***Pair work*** Look at these clocks. What time is it?

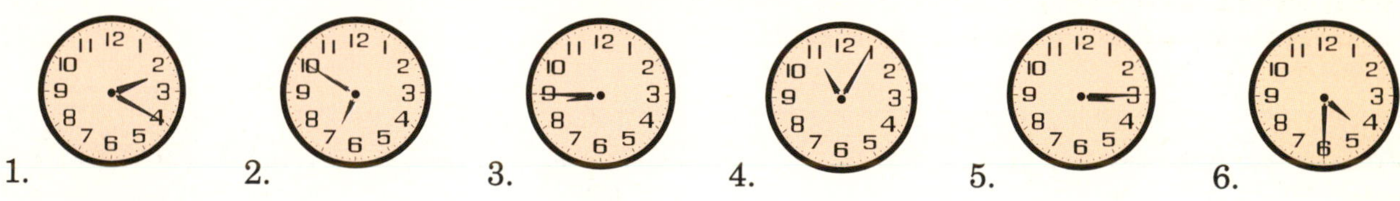

1. 2. 3. 4. 5. 6.

A: What time is it?
B: It's twenty after two. **OR** It's two-twenty.

6 CONVERSATION

 Listen and practice.

Steve: Hi, Mom.
Mrs. Dole: What are you doing, Steve?
Steve: I'm hungry, so I'm cooking.
Mrs. Dole: You're cooking? It's two o'clock in the morning!
Steve: Yeah, but I'm *really* hungry!
Mrs. Dole: What are you making?
Steve: Pizza.
Mrs. Dole: Mmm, pizza. So let's eat!

5 TELLING TIME (2)

This exercise presents and practices expressions for telling more exact time before or after the hour. It introduces the prepositions *after* and *to* for telling time.

(*Note:* There are many ways of saying time in English. Ss may hear the following variants:
a quarter to nine = a quarter of nine
twenty to nine = twenty before nine
twenty of nine
nine thirty = half past nine
nine twenty = twenty past nine
It is not necessary to present these forms at this point.)

A 

- Books open. Have Ss study the illustrations. Play the audio program. Ss read and listen.
- Point out the uses of *after* and *to*. Also point out that *o'clock* is for hours only, not hours + minutes. Mention that the word *minutes* can be used in giving the time with numbers like five, ten, or twenty-five *after* and *to* the hour.
- Play the program again, or model the sentences line by line. Ss listen and repeat.
- **Optional:** Write clock times in numbers on the board. Use minutes in multiples of five (e.g., 7:25, 12:50, 8:15). Lead choral and individual repetition of the times. When possible use two ways of saying the time. If you wish, interrupt your practice every so often and ask, "What time is it now?"

B ***Pair work***

- Use the example conversation to demonstrate the task with a S.
- Ss work in pairs, using the clocks to tell the time.
- Elicit all the possible answers from Ss. (*Note:* The last clock has only one answer.)

Answers

1. It's twenty (minutes) after two./It's two-twenty.
2. It's ten (minutes) to seven./It's six-fifty.
3. It's a quarter to nine./It's eight forty-five.
4. It's five (minutes) after eleven./It's eleven-oh-five.
5. It's three-fifteen./It's a quarter after three.
6. It's four-thirty.

- **Optional:** Draw more clocks on the board. Ss change partners and continue practicing.

 ***Workbook***

Workbook Exercises 1–4 on pages 25–26 correspond to Cycle 1, Exercises 1–5 of the Student's Book. Answers to the Workbook exercises begin on page T-182 of this Teacher's Edition.

Cycle 2, Exercises 6–11

6 CONVERSATION

This conversation introduces questions with *what* + *doing* in the present continuous. It also introduces the conjunction *so*.

- Books open. Set the scene by looking at the picture. Ask, "What are the boy and the woman wearing? (He's wearing jeans, a T-shirt, and sneakers. She's wearing pajamas and a robe.)
- Write this question on the board:
  What time is it?
  (It's 2:00.)

  Ask Ss to guess if it is 2:00 in the morning or in the afternoon.
- Play the audio program while Ss read and listen to confirm the answer. Elicit the answer.
- Play the tape again. Ss read and listen. Try to elicit the meanings of *hungry, cooking, making,* and *pizza.* Encourage guessing.
- Play the audio program again, or model the conversation line by line. Ss listen and read, then look up and repeat.
- Ss practice the conversation in pairs using the Look Up and Say technique.
- **Optional:** Have a few students act out the conversation for the class.

7 GRAMMAR FOCUS What + doing; *conjunction* so

This grammar focus presents the conjunction *so* and present continuous Wh-questions, focusing on *what + doing.* It also teaches the meanings of several new verbs.

(*Note:* The times are all at the same moment in real time. When it is 4 A.M. in Los Angeles, it is 6:00 A.M. in Mexico City, and so on.)

- Books open. Point out the captions naming the city and giving the local time in each picture. Ask about a few of the cities in random order. (Skip *your city* for now.)

  T: What time is it in New York City?
  Ss: 7:00 A.M.

- Play the audio program to present the questions and answers. Ss read and listen.
- Point out the meaning of *so*. Read Marcos's statement: "It's 6:00 A.M., so he's getting up." Ask, "Why is Marcos getting up?" Elicit the answer, "It's 6:00 A.M."
- Play the audio program again, or model the sentences line by line. Ss listen and repeat. For the last picture, have Ss say what they are doing now (e.g., studying English, thinking about lunch).
- **Optional:** Ss imagine different hours of the day. They use their imaginations to say what they "are doing." Help with vocabulary if necessary, and elicit statements from the Ss like this:

  T: What are you doing, John?
  S: It's 5:00, so I'm cooking dinner.

A *Pair work*

- Demonstrate the task with one or two Ss.
- Ss practice asking and answering the questions in pairs. (Tell Ss to skip the woman illustrated in *your city.*) Help Ss with the use of *who* in the present continuous.
- To check, call on pairs to ask and answer a question for the class. If the answer is not complete, elicit other answers from other Ss.

Answers

1. It's four in the morning./It's 4:00 A.M.
2. She's sleeping.
3. They're in New York City.
4. Victoria and Marcos are wearing pajamas. Celia, James, Anne, and Andrei are wearing suits.
5. Andrei is working.
6. He's getting up.
7. She's going to work.
8. Sue, Tom, James, Anne, and Permsak are eating.

B *Group work*

- Play the audio program to present the information in the spelling box. The examples illustrate these rules for spelling verbs in the continuous:
  1. For most verbs, just add *-ing* to the base form. (sleeping)
  2. If the base form ends in a vowel + a consonant, double the final consonant and add *-ing*. (getting)
  3. If the base form ends in a silent *e*, drop the *e* and add *-ing*. (having)
- Ss write their questions individually. Have Ss write at least one question with each of the following: *who, what,* and *where*. As they write, go around the class to check their work.
- Ss ask and answer their questions in groups. Let the group decide which questions are best. Have a "secretary" from each group put the group's three best questions on the board.
- Correct the questions with the class. Elicit answers from the class.

Optional activity: *Diary*

- See page T-150.

7 GRAMMAR FOCUS What + doing; *conjunction* so 

Los Angeles 4:00 A.M.

What's Victoria **doing**?
She**'s sleeping** right now.

Mexico City 6:00 A.M.

What's Marcos **doing**?
It's 6:00 A.M., **so** he**'s getting up**.

New York City 7:00 A.M.

What are Sue and Tom **doing**?
They**'re having** breakfast.

Brasília 9:00 A.M.

What's Celia **doing**?
She**'s going** to work.

London 12:00 NOON

What are James and Anne **doing**?
It's noon, **so** they**'re having** lunch.

Moscow 3:00 P.M.

What's Andrei **doing**?
He**'s working**.

Bangkok 7:00 P.M.

What's Permsak **doing**?
He**'s eating** dinner right now.

Tokyo 9:00 P.M.

What's Hiroshi **doing**?
He's **watching** television.

Your city 00:00

What are you **doing**?
It's . . . , **so I'm** . . . .

A ***Pair work*** Ask and answer the questions about the pictures.

1. What time is it in Los Angeles?
2. What's Victoria doing?
3. Where are Sue and Tom?
4. Who's wearing pajamas? suits?
5. Who's working right now?
6. What's Marcos doing?
7. What's Celia doing?
8. Who's eating right now?

Spelling

sleep → **sleeping**
get → **getting** (+ *t*)
have → **having** (– e)

B ***Group work*** Write five more questions about the pictures. Ask and answer your questions in groups.

8 PRONUNCIATION *Intonation of yes/no and Wh-questions*

A Listen and practice. Notice the intonation of the questions.

A: Is Victoria getting up? ↗
B: No, she isn't.

A: What's Victoria doing? ↘
B: She's sleeping.

B Listen to the questions. Write ↗ for rising intonation or ↘ for falling intonation.

1. ..↗.. 2. .... 3. .... 4. .... 5. .... 6. ....

9 WORD POWER *Activities*

A Listen and practice. *"He's playing tennis."*

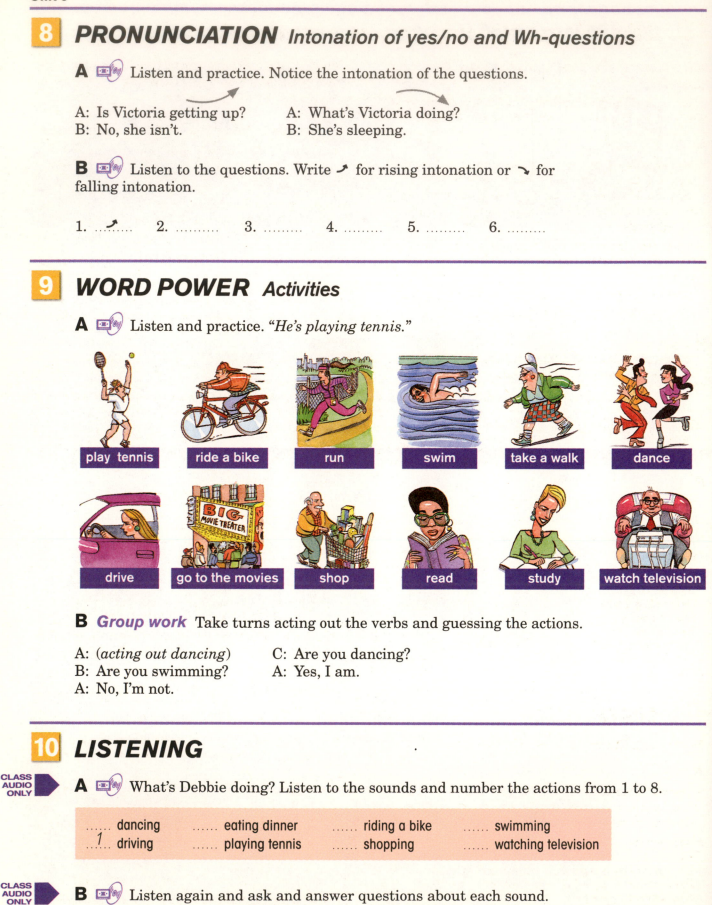

B ***Group work*** Take turns acting out the verbs and guessing the actions.

A: (*acting out dancing*)
B: Are you swimming?
A: No, I'm not.
C: Are you dancing?
A: Yes, I am.

10 LISTENING

A What's Debbie doing? Listen to the sounds and number the actions from 1 to 8.

...... dancing	...... eating dinner	...... riding a bike	...... swimming
..1.. driving	...... playing tennis	...... shopping	...... watching television

B Listen again and ask and answer questions about each sound.

A: What's Debbie doing right now?
B: She's driving.

8 PRONUNCIATION *Intonation of yes/no and Wh-questions*

In this exercise, Ss practice intonation patterns for questions.

(*Note:* Yes/no questions generally end with rising intonation. Wh-questions generally end with falling intonation.)

A

- Write the two short conversations on the board, including the arrows. Books closed. Play the audio program. When the speaker's voice goes up, point to the rising arrow. When the voice goes down, point to the falling arrow.
- Books open. Ss say the conversations in pairs. Have them change partners several times. Walk around to help.
- Ask pairs of Ss to say the conversations for the class. Correct their intonation if necessary.

B

- Books open. Play the first item on the audio program, and use the example to demonstrate the task.
- Play the audio program as many times as necessary. Have one or two Ss work at the board.

Audio script

1. WOMAN: Are you wearing a coat? *(up)*
   MAN: Yes, I am.
2. MAN: What are you doing now? *(down)*
   WOMAN: I'm having lunch.
3. WOMAN: What time is it? *(down)*
   MAN: It's noon.
4. MAN: Is it midnight? *(up)*
   WOMAN: No, it's a quarter to twelve.
5. WOMAN: What color is his T-shirt? *(down)*
   MAN: It's purple.
6. WOMAN: Are you from Thailand? *(up)*
   MAN: Yes, I am.

- Check answers by playing the audio program again. Ss check the answers on the board and their own answers.

Answers

1. ↗ 2. ↘ 3. ↘ 4. ↗ 5. ↘ 6. ↗

9 WORD POWER *Activities*

This exercise introduces and practices new action verbs.

A

- Books open. Ss study the illustrations. Read the activities aloud. Ss listen and read.
- Play the audio program. Ss listen and repeat.

Audio script

He's playing tennis
He's riding a bike.
She's running.
He's swimming.
She's taking a walk.
They're dancing.
She's driving.
They're going to the movies.
He's shopping.
She's reading.
She's studying.
He's watching television.

- Have volunteers make the statements about each picture. If necessary, correct the statements. Then Ss repeat.
- Say the verbs or phrases under the pictures in random order. Call on Ss to say the complete sentences.

B *Group work*

- Model the example conversation with two Ss.
- In groups, Ss take turns acting out verbs, while the others guess what they're doing. The S who is acting out a verb can look at the book to choose one.
- **Optional:** Have Ss act out other action verbs. Let each group act out one verb for the class.

10 LISTENING

This fun exercise checks Ss' recall of the verbs.

A

- Use the example in the book and the first part of the audio program to demonstrate and explain the task. Then play the audio program.

Audio script

1. *(a car on a busy highway)*
2. *(swimming in a pool)*
3. *(people eating dinner)*
4. *(a television)*
5. *(a nightclub with dance music)*
6. *(riding a bicycle)*
7. *(playing tennis)*
8. *(shopping in a mall)*

- To check answers, play one sound at a time. Let Ss call out the answers. Write the answers on the board.

Answers

5. dancing
1. driving
3. eating dinner
7. playing tennis
6. riding a bike
2. swimming
8. shopping
4. watching television

B

- Books closed. Model the example conversation with a S.
- Play the sounds on the audio program one by one. Pairs take turns asking and answering the questions.

11 READING *It's Saturday! What are you doing?*

In this article, Ss read about what four people are doing on a Saturday. The exercises practice reading for main ideas, making inferences, and writing about what people are doing.

(*Note:* See the Introduction to this Teacher's Edition, pages iv and xiii, for general suggestions about teaching reading with *Intro* Student's Book.)

- Books open. Read the title aloud, and write it on the board.
- The prereading task is in the blue bar under the title. Introduce the task. Hold up your book, and point to the four photographs. Say, "It's Saturday. What are *they* doing?"
- Use the example to demonstrate the task. Point to the first sentence of paragraph 1 and read it aloud: "We're washing people's cars." Try the sentence with each photograph:

  T: (pointing to photograph a) Is she washing people's cars?
  Ss: No.

  Continue with photographs b – d. Ss answer yes for photograph d.
- Have Ss complete the task individually. Help Ss with key words if necessary *(cars, movie, granddaughter, park,* and *computer).*
- Go over the answers as a class. Have Ss point out the key words that helped them find the answers.

Answers

1. d	2. c	3. a	4. b

A

(*Note:* A class activity is recommended because this is the first reading exercise in this book.)

- Have Ss read the article. If you wish, play the audio program as Ss listen and read.
- **Optional:** Ss underline words they do not know. Encourage Ss to guess the meaning from the context of the paragraph of the accompanying photo. Ss will be able to do the exercise without understanding all the words.
- Use the example to demonstrate the task. Ss need to find the first part of each sentence. Let Ss discover that the first clause of the example (Her parents are working today) comes from paragraph 3.
- Let Ss ask about key vocabulary in the exercise (e.g., *full* and *fun*). Complete the exercise as a class activity. Put the answers on the board for Ss to see.
- **Alternate presentation:** If your Ss are ready, let them do the exercise individually or in pairs. Walk around as they work. Put the answers on the board so that Ss can check their work.

Answers

1. **Her parents are working today**, so she's with me for the day. (paragraph 3)
2. **It's 11:00 at night**, so I'm not working. (paragraph 4)
3. **It's noon**, so the movie theater isn't full. (paragraph 2)
4. **My friends and I are working together**, so the work is actually fun. (paragraph 1)

B *Group work*

- Put the Ss in groups of three to five. Ask Ss to imagine today is Saturday. Ss decide where they are and what they are doing. Then they write five sentences. Point out the written example in the book.
- Bring the class back together. Have groups take turns reporting to the class.
- **Optional:** Tell Ss that you will collect their papers and check them. Give the groups three to five minutes to correct their papers. Have them write all their names on the paper.

  Collect the papers and check them. Do not correct the papers. Just mark an X for a mistake.

  Return the papers and give the groups another chance to correct them. Walk around to check the final corrections.

  Finally, announce the group with the fewest mistakes on their paper.

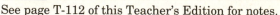

INTERCHANGE 5 Time zones

See page T-112 of this Teacher's Edition for notes.

Workbook

Workbook Exercises 5–9 on pages 27–30 correspond to Cycle 2, Exercises 6–11 of the Student's Book. Answers to the Workbook exercises begin on page T-182 of this Teacher's Edition.

Optional activities

1. *Action verbs*

- See page T-150.

2. *Complete the word*

- See page T-150.

11 READING

It's Saturday! What are you doing?

Read the first sentence of each paragraph. Find the picture for each paragraph.

a

b

c

1. ...d... We're washing people's cars. My friends and I are working together. The money from the car wash is for our school football team.

2. .... I'm watching a funny movie with my friend. It's noon. My friend is laughing at something, so now I'm laughing, too. We're laughing at *everything*!

3. .... I'm with my granddaughter in the park. Her parents are working today. We're playing and talking. She's telling me about school. She and I are good friends.

4. .... I'm sitting in bed with my laptop computer. It's 11:00 at night. I'm writing letters to friends. They're in other countries. But I'm thinking about them, so I'm not sad.

d

A Read the article. Then add these clauses to the appropriate paragraph.

1. . . . , so she's with me for the day.
   Her parents are working today, so she's with me for the day.
2. . . . , so I'm not working.
3. . . . , so the movie theater isn't full.
4. . . . , so the work is actually fun.

B ***Group work*** Imagine it is Saturday. You and your classmates are together. Where are you? What are you doing? Write five sentences.

We're in the park. We're riding our bikes. . . .

interchange 5

Time zones

What are people doing in different cities of the world?
Turn to page IC-8.

6 We live in the suburbs.

1 SNAPSHOT

Listen and practice.

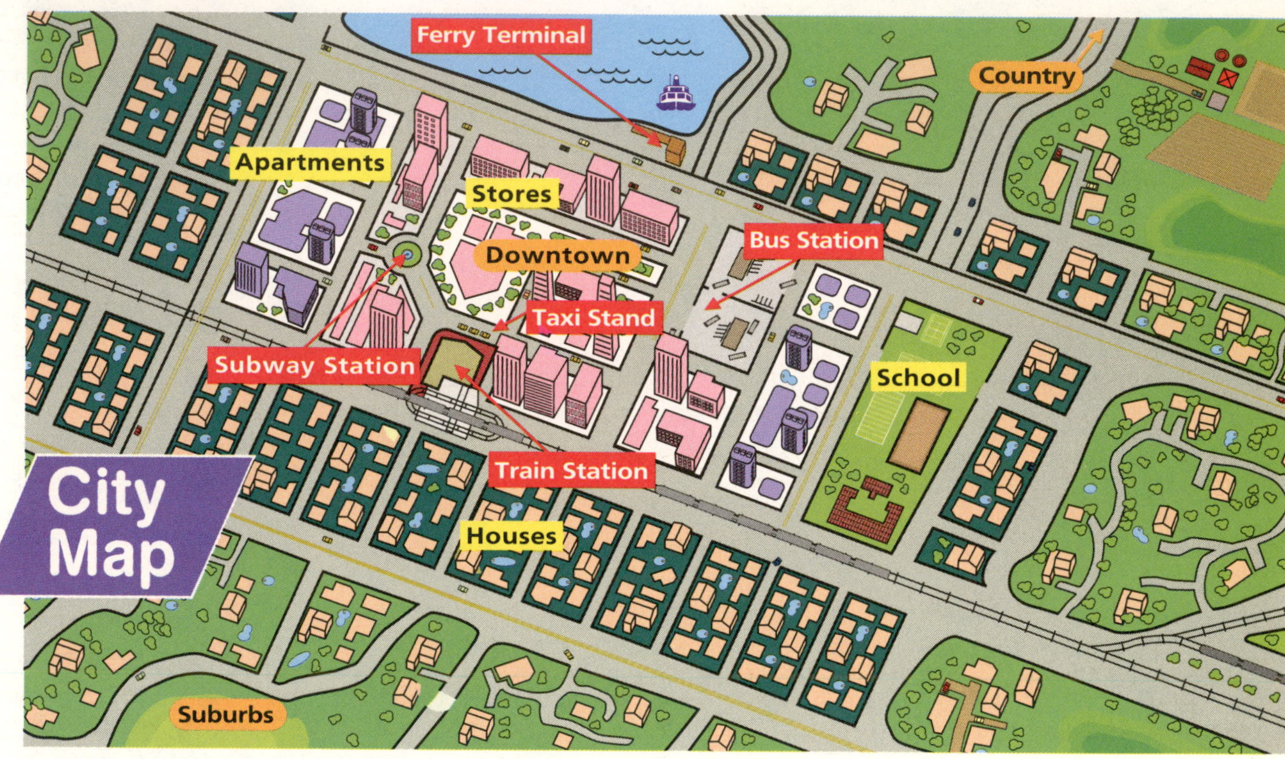

Which of these places are in your hometown?
What public transportation do you have? buses? trains? a subway? taxis? ferries?
Can you name other places in your hometown?

2 CONVERSATION

 Listen and practice.

Ashley: Hey, Jason. What are you doing?
Jason: Oh, I'm waiting for my mom. My bike has a flat tire.
Ashley: Is she coming right now?
Jason: Yeah. She works near here.
Ashley: Oh, that's good.
Jason: So what are *you* doing?
Ashley: I'm going home. I don't live far from here, so I walk to school.
Jason: You're lucky!

6 We live in the suburbs.

This unit introduces the topics of places, transportation, family, and daily routines. It presents simple present statements and questions with regular and irregular verbs.

Cycle 1, Exercises 1–7

1 SNAPSHOT City Map

This map presents vocabulary for places in a typical (but imaginary) small city in Canada or the United States. The questions relate the information to Ss' own lives.

- Introduce the information on the map by playing the audio program. Ss listen and read.
- Point out that the words are in different colors for the three vocabulary groups: orange for urban and nonurban areas; yellow for places to live and shop; and red for transportation facilities. Write the words in three lists on the board like this:

Areas	Places	Transportation
country	apartments	bus station
downtown	houses	ferry terminal
suburb	school	subway station
	stores	taxi stand
		train station

- Ss work in groups to study the map and understand the words. Encourage guessing. Let groups consult with each other if necessary.
- Play the audio program again or say the words one at a time. Ss listen and repeat.
- Ask the questions one by one. If your Ss are not studying in their hometowns, first ask, "Which of these places are in this town?" Elicit answers from the Ss.

  For the second question, if your town does not have much public transportation, ask about a larger city that Ss know about.

  For the last question, some possible answers are *park, airport, shopping center* or *mall, movie theater, hospital,* and *bank.*

2 CONVERSATION

This conversation introduces statements in the simple present with both regular and irregular verbs for talking about daily routines. It also introduces the topic of family.

- Books open. Use the picture to set the scene. Ashley and Jason are talking in front of their school. Write these questions on the board:

  What is Jason doing? (He's waiting for his mother.)
  What is Ashley doing? (She's going home.)

- Play the audio program while Ss read and listen for the answers. Elicit the answers.
- Play the audio program again. Ss read and listen. Try to elicit the meanings of *mom, bike, flat tire, far,* and *lucky.* Encourage Ss to use the illustration and the context to guess meanings.
- Play the audio program again, or model the conversation line by line. Ss listen and read, then look up and repeat.
- Ss practice the conversation in pairs using the Look Up and Say technique. Walk around the room, and encourage Ss to speak with expression.
- **Optional:** Have a few students act out the conversation for the class.

3 WORD POWER *Family relationships*

This exercise presents vocabulary about family relationships. This is the family of the character of Jason from Exercise 2.

A *Pair work*

- Books open. Ss study the illustration. Read the words aloud. Start with the names, then read the words for family relationships. Ss listen and read.
- Read the words again. Ss listen and repeat. Point out the green box at the left. The words on the left are often used in speech, but not in formal writing. Read all the words, and have Ss repeat them.
- Use the example to demonstrate the task. Ss work in pairs to complete the sentences.
- Play the audio program for Ss to check their answers.

Answers and audio script

1. Anne is Charles's **wife**.
2. Jason and Emily are their **children (kids)**.
3. Charles is Anne's **husband**.
4. Jason is Anne's **son**.
5. Emily is Charles's **daughter**.
6. Jason is Emily's **brother**.
7. Emily is Jason's **sister**.
8. Charles and Anne are Jason's **parents**.

- **Optional:** Play the audio program again sentence by sentence. Ss repeat.

B *Pair work*

- **Optional:** Tell the class about your own family.
- Have a S read the example aloud to demonstrate the task. Have two or three volunteers each say a sentence about their families.
- Ss talk about their families in pairs.
- **Optional:** Have Ss take notes about their partner's family. Then ask Ss to report back to the class or small group. For example, "My partner's name is . . . . His mother's name is . . . , and his father's name is . . . . He has two brothers," etc.

4 GRAMMAR FOCUS *Simple present statements*

This grammar focus has two grammar boxes. This first box presents simple present affirmative and negative statements with regular verbs.

(*Note:* The simple present is used to talk about things that happen regularly (e.g., I walk to school) or things that are true in general (e.g., I live in Thailand). This is different from things happening in the immediate present, which are expressed with the present continuous.)

- Play the audio program to present the information in the first grammar box. Ss read and listen.
- Point out the *-s* ending on the verbs in affirmative sentences with *he* and *she*.
- Point out *don't* and *doesn't* in the negative sentences. *Don't* and *doesn't* are contractions of the full forms *do not* and *does not.*
- Try to elicit the meanings of *take the bus, use,* and *need.* Encourage Ss to guess.
- Play the audio program again, or model the sentences. Ss listen and repeat.

A

- Books open. Refer Ss to the picture in Exercise 3. Charles Carter is talking about his family. In paragraph 1, he's talking about the people in the picture. In paragraph 2, he's talking about his own mother and father.
- Demonstrate the task. Show Ss that *my family and I* = *we.* Point to the grammar box, and show Ss that the verb does not have an *-s* with *we.*
- Ss complete the paragraphs individually. Then they compare their answers with a partner, making changes if they wish.
- Elicit answers from Ss. Write them on the board so Ss can check their work.

Answers

1. My family and I **live** in the suburbs. My wife **works** near here, so she **drives** to her office. I **don't** work in the suburbs. I **take** the bus to the city. Our son **rides** his bike to school, but our daughter **doesn't** go to school yet.
2. My parents **live** in the city. My mother **takes** a train to work. My father **doesn't** work now. He's retired. He also **uses** public transportation, so they **don't** need a car.

Optional activity: *Thinking about grammar*

- See page T-151.

3 WORD POWER *Family relationships*

A ***Pair work*** Complete the sentences about the Carter family. Then listen to check your answers.

1. Anne is Charles's ...*wife*... .
2. Jason and Emily are their ....
3. Charles is Anne's ....
4. Jason is Anne's ....
5. Emily is Charles's ....
6. Jason is Emily's ....
7. Emily is Jason's ....
8. Charles and Anne are Jason's ....

kids	=	children
mom	=	mother
dad	=	father

B ***Pair work*** Tell your partner about your family.

"My mother's name is Angela. David and Daniel are my brothers."

4 GRAMMAR FOCUS

Simple present statements

I	**walk**	to school.	I	**don't live**	far from here.	**don't = do not**
You	**ride**	your bike to school.	You	**don't live**	near here.	**doesn't = does not**
He	**works**	near here.	He	**doesn't work**	downtown.	
She	**takes**	the bus to work.	She	**doesn't drive**	to work.	
We	**live**	with our parents.	We	**don't live**	alone.	
They	**use**	public transportation.	They	**don't need**	a car.	

A Charles Carter is talking about his family. Complete the sentences. Choose the correct verb form. Then compare with a partner.

1. My family and I ...*live*... (live/lives) in the suburbs. My wife .... (work/works) near here, so she .... (drive/drives) to her office. I .... (don't/doesn't) work in the suburbs. I .... (take/takes) the bus to the city. Our son .... (ride/rides) his bike to school, but our daughter .... (don't/doesn't) go to school yet.

2. My parents .... (live/lives) in the city. My mother .... (take/takes) a train to work. My father .... (don't/doesn't) work now. He's retired. He also .... (use/uses) public transportation, so they .... (don't/doesn't) need a car.

Simple present statements with irregular verbs

I/you/we/they	he/she/it
I **have** a bike.	It **has** a flat tire.
We **do** our homework every day.	My father **does** a lot of work at home.
My parents **go** to work by car.	My sister **goes** to school by bus.

B Ashley is talking about her family and her friend Jason. Complete the sentences. Then compare with a partner.

1. I live with my parents. We ..*have*.. (have/has) a house in the suburbs. My mom and dad both .... (go/goes) downtown to work. They both .... (have/has) cars and drive to work every day. I .... (do/does) a lot of work at home because my parents are very busy.

2. My brother doesn't live with us. He .... (have/has) an apartment in the city. He .... (go/goes) to school all day, and he .... (do/does) office work at night.

3. I .... (have/has) a new friend. His name is Jason. He doesn't have a car, but he .... (have/has) a cool bike. Jason and I .... (do/does) our homework together after school.

5 LISTENING

Pair work How do these people go to work or school? Do they walk? take the bus? ride a bike? drive? Write one guess in the chart for each person.

Then listen and complete the chart.

Your guess	How they actually go to work or school
Jeremy *rides a bike to school*	Jeremy ....
Tina	Tina ....
Rosie	Rosie ....
Louis	Louis ....

Simple present statements with irregular verbs

This grammar focus has two grammar boxes. This second box presents simple present statements with some irregular verbs.

- Play the audio program to present the information in the second grammar box. Ss read and listen.
- Point out the irregular forms *has, does,* and *goes.* Regular verbs just add *-s* with *he* and *she.* Irregular verbs make other changes.
- The main verb *do* is new here, but the context makes it clear. Encourage Ss to guess the meaning, if necessary.
- Play the audio program again, or model the sentences. Ss listen and repeat.

B

- Introduce the completion exercise. Refer Ss to the picture in Exercise 2.
- Ss complete the paragraphs individually, then compare their answers with a partner, making changes if they wish.
- Elicit answers from Ss. Write them on the board so Ss can check their work.

Answers

1. I live with my parents. We **have** a house in the suburbs. My mom and dad both **go** downtown to work. They both **have** cars and drive to work every day. I **do** a lot of work at home because my parents are very busy.
2. My brother doesn't live with us. He **has** an apartment in the city. He **goes** to school all day, and he **does** office work at night.
3. I **have** a new friend. His name is Jason. He doesn't have a car, but he **has** a cool bike. Jason and I **do** our homework together after school.

5 LISTENING

In this exercise, Ss listen to statements in the simple present about how people get to where they need to go.

- Books closed. Write these choices on the board:

  walk? take the bus? ride a bike? drive?

  Ask, "How do you go to school?" If appropriate, also ask, "How do you go to work?" Elicit answers.

Pair work

- Books open. Have Ss look at the photos. Explain the task: Ss look at the photos and guess about how the people go to work or school.
- Show the "guess" about Jeremy in the book. Ask for reasons why someone would make that guess. (He's young. He doesn't drive. He probably has a bike.)
- Ss work in pairs to make guesses and write sentences about the other three people. Walk around while they work to make sure they understand the task.

- Point out the right side of the chart. Explain the task: Ss listen to the people say how they *actually* get to school or work and write new sentences.
- Use the first conversation to demonstrate the task. Play the first part of the audio program.

Audio script

Jeremy
WOMAN: How do you go to school, Jeremy?
JEREMY: Well, I live with my parents in the country. The bus doesn't come near my house, so I ride my bike to school almost every day.

Tina
MAN: Tina, how do you go to work?
TINA: I go to work very early in the morning, so I drive. I live near my office, so it only takes me fifteen minutes.

Rosie
MAN: How do you go to school, Rosie?
ROSIE: My classes are in the afternoon, so I get up late and then I walk to school. I have lots of time.

Louis
WOMAN: How do you go to work, Louis?
LOUIS: Well, I don't work now. I'm retired. But I take a class at the community college downtown. Every Monday, Wednesday, and Thursday, I take the bus to school.

- Play the rest of the audio program as many times as necessary. Ss listen and write the answers individually.
- Ss compare answers in pairs, changing them if they wish.
- Play the audio program again so that Ss can verify their answers. While the program is playing, write the correct answers on the board.

Answers

How they actually go to work or school
Jeremy **rides a bike to school**.
Tina **drives to work**.
Rosie **walks to school**.
Louis **takes the bus to school**.

6 PRONUNCIATION *Third-person singular s*

In this exercise, Ss practice the pronunciation of verbs in the third-person singular of the simple present.

(*Note:* The pronunciation of *-s* endings for regular verbs in the simple present follow the same rules as the pronunciation of *-s* endings for regular plural nouns. See page T-9 of this Teacher's Edition.)

- Books open. Play the audio program. Ss listen and read.
- Model the *s* sounds in isolation: /s/, /z/, and /ɪz/. Point out that *do* and *say* are considered irregular because the vowel sounds change in the third-person singular: /duw/ /dʌz/, /sey/ /sɛz/. *Have* is considered irregular because the ending of the word changes entirely: /hæv/ /hæz/.
- Play the audio program again, or model the words one at a time as Ss listen and repeat.
- **Optional:** Ss repeat the words one S at a time. Correct their intonation individually.
- If Ss have trouble producing or distinguishing /s/ and /z/, tell them to put their fingers on their throats as they try to say the sounds. Voiced /z/ causes vibration when it is pronounced; voiceless /s/ does not.

7 WHO IS IT?

In this free-writing exercise, Ss communicate real information about themselves in English.

A

- Books open. Use the model to demonstrate the task. Point out that in the model the writer put *(Female)* at the beginning of her paper. Have a S read the statements about the writer and her family. Point out that the writer's name is not on the paper.
- **Optional:** Demonstrate the task further by writing on the board about yourself. First write *male* or *female*. Write five statements about yourself, your friends, and your family on the board.
- Ss write their own sentences individually. As they write, circulate to give help.
- Collect the papers and mix them up.

B *Class activity*

- Books open. Demonstrate the task and model the conversation. You are A. Choose four Ss to be B, C, D, and E. Read A's sentences from the model one at a time. Point out that you are changing each statement from the first-person *(I)* form to the third-person *(he/she)* form. You are using "she" because the writer wrote *Female* on her paper.
- **Optional:** Further demonstrate the task with your sentences on the board. Ask a volunteer to read your sentences from the board, changing each one from the first-person to third-person form. After the S reads your sentences from the board, "guess" one of the Ss in the class. Let the conversation continue until a S "guesses" you.
- Pass out the mixed up papers. If necessary, give Ss time to think about how to change the papers from the first-person to third-person form.
- Each S reads the sentences aloud. The other Ss try to guess the writer. When they guess the writer, give the paper back to the writer. Then continue the activity.
- **Alternate presentation:** If the class is large, do this activity in groups.

Workbook

Workbook Exercises 1–4 on pages 31–33 correspond to Cycle 1, Exercises 1–7 of the Student's Book. Answers to the Workbook exercises begin on page T-182 of this Teacher's Edition.

Cycle 2, Exercises 8–11

8 CONVERSATION

This conversation introduces simple present questions about daily activities.

- Books open. Set the scene. Have Ss look at the illustration and the names in the conversation. Ask, "What are Jack and Amy talking about?" (Harry's Restaurant, Sunday, and breakfast.)
- Write the question on the board:

  What are Jack and Amy talking about?
  (breakfast at Harry's Restaurant on Sunday)
- Play the audio program while Ss read and listen to confirm the answer. Elicit the answer.
- Play the audio program again. Ss read and listen. Try to elicit the meaning of *sleep late*. Encourage guessing. If necessary, clarify other new vocabulary.
- Play the audio program again, or model the conversation line by line. Ss listen and read, then look up and repeat.
- Ss practice the conversation in pairs using the Look Up and Say technique.
- **Optional:** Have a few students act out the conversation for the class.

6 PRONUNCIATION *Third-person singular* s

Listen and practice. Notice the pronunciation of **s** endings.

s = /s/		*s* = /z/		*(e)s* = /ɪz/		*irregular*	
take	take**s**	go	go**es**	dance	danc**es**	do	**does**
sit	sit**s**	live	live**s**	use	us**es**	say	say**s**
walk	walk**s**	study	stud**ies**	watch	watch**es**	have	**has**

7 WHO IS IT?

A Write five sentences about you, your family, and your friends. Write "Male" or "Female" on your paper, but not your name.

(Female) I live with my parents. I have two sisters. We go to Europe in the summer. . . .

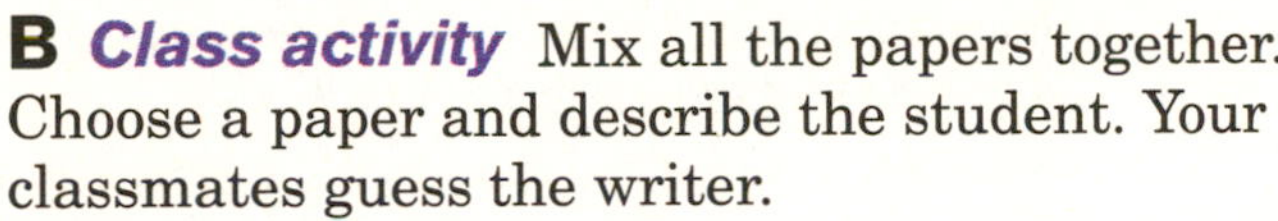

B ***Class activity*** Mix all the papers together. Choose a paper and describe the student. Your classmates guess the writer.

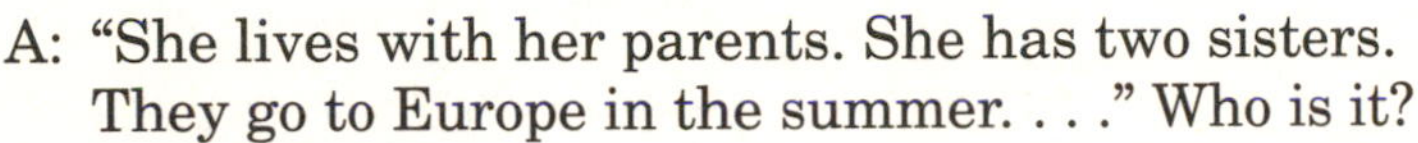

A: "She lives with her parents. She has two sisters. They go to Europe in the summer. . . ." Who is it?
B: Is it Michelle?
C: No, it's not me.
D: Is it Christine?
E: Yes, it's me!

8 CONVERSATION

Listen and practice.

Jack: Let's go to the park on Sunday.
Amy: OK, but let's not go early. I sleep late on weekends.
Jack: What time do you get up on Sundays?
Amy: At ten o'clock.
Jack: Oh, that isn't very late. I get up at noon.
Amy: Do you eat breakfast then?
Jack: Sure. I have breakfast every day.
Amy: Then let's meet at Harry's Restaurant at one o'clock. They serve breakfast all day on Sundays – for people like us.

9 LISTENING Days of the week

A Listen and practice.

B Listen to four conversations. What days do the people talk about? Write the number of the conversation on the day of the week.

10 GRAMMAR FOCUS

Simple present questions

Do you **get up** early on weekends?	No, I **get up** late.
What time **do** you **get up**?	At ten o'clock.
Does he **have** breakfast on Sundays?	Yes, he **eats** breakfast every day.
What time **does** he **have** breakfast?	At noon.
Do they **shop** together?	Yes, they **shop** together a lot.
When **do** they **shop**?	On Saturdays.

Time expressions

early	**on** Sundays	**in** the morning	**at** nine o'clock
late	**on** weekends	**in** the afternoon	**at** noon/**at** midnight
every day	**on** weekdays	**in** the evening	**at** night

A *Pair work* Ask and answer questions about your daily life. Add three more questions to the list.

1. What time do you get up? Do you get up early on weekends?
2. How do you go to school or work? Do you take the bus?
3. What time do you go home? Do you eat with your family?
4. When do you have English class?
5. Do you see your friends in the evening? Do you call your friends?
6. Do you have a computer at home? Do you go on the Internet at night?
7. What time do you go to bed?
8. ....
9. ....
10. ....

B *Class activity* Are you and your partner the same or different? Tell the class.

"Wen Pin and I get up early on weekdays. Wen Pin gets up early on weekends, but I get up late. . . ."

9 LISTENING *Days of the week*

This exercise presents the days of the week. Ss listen for specific information: the days of the week.

A

- Books open. Show Ss the graphic with the days of the week. Point out the five weekdays and the two days of the weekend.
- Play the audio program. Ss listen and read.
- Play the audio program again, or model the words one at a time. Ss listen and repeat.
- **Optional:** To practice, say a day of the week and have Ss quickly say the day that follows.

B

- Books open. Play the first item on the audio program, and use the example to demonstrate the task.
- Play the audio program as many times as necessary for Ss to complete the task.

Audio script

1. MAN: Do you sleep late on weekends?
   WOMAN: Oh, no. I get up early on Saturdays.
   MAN: When do you get up?
   WOMAN: At 4:30 A.M. I go to work at 5:30.
2. WOMAN: Let's go to the movies this week.
   MAN: OK. When?
   WOMAN: How about tonight?
   MAN: No, I'm busy tonight.
   WOMAN: Well, then, tomorrow . . . Thursday.
   MAN: OK. Thursday is fine.
3. MAN: Do you have dinner with your family every night?
   WOMAN: No. I go to school at night on weekdays, so I get home late.
   MAN: So do you have dinner with your family on the weekend?
   WOMAN: Well, we always have dinner together on Sundays.
4. WOMAN: Excuse me. When does the train come?
   MAN: The train isn't running tonight. It doesn't run at night on Mondays.
   WOMAN: Oh, no! I guess I need a taxi!

- Elicit the answers from the class, and write them on the board. If there is disagreement, read the conversation aloud to verify the answer.

Answers

1. Saturday 2. Thursday 3. Sunday 4. Monday

Optional activity: ***Days of the week***

- See page 151.

10 GRAMMAR FOCUS *Simple present questions*

This grammar focus presents simple present questions with *do* and *does* – with both yes/no and Wh-questions. It also introduces time expressions.

- Play the audio program to present the questions and answers. Ss read and listen. Show Ss the relationship between the statements and the questions. Statements with *he* and *she* need an *-s* on the verb. Questions with *he* and *she* need *does*.
- Play the audio program again or model the sentences. Ss listen and repeat.
- Now play the audio program to present the time expressions. Ss read and listen. Explain the meaning of *early, late,* and *every* with examples from your own daily activities. "I get up at 6:00 on weekdays. That's early." "I get up late on Sundays – about noon." "I go to bed at 10:00 every day – on weekdays and weekends."
- Play the audio program again or model the expressions. Ss listen and repeat.

A ***Pair work***

- With the class, make a list of additional questions on the board:

  What time do you get up on weekends?
  What do you do in the evening?
  How do you go home from school?
  Where do you live?

- Each S chooses three questions for numbers 8–10. Ss can write their own questions if they wish.
- Demonstrate the task with one or two Ss. Tell Ss to keep notes of their partners' responses.
- While Ss are practicing, listen and choose a S to help you demonstrate the class activity in part B.

B ***Class activity***

- Write this on the board to remind Ss of the meanings of *and* and *but*:

  and = same *but = different*

- Ask a S to read the model, using the Look Up and Say technique.
- Demonstrate the task with the S you have chosen. Tell how you and the S are the same and different.
- Let Ss volunteer to talk about themselves and their partners.

Optional activity: ***Game – Tic-Tac-Toe***

- See page T-151.

11 READING *What's your schedule like?*

In this article, Ss read about the work and sleep schedules of three people. The exercises practice scanning for specific information, making inferences, and writing about Ss' own daily schedules and habits.

- Books open. Read the title aloud, and write it on the board. Clarify the meaning of *schedule* by talking about your own schedule: "I work from 9 A.M. to 5 P.M. That's my work schedule. I sleep from 11 P.M. to 7 A.M. That's my sleep schedule."
- Introduce the prereading task. Read the questions aloud one at a time. Ss look at the photos and guess the answers. Elicit guesses from several Ss. Ask Ss for reasons for their guesses.

A

- Ss read the article. If you wish, play the audio program as Ss listen and read.
- Go over questions 1–4 with the Ss. Ss scan the article silently to find the answers.
- Elicit the answers from the Ss. Write the information on the board. Complete sentences are not necessary.

Answers 1–4

1. Brittany – 7:00 A.M.
   Joshua – 6:30 A.M.
   Maya – 2:00 P.M.
2. Weekends – Maya and Brittany
   Weekdays – Brittany, Joshua, and Maya
3. Eats breakfast in the morning – Brittany and Joshua
4. Works five days a week – Joshua

- Let Ss ask questions about vocabulary, but remind them that they have already answered questions 1–4 without any explanation. Try to get Ss to answer instead of you. Help them guess.
- **Optional:** Tell Ss you will give them definitions for only three vocabulary words in the article. Let Ss make requests and vote to choose which words you explain.
- Go over questions 5 and 6. If you wish, play the audio program while Ss skim the article again.
- Elicit answers for questions 5 and 6 from several Ss.

Possible answers 5 and 6

1. Brittany sleeps until noon on Sundays.
   Joshua works at home.
   Maya only works three nights a week.
2. Brittany works on Saturdays.
   Joshua sometimes works all night.
   Maya works at night.

B *Pair work*

- Go over the explanation of "early birds" and "night owls." Elicit who in the article is an early bird (Joshua) and who is a night owl (Maya and sometimes Joshua). Brittany gets up and goes to bed at normal hours. She isn't an early bird or a night owl.
- Ask who in the class is an early bird, who is a night owl, and who isn't either. Ss raise their hands.
- Demonstrate the task. Write a few sentences about your own schedule. Elicit from the Ss if you are an early bird, a night owl, or neither.
- Ss work individually to write five sentences about their own schedules. Walk around as they work. Comment on their information (not their grammar or spelling).
- Put Ss in pairs. Ss take turns reading their sentences to a partner. The partner says, "You're an early bird," "You're a night owl," or "You aren't an early bird or a night owl."
- **Optional:** Bring the class back together. Have Ss take turns reporting to the class about their partners.
- **Optional:** Have each S circle one or two sentences on their papers for you to correct. Collect their papers, correct them, and return them in the next class.

INTERCHANGE 6 Class survey

See page T-113 of this Teacher's Edition for notes.

Workbook

Workbook Exercises 5–10 on pages 34–36 correspond to Cycle 2, Exercises 8–11 of the Student's Book. Answers to the Workbook exercises begin on page T-182 of this Teacher's Edition.

11 READING

WHAT'S YOUR SCHEDULE LIKE?

Look at the pictures. Who gets up early? Who gets up late?

Brittany Davis
College Student

"My classes all start at 8:00 A.M., so I get up at 7:00, eat a quick breakfast, and take the bus to the university. In the afternoon, I have a job at the library. My only time to study is in the evening, from eight until midnight. I work at the library on Saturdays, too. But on Saturday nights I stay out late, and on Sundays I sleep until noon!"

Joshua Burns
Web-Site Designer

"I design Web sites for small companies. I'm self-employed, so I work at home. I get up at 6:30 and go for a run before breakfast. I'm at my computer by 8:00, and I work until 6:00. Around one o'clock, I take a lunch break, and I 'surf the Net' to look at other Web sites. I work hard – sometimes I work all night to finish a project. But I never work on weekends!"

Maya Black
Rock Musician

"I go to work at ten o'clock in the evening, and I play until 3:00 A.M. I take a break at midnight, though. After work, I have dinner at an all-night restaurant. Then I take a taxi home. I go to bed at five in the morning and sleep until two in the afternoon. I only work three nights a week – Friday, Saturday, and Sunday – but I practice every afternoon."

A Read the article and answer the questions.

1. What time does each person get up?
2. Who works on weekends? Who works on weekdays?
3. Who eats breakfast in the morning?
4. Who works five days a week?
5. Find one thing you like about each person's schedule.
6. Find one thing you don't like about each person's schedule.

B ***Pair work*** Write five sentences about your schedule. Compare with a partner. Are you an "early bird" or a "night owl"? (Early birds get up early in the morning. Night owls stay up late at night.)

interchange 6

Class survey

Find out more about your classmates. Turn to page IC-9.

Does the apartment have a view?

1 SNAPSHOT

Listen and practice.

Houses and Apartments

second floor
bedroom
bedroom
closet
hall
stairs
bedroom
bathroom
first floor
dining room
kitchen
laundry room
living room
stairs
garage
yard
House

bathroom
bedroom
closet
dining room
kitchen
living room
elevator
Apartment
lobby

Which rooms are in houses in your country?
Which rooms are in apartments in your country?

2 CONVERSATION

 Listen and practice.

Linda: Guess what! I have a new apartment.
Chris: That's super. What's it like?
Linda: It's really beautiful.
Chris: How many rooms does it have?
Linda: Well, it has a bedroom, a bathroom, a kitchen, and a living room. Oh, and a big closet in the hall.
Chris: Where is it?
Linda: It's on Lakeview Drive.
Chris: Oh, nice. Does it have a view?
Linda: Yes, it does. It has a great view of my neighbor's apartment!

7 Does the apartment have a view?

This unit introduces expressions for talking about homes and furniture. It introduces short answers to yes/no questions, *how many* questions, *there is/there are* statements, and *some/any*.

Cycle 1, Exercises 1–4

1 SNAPSHOT *Houses and apartments*

This graphic shows floor plans of a typical two-story house and a one-bedroom apartment in the United States. The captions introduce vocabulary related to housing. The questions relate the information to Ss' own lives.

- Books open. Give Ss a moment to study the graphic.
- Explain that the Ss are going to hear people describing the home and apartment in the Snapshot. Ss should listen and follow along with the description.
- Play the audio program.

Audio script

House
WOMAN: The house has two floors, a garage, and a yard.
MAN: The first floor has a living room, a dining room, a kitchen, a laundry room, and stairs to the second floor.
WOMAN: The second floor has a hall, three bedrooms, and a bathroom. Every bedroom has a closet.

Apartment
WOMAN: The apartment building has a lobby and an elevator.
MAN: Every apartment has a living room, a kitchen, a dining room, a bedroom, a bathroom, and a closet.

- Read the words in the Snapshot aloud. Students listen and repeat. You may mention that in the United States, "the first floor" is also sometimes called "the ground floor."
- Ask the questions one by one. Elicit answers from Ss. Make a chart of their responses on the board:

Houses	*Apartments*
living room	*living room*
. . .	. . .

- If your Ss are from different countries, write the names of the countries next to the responses as well. Make sure to find out what *other* rooms are in houses and apartments in your Ss' countries. What do the rooms look like? What do they do in the rooms?

2 CONVERSATION

This conversation introduces expressions for talking about homes. It also introduces questions with *how many* and short answers to yes/no questions.

- Books open. Use the illustration to set the scene. Say, "This is Linda. She's talking about her new apartment." Write these questions on the board:

  What rooms does the apartment have?
  (a bedroom, a bathroom, a kitchen, and a living room)
  Where is the apartment? (on Lakeview Drive)
- Play the audio program while Ss read and listen for the answers. Elicit the answers.
- Play the audio program again. Ss read and listen. Try to elicit the meanings of *guess what* and *a great view.* Encourage guessing.
- You may ask, "Does Linda's apartment have a view?" Elicit answers from Ss. (No. A view of another apartment is not considered a view. Linda is joking.)
- Play the audio program again, or model the conversation line by line. Ss listen and read, then look up and repeat.
- Ss practice the conversation in pairs using the Look Up and Say technique.
- **Optional:** Have a few students act out the conversation for the class.

3 GRAMMAR FOCUS Simple present short answers; how many

This grammar focus presents and practices simple present short answers and questions with *how many.*

(*Note:* In the pronunciation of questions, the auxiliaries *do, don't, does,* and *doesn't* are not usually stressed. In the pronunciation of short answers, they are stressed.)

- Play the audio program to present the questions and answers. Ss read and listen. If necessary, first review the formation of simple present questions (see Unit 6, Exercise 10). Then explain that short answers to yes/no questions use the auxiliary verb *do,* not the main verb.
- Point out the structure of the question *how many* + noun – *how many rooms.* Explain that *how many* questions usually require a number in the response – *four rooms.*
- Play the audio program again, or model the sentences. Ss listen and repeat.

A

- Use the example to demonstrate the task. Tell Ss to use the verbs in the grammar box.
- Ss complete the conversation individually.
- Read the conversation aloud with the correct answers. Ss verify their answers. Then Ss practice the conversation in pairs.

Answers

LINDA: **Do** you **live** in an apartment?
CHRIS: No, I **don't**. I **live** in a house.
LINDA: What's it like? **Does** it **have** a yard?
CHRIS: Yes, it **does**. And it's next to the river.
LINDA: That sounds nice. **Do** you **live** alone?
CHRIS: No, I **don't**. I **live** with my parents and my sisters.
LINDA: How many sisters **do** you **have**?
CHRIS: I **have** four.
LINDA: That's a big family. **Do** you **have** a big house?
CHRIS: Yes, we **do**. It **has** ten rooms.
LINDA: Ten rooms! How many bedrooms **does** it **have**?
CHRIS: It **has** four.
LINDA: **Do** you **have** your own bedroom?
CHRIS: Yes, I **do**. I'm really lucky.

B *Pair work*

- Use the example to demonstrate the task. Give Ss time to find the answers to questions 2–5. Then, in pairs, Ss take turns asking and answering the questions.
- Call on pairs to ask and answer a question for the class. If the answer is not correct, let other Ss correct it.

Answers

1. No, he doesn't. He lives in a house.
2. Yes, it does.
3. No, he doesn't. He lives with his parents and his sisters.
4. No, he doesn't. He has four sisters.
5. Yes, he does.

C

- Demonstrate the task. Elicit some questions about your home. Answer the questions and write the questions and answers on the board.
- Ss work individually to write five questions for their partners. As they work, go around the class to give help if necessary. Comment on interesting questions.
- In pairs, Ss take turns asking and answering questions.
- Bring the class back together. Ask volunteers to share questions and answers with the class.

4 LISTENING

In this exercise, Ss listen for the gist in descriptions of houses and apartments.

- Books open. Have Ss study the photographs.
- Play the first item on the audio program, and use the example to demonstrate and explain the task.
- Play the audio program as many times as necessary. Ss fill in the numbers.

Audio script

1. WOMAN: My apartment is very small. It has just one room with a very small kitchen. It doesn't have a bedroom, so I sleep on the sofa.
2. MAN: My house is on the water. In fact, I have a view of the water from my living room. My house is very big – I have ten rooms.
3. WOMAN: My family and I live in the country in an old house. We have a yard and a garden, but the house isn't big. Our bedroom is downstairs, and the kids' bedrooms are upstairs.
4. MAN: I live in an apartment downtown. It's a beautiful apartment with two bedrooms and lots of windows. It has a big living room with a great view of the city.

- Elicit answers. In case of confusion, read the audio script or play the audio program again.

Answers

4, 3, 1, 2

Workbook

Workbook Exercises 1–4 on pages 37–38 correspond to Cycle 1, Exercises 1–4 of the Student Book. Answers to the Workbook exercises begin on page T-182 of this Teacher's Edition.

Optional activity: *My home*

- See page T-151.

3 GRAMMAR FOCUS

Simple present short answers; how many

Do you **live** in an apartment? Yes, I **do**. No, I **don't**.	**Do** the bedrooms **have** closets? Yes, they **do**. No, they **don't**.
Does the apartment **have** a view? Yes, it **does**. No, it **doesn't**.	**How many** rooms **does** the apartment **have**? It **has** four rooms.

A Complete the conversation. Then practice with a partner.

Linda: ...Do... you ...live... in an apartment?
Chris: No, I .... I .... in a house.
Linda: What's it like? .... it .... a yard?
Chris: Yes, it .... And it's next to the river.
Linda: That sounds nice. .... you .... alone?
Chris: No, I .... I .... with my parents and my sisters.
Linda: How many sisters .... you .... ?
Chris: I .... four.
Linda: That's a big family. .... you .... a big house?
Chris: Yes, we .... It .... ten rooms.
Linda: Ten rooms! How many bedrooms .... it .... ?
Chris: It .... four.
Linda: .... you .... your own bedroom?
Chris: Yes, I .... I'm really lucky.

B ***Pair work*** Read the conversation in part A again. Ask and answer these questions. For "no" answers, give the correct information.

1. Does Chris live in an apartment?
   "No, he doesn't. He lives in a house."
2. Does Chris's home have a yard?
3. Does Chris live alone?
4. Does he have four brothers?
5. Does he have his own room?

C Write five questions like the ones in part B about a partner's home. Ask and answer your questions with your partner.

4 LISTENING

 Listen to people describe their homes. Number the pictures from 1 to 4.

5 WORD POWER Furniture

A Listen and practice.

B Where do these things go? Complete the chart.

Kitchen	*table* *stove*
Dining room	*table*
Living room	
Bedroom	

C ***Group work*** Compare your charts.

A: The table goes in the kitchen.
B: The table goes in the dining room, too.

6 CONVERSATION

 Listen and practice.

Chris: This apartment is great.
Linda: Thanks. I love it, but I really need some furniture.
Chris: What do you need?
Linda: Well, there are some chairs in the kitchen, but there isn't a table.
Chris: And there's no sofa here in the living room.
Linda: And there aren't any chairs. There's only this lamp.
Chris: So let's go shopping next weekend!

Cycle 2, Exercises 5–11

5 WORD POWER *Furniture*

This exercise introduces and practices vocabulary for household furnishings.

A

- Books open. Ss study the illustrations. Play the audio program or model the words in the picture. Ss listen and read, then listen and repeat.
- If necessary, give extra practice with words that are difficult for your Ss.

B

- Use the examples to demonstrate the task. Point to the illustration and say, "This furniture goes in the kitchen, the dining room, the living room, and the bedroom." Ask, "Where does the table go?" (in the kitchen and the dining room) "Where does the stove go?" (in the kitchen).
- Ss work individually to fill in the chart.

C *Group work*

- Model the example conversation with a S.
- Put Ss in groups of four or five. In group conversations, Ss compare their charts and make one chart for the group.
- As a class, Ss discuss the lists. Opinions will vary, so accept all reasonable answers.

Possible answers

Kitchen: chairs, clock, curtains, microwave oven, pictures, refrigerator, rug, stove, table, television
Dining room: chairs, curtains, mirror, pictures, rug, table
Living room: armchairs, bookcase, coffee table, curtains, desk, lamps, mirror, pictures, rug, sofa, television
Bedroom: bed, chairs, clock, curtains, desk, dresser, lamps, mirror, pictures, rug, television

6 CONVERSATION

This conversation introduces *there is/there are* and *some/any.*

- Books open. Set the scene. Linda and Chris are from Exercise 2. Chris is visiting Linda's new apartment. Write this question on the board.

  What does Linda need for her apartment?
  (a table, a sofa, and chairs)
- Play the audio program while Ss read and listen for the answers. Elicit the answers.
- Play the audio program again. Ss read and listen. Let Ss ask about key vocabulary. Encourage guessing.
- Play the audio program again or model the conversation line by line. Ss listen and read, then look up and repeat.
- Ss practice the conversation in pairs using the Look Up and Say technique.
- **Optional:** Have a few students act out the conversation for the class.

7 GRAMMAR FOCUS There is, there are

 This grammar focus presents statements with *there is, there are* with *no, some,* and *any.*

(*Note:* In this unit, all the new nouns for productive use are countable. Uncountable nouns are taught in Unit 9.)

- Play the audio program to present the statements. Ss read and listen.
- Point out that *a/an* and *no* are used with singular nouns. *Some* and *any* are used with plural nouns. *Some* is used in affirmative statements. *Any* is used in negative statements.
- Play the audio program again, or model the sentences. Ss listen and repeat.

A

- Use the examples to demonstrate the task. (*Note:* In this exercise, there are two other ways to say negative sentences. There is one other way to say affirmative sentences.)
- Read the first sentence aloud. Elicit the first example from a S. Ss repeat each sentence.
- Elicit another way to say the same sentence. (There isn't a table in the kitchen.) Ss repeat.
- Follow the same procedure for the second example. Then lead the Ss through the exercise as a class activity.

Answers

3. There's a stove in the kitchen.
4. There isn't a refrigerator. / There's no refrigerator.
5. There are some curtains on the windows.
6. There aren't any rugs on the floor. /
   There are no rugs on the floor.

B *Pair work*

- Books open. Ss study the illustration of Linda's apartment.
- **Optional:** Let Ss ask about vocabulary in the picture. Have the S ask "What's this called in English?" and show you what he or she is asking about. Try to get Ss to answer before you do. Answer questions about these things: *pillow, bedspread* or *quilt, TV stand, counter, sink,* and *cabinets.*
- Have two Ss demonstrate the task using the example conversation.
- Ss talk about the illustration in pairs. After a few minutes, have Ss change partners and continue practicing.
- Bring the class back together. Ask several Ss to tell you one thing Linda has and one thing she doesn't have.

C

- Demonstrate the task by reading the examples aloud. Elicit one or two examples from Ss about the school and write them on the board.
- Ss write five sentences individually. Go around the class to help. Comment on interesting sentences.
- Ss compare their sentences in pairs, making changes if they wish.
- Ask each S to read a sentence to the class. If the class is large, do this in groups.

Optional activity: *I need some furniture!*

- See page T-151.

7 GRAMMAR FOCUS

There is, there are

There's a lamp in the living room.	**There are some** chairs in the kitchen.
There's no sofa in the living room.	**There are no** chairs in the living room.
There isn't a table in the kitchen.	**There aren't any** chairs in the living room.

There's = **There is**

A Say each sentence another way.

1. I don't have a table in the kitchen. *"There's no table in the kitchen."*
2. I have some chairs in the kitchen. *"There are some chairs in the kitchen."*
3. I have a stove in the kitchen.
4. I don't have a refrigerator.
5. I have some curtains on the windows.
6. I don't have any rugs on the floor.

B ***Pair work*** Look at the picture of Linda's apartment. Take turns saying what things Linda has and doesn't have in her apartment.

A: There's a mirror in the bedroom.
B: But there aren't any pictures in the bedroom.

C Write five sentences about things you have or don't have in your classroom and school. Then compare with a partner.

There are twenty desks in the classroom.
There aren't any computers.

8 PRONUNCIATION Words with th

A Listen and practice. Notice the two pronunciations of **th**.

/ð/ /θ/ /ð/ /ð/ /θ/ /θ/
There are **th**irteen rooms in **th**is house. **Th**e house has **th**ree ba**th**rooms.

B Think of three other /ð/ words and three other /θ/ words.
Write three funny sentences using them, and read them aloud.

On Thursdays, their mother and father think for thirteen minutes.

9 LISTENING

Listen to Linda and Chris shopping. What does Linda buy?
Check (✓) the things.

What does Linda buy?			
☑ chairs	☐ a sofa	☐ a rug	☐ a table
☐ a refrigerator	☐ a dresser	☐ a coffee table	☐ curtains

10 DREAM HOUSE

A Write a description of your dream house.

Where is your dream house?
How many rooms does it have?
What are the rooms?
What's in the rooms?
What else does it have?

My dream house is in the country.
There are twenty rooms. . . .

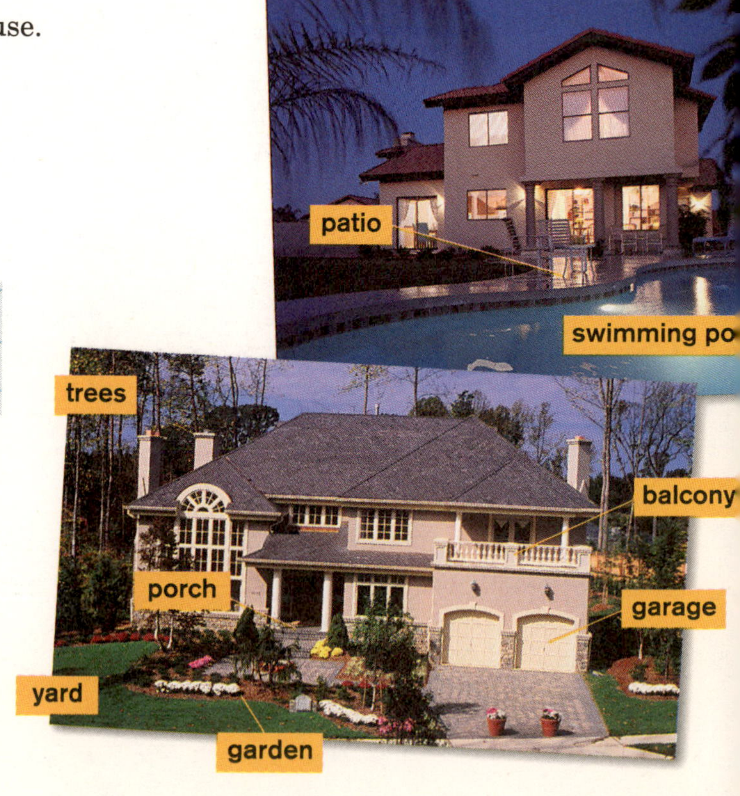

B ***Pair work*** Ask your partner about his or her dream house.

A: Does it have a swimming pool?
B: Yes, it does. There's a really big pool.

8 PRONUNCIATION Words with th

A

- Write the sentence on the board. Play the audio program. Underline the *th* words as the audio plays.
- Books open. Make sure Ss notice the phonetic symbols. Play the audio program again. Ss listen and read.
- Play the audio program again, or model the sentence. (*Note*: Have Ss hold one hand in front of their mouths to feel for air. Correct pronunciation of ð sounds will not produce air through the mouth whereas θ sounds will.)

B

- As a whole class, create a list of *th* words on the board. Use the Unit Summaries in the back of the Student's Book. If Ss know more *th* words, add them to the list. Then practice the pronunciation.

Sample answers

/ð/	/θ/
brother/mother/father	math
their	month
them	thank
this/these	thing
weather	think

- Ss write sentences as a group activity. Walk around and give help. When you see a good sentence, send a S to write it on the board.
- If necessary, correct the sentences on the board as a class. Write the number of *th* sounds each sentence has next to each one. Model the sentences. Ss repeat.

9 LISTENING

This exercise practices listening for key words in a conversation about furniture.

- Set the scene. Linda and Chris are shopping for furniture for Linda's new apartment. Use the example in the book and the first part of the audio program to demonstrate and explain the task.
- Play the audio program. Ss listen and check the correct items in the chart.

Audio script

CHRIS: What are you looking for?
LINDA: Oh, I'm only buying a few things for the living room. Furniture is expensive!
CHRIS: Yeah, it is.
LINDA: Ooh! Look at those blue chairs.
CHRIS: Yeah, they're cool.
LINDA: I need two for the living room.
CHRIS: Uh-huh. But what about a sofa?
LINDA: I have a sofa now – from my parents. And it's blue, too!
CHRIS: Oh. Hey, look! You know, this rug is nice. And it matches the chairs.
LINDA: Umm . . . it's nice, but it's a little boring. Oh, wait a minute. That coffee table is great.
CHRIS: Yeah, I like it, too.
LINDA: So the chairs, the coffee table . . . . What else? I don't need any lamps. Oh, I know. I want some curtains, too.
CHRIS: How about the curtains over there?
LINDA: Where?
CHRIS: Right there. They're red.
LINDA: Oh, yes! They're perfect.

- Elicit answers. In case of confusion, read the audio script or play the audio program again.

Answers

chairs, a coffee table, curtains

10 DREAM HOUSE

This writing and speaking activity reviews some of the grammar and vocabulary of the unit. It also presents new vocabulary about houses.

A

- Books open. Clarify the meaning of *dream house*. Ask, "Where do you want to live? What kind of house do you want?" Model the vocabulary in the photos. Ss listen and repeat.
- Use the questions and the model to explain the task.
- Elicit some words (adjectives) for talking about a dream house, for example, *beautiful, nice, big, cool, new*. Write the words on the board. Remind Ss that they can also use *very* and *really*. Most of their sentences will use *has, there is,* or *there are*.
- Ss work individually to write a description of their dream house by answering the questions. Some answers may need more than one sentence.
- Have a few Ss read their descriptions aloud to the class. Or have Ss read them in groups.

B ***Pair work***

- Have two Ss demonstrate the task with the model conversation. Have another pair demonstrate with another question and answer.
- In pairs, Ss ask and answer questions about their dream houses.

11 READING *Two Special Houses in the American Southwest*

In this article, Ss read about two unusual houses: Sandra Cisneros's colorful house in San Antonio, Texas and a Navajo *hogan* in Arizona. The exercises practice reading for main ideas and giving opinions.

- Books open. Read the title aloud, and write it on the board. If necessary, use the photograph on the right to clarify *the American Southwest.*
- Introduce the prereading task. Point to the photograph on the left. Ask, "What is special – what is different – about this house?" (The colors.) Ask about the photograph on the right. Ss may not be able to answer in English. Accept any answer that you can understand, or tell Ss to look for words in the paragraph.

A

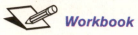

- Use the example and the photograph to demonstrate the task. Go over the list of possible answers. Let Ss ask about key vocabulary in the exercise.
- Ss read the article and work individually to complete the chart. If you wish, play the audio program as Ss listen and read.
- **Optional:** Ss underline words they do not know as they read. Let Ss ask a few questions about vocabulary, but encourage Ss to guess the meaning from the context of the paragraph. Ss will be able to do the exercise without understanding all the words.
- Ask for volunteers to read the answers aloud, or write the answers on the board for Ss to see.

Answers

Sandra Cisneros's house
1. There is **a porch with a pink floor**.
2. There are **many books**.
3. There are **colorful paintings**.

Lorraine Nelson's hogan
4. There is a **wood-burning stove**.
5. There are **three chairs**.
6. There are **two beds on the floor**.

B *Group work*

- Read the instructions aloud, and go over the questions.
- Put the Ss in groups of three to five. Ss answer the questions in groups. They give reasons if they can. Appoint a "secretary" in each group to write down the group's choices. (What colors do you choose? Do you stay in a house or a *hogan*?)
- Bring the class back together. Secretaries report their groups' choices to the class.

INTERCHANGE 7 Find the differences

See page T-114 of this Teacher's Edition for notes.

Workbook

Workbook Exercises 5–10 on pages 39–42 correspond to Cycle 2, Exercises 5–11 of the Student's Book. Answers to the Workbook exercises begin on page T-182 of this Teacher's Edition.

Optional activity: ***My favorite room***

- See page T-152.

11 READING

TWO SPECIAL HOUSES IN THE AMERICAN SOUTHWEST

Look at the pictures. What is special about the two houses?

In San Antonio, Texas, there is a purple house. This house is the home of Sandra Cisneros. Ms. Cisneros is a Mexican-American writer. She is famous for her interesting stories. The house has a porch with a pink floor. The rooms are green, pink, and purple. There are many books and colorful paintings. Many other houses near Ms. Cisneros's house are white or beige, so her house is very different. Some of her neighbors think her house is too colorful, but Ms. Cisneros loves it.

Every year many people visit the land of the Navajos, the largest Native American tribe in the Southwest. Most people stay in hotels, but some are now staying in traditional Navajo homes, called *hogans*. Hogans are made of logs and mud and have dirt floors. Lorraine Nelson, a schoolteacher from Arizona, now invites visitors to stay in a hogan on her property. Her hogan has three chairs, two beds on the floor, and a wood-burning stove. Ms. Nelson teaches guests about Navajo traditions.

A Read the article. What's in the two houses? Complete the chart.

three chairs
many books
colorful paintings
✓porch with a pink floor
two beds on the floor
wood-burning stove

Sandra Cisneros's house	Lorraine Nelson's hogan
1. There is a *porch with a pink floor* .	**4.** There is a ....
2. There are	**5.** There are ....
3. There are	**6.** There are ....

B ***Group work*** Talk about these questions.

1. Imagine that you want to paint your house. What colors do you choose? Why?
2. Imagine that you are visiting Arizona. Do you stay in a hogan or in a hotel? Why?

Find the differences

Compare two apartments. Turn to page IC-10.

What do you do?

1 WORD POWER *Jobs*

A Listen and practice. Then match the occupations to the pictures. *"He's a receptionist."*

a. cashier
b. cook/chef
c. doctor
d. flight attendant
e. judge
f. lawyer
g. musician
h. nurse
i. pilot
j. police officer
✓k. receptionist
l. salesperson
m. security guard
n. singer
o. waiter
p. waitress

B ***Pair work*** Compare your answers.

A: What's his job?
B: He's a receptionist.

8 What do you do?

This unit introduces expressions for talking about work. It presents Wh-questions with do and the pattern a/an + adjective + noun. It also presents adjectives for giving opinions.

Cycle 1, Exercises 1–6

1 WORD POWER Jobs

This exercise teaches the names of some jobs.

A

- Books open. To illustrate *job* and *occupation,* write on the board:

  I'm a teacher. My job or occupation = teacher.

- Ss study the illustrations. Play the audio program. (The audio program follows the illustrations in order from 1–16.) Ss listen and study the illustrations.

Audio script

He's a receptionist.
She's a doctor.
She's a nurse.
He's a pilot.
She's a flight attendant.
He's a musician.
She's a singer.
She's a judge.
He's a police officer.
He's a lawyer.
He's a cook./He's a chef.
He's a waiter.
She's a waitress.
He's a salesperson.
She's a cashier.
She's a security guard.

- Play the audio program again, or model the sentences line by line. Ss listen and repeat.
- Read the names of the jobs in the blue box aloud. Ss listen and repeat.
- Use the example to demonstrate the task. Ss match the occupations in the box with the illustrations.
- If necessary, play the audio program again to help Ss match more occupations.

B *Pair work*

- Books open. Model the example conversation with a S. Hold up your book and point to picture 1 when you ask the question. Ss listen and repeat.
- Ask a pair of Ss to demonstrate the task, talking about another person in the illustrations. The first S holds up the book and points to the picture he or she is asking about.
- Ss work in pairs to compare their answers, pointing to the people they are asking about.
- When Ss have finished, elicit the answers and write them on the board so that Ss can check their work.

Answers

1. k	5. d	9. j	13. p
2. c	6. g	10. f	14. l
3. h	7. n	11. b	15. a
4. i	8. e	12. o	16. m

2 THE WORLD OF WORK

This exercise presents vocabulary for workplaces and practices some of the job vocabulary from Exercise 1.

A *Pair work*

- Books open. Point out that the illustrations show a hospital, an office, a store, and a hotel.
- Ask, "Who works in a hospital?" Use the example conversation and the examples in the chart to explain and demonstrate the task: Ss write three occupations from Exercise 1 for each workplace. Then they add one more occupation. This can be a new vocabulary word or another occupation from Exercise 1 if necessary. Students can use some occupations in more than one list.
- Ss complete the chart in pairs.
- Elicit answers from Ss. Make a list on the board of possible occupations for each workplace. Explain new jobs or have Ss explain them if possible.

Possible answers *(Additional answers will vary)*

In a hospital: cook/chef, doctor, nurse, receptionist, security guard
In an office: doctor, lawyer, nurse, police officer, receptionist, salesperson
In a store: cashier, security guard, salesperson
In a hotel: cook/chef, musician, receptionist, security guard, singer, waiter, waitress

B *Class activity*

- Use the illustrations on pages 46 and 47, actual objects, or gestures to explain *uniform, handles money, works hard,* and *carries a gun.*
- Have three Ss read the model conversation using the Look Up and Say technique.
- Ss ask and answer the questions around the class. Answers may vary (e.g., police officers carry guns in some countries but not in others).
- **Alternate presentation:** In a large class, do the activity in groups so that Ss get to speak more often.

3 CONVERSATION

This conversation introduces Wh-questions in the simple present.

- Books open. Set the scene. Rachel and Angela are talking about their brothers. Have Ss look at the illustration. Write this question on the board:

  What are the men's jobs? (a chef and a security guard)
- Play the audio program while Ss read and listen for the answers. Elicit the answers.
- Play the audio program again. Ss read and listen. It should not be necessary to explain vocabulary.
- Play the audio program again, or model the conversation line by line. Ss listen and read, then look up and repeat.
- Ss practice the conversation in pairs using the Look Up and Say technique.
- **Optional:** Have a few students act out the conversation for the class.

2 THE WORLD OF WORK

A ***Pair work*** Who works in these places? Complete the chart with occupations from Exercise 1. Add one more occupation to each list.

A: A doctor works in a hospital.
B: A nurse works in a hospital, too.

In a hospital	In an office	In a store	In a hotel
doctor			
nurse			

B ***Class activity*** Ask and answer questions about occupations.

Who . . . ?

wears a uniform	talks to people
stands all day	works hard
sits all day	works at night
handles money	carries a gun

A: Who wears a uniform?
B: A police officer wears a uniform.
C: And a security guard . . . .

3 CONVERSATION

 Listen and practice.

Rachel: Where does your brother work?
Angela: In a hotel.
Rachel: Oh, that's interesting. My brother works in a hotel, too.
Angela: Really? What does he do, exactly?
Rachel: He's a chef in the restaurant. What about your brother?
Angela: He's a security guard, but he doesn't like it.
Rachel: That's too bad.
Angela: Yeah. He's looking for a new job.

4 GRAMMAR FOCUS

Simple present Wh-questions with do

Where do you work? I work in a hotel.	Where does she work? She works in a store.	Where do they work? They work in a hospital.
What do you do there? I'm a receptionist.	**What does she do** there? She's a cashier.	**What do they do** there? They're nurses.

a doctor — a salesperson — a computer repairperson

Complete these conversations with questions. Then practice with a partner.

1. A: *What does your sister do* ?
   B: My sister? She's a doctor.
   A: .... ?
   B: In a hospital. And she has an office, too.
2. A: .... ?
   B: I work in an electronics store.
   A: .... , exactly?
   B: I sell CD players, televisions, and telephones.
3. A: .... ?
   B: Tom works in a computer factory.
   A: .... there, exactly?
   B: He's a repairperson. He repairs computers.

5 PRONUNCIATION Reduction of do and does

A Listen and practice. Notice the reduction of **do** and **does** in these questions.

Where **do you** work? — What **do you** do?
Where **does he** work? — What **does he** do?
Where **do they** work? — What **do they** do?

B Practice the conversations in Exercise 4 again. Pay attention to your pronunciation of **do you**, **does she**, and **does he**.

4 GRAMMAR FOCUS *Simple present Wh-questions with* do

 This grammar focus presents *do* as a main verb in questions about occupations.

- Books open. Play the audio program to present the questions and answers. Ss read and listen.
- Point out the questions with *do* as both the auxiliary and the main verb. The answers use *be*.
- Point out that both "What do you do?" and "Where do you work?" can be answered, "I work in a hotel."
- Play the audio program again or model the sentences. Ss listen and repeat.
- Demonstrate the task. Lead Ss through the example.
- Ss complete the conversations individually. Go around the class to help as they write.
- Ss practice the conversations in pairs, correcting their answers as they practice.

Answers

1. A: **What does your sister do**?
   B: My sister? She's a doctor.
   A: **Where does she work**?
   B: In a hospital. And she has an office, too.
2. A: **Where do you work?/ What do you do**?
   B: I work in an electronics store.
   A: **What do you do**, exactly?
   B: I sell CD players, televisions, and telephones.
3. A: **Where does Tom work?/What does Tom do**?
   B: Tom works in a computer factory.
   A: **What does he do** there, exactly?
   B: He's a repairperson. He repairs computers.

- To check, call on pairs to say each conversation for the class using the Look Up and Say technique. Write their questions on the board and have the whole class correct the questions together.

5 PRONUNCIATION *Reduction of* do *and* does

This exercise highlights and practices the reduction of *do* and *does* before pronouns.

(*Note:* The pronunciation of auxiliary verbs is reduced in conversation. Notice that *you* is also reduced and that the *h* of *he* is not pronounced. The elision marks under the words show blending – the two words are pronounced as one. Main verbs are not reduced.)

A 

- Write the six sentences on the board. Books closed. Play the audio program.
- Mark the blending of *do you, does he,* and *do they* in the sentences on the board while Ss listen.
- Books open. Play the audio program again, or model the sentences line by line. Ss repeat the sentences.
- Ss say the conversations in pairs. Have them change partners several times. Walk around to help.
- Ask pairs of Ss to say the conversations for the class. Correct their intonation if necessary.

B

- Books open. Direct Ss to the conversations they completed in Exercise 4.
- In pairs, Ss practice the conversations again, with special attention to reductions and blending. Walk around while they practice to help with pronunciation. If necessary, model the conversations line by line.

6 WORKDAYS

In this fluency exercise, Ss ask and answer questions about jobs. They also prepare and deliver brief reports to the class.

Group work

- Explain the task. Show Ss the two lists of questions in the book. Call on Ss to read the questions. Make sure Ss understand the questions.
- Write this on the board:

  A: Do you have a job?

  B: Yes, I do. **OR** *B: No, I don't, but my brother has a job.*

  Read the question aloud with each answer. Tell Ss that if the S they are questioning has a job, they use the questions on the left. If the S doesn't have a job, they use the questions on the right.
- **Optional:** Some Ss may want to role play. They can talk about jobs they don't really have. They will need to invent all the details.
- Tell Ss to take notes of the answers in their groups.
- Demonstrate the task with three Ss. One S asks another S the questions. The third S takes notes of the answers. Have the demonstrating S take notes on the board. If necessary, show the S how to write just a few words, not complete sentences.
- Ss practice in groups of three. S should change roles so that each S is secretary only once. While they work, walk around to help.
- Point out the models for reporting about a S. Have two Ss read the models.
- Each S writes a report about the S that he or she took notes about. Have Ss practice their reports for their group members. Group members help the reporter make corrections.
- Bring the class back together. Ask for volunteers, or call on Ss to read their reports.

Workbook

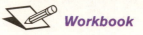

Workbook Exercises 1–4 on pages 43–46 correspond to Cycle 1, Exercises 1–6 of the Student's Book. Answers to the Workbook exercises begin on page T-182 of this Teacher's Edition.

Optional activity: ***Game – What's the question?***

- See page T-149. Ss write statements about their jobs or a friend or family member's job.

Cycle 2, Exercises 7–11

7 SNAPSHOT *Job Survey: People's opinions of different jobs*

This exercise gives people's opinions of different jobs. It also introduces adjectives for describing jobs and the names of eleven more occupations. The questions relate the information to Ss' own lives.

- Books open. Read the title aloud. Explain *survey* and show Ss the source note under the chart. Explain *opinion*.
- Model the names of the jobs one by one. Ss repeat. If possible, try to elicit the explanations of the jobs from S. Explain the new jobs if necessary.
- Read the adjectives aloud. Ss repeat. Show Ss that the adjectives are in contrasting pairs: *exciting* is the opposite of *boring,* and so on. Clarify meaning with mime, gestures, examples, or paraphrase.
- If necessary, illustrate the concept of "opposite" like this. Write on the board:

  easy — $2 \times 2 =$

  difficult — $(187.99 \times 37.8)^2 \div 6 =$
- Ss work individually to make Xs on the chart to show their own opinions. Tell Ss they may have the same opinion as the ones listed on the chart.
- Bring the class back together, and discuss the questions. Go over each one of the jobs. Say, for example, "An actor's job is difficult. Do you agree?" Have Ss who agree raise their hands or call out "Yes."

  Then ask, "Do you disagree?" The other Ss say "Yes." Elicit other adjectives. Let Ss give reasons for their opinions, if they can.

Optional activities: Vocabulary for names of jobs and opinion adjectives can be reviewed using any of the following games or exercises.

1. ***Scrambled letters***

- See page T-147.

2. ***Game – Word bingo***

- See page T-150.

3. ***Complete the word***

- See page T-150.

4. ***Game – Twenty questions***

- See page T-152.

6 WORKDAYS

Group work Ask three classmates about their jobs. If they don't have a job, ask them about a friend or family member. Then tell the class.

Ask about a classmate
Do you have a job?
Where do you work?
What do you do, exactly?
What time do you start work?
When do you finish work?
Do you take a break in the afternoon?
What do you do after work?
Do you watch television? read? study?

"Victor is a cashier. He works in a department store. He starts work at 10:00 A.M., and he finishes at 6:00 P.M. . . ."

Ask about a classmate's friend or relative
Tell me about your brother (sister). . . .
Where does he work?
What does he do, exactly?
What time does he start work?
When does he finish work?
Does he like his job?
What does he do after work? . . .

"Tomoko doesn't have a job, but her brother is a waiter. He works in a restaurant. He starts work . . . ."

7 SNAPSHOT

Job Survey — People's opinions of different jobs

	Exciting	Boring	Easy	Difficult	Safe	Dangerous	Relaxing	Stressful
actor				X				
air traffic controller								X
artist							X	
athlete	X							
carpenter						X		
DJ (disc jockey)			X					
fashion designer	X							
flight attendant		X						
florist					X			
gardener							X	
librarian					X			
pilot						X		
police officer						X		
receptionist		X						
teacher				X				
waiter/waitress								X

Source: Interviews with people between the ages of 18 and 50

Complete the chart with your opinions.
Which opinions do you agree with?
Which opinions do you disagree with? Why?

8 CONVERSATION

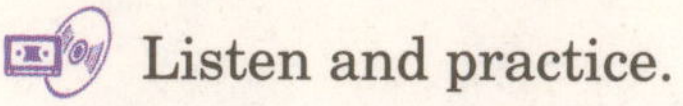

Listen and practice.

Richard: Hi, Stephanie. I hear you have a new job.
Stephanie: Yes. I'm teaching math at Lincoln High School.
Richard: How do you like it?
Stephanie: It's great. The students are terrific. How are things with you?
Richard: Not bad. I'm an air traffic controller now, you know.
Stephanie: Now, that's exciting!
Richard: Yes, but it's a very stressful job.

9 GRAMMAR FOCUS

Adjectives before nouns

be + adjective	*adjective + noun*
A police officer's job **is dangerous**.	A police officer has **a dangerous job**.
A doctor's job **is stressful**.	A doctor has **a stressful job**.

A ***Pair work*** Say each sentence another way.

1. A photographer's job is interesting.
   "A photographer has an interesting job."
2. An athlete's job is exciting.
3. A lawyer's job is stressful.
4. A gardener's job is relaxing.
5. An accountant's job is difficult.
6. A firefighter's job is dangerous.

B ***Class activity*** Think of two jobs for each category. Do you and your classmates agree?

a boring job	....	....
an easy job	....	....
a dangerous job	....	....
an exciting job	....	....
a difficult job	....	....
a stressful job	....	....

A: A musician has a boring job.
B: I disagree. A rock musician doesn't have a boring job.
C: I agree. A rock musician's job is very exciting.

8 CONVERSATION

This conversation introduces expressions for talking about how people like their jobs.

- Books open. Introduce the conversation with a quick-reading exercise. Ask, "What do Stephanie and Richard do?" Give Ss a few seconds to find the answers in the conversation. (She's a teacher. He's an air traffic controller.)
- Write these questions on the board:

  Does Stephanie like her job? (Yes.)
  Does Richard like his job? (Yes and no.)
- Play the audio program while Ss read and listen for the answers. Go over the answers. Stephanie says her job is great, so her answer is yes. Richard says his job is not bad, but stressful, so his answer is yes and no.
- Play the audio program again. Ss read and listen. It should not be necessary to explain vocabulary.
- Play the audio program again, or model the conversation line by line. Ss listen and read, then look up and repeat.
- Ss practice the conversation in pairs using the Look Up and Say technique.
- **Optional:** Have a few students act out the conversation for the class.

9 GRAMMAR FOCUS *Adjectives before nouns*

This grammar focus presents and practices the patterns *be* + adjective and adjective + noun. (Both forms were first seen in Unit 4.)

- Books open. Direct Ss' attention back to the chart in Exercise 7. Tell them that the words across the top (*exciting, boring*, etc.) are called adjectives.
- Play the audio program to present the information in the grammar box. Ss read and listen.
- Point out that the pairs of sentences have the same meaning, but different grammar. Have them identify the adjectives in each pair.
- Play the audio program again or model the sentences. Ss listen and repeat.

A *Pair work*

- Show Ss that three new occupations in the sentences are illustrated at the right. Model the name of each occupation. Ss repeat.
- In pairs, Ss take turns reading the sentences and saying them another way. Ss should do the exercise twice so that each S says every sentence two ways.
- **Optional:** Let Ss disagree with the statements. For example, in item 1, a S might say, "No, a photographer has a boring job."
- As they work, go around the class to check Ss' accuracy and pronunciation. Pay special attention to the pronunciation of the possessive *'s*.
- To check, call on pairs to sentences for the class. If the answer is incorrect, elicit the answer from other Ss.

Answers

1. A photographer has an interesting job.
2. An athlete has an exciting job.
3. A lawyer has a stressful job.
4. A gardener has a relaxing job.
5. An accountant has a difficult job.
6. A firefighter has a dangerous job.

B *Class activity*

- Demonstrate the first task. Write the first line of the chart on the board. Elicit from Ss the names of two "boring" jobs and fill them in.
- Ss work individually to complete the chart according to their own opinions.
- Use the example conversation to demonstrate the class activity.
- Ss volunteer their opinions about different jobs. Act as moderator and helper to keep the discussion going.

10 LISTENING

This activity practices listening for the names of people's jobs and their opinions about their jobs.

- Books open. Have Ss look at the photographs. Ask "What do these women do? Where do you think they work?" Elicit answers.
- Explain the first task. Use the example in the book and the first part of the audio program to demonstrate.
- Play the audio program. Ss listen and number the pictures.

Audio script

1. MAN: Where do you work now, Theresa?
   THERESA: I have a job at a hotel.
   MAN: What do you do, exactly?
   THERESA: I'm a security guard.
   MAN: Wow! That's exciting.
   THERESA: Not really. It's pretty boring. I stand around all day.
2. MAN: What do you do, Cecilia?
   CECILIA: I work in a restaurant.
   MAN: Really. What do you do, exactly?
   CECILIA: I'm a chef. I cook lunch and dinner there.
   MAN: That's not an easy job!
   CECILIA: No, it isn't. I have a difficult job, but I like it.
3. MAN: Where do you work, Christine?
   CHRISTINE: At a restaurant.
   MAN: Uh, are you a chef? A waitress?
   CHRISTINE: No, actually, I'm a singer. I sing with the band there.
   MAN: How exciting!
   CHRISTINE: Yes, it is.
4. MAN: What do you do, Kathleen?
   KATHLEEN: I work for Transnational Airlines.
   MAN: What do you do, exactly?
   KATHLEEN: I'm a pilot.
   MAN: Now, that's a stressful job.
   KATHLEEN: Yeah, but I really like the work.

- Elicit answers from Ss. Write them on the board so that Ss can check.

Answers

3, 2, 1, 4

- Explain the second task. Use the example in the book and the first part of the audio program to demonstrate.
- Play the audio program again. Ss listen and write the adjectives under the photographs.

Answers *(from left to right)*

exciting, difficult, boring, stressful

11 READING *What do you do, exactly?*

In this article, Ss read about what three people do. The exercises practice making inferences and writing descriptions.

- Books closed. Read the title aloud, and write it on the board. Tell Ss that they will read about people's jobs.
- Lead Ss through the prereading task. Ss find a piece of paper, open their books, and cover the text. Ss guess the jobs of the people in the photographs. Then they uncover the words to check their answers.

A

- Books open. Read the sentences aloud. Explain the task: These sentences are not in the article, but the people in the article might say them. Who says each sentence?
- Ss guess which person made each statement. They can guess as a class activity, in pairs, or individually.
- Ss read the article. Tell Ss they can change their guesses after they read. If you wish, play the tape as Ss read.
- Elicit answers from Ss. Have them try to explain their choices.

Answers

1. Molly Swift, the carpenter
2. Benjamin Morse, the teacher
3. Joseph Todd, the judge

B *Group work*

- Explain the task. Have a S read the example sentences. Tell Ss to choose a job to describe.
- Give Ss some ideas about what to say:

  Where do you work?
  What days do you work? Do you work at night?
  What do you wear? Do you wear a uniform?
  What do you do, exactly?

- Ss write descriptions individually on a separate piece of paper. They do not write the name of the job.
- Put the Ss in groups of three to five. Ss describe their jobs. The other Ss guess the name of the job.
- **Optional:** Groups choose one of the descriptions from their group. The S stands and gives the description for the whole class to guess.

INTERCHANGE 8 The perfect job

See page T-115 of this Teacher's Edition for notes.

Workbook

Workbook Exercises 5–7 on pages 47–48 correspond to Cycle 2, Exercises 7–11 of the Student's Book. Answers to the Workbook exercises begin on page T-182 of this Teacher's Edition.

10 LISTENING

Listen to these women talk about their jobs. Number the pictures from 1 to 4. Then listen again. Are their jobs boring, stressful, difficult, easy, or exciting? Write the correct adjective under the picture.

1
boring

11 READING

What do you do, exactly?

Cover the reading and look at the pictures. What does each person do?

Joseph Todd

As a judge, I am in charge of trials. I listen to people and their lawyers, and I make decisions. These decisions are sometimes very difficult. Of course, I know the law well, but each person's case is different, and I try to be fair.

Molly Swift

I do many kinds of carpentry. That way, I work all year. I build furniture, and I also build houses. My work is sometimes difficult and dangerous. These days, a lot of things are "prefabricated" – already made. As a result, my job is easier, but there is less work.

Benjamin Morse

My job keeps me busy. I plan lessons, give tests, grade homework, talk to parents, help with after-school activities – and, of course, I teach! My salary isn't great, but that's OK. My students are excited about learning, so I'm happy.

A Read the article. Who do you think says this? Write the name of the person.

1. "Sometimes I work a lot, but sometimes I don't." ....
2. "This year, I'm helping with the soccer team." ....
3. "I'm not always happy about my decisions." ....

The perfect job

What do you want in a job? Turn to page IC-11.

B ***Group work*** Write a description of a job in two or three sentences. Can the other people in your group guess the job?

"Every year, many people see me. I'm always playing other people." (actor)

Review of Units 5–8

1 LISTENING

Pair work Victoria is calling friends in different parts of the world. Where are they? What time is it there? What are they doing? Complete the chart.

	City	Time	Activity
1. Sue	....	....	....
2. Marcos	....	....	....
3. Jim	....	....	....

2 TRUE OR FALSE?

A Write three true statements and one false statement about your classroom.

Our classroom has a nice view.
There's a cassette player on the teacher's desk.

It has . . . .
It doesn't have . . . .
There's a/an . . . .
There are . . . .
There isn't a/an . . . .
There's no . . . .
There aren't any . . . .
There are no . . . .

B ***Pair work*** Take turns reading your statements. Say "True" or "False" for each statement. For false statements, give the true information.

A: Our classroom has a nice view.
B: False. There aren't any windows in our classroom.

Review of Units 5–8

This unit reviews the present continuous and the simple present including has/have, there is/there are, *Wh-questions, and yes/no questions. It focuses on vocabulary and functions relating to time, daily activities, daily routines, and jobs.*

1 LISTENING

In this exercise, Ss listen to three telephone conversations and extract specific information.

Pair work

- Books open. Have Ss look at the illustration. Explain the task: Ss listen to Victoria call friends around the world. Ss listen for city, the time, and what the people are doing.
- Play the audio program once. Ss fill in as much information in their charts as they can.
- Give Ss a few minutes to compare their answers in pairs and identify problems. Play the audio program again. Ss compare answers again.

Audio script

1. **Sue**

SUE: *(phone rings)* Hello?
VICTORIA: Hello, Sue? This is Victoria. I'm calling from Los Angeles.
SUE: Hi, Victoria. How are you?
VICTORIA: I'm good. So, how are things in New York?
SUE: Oh, fine . . . just fine, thanks.
VICTORIA: What time is it in New York?
SUE: It's about twelve o'clock.
VICTORIA: It's noon? Oh, I'm sorry. Are you having lunch right now?
SUE: No, no, it's OK. I'm just watching television.
VICTORIA: Oh. What are you watching?
SUE: The news. Right now, they're giving the . . .

2. **Marcos**

MARCOS: *(phone rings)* Bueno?
VICTORIA: Hello, Marcos. This is Victoria in Los Angeles. How are you?
MARCOS: I'm not sure, Victoria. I'm not very awake.
VICTORIA: Really? What time is it there in Mexico City?
MARCOS: Well, it's a quarter after eleven in the morning here.
VICTORIA: Eleven-fifteen A.M.?
MARCOS: Yeah. I'm having breakfast right now.
VICTORIA: You're having breakfast?
MARCOS: Yeah. I always get up late on Saturday. So, what's up with you? How are things in Los Angeles? Are you working . . . ?

3. **Jim**

JIM: *(phone rings)* Hello?
VICTORIA: Is this Jim?
JIM: Yes, it is. Who's calling, please?
VICTORIA: This is Victoria. I'm calling from Los Angeles.
JIM: Oh, hi, Victoria.
VICTORIA: Hi, Jim. So, how are things in Sydney?
JIM: Things are fine here in Sydney, but . . . do you know it's three-thirty in the morning here?
VICTORIA: Oh, my gosh. I'm sorry. Let me call back tomorrow!
JIM: No, it's OK. Luckily, I'm not sleeping.
VICTORIA: What are you doing?
JIM: I'm reading a really great book. It's about a lawyer who . . .

- To check answers, go over the answers with the class.

Answers

	City	*Time*	*Activity*
Sue:	New York	12:00 P.M./noon	watching TV
Marcos:	Mexico City	11:15 A.M.	having breakfast
Jim:	Sydney	3:30 A.M.	reading a book

2 TRUE OR FALSE?

This exercise reviews expressions for describing rooms and furniture, and recycles the names of classroom objects.

A

- Books open. Use the model to explain and demonstrate the task. Show Ss that they can use the incomplete sentences in the box at the right. Then elicit one true and one false statement from Ss and write them on the board. Leave them on the board for part B.
- Remind Ss of the vocabulary they know for classroom objects. Elicit a list of things that can be in a classroom. Write the list on the board.
- Ss write their true and false statements individually. Circulate while they work to be sure they are following the instructions.
- **Optional:** Ask for more than three sentences. Do not limit true or false statements.

B *Pair work*

- Demonstrate the conversation with the two sentences on the board. Read the true statement, and elicit the response "true" from Ss. Read the false statement, and elicit "false," plus the correct true statement.
- Ss work in pairs to read their statements and respond to each other. Circulate to listen and help if necessary.
- **Optional:** Make it a class activity. Have Ss read sentences aloud to the whole class. To each statement, the other Ss call out either "true!" or "false!" For a false statement, choose one S to correct it.

3 HABITS

This exercise reviews the use of the simple present for habitual actions.

A

- Books open. Use the model to introduce the task. Elicit two things that Ss do in the morning and two things that they don't do. Write them on the board:

  I get up at 7:00 A.M.
  I have breakfast in the morning.
  I don't drink coffee in the morning.

- Refer Ss to the Unit Summaries for Units 5–8. The lists of verbs can give them ideas for this exercise. Ss write their eight statements individually.

B *Group work*

- Introduce the task. Read the model conversation with two Ss. Point out the negative question, "What don't you do . . . ?"
- Ss work in groups to compare the sentences they wrote in part A.
- **Optional:** While Ss are doing parts A and B, notice the most common things they do and don't do. Take a class survey by asking questions about those things. Write the questions on the board. Write the number of Ss who raise their hands next to each question, for example:

  Who eats breakfast in the morning? (19)
  Who doesn't drink coffee in the morning? (6)

4 WHAT'S THE QUESTION?

This exercise reviews Wh-questions.

A

- Books closed. Have Ss tell you the Wh-words they know *(where, when, who, what, what time, what color, how, how many)*. Make a list on the board.
- Books open. Use the example to demonstrate the task.
- Ss work individually to write a question for each answer. Then Ss compare their answers with a partner. Let them make changes if they wish.
- Write the numbers 1–10 on the board. Have volunteers write their questions. Go over the questions on the board with the class. Have Ss make corrections if needed. If Ss have other possible answers, write them on the board, too. Ss correct their own papers from the board.

Answers

1. Where do you work?
2. What do you do (there)?
3. How do you like your job?
4. Where do you live?
5. How many rooms does it have?/ What is your apartment like?
6. What do you need (for your apartment)?
7. How do you go to class?
8. What time do you get up?/When do you get up?
9. What time is it?
10. What are you doing?

B *Pair work*

- Demonstrate the task with two Ss and one or two questions.
- In pairs, Ss take turns asking and answering the questions they wrote in part A.
- Ask each pair to share an exchange with the class.

5 TWENTY QUESTIONS

This game provides communicative practice of questions.

Group work

- Introduce the game. Ask Ss to name some famous people.
- Ask for volunteers to model the list of questions.
- Demonstrate the game. Think of a famous person. Write the name on a piece of paper, and answer the Ss' questions. Give hints so that Ss ask the right questions to guess your famous person. Then show them the name you wrote.
- Put Ss in groups. Choose one S in each group to start. The S writes down the person's name before answering questions. When the person is guessed, or after twenty questions, the first S shows the name to the other Ss.

Test 2

See page T-158 of this Teacher's Edition for general instructions on using the tests. Test 2 covers Units 5–8. Photocopy the test (pages T-163–T-166) and give a copy to each S. Allow 45–60 minutes for the test. Listening material for the tests is at the end of the Class Audio Program. The Test Audio Scripts and Answer Key start on page T-175 of this book.

Optional activities: Vocabulary from Units 5–8 can be reviewed using any of the following games or exercises.

1. *Spelling contest*

- See page T-148.

2. *Game – Hangman*

- See page T-148.

3. *Crossword puzzle*

- See page T-148.

4. *Opposites*

- See page T-152.

3 HABITS

A Write eight sentences about yourself. Name two things . . . .

you do in the morning
you don't do in the morning
you do on weekends
you don't do on weekends

I have breakfast in the morning.

B ***Group work*** Compare. Who has similar habits?

A: What do you do in the morning?
B: I have breakfast in the morning.
C: What don't you do in the morning?
B: I don't read the newspaper.

4 WHAT'S THE QUESTION?

A Look at these answers. What are the questions? Write them down. Then compare with a partner.

1. A: *Where do you work?*
   B: I work in a store.
2. A: ....
   B: I'm a salesperson.
3. A: ....
   B: I really like my job.
4. A: ....
   B: I live in an apartment downtown.
5. A: ....
   B: My apartment has five rooms.
6. A: ....
   B: I need a sofa, a rug, and a lamp.
7. A: ....
   B: I go to class by subway.
8. A: ....
   B: I get up at 6:00 A.M. every morning.
9. A: ....
   B: It's four o'clock in the morning!
10. A: ....
    B: I'm watching television right now.

B ***Pair work*** Take turns. Ask the questions in part A. Answer with your own information.

5 TWENTY QUESTIONS

Group work Take turns. One student thinks of a famous person. The group asks up to twenty questions like the ones below. The student answers with "Yes" or "No."

Is it a man?/Is it a woman?
Does he/she live in the United States?
Is he/she Canadian?
Is he/she a singer/an actor/. . . ?
Does he/she wear glasses?
Is he/she young/middle-aged/old?

When you think you know the person's name, ask, "Is his/her name . . . ?"

9 Broccoli is good for you.

1 SNAPSHOT

Listen and practice.

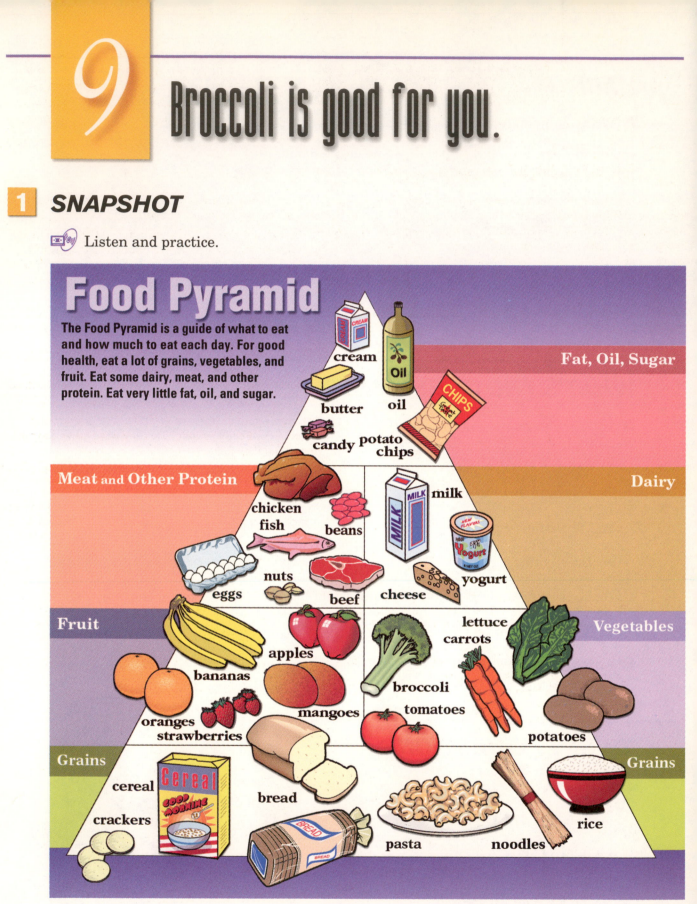

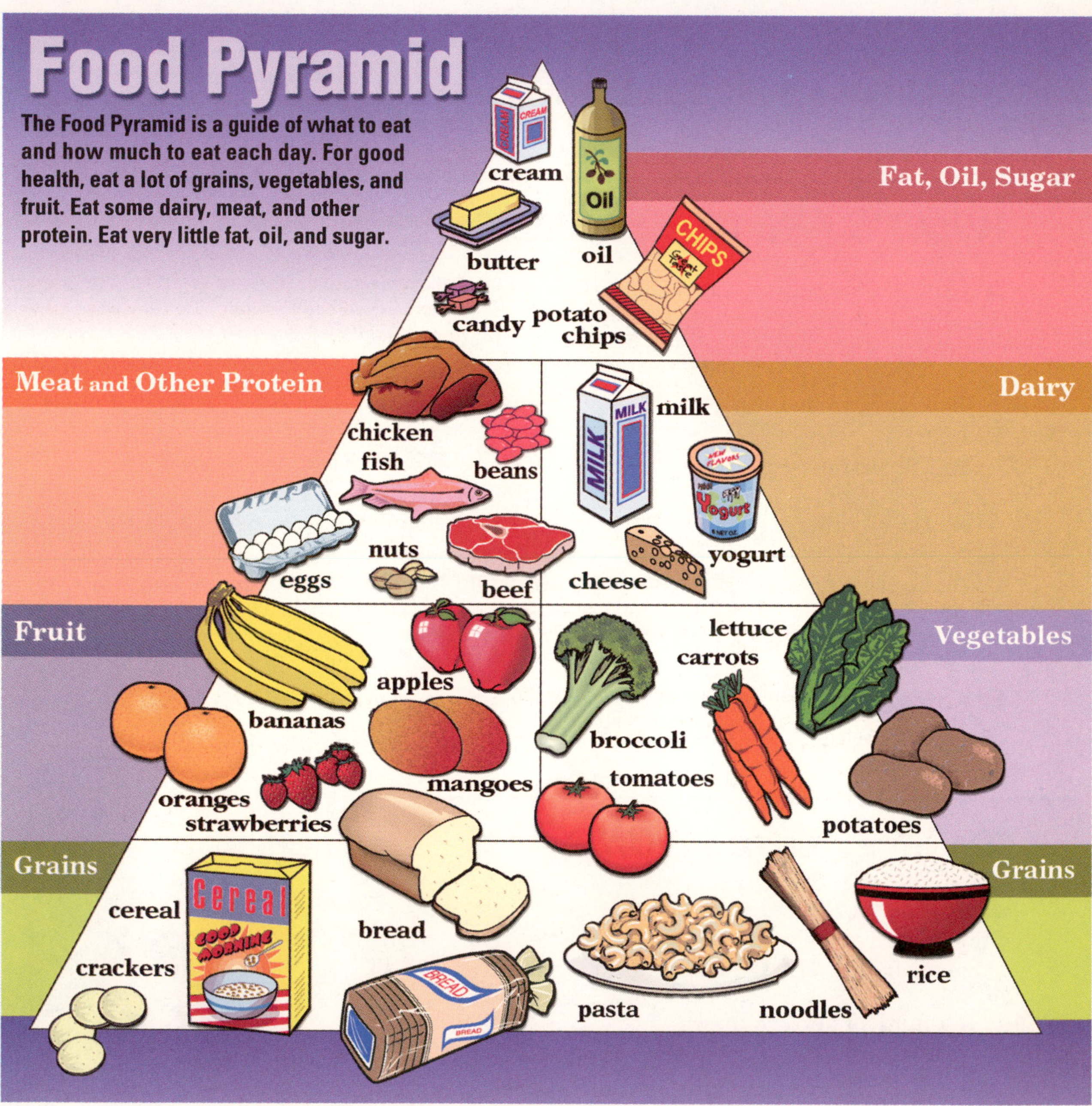

Source: Adapted from the U.S. Department of Agriculture Food Guide Pyramid

According to this Food Pyramid, which foods are good for you? bad for you?
Do you agree with the idea of a Food Pyramid?
Which foods do you eat? Which foods don't you eat?

9 Broccoli is good for you.

This unit introduces the topic of food. It presents expressions for talking about likes and dislikes and about eating habits. It also presents countable and uncountable nouns, some *and* any, *and adverbs of frequency.*

Cycle 1, Exercises 1–5

1 SNAPSHOT Food Pyramid

This illustration gives information about food and nutrition from the United States Department of Agriculture. It introduces the names of some common foods. The questions relate the information to Ss' own lives.

(*Note:* In 1992, the U.S. Department of Agriculture (USDA) released the Food Guide Pyramid, a tool for nutrition education. The Food Guide Pyramid is simply a basic outline of how much food to eat from each of the five food groups. Food groups – which are made up of foods with similar nutrients – form the building blocks of the pyramid. Like a giant puzzle, the pyramid is incomplete if any piece is removed. The same is true of a nutritious diet. Each food group is equally important because each plays a unique role in health.)

- Books open. Have Ss study the food pyramid. Show them the paragraph under the title. Play the first part of the audio program while Ss listen and read the paragraph.
- Write these incomplete sentences on the board:

  Eat very little . . . (fat, oil, and sugar)
  Eat some . . . (dairy, meat, and other protein)
  Eat a lot of . . . (grains, vegetables, and fruit)
- Use hand gestures to show the meanings of *a lot of, some,* and *very little.*
- Ss look for the answers in the paragraph. Have them tell you the answers to complete the sentences on the board.
- Books open. Have Ss look at the food pyramid. Play the rest of the audio program with the names of the food groups and foods. Ss listen and read.
- Play the audio program again or model the food words one by one. Ss listen and repeat.
- Books open or closed. Write the names of the six food groups on the board. Then call out each one. Have Ss give examples of the foods in that group. Ss then come to the board and write the name of the food under the food group.
- **Optional:** Have Ss call out the names in English of other foods that can fit under each food group.
- Ask the first discussion question. Elicit answers from the Ss.
- **Optional:** Ask the Ss their own opinions. What foods do they think are good for you? bad for you?
- Ask the second discussion question. Do Ss follow the ideas in the Food Pyramid? Do they have other diets or diet plans they follow?
- Ask the third discussion question. You may wish to have Ss answer this question in pairs or groups.
- **Optional:** Have Ss give opinions about their own eating habits. According to the Food Pyramid, do Ss eat more foods that are good for them or more foods that are bad for them?

2 WORD POWER Foods: countable and uncountable

This exercise presents and contrasts countable and uncountable nouns using food vocabulary.

(*Note:* Working with countable and uncountable nouns is sometimes difficult for Ss:

1. The distinction between countable and uncountable nouns does not exist in all languages.
2. Things that are countable in English may be uncountable in another language and vice versa.
3. Some nouns may be either countable or uncountable in English, depending on the context:
   Do you want some *pie*? (uncountable)
   We need three *pies* for the party. (countable)

It is not necessary to discuss exceptions to the rules at this point. The *Intro* level generally presents nouns as either countable or uncountable, not both.)

A

- Books open. Ss study the photo. Set the scene: people are shopping for groceries in a supermarket. If necessary, explain *supermarket* and *groceries.*
- Play the audio program to present the information under the photograph. Ss listen and read.
- Answer any questions about vocabulary. Try to elicit the meaning of *delicious*. Encourage guessing.
- Play the audio program again or model the sentences. Ss listen and repeat.
- Explain countable nouns, for example *orange*.

  It has a singular form that uses *a/an: an orange.*
  It has a plural form: *oranges.*
  And you can really count them: *one orange, two oranges . . .*
- Explain uncountable nouns, for example *broccoli.*

  It has only one form.
  It does not use *a/an.*
  It does not use the plural *s* ending.
  And you cannot count it.
- Explain *specific: An* and *some* are specific. "I'm buying an orange" and "I'm buying some broccoli" are specific because the people are talking about "this orange and this broccoli, right here."
- Explain *general:* The plural form *oranges* is general. *Broccoli* without *some* is general. "I like oranges" and "I like broccoli" are general because the people are talking about all oranges and all broccoli.

B

- Use the instructions and the examples to demonstrate the task.
- Tell Ss that countable nouns have singular and plural forms, but all the countable nouns in the Food Pyramid are plural.
- Ss fill in the chart nouns from the Food Pyramid. Then Ss add two more foods to each list. If necessary, brainstorm the names of foods with the class, and write them on the board.
- To check answers, make two lists on the board: *Countable* and *Uncountable.* Starting at the top of the Food Pyramid, Ss tell you where to write each food. Let them correct each other. (There are fourteen countable nouns and sixteen uncountable nouns in the Food Pyramid.)
- Add the other words Ss thought of under *Countable* and *Uncountable.*

Possible answers

From top to bottom of the Food Pyramid:
Countable: potato chips, beans, eggs, nuts, apples, bananas, oranges, strawberries, mangoes, carrots, tomatoes, potatoes, crackers, noodles
Uncountable: cream, butter, oil, candy, beef, chicken, fish, milk, cheese, yogurt, broccoli, lettuce, cereal, bread, pasta, rice

C *Pair work*

- Use the example to demonstrate the task. Remind Ss that plural nouns need *are*. Singular nouns and uncountable nouns need *is*. (*Note:* There are only plural nouns and uncountable nouns in this exercise.)
- Ss complete the sentences individually.
- Ask the Ss who finish first to write the answers on the board. Correct the answers with the class.

Answers

1. Carrots **are** my favorite vegetable.
2. I think mangoes **are** delicious.
3. Broccoli **is** very good for you.
4. Strawberries **are** my favorite fruit.
5. I think yogurt **is** awful.
6. Chicken **is** my favorite meat.

- Use the two sentences in the model conversation to demonstrate the next writing task. Ss rewrite the six sentences on a separate piece of paper. They give true information about food they like and don't like.
- Have two Ss demonstrate the conversation using their rewritten sentences and the Look Up and Say technique.
- In pairs, Ss take turns reading their sentences using the Look Up and Say technique. Walk around as they practice to give help. Pay special attention to nouns and verbs.

2 WORD POWER *Foods: countable and uncountable*

A Listen and practice.

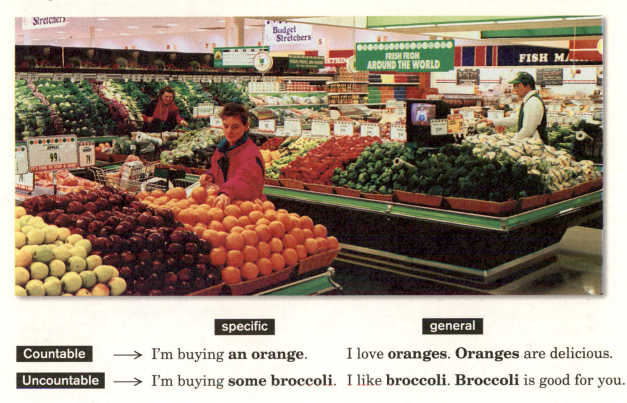

	specific	general
Countable →	I'm buying **an orange**.	I love **oranges**. **Oranges** are delicious.
Uncountable →	I'm buying **some broccoli**.	I like **broccoli**. **Broccoli** is good for you.

B Divide the words in the Food Pyramid into two lists: countable and uncountable nouns. Add two more foods to each list.

Countable (singular and plural)			Uncountable (only singular)		
bananas			beef		

C ***Pair work*** Complete these general statements with **is** or **are**. Then rewrite the sentences with your own information. Compare with a partner.

1. Carrots ...*are*... my favorite vegetable.
2. I think mangoes .... delicious.
3. Broccoli .... very good for you.
4. Strawberries .... my favorite fruit.
5. I think yogurt .... awful.
6. Chicken .... my favorite meat.

A: Tomatoes are my favorite vegetable.
B: Broccoli is my favorite vegetable.

3 CONVERSATION

A Listen and practice.

Adam: What do you want for the barbecue?
Amanda: Hmm. How about chicken and hamburgers?
Adam: OK. We have some chicken in the freezer, but we don't have any hamburger meat.
Amanda: And there aren't any hamburger rolls.
Adam: Do we have any soda?
Amanda: No, we don't. We need some. Oh, and let's get some lemonade, too.
Adam: All right. And how about potato salad?
Amanda: Oh, yeah. Everyone likes potato salad.

B Listen to the rest of the conversation. Check (✓) the desserts Adam and Amanda want for their barbecue.

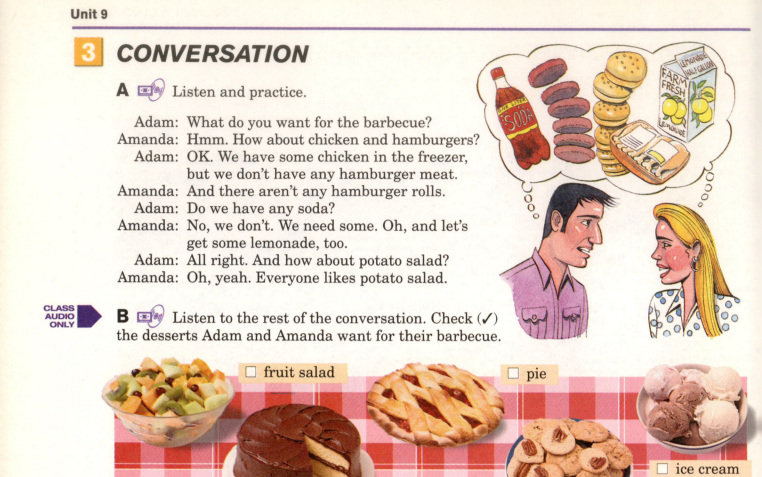

4 GRAMMAR FOCUS

Some *and* any

Do we need **any** meat?	We need **some** hamburger meat.	We don't need **any** chicken.
Do we need **any** soda?	Yes, let's get **some** soda.	No, we don't need **any** soda.
	Yes, let's get **some**.	No, we don't need **any**.

Complete this conversation with **some** or **any**. Then compare with a partner.

Amanda: Hmm. Let's not buy ...*any*... potato salad. Let's make ...*some*... at home.
Adam: OK. So we need .... potatoes. Is there .... mayonnaise at home?
Amanda: No, we need to buy ....
Adam: OK. And we need .... onions, too.
Amanda: Oh, I don't want .... onions in the salad. I hate onions!
Adam: Then let's buy .... celery. That's delicious in potato salad.
Amanda: Good idea. And .... carrots, too.

3 CONVERSATION

This conversation introduces food vocabulary and presents statements with *some* and *any*. Ss then listen for the names of desserts.

A

- Books open. Use the illustration to set the scene: Adam and Amanda are planning a barbecue. Explain that *a barbecue* is a picnic where you cook some of the food outdoors.
- Play the audio program while Ss read and listen.
- Play the audio program again. Ss read and listen. If necessary, explain vocabulary that is not illustrated. There is a photograph of *potato salad* at the bottom of the page.
- Play the audio program again or model the conversation line by line. Ss listen and read, then look up and repeat.
- Ss practice the conversation in pairs using the Look Up and Say technique.
- **Optional:** Have a few Ss act out the conversation for the class.

B

- Set the scene: Adam and Amanda are continuing their conversation about the barbecue. They are talking about dessert.
- Read the names of the desserts one by one. Ss repeat.
- Play the audio program as many times as necessary. Ss listen and check off the answers.

Audio script

ADAM: Let's not forget about dessert.
AMANDA: Yeah. How about a fruit salad? Maybe grapes, melon, and . . . .
ADAM: Hmm. But, I don't really like fruit.
AMANDA: Oh, well . . . . Then let's have *your* favorite dessert, cake.
ADAM: Yeah. *Chocolate* cake . . . and ice cream.
AMANDA: *(laughs)* OK. So let's add chocolate cake and ice cream to the shopping list.

- Elicit the answers from Ss. If there is disagreement, play the audio program again so that Ss can confirm their answers.

Answers

chocolate cake, ice cream

4 GRAMMAR FOCUS Some *and* any

This grammar focus presents *some* and *any* in simple present questions and statements.

(*Note: Some* and *any* are used with uncountable nouns and plural countable nouns. *Some* is most frequently used in affirmative statements. *Any* is most frequently used in questions and negative statements.)

- Play the audio program to present the questions and statements. Ss read and listen.
- Point out the use of *some* and *any* without a noun. When *some* and *any* are used in response to a question, the noun is usually dropped in the response.
- Play the audio program again or model the sentences. Ss listen and repeat.
- Check Ss' understanding. Write sentences like these on the board. Ss supply the missing words:

  Do we need _____ vegetables? (any)
  We need _____ carrots. (some)
  We don't need _____ potatoes. (any)
- Use the instructions and the examples to demonstrate the task. Refer Ss to the photographs for new vocabulary.
- Ss complete the conversation individually.
- In pairs, Ss compare their answers, making changes if they wish.
- Elicit answers from Ss. Write the correct answers on the board or have a S write them. Ss correct their answers from the board.

Answers

AMANDA: Hmm. Let's not buy **any** potato salad. Let's make **some** at home.
ADAM: OK. So we need **some** potatoes. Is there **any** mayonnaise at home?
AMANDA: No, we need to buy **some**.
ADAM: OK. And we need **some** onions, too.
AMANDA: Oh, I don't want **any** onions in the salad. I hate onions!
ADAM: Then let's buy **some** celery. That's delicious in potato salad.
AMANDA: Good idea. And **some** carrots, too.

- **Optional:** Model the conversation line by line. Ss listen and read, then look up and repeat. Then Ss practice the conversation in pairs using the Look Up and Say technique.

5 PRONUNCIATION Sentence stress

In this exercise, Ss practice sentence stress patterns.

A

- Write the conversation on the board. Books closed. Play the audio program once or twice. Tell Ss to listen for the stressed words in each sentence. Mark the stress the Ss tell you. (It is not important for S to get the right answers, only to begin listening for the stress.)
- Books open. Play the audio program again. Ss listen and read. Ask them which words are stressed, or loudest (they are printed in boldface type).
- Play the audio program again. Ss listen and repeat. Encourage them to mimic the speed, rhythm, and stress as closely as possible.
- Have pairs of Ss read the conversation aloud. Give feedback on stress.
- Ss practice saying the conversation in pairs. Go around the classroom to check for correct stress.

B

- Use the instructions and the grocery list at the right to demonstrate the task.
- Ss make their grocery lists individually. Ask them to list at least five things.
- In pairs, Ss use the model conversation from part A to compare their lists.

Workbook

Workbork Exercises 1–5 on pages 49–52 correspond to Cycle 1, Exercises 1–5, of the Student's Book. Answers to the Workbook exercises begin on page T-182 of this Teacher's Edition.

Optional activities:

1. *Shopping lists*

- See page T-152.

2. *Favorite snacks*

- See page T-153.

Cycle 2, Exercises 6–10

6 CONVERSATION

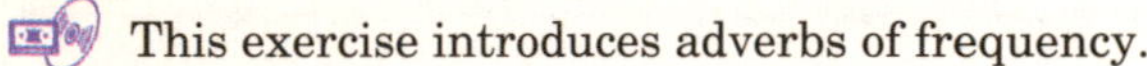

This exercise introduces adverbs of frequency.

- Books open. Ask Ss to identify the foods in the photograph (fish, rice, soup, salad, green tea). Let them scan the conversation to find the words, if necessary.
- Play the audio program while Ss read and listen.
- Play the audio program again. Ss read and listen. If Ss have questions about *always, usually,* or *never,* provide a brief explanation.
- Play the audio program again or model the conversation line by line. Ss listen and read, then look up and repeat.
- Ss practice the conversation in pairs using the Look Up and Say technique.
- **Optional:** Have a few Ss act out the conversation for the class.

7 GRAMMAR FOCUS Adverbs of frequency

This grammar focus presents adverbs of frequency in simple present questions and short answers.

- Books open. Play the audio program to present the information in the boxes. Ss listen and read.
- Point out the box on the right that shows the general meanings of six frequency adverbs. Also point out word order in these sentences. Note that *sometimes* often goes at the beginning of a statement. *Ever* is used in questions. Answers to *ever* questions generally need frequency adverbs or other time expressions.
- Play the audio program again or model the sentences. Ss listen and repeat.

A

- Use the instructions and the example to demonstrate the task. Copy the example on the board. Show Ss how to make a carat (^) to show where the frequency adverb goes in the sentence. Then write the frequency adverb above the carat.
- Ss work individually to put the adverbs in the correct places.
- Have five Ss come to the board. Each S copies and completes one sentence.
- Correct the sentences on the board with the class. Ss correct their own work from the board.

Answers

A: What do you **usually** have for breakfast?
B: Well, on Sundays I **often** have eggs, bacon, and toast.
A: Do you **ever** eat breakfast at work?
B: I **sometimes** have breakfast at my desk./ **Sometimes** I have breakfast at my desk.
A: Do you **usually** eat rice for breakfast?
B: No, I **seldom** have rice.

5 PRONUNCIATION Sentence stress

A Listen and practice. Notice the words with the most stress.

A: What do you **néed**?
B: I need some **bréad** and some **físh**.
A: Do you need any **frúit**?
B: **Yés**. I want some banánas.

B What do you need from the grocery store today? Make a list. Then compare your list with a partner.

6 CONVERSATION

 Listen and practice.

Sarah: Let's have breakfast together on Sunday.
Kumiko: OK. Come to my house. My family always has a Japanese-style breakfast on Sundays.
Sarah: Really? What do you have?
Kumiko: We usually have fish, rice, and soup.
Sarah: Fish for breakfast? That's interesting.
Kumiko: Sometimes we have a salad, too. And we always have green tea.
Sarah: Well, I never eat fish for breakfast, but I love to try new things.

7 GRAMMAR FOCUS

Adverbs of frequency

I **always** eat breakfast. **usually** **often** **sometimes** **seldom** **never** **Sometimes** I eat breakfast.	Do you **ever** have fish for breakfast? Yes, I **always** do. **Sometimes** I do. No, I **never** do.	100% **always** **usually** **often** **sometimes** **seldom** 0% **never**

A Add the adverbs in the correct places. Then practice with a partner.

A: What do you ^usually have for breakfast? (usually)
B: Well, on Sundays I have eggs, bacon, and toast. (often)
A: Do you eat breakfast at work? (ever)
B: I have breakfast at my desk. (sometimes)
A: Do you eat rice for breakfast? (usually)
B: No, I have rice. (seldom)

B ***Pair work*** Put the words in order to make sentences. Then rewrite the sentences with your own information. Compare with a partner.

1. *I never have breakfast on weekends.*
   I never breakfast on have weekends
2. ....
   work I snacks eat at seldom
3. ....
   eat for pasta dinner sometimes I
4. ....
   have I dinner with often family my

A: I always have breakfast on weekends.
B: I seldom have breakfast on weekends. I get up very late.

8 LISTENING

CLASS
AUDIO
ONLY

Listen to Paul and Megan talk about food. How often does Megan eat these foods? Check (✓) **often**, **sometimes**, or **never**.

	Often	Sometimes	Never
pasta	✓	☐	☐
hamburgers	☐	☐	☐
fish	☐	☐	☐
eggs	☐	☐	☐
broccoli	☐	☐	☐

9 BREAKFAST, LUNCH, AND DINNER

A ***Pair work*** Add three questions to the list. Then ask and answer the questions with a partner.

1. Do you usually have breakfast in the morning?
2. What time do you eat?
3. Do you ever eat meat or fish for breakfast?
4. Do you ever go to a restaurant for breakfast?
5. Do you always drink the same thing in the morning?
6. What is something you never have for breakfast?
7. ....
8. ....
9. ....

interchange 9
Eating habits
What foods do you eat?
Turn to page IC-12.

B ***Group work*** Ask and answer similar questions about lunch and dinner.

B *Pair work*

- Books closed. Copy the words for the first item on the board as they are in the book. Have Ss tell you the correct order.
- Books open. Ss work individually to write the other sentences.
- Ss compare their sentences in pairs, making changes if they wish.
- Volunteers write their sentences on the board. Correct the sentences with the whole class. Leave the sentences on the board.

Answers

2. I seldom eat snacks at work.
3. I sometimes eat pasta for dinner./ Sometimes I eat pasta for dinner.
4. I often have dinner with my family.

- Demonstrate the second task. Rewrite the example sentence on the board. Change the frequency adverb to make it true about you.
- Ss rewrite the sentences.
- In pairs, Ss take turns reading their sentences to each other, using the Look Up and Say technique.

8 *LISTENING*

In this exercise, Ss practice listening for adverbs of frequency.

- Use the illustration to set the scene. Ask, "Where are Paul and Megan?" (In a restaurant.)
- Play the first part of the audio program, and use the example to demonstrate the task.
- Play the audio program as many times as necessary. Ss listen and check the boxes.

Audio script

PAUL: So, what looks good?
MEGAN: I don't know yet.
PAUL: Well, do you like pasta?
MEGAN: Oh, yeah. I often eat pasta for dinner. I just don't want it tonight.
PAUL: What about a hamburger?
MEGAN: Oh, no. I never eat hamburgers. I don't eat meat.
PAUL: Really? Never?
MEGAN: No, never. I sometimes have fish or eggs, but never beef.
PAUL: So, do you eat a lot of vegetables?
MEGAN: Yes. Broccoli is my favorite. I often just have a big plate of broccoli or some other vegetable for dinner.
PAUL: Really?
MEGAN: Really.

- In pairs, Ss compare answers making changes if they wish. Then play the audio program again. Ss can confirm the answers.
- Elicit the correct answers. Ss correct their work.

Answers

pasta:	**often**	eggs:	**sometimes**
hamburgers:	**never**	broccoli:	**often**
fish:	**sometimes**		

9 *BREAKFAST, LUNCH, AND DINNER*

In this exercise, Ss use adverbs of frequency in conversations about their own eating habits. In part A, Ss write questions about personal eating habits.

A *Pair work*

- Have volunteers read the questions aloud.
- If necessary, model each question. Ss listen and repeat.
- In pairs, Ss think of three more questions with frequency adverbs. Each S writes the questions individually.
- While Ss are writing, go around the room and read their questions. Send Ss to the board to write as many different questions as possible.

Possible additional questions

What is something you always have for breakfast?
Do you usually make your own breakfast?
Do you ever make breakfast for other people?
Do you ever eat breakfast alone?
Do you have a different breakfast on weekends?
Do you usually watch TV while you eat breakfast?

- Correct the questions on the board with the whole class. Ss correct their own work from the board.
- Put Ss in new pairs to ask and answer the questions.
- **Optional:** Ask a few of the most interesting questions, and count the different answers Ss give. Write the results on the board as a class survey. Alternatively, have Ss take the survey.

B *Group work*

- Demonstrate the task. Ask, for example, "Do you usually have lunch at noon? What time do you eat dinner?" Elicit answers from Ss.
- In groups, Ss take turns asking and answering questions about lunch and dinner habits.

INTERCHANGE 9 Eating habits

See page T-116 of this Teacher's Edition for notes.

Optional activity: *Breakfast at my house*

- See page T-153.

10 READING *Eating for Good Luck*

In this article, Ss read about foods people eat for good luck on New Year's Day in different countries and cultures.

- Books open. Read the title aloud, and write it on the board. Elicit or explain the meaning of *good luck*.
- Help Ss with the prereading question. Elicit or give examples of "special occasions."
- Point to the photographs. Ask, "Do you ever eat these things? Do you eat them on special occasions? When?"
- **Optional:** Have Ss scan the text to find and circle the names of the foods in the photographs.

A

- Ss read the article. If you wish, play the audio program as Ss listen and read.
- **Optional:** Ss underline words they do not know. Encourage Ss to guess the meaning from the context of the paragraph. Ss will be able to do the exercise without understanding all the words.
- Use the instructions and the example to demonstrate the task. Have volunteers read the rest of the sentences aloud.
- Ss scan the article again to find the mistake in each sentence and write their corrections.
- In pairs, Ss compare their answers, making changes if they wish. Walk around while Ss are working. Send Ss with correct answers to the board to write the sentences.
- Go over the answers on the board with the whole class.

Answers

2. Some Jewish people eat apples with ~~candy~~ *honey* for a sweet new year.
3. Greeks eat vasilopitta, bread with ~~beans~~ *a coin* inside.
4. In ~~Europe~~ *(Spain and some Latin American countries)*, people eat twelve grapes for good luck in the new year.
5. The Japanese eat ~~chocolate cake~~ *rice cakes* for strength in the new year.
6. Some Americans eat black-eyed peas. Black-eyed peas are like ~~dollars~~ *coins*.

B *Group work*

- Introduce the task, and read the questions. Tell Ss that if the answer is "no" to either question, they need to add some information.
- Demonstrate with two Ss:

  S1: Do you eat anything special on New Year's Day for good luck?
  T: No, I don't. But my grandmother always eats twelve grapes on New Year's Eve.
  S2: Do you do anything special on New Year's Day for good luck?
  T: No, I don't. But my friend John always gives money to a person that he doesn't know.
- Ask one or two Ss the questions. Elicit answers about the Ss themselves or people they know.
- Put the Ss in groups of three to five. Ss answer the questions in groups.
- **Optional:** Have Ss discuss their New Year's traditions regardless of whether the traditions are "for luck." Ask Ss, "Do you eat anything special on New Year's Day?" and "Do you do anything special on New Year's Day?"
- **Optional:** Have each group prepare a report about the people in the group. Give Ss time to practice their reports. Then choose one S from each group to make the group's report to the class. If possible, have Ss speak extemporaneously rather than read their reports. Allow other Ss in the group to give help as the chosen S speaks.

Workbook

Workbook Exercises 6–9 on pages 53–54 correspond to Cycle 2, Exercises 6–10, of the Student's Book. Answers to the Workbook exercises begin on page T-182 of this Teacher's Edition.

Optional activities: Vocabulary for names of foods and adverbs of frequency can be reviewed using any of the following games or exercises.

1. *Scrambled letters*
- See page T-147.

2. *Game – Hangman*
- See page T-148.

3. *Game – Word bingo*
- See page T-150.

4. *Complete the word*
- See page T-150.

10 READING

Eating for Good Luck

On special occasions, do you ever eat any of the foods in these pictures?

On New Year's Day, many people eat special foods for good luck in the new year.

Some Chinese people eat tangerines. Tangerines are round. Round foods end and begin again, like years.

It is a Jewish custom to eat apples with honey for a sweet new year.

Greeks eat *vasilopitta,* bread with a coin inside. Everyone tries to find the coin for luck and money in the new year.

In Spain and some Latin American countries, people eat twelve grapes at midnight on New Year's Eve – one grape for good luck in each month of the new year.

On New Year's Day in Japan, people eat *mochi* – rice cakes – for strength in the new year.

Some Americans from southern states eat black-eyed peas and rice with collard greens. The black-eyed peas are like coins, and the greens are like dollars.

A Read the article. Then correct the information in these sentences.

1. Some Chinese people eat tangerines. Tangerines are ~~sweet~~ *round*, like years.
2. Some Jewish people eat apples with candy for a sweet new year.
3. Greeks eat vasilopitta, bread with beans inside.
4. In Europe, people eat twelve grapes for good luck in the new year.
5. The Japanese eat chocolate cake for strength in the new year.
6. Some Americans eat black-eyed peas. Black-eyed peas are like dollars.

B ***Group work*** Talk about these questions.

1. Do you eat anything special on New Year's Day for good luck? What?
2. Do you do anything special on New Year's Day for good luck? What?

You can play baseball really well.

1 SNAPSHOT

Listen and practice.

SPORTS SEASONS IN THE UNITED STATES AND CANADA

In the winter, people . . . .

play hockey
play basketball
go ice-skating
go skiing

In the spring, people . . . .

play golf
play soccer

In the summer, people . . . .

play baseball
play tennis
play volleyball
go swimming

In the fall, people . . . .

play football
go bike riding
go hiking

Sources: Adapted from *ESPN Information Please Sports Almanac* and interviews with people between the ages of 18 and 50

What sports do people play in your country?
Do you like sports? What sports do you play?

10 You can play baseball really well.

This unit presents expressions for talking about sports, especially likes and dislikes. It reviews Wh-questions in the simple present and introduces can *and* can't *for talking about talents and abilities.*

Cycle 1, Exercises 1–4

1 SNAPSHOT Sports Seasons in the United States and Canada

This graphic introduces information about and basic vocabulary for sports in the United States and Canada.

(*Note:* The verb *go* is only used when the person is doing the sport for fun, not for competition.)

- Books open. Have Ss study the illustrations. All of the sports are illustrated in the graphic. Play the audio program. Ss listen and read.
- Play the audio program again or model the sentences line by line. Ss listen and repeat.
- Ask the first discussion question. When Ss answer, write the names of the sports on the board. If Ss are from different countries, write the names of the countries on the board. Write the names of the sports under the countries.
- Ask the second discussion question. Write the names of the sports Ss play on the board.

Optional activity: ***Olympic sports***

- See page T-153.

2 CONVERSATION

This conversation introduces expressions for talking about favorite sports.

- Books open. Have Ss study the illustration. Ask, "What sports are in the picture?" (hockey, baseball, and skiing).
- Write these questions on the board:

  Does Justin like sports? (yes)
  What sports does he like? (hockey, baseball, and skiing)
  What sports does he play? (He doesn't play sports.)

- Play the audio program while Ss read and listen for the answers. Elicit the answers.
- Play the audio program again. Ss read and listen. Try to elicit the meanings of *free time* and other new vocabulary. Encourage guessing.
- Play the audio program again or model the conversation line by line. Ss listen and read, then look up and repeat.
- Ss practice the conversation in pairs using the Look Up and Say technique.
- **Optional:** Have a few Ss act out the conversation for the class.

3 GRAMMAR FOCUS *Simple present Wh-questions*

This grammar focus reviews and practices the meanings of Wh-words. The question *Who... with?* is new here.

(*Note:* The questions and answers in this grammar box are a conversation.)

- Books open. Play the audio program to present the questions and answers. Ss read and listen.
- Point out the meaning of the new question *Who do you play baseball with?* and the answer. Ss can guess most new vocabulary from the context. You may need to clarify the difference between *practice* and *play*.
- Play the audio program again or model the sentences. Ss listen and repeat.

A

- Use the example to demonstrate the task.
- Ss write questions individually.
- In pairs, Ss compare their questions. They may change them if they wish.
- Elicit Ss' questions from around the class. Write them on the board so that Ss can check their work.

Answers

1. What sports do you like?
2. When do you play volleyball?
3. Who do you play with?
4. Where do you play?
5. What do your parents think of volleyball?

- **Optional:** Have Ss practice the conversation in pairs.

B *Pair work*

- Demonstrate the task. Show Ss that the conversations in part A are examples for part B.
- In pairs, Ss ask each other to name their favorite sports.
- Individually, Ss write five questions for their partner about his or her favorite sports.
- In pairs, Ss take turns asking and answering questions.
- **Optional:** Do the activity again with new partners.

2 CONVERSATION

Listen and practice.

Lauren: So, Justin, what do you do in your free time?
Justin: Well, I love sports.
Lauren: Really? What sports do you like?
Justin: Hmm. Hockey, baseball, and skiing are my favorites.
Lauren: Wow, you're a really good athlete!
Justin: Oh, no, I'm not. I don't *play* those sports. I just watch them on TV!

3 GRAMMAR FOCUS

Simple present Wh-questions

What sports do you play?	I play **baseball** and I **go skiing**.
Who do you play baseball **with**?	**With some friends from work.** We have a team.
When does your team practice?	We practice **on Saturdays**.
What time do you practice on Saturdays?	We start **at ten o'clock in the morning**.
Where do you go skiing?	I go skiing **in Colorado**.
What do your parents **think of** skiing?	They **think it's dangerous**.

A Write questions for these answers. Then compare with a partner.

1. A: *What sports do you like?*
   B: I like ice-skating, but I really love volleyball!
2. A: ....
   B: Volleyball? I play it in the summer.
3. A: ....
   B: My brother and sister play with me.
4. A: ....
   B: We usually play in our yard or at the beach.
5. A: ....
   B: Our parents think it's a great sport. They enjoy it, too.

B ***Pair work*** Find out what sports your partner likes. Then write five questions about the sports. Take turns asking the questions.

4 LISTENING

Listen to Lisa, John, Sue, and Henry talk about sports. Complete the chart.

	Favorite sport	Does he/she play or do it? Yes	No
1. Lisa	*ice-skating*	☑	☐
2. John	....	☐	☐
3. Sue	....	☐	☐
4. Henry	....	☐	☐

5 CONVERSATION

Listen and practice.

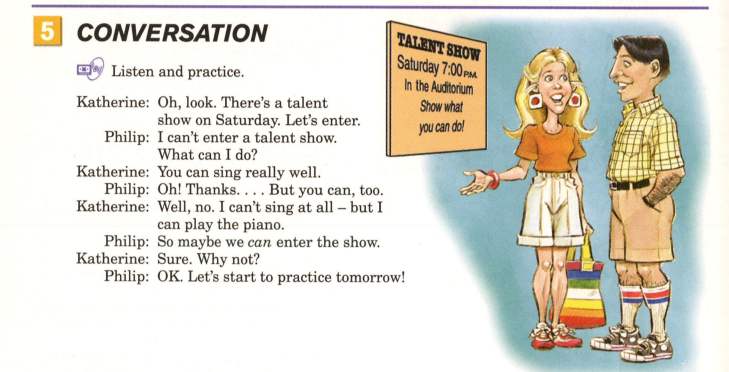

Katherine: Oh, look. There's a talent show on Saturday. Let's enter.
Philip: I can't enter a talent show. What can I do?
Katherine: You can sing really well.
Philip: Oh! Thanks. . . . But you can, too.
Katherine: Well, no. I can't sing at all – but I can play the piano.
Philip: So maybe we *can* enter the show.
Katherine: Sure. Why not?
Philip: OK. Let's start to practice tomorrow!

TALENT SHOW
Saturday 7:00 P.M.
In the Auditorium
Show what
you can do!

6 PRONUNCIATION Can *and* can't

A Listen and practice. Notice the pronunciation of **can** and **can't**.

/kən/ /kænt/
I **can** play the guitar, but I **can't** sing very well.

B ***Pair work*** Do you hear **can** or **can't**? Read a sentence from the left or right column. Your partner says **can** or **can't**.

I can dance.	I can't dance.
He can swim very well.	He can't swim very well.
She can sing.	She can't sing.
They can skate very well.	They can't skate very well.

4 LISTENING

In this exercise, Ss listen for information about sports in four conversations.

- Books open. Play the first part of the audio program and use the example to demonstrate the task.
- Play the audio program as many times as necessary. Ss listen and complete the chart.

Audio script

1. MAN: What sports do you like, Lisa?
   LISA: Oh, I don't like sports very much.
   MAN: So you never play sports.
   LISA: Well, not much. But I do love ice-skating.
   MAN: So do you go ice-skating in the winter?
   LISA: Yes, I do!
   MAN: Who do you go with?
   LISA: I usually go with my sister. We go as often as possible.
2. WOMAN: What do you think of ice-skating, John?
   JOHN: It's OK, but I don't do it . . . . And I don't usually watch it.
   WOMAN: But you enjoy sports.
   JOHN: Oh, yeah. Swimming and bike riding, but *especially* baseball. It's my favorite.
   WOMAN: When do you play it?
   JOHN: Every summer.
3. MAN: Do you play baseball, Sue?
   SUE: Uh, no. I think it's a little boring.
   MAN: Do you play any sports?
   SUE: Oh, sure. I play golf and tennis.
   MAN: Which is your favorite?
   SUE: That's tough. Hmm . . . I think golf is my favorite.
4. WOMAN: What do you think of golf, Henry?
   HENRY: Well, it's not my favorite. I really enjoy skiing, and I like to go hiking, too.
   WOMAN: What's your favorite sport?
   HENRY: Actually, my favorite sport is basketball.
   WOMAN: Really! Where do you play basketball?
   HENRY: Oh, I don't play basketball. I just watch it on TV a lot.

- Ss compare answers, changing them if they wish.
- Play the audio program again so that Ss can verify their answers. Write the correct answers on the board.

Answers

	Favorite sport	*Does he / she play or do it?*
1. Lisa	ice-skating	yes
2. John	baseball	yes
3. Sue	golf	yes
4. Henry	basketball	no

Workbook

Workbook Exercises 1–3 on pages 55–56 correspond to Cycle 1, Exercises 1–4, of the Student's Book. Answers to the Workbook exercises begin on page T-182 of this Teacher's Edition.

Cycle 2, Exercises 5–10

5 CONVERSATION

This conversation introduces *can* and *can't* to express ability and inability.

- Books open. Have Ss look at the illustration. Write these questions on the board:

  What can Katherine do? (play the piano)
  What can Philip do? (sing)

- Play the audio program while Ss read and listen for the answers. Elicit the answers.
- Play the audio program again. Ss read and listen. Try to elicit the meanings of the adverbs *really well* and *not at all.* Help Ss guess other new vocabulary.
- Play the audio program again or model the conversation line by line. Ss practice the conversation in pairs.

6 PRONUNCIATION Can *and* can't

In this exercise, Ss practice the pronunciation of *can* and *can't.*

(*Note:* Beginning Ss usually listen for the /t/ to distinguish *can't* from *can.* Because the /t/ in *can't* is not usually pronounced strongly, Ss should listen to the vowel instead. Statements with *can* generally use the reduced vowel /ə/. Negative statements with *can't* and both short answers (*Yes, I can / No, I can't*) use the full vowel /æ/.)

A

- Books open. Play the audio program. Ss listen and read.
- Play the audio program again. Ss listen and repeat. Ss practice until they are pronouncing the sentence correctly.

B Pair work

- Books closed. Write the first sentences on the board.
- Without pointing to the sentences on the board, read them aloud a few times in random order. If Ss hear *can,* they raise their hands and say "can." If they hear *can't,* they don't raise their hands, but they say "can't."
- Books open. In pairs, Ss take turns reading the sentences and identifying them by saying *can* or *can't.*

7 GRAMMAR FOCUS Can for ability

 This grammar focus presents the modals *can* and *can't* for expressing ability.

(*Note:* In this unit, *can* is used to talk about abilities. It is not necessary to discuss other meanings of *can* at this stage.)

- Play the audio program to present the information in the boxes. Ss read and listen.
- Remind Ss that the vowel of *can* is reduced in statements and questions, but it is not reduced in short answers.
- Play the audio program again or model the sentences. Ss listen and repeat.

A

- Books open. Use the example to demonstrate the task.
- Ss work individually to complete the sentences with *can* or *can't.*
- In pairs, Ss compare their answers, making changes if they wish.
- Elicit the correct answers from Ss and write them on the board. Ss correct their own work.

Answers

1. I **can** draw.
2. I **can** write poetry.
3. I **can** fix cars.
4. I **can't** sing very well.
5. I **can** play the piano.
6. I **can't** cook very well.

B *Pair work*

- Use the example conversation to demonstrate the task.
- Ss take turns asking and answering questions about the pictures in part A. Have them change roles and practice again so that every Ss asks and answers every question.

7 GRAMMAR FOCUS

Can for ability

I				you			I	
You				I			you	
He	**can**	sing very well.	**Can**	he	sing?	Yes,	he	**can.**
She	**can't**	sing at all.		she		No,	she	**can't.**
We				we			we	
They				they			they	

A Katherine is talking about things she can and can't do. Complete these sentences. Then compare with a partner.

1. I ...*can*... draw.

2. I .... write poetry.

3. I .... fix cars.

4. I .... sing very well.

5. I .... play the piano.

6. I .... cook very well.

B ***Pair work*** Ask and answer questions about the pictures. Respond with short answers.

A: Can Katherine draw?
B: Yes, she can.

8 LISTENING

Listen to Peter, Liz, and Scott talk about their talents. Check (✓) the things they say they can do well.

9 WORD POWER *Abilities and talents*

A Complete the word map with abilities and talents from the list. Add two more expressions to each category.

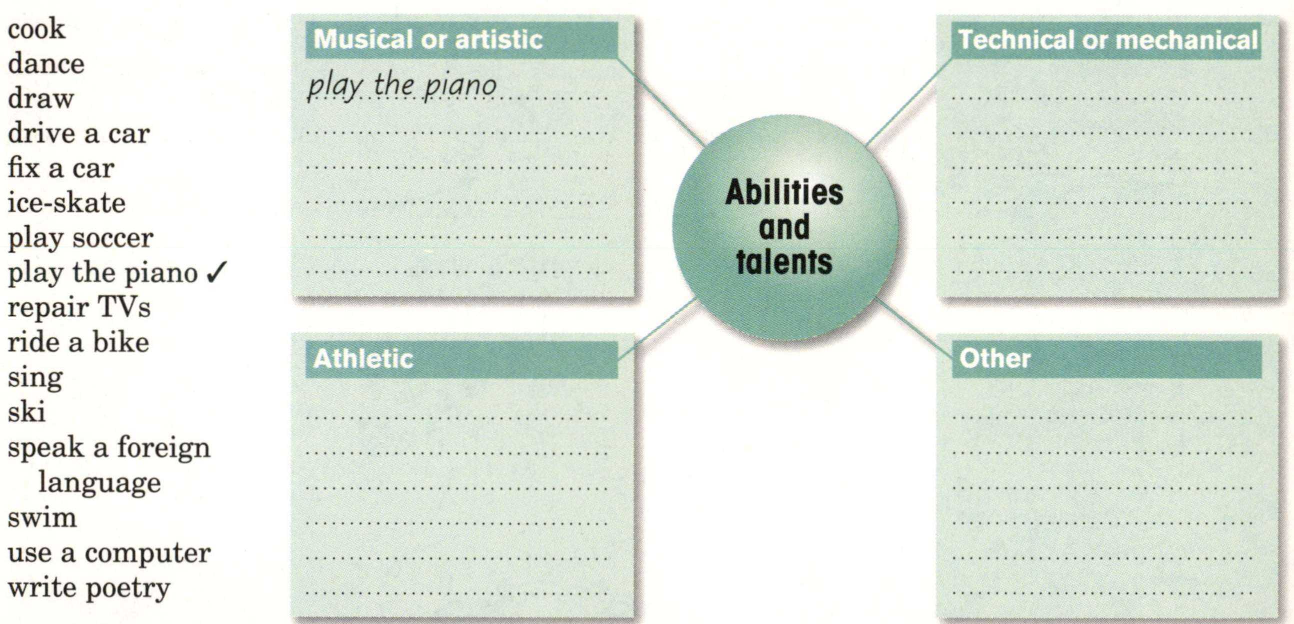

B ***Group work*** Sit in a circle. Take turns asking about the abilities and talents in the word map.

A: Sawit, can you play the piano?
B: Yes, I can. Can you play the piano, Amara?
C: No, I can't. Can you play the piano, Somsak?

C ***Class activity*** Tell the class about the people in your group. Who is musical or artistic? athletic? Who has technical or mechanical skills? Who has other talents?

"Sawit is musical. He can play the piano and the guitar. . . . "

8 LISTENING

In this exercise, Ss listen for specific things that three people can do well.

- Have Ss look at the illustrations in the chart. Try to elicit the talent (the verb) that each picture represents: play the piano, dance, sing, draw, swim, take photos, cook, use a computer. List the verbs on the board as Ss name them. Encourage Ss to guess, but give help as needed. Ss need to understand the vocabulary in order to do the task.
- Explain the task. If necessary, play the first part of the audio program to help further demonstrate the task.
- Play the audio program as many times as necessary. Ss listen and check the correct boxes.

Audio script

1. PETER: I'm a musician. So I can sing and play the piano really well.
2. LIZ: I can cook really well – I'm a chef. And I love to take photos on weekends with my camera. I think I can do that really well, too.
3. SCOTT: Well, I'm an artist, so I can draw really well. I often do my work on a computer, so I can use computers really well, too.

- Elicit the correct answers from the Ss and write them on the board. Play the audio program again so that Ss can confirm them.

Answers

1. PETER: play the piano, sing
2. LIZ: take photos, cook
3. SCOTT: draw, use a computer

9 WORD POWER *Abilities and talents*

This exercise introduces and practices verbs that express abilities and talents.

A

- Write the names of the four categories on the board. Fill in the example under *Musical or artistic.* Elicit examples for *Technical or mechanical, Athletic,* and *Other.*
- Tell Ss to complete the word map using all the words in the list. Tell them that some categories have more words than others.
- Ss work individually to complete the word map and then add two more verbs to each category. If necessary, brainstorm the words for other talents or abilities with the class and write them on the board.
- Elicit Ss' answers. Write them on the board under the correct categories so that Ss can check their work. Accept any reasonable answer. (*Note:* There may be reasonable disagreement about categories for some expressions. For example, *dance* might be *Musical or artistic, Athletic,* or *Other,* depending on the kind of dancing Ss are thinking of.)
- Add the other words Ss thought of under the categories.

Possible answers

Musical or artistic: play the piano, dance, draw, sing, write poetry
Technical or mechanical: drive a car, fix a car, repair TVs, use a computer
Athletic: ice-skate, play soccer, ride a bike, ski, swim
Other: cook, speak a foreign language

B *Group work*

- Model the example conversation with two Ss.
- Ask three Ss to demonstrate the conversation using another verb from part A and their own names.
- Ss ask and answer questions in groups. Walk around to check on the pronunciation of *can.*
- **Optional:** Encourage Ss to volunteer information about their other talents and abilities, for example, "I can make clothes," "I can grow vegetables."
- **Optional:** To help Ss prepare for part C, assign a secretary in each group to take notes on people's talents and abilities.

C *Class activity*

- In groups, Ss list the people in their group under each category from part A. Some Ss may be in more than one category.
- Have each group prepare a report for the class. They name each person and say exactly what he or she can do. Give Ss time to practice their reports. Then choose one S from each group to make the group's report to the class. If possible, have Ss speak extemporaneously rather than read their reports. Allow other Ss in the group to give help as the chosen S speaks.
- **Optional:** In a large class, choose two people from each group to report.

10 READING Race the U.S.!

In this article, Ss read about three unusual races in the United States. The exercises practice reading for main ideas and making inferences.

- Books open. Read the title aloud and write it on the board. If necessary, use the photographs to clarify *race*.
- Introduce the prereading task. Begin with a few of your own ideas, such as "Run, bike, . . ." Elicit more kinds of races from Ss, and list them on the board. Allow any reasonable response. Ss do not need to know the correct name of a race (e.g., marathon, triathlon).

Possible answers

run, bike, swim, car/drive, ski, ice-skating, walking, eating

- Read the lead sentence aloud, "Here are three unique races." Try to elicit the meaning of *unique* (special, the only one).

A

- Ss read the article. If you wish, play the audio program as Ss listen and read.
- **Optional:** Ss underline words they do not know. Encourage Ss to guess the meaning from the context of the paragraph or the accompanying photo. Ss will be able to do the exercise without understanding all the words.
- Go over the information needed in the chart.
- Be sure Ss understand the task. Have Ss fill in the chart for the first paragraph only.
- Elicit answers from Ss and write them on the board.
- Ss complete the chart then compare their answers in pairs, making changes if they wish.
- Elicit the rest of the answers and write them on the board so that Ss can check their work.
- **Optional:** Sketch a map of the United States or bring one to class. Show the places named in the article.

Answers

1. Empire State Building Run-Up
   Place(s): New York City/the Empire State Building
   Distance: 1,050 feet/320 meters/86 floors/1,575 steps
   Winning times: 10 or 11 minutes
2. Badwater Run
   Place(s): Death Valley to Mount Whitney
   Distance: 139 miles/224 kilometers
   Winning times: about 28 hours
3. Race Across America
   Place(s): Irvine, California, to Savannah, Georgia
   Distance: 2,900 miles/4,667 kilometers
   Winning times: eight to ten days

B *Group work*

- Read the instructions aloud, and go over the questions.
- Put the Ss in groups of three to five. Ss answer the questions and give reasons.
- **Optional:** Have each group come to a consensus. Appoint a "secretary" in each group to write down the group's choices. Bring the class back together. Secretaries report their groups' choices to the class.

IC INTERCHANGE 10 Hidden talents

See page T-117 of this Teacher's Edition for notes.

Workbook

Workbook Exercises 4–9 on pages 57–60 correspond to Cycle 2, Exercises 5–10, of the Student's Book. Answers to the Workbook exercises begin on page T-182 of this Teacher's Edition.

Optional activities: Vocabulary for names of sports and abilities and talents can be reviewed using any of the following games or exercises.

1. *Scrambled letters*

- See page T-147.

2. *Game – Hangman*

- See page T-148.

3. Game – *Word bingo*

- See page T-150.

4. *Complete the word*

- See page T-150.

5. *In my free time*

- See page T-153.

10 READING

Race the U.S.!

How many different kinds of races can you think of?

Here are three unique races:

One race takes place in a building. In the Empire State Building Run-Up, racers run up the stairs to the top of New York City's Empire State Building. The climb is 1,050 feet (320 meters) – 86 floors, or 1,575 steps. Winners can reach the top in just 10 to 11 minutes.

Racers in the Badwater Run in California run 139 miles (224 kilometers), climbing 8,653 feet (2,637 meters). The race begins in Death Valley, a desert. The temperature is about 130° F (54° C), and contestants sometimes run through sandstorms. The race ends near the top of Mount Whitney, where the temperature is only 30° F (-1° C), and there are sometimes ice storms. Amazingly, winners can usually finish in about 28 hours.

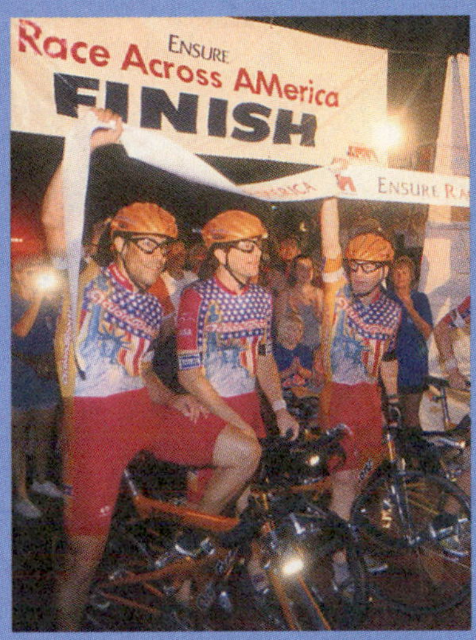

Race Across America is a bicycle race all the way across the U.S., from Irvine, California, to Savannah, Georgia. In this race, there are no "time-outs" for sleep, so the racers can sleep only about three hours each day. Winners complete the 2,900 miles (4,667 kilometers) in just eight to ten days.

A Read the article. Then complete the chart.

	Place(s)	Distance	Winning times
1. Empire State Building Run-Up	....	....	....
2. Badwater Run	....	....	....
3. Race Across America	....	....	....

B ***Group work*** Talk about these questions.

1. Which race is most interesting to you? Why?
2. Which race do you think is the most difficult? Why?

interchange 10

Hidden talents

Learn about your classmates' special abilities. Turn to page IC-13.

11 What are you going to do?

1 WORD POWER Dates

A Listen. Practice the months and the ordinal numbers.

January February	March April	May June	July August	September October		November December
1st first	2nd second	3rd third	4th fourth	5th fifth	6th sixth	7th seventh
8th eighth	9th ninth	10th tenth	11th eleventh	12th twelfth	13th thirteenth	14th fourteenth
15th fifteenth	16th sixteenth	17th seventeenth	18th eighteenth	19th nineteenth	20th twentieth	21st twenty-first
22nd twenty-second	23rd twenty-third	24th twenty-fourth	25th twenty-fifth	26th twenty-sixth	27th twenty-seventh	28th twenty-eighth
29th twenty-ninth	30th thirtieth	31st thirty-first				

B ***Pair work*** Practice saying these dates.

1. January 1 *"January first"*
2. 6/30 *"June thirtieth"*
3. July 4
4. May 18
5. October 31
6. 2/14
7. 5/25
8. 11/2

2 CONVERSATION

A Listen and practice.

Amy: Are you going to do anything exciting this weekend?
Philip: Well, I'm going to celebrate my birthday.
Amy: Fabulous! When is your birthday, exactly?
Philip: It's August ninth – Sunday.
Amy: So what are your plans?
Philip: Well, my friend Katherine is going to take me to a restaurant.
Amy: Nice! Is she going to order a cake?
Philip: Yeah, and the waiters are probably going to sing "Happy Birthday" to me. It's so embarrassing!

B ***Class activity*** Make a list of your classmates' birthdays. How many people have birthdays this week? this month? in the same month? on the same day?

A: When's your birthday?
B: July 21st. When's *your* birthday?

11 What are you going to do?

This unit provides language for talking about birthdays, holidays, and celebrations, including months and dates. It introduces the future with be going to and future time expressions.

Cycle 1, Exercises 1–5

WORD POWER Dates

This exercise introduces and practices the months of the year and dates expressed with the ordinal numbers *first* through *thirty-first.*

A

- Play the audio program to present the months. Ss listen and read.
- Play the audio program again or model the months one at a time. Ss listen and repeat.
- Have Ss repeat the months a few times in order, first chorally, then individually.
- **Optional:** Practice with a game. In two teams, Ss take turns saying the name of a month in random order. The other team says the month just after it. Keep time, and score based on the time. For a second round, Ss name the month just before the one named.
- Play the audio program to present the ordinal numbers. Ss listen and read.
- Play the audio program again or model the numbers one at a time. Ss listen and repeat.
- Have Ss repeat the ordinal numbers a few times in order, first chorally, then individually.
- Write the cardinal numbers 1–31 on the board. Point to them in random order. Ss say the equivalent ordinal numbers.
- **Optional:** Books closed. In pairs, taking turns, one S says and writes the word for a cardinal number. The other S says and writes the corresponding word for the ordinal number. When they finish, they can check the written ordinal numbers against the list in the book.

B ***Pair work***

- Books closed. Write a few dates in each style on the board (e.g., June 15, 10/7). Model the way each is pronounced (June fifteenth, October seventh).
- Point out that in the United States, when the date is written with two numbers (i.e., 10/7), the first number represents the month and the second represents the day. In many other countries, this is reversed.
- Books open. Use the examples to demonstrate the task.
- In pairs, Ss take turns reading the dates aloud.
- **Optional:** Extend the practice. Write more dates on the board in both styles, or have Ss write them. Ss continue practicing in new pairs.

2 CONVERSATION

This conversation introduces *be going to* for talking about the future. It introduces expressions for talking about birthdays.

A

- Books open. Have Ss look at the illustration and name the things they see (a man, a woman, a restaurant, a birthday cake, waiters, a waitress). Ask, "What are they doing?" Elicit simple responses from Ss.
- Play the audio program while Ss read and confirm their answers.
- Play the audio program again. Ss read and listen. Try to elicit the meaning of *embarrassing* from the situation and from Philip's expression. Encourage guessing.
- Play the audio program again or model the conversation line by line. Ss listen and read, then look up and repeat.
- Ss practice the conversation in pairs using the Look Up and Say technique.
- **Optional:** Have a few Ss act out the conversation for the class.

B ***Class activity***

- Have Ss take out a sheet of paper and make two columns titled *Name* and *Birthday.*
- Use the model conversation to demonstrate the task.
- Tell Ss to take notes during the activity. Elicit birthdays from two or three Ss and write them on the board:

Name	Birthday
Helen	9/10
Daniel	3/23

- Ss stand and walk around the room asking one another's birthdays. Give Ss a time limit, perhaps four minutes.
- Bring the class back together. Make a list of names and birthdays on the board. Call out the names of the Ss one by one. Ss tell you the birthdays.
- Use the list on the board to answer the questions about birthdays this week, this month, the same month, and the same day.

Optional activity: *Birthday parties*

- See page T-153.

3 GRAMMAR FOCUS *The future with* be going to

This grammar focus presents and practices yes/no questions, short answers, and statements with *be going to.*

(*Note: Be going to* + verb is used to talk about future plans and intentions: *Are you going to work late?* = *Are you planning to work late?* It differs from the use of *go* in the present continuous for describing actions that are happening right now: *I'm going to class right now.*)

- Books open. Play the audio program to present the questions and answers. Ss read and listen.
- Point out that the short answer for yes/no *be going to* questions uses only the verb *be.*
- Play the audio program again or model the sentences. Ss listen and repeat.

A

- Books open. Have Ss identify the activities in the photographs. Make a list of verbs on the board for reference (cook, read, walk/go walking, watch TV, swim/go swimming, have lunch at a restaurant/go out with a friend, see a movie, see friends, go dancing, work).
- Use the examples to demonstrate the task.
- Working alone, Ss write ten sentences in two lists: things they are going to do this weekend and things they are not going to do. As they write, give help and check Ss' work.
- In pairs, Ss compare their sentences, making changes if they wish.

Possible answers

I'm (not) going to cook.
I'm (not) going to read.
I'm (not) going to walk./I'm (not) going to go walking.
I'm (not) going to watch TV.
I'm (not) going to swim./
I'm (not) going to go swimming.
I'm (not) going to have lunch at a restaurant./
I'm (not) going to go out with a friend.
I'm (not) going to see a movie.
I'm (not) going to see friends.
I'm (not) going to go dancing.
I'm (not) going to work.

- **Optional:** Encourage Ss to write about activities that are not in the photographs. Let them use dictionaries if necessary or ask you for vocabulary.
- **Optional:** In pairs, Ss identify things they are both going to do and not do. They write sentences beginning "We are going to . . ." and "We are not going to . . ." Have pairs read their sentences to the class.

B *Pair work*

- Demonstrate the task. Have two Ss model the example conversation.
- Show Ss that a short answer is not enough. They need to add a statement with more information.
- Ss work in pairs to ask each other about their weekend plans.
- **Optional:** Ss exchange partners with another pair. They tell their new partner about their first partner's weekend plans.

3 GRAMMAR FOCUS

The future with be going to

Are you **going to do** anything exciting this weekend?	Yes, I am. **I'm going to celebrate** my birthday. No, I'm not. **I'm going to stay** home.
Is Katherine **going to have** a party for you?	Yes, she is. She**'s going to invite** all my friends. No, she isn't. She**'s going to take** me out to a restaurant.
Are the waiters **going to sing** to you?	Yes, they are. They**'re going to sing** "Happy Birthday." No, they aren't. But they**'re going to give** me a cake.

A Are you going to do any of these things this weekend? Write ten sentences. Then compare with a partner.

Things I'm going to do this weekend	*Things I'm not going to do this weekend*
I'm going to see friends.	*I'm not going to watch TV.*

B ***Pair work*** Ask questions about your partner's plans for the weekend.

A: Are you going to see a movie this weekend?
B: Yes, I am. I'm going to see the new Tom Cruise movie.
A: Are you going to go with a friend? . . .

4 PRONUNCIATION *Reduction of* going to

A Listen and practice. **Going to** is sometimes pronounced /gənə/ in conversation.

A: Are you **going to** have a party for your birthday?
B: No, I'm **going to** go out with a friend.

A: Are you **going to** go to a restaurant?
B: Yes. We're **going to** go to Nick's Café.

B Ask another classmate about weekend plans. Try to reduce **going to** to /gənə/.

5 LISTENING

A It's five-thirty in the evening, and these people are waiting for the bus. What are their plans for tonight? Write one guess for each person.

B Listen to the people talk about their evening plans. What are they really going to do? Complete the chart.

Your guess	What they're really going to do
Michelle *is going to go to the gym.*	Michelle ....
Kevin	Kevin ....
Robert	Robert ....
Jane	Jane ....

6 SNAPSHOT

Do you know these holidays in the United States?

New Year's Day
January 1

Valentine's Day
February 14

Independence Day
July 4

Halloween
October 31

Thanksgiving
4th Thursday in November

Christmas
December 25

Do you celebrate any similar holidays? How?
What are some holidays in your country? What's your favorite holiday? Why?

4 PRONUNCIATION Reduction of going to

This exercise, presents the reduced form of *going to:* /gənə/.

(*Note:* The pronunciation of *going to* is often reduced when used to talk about the future. It is not reduced in the present continuous. Compare: "I'm going to go to the store" and "I'm going to the store.")

A

- Write the two short conversations on the board. Books closed. Play the audio program. Underline *going to* in each sentence and say /gənə/. Ss repeat.
- Books open. Ss say the conversations in pairs. Have them change partners several times. Walk around to help.
- Ask pairs of Ss to say the conversations for the class. Correct their intonation if necessary.

B *Pair work*

- Ss work in pairs to ask each other about their weekend plans. They should pay attention to the pronunciation of *going to.*

5 LISTENING

This exercise practices listening for plans.

A

- Books open. Have Ss look at the illustration. Explain the task. Ss work individually to write their guesses in the chart. Ask several Ss to share their guesses.

B

- Explain the task. Play the audio program. Ss listen only. Then play the audio program as many times as necessary. Ss listen and write the answers.

Audio script

INTERVIEWER: Good evening. I'm Al Rivers with KXQ News Radio. I'm talking with people waiting for the bus tonight. I'm finding out how they're going to spend their evening.
INTERVIEWER: What's your name?
MICHELLE: It's Michelle.
INTERVIEWER: I bet you're going to go to the gym tonight.
MICHELLE: No, not tonight. I'm going to meet a friend. We're going to run together in the park.
INTERVIEWER: And what's your name?
KEVIN: Kevin.
INTERVIEWER: Are you going home now, Kevin?
KEVIN: No, not right now. First, I'm going to go to the video-game arcade.
INTERVIEWER: Oh, so you're going to play video games.
KEVIN: Yeah, I am.
INTERVIEWER: Can I ask your name?
ROBERT: Yes. My name's Robert.
INTERVIEWER: Are you going to do anything interesting tonight?
ROBERT: Well, my friend Chris is going to have a party, but I'm going to work at home. I have all my work right here in my briefcase.
INTERVIEWER: So you can't go to the party. You're going to work tonight.
ROBERT: That's right.
INTERVIEWER: And what's your name?
JANE: I'm Jane.
INTERVIEWER: Do you have any plans for this evening?
JANE: I just bought some new CDs, so I'm going to listen to music tonight.
INTERVIEWER: What kind of music is it?
JANE: Jazz. I always listen to jazz.

- Have four Ss write the answers on the board. Correct the answers with the class.

Possible answers

Michelle is going to meet a friend. / is going to run in the park.
Kevin is going to play video games.
Robert is going to work at home.
Jane is going to listen to music.

Workbook

Workbook Exercises 1–4 on pages 61–63 correspond to Cycle 1, Exercises 1–5, of the Student's Book. Answers to the Workbook exercises begin on page T-182 of this Teacher's Edition.

Cycle 2, Exercises 6–11

6 SNAPSHOT Do you know these holidays in the United States?

This graphic gives information about holidays and celebrations in the United States.

- Books open. Have Ss study the illustrations. Read the information as Ss listen. Then Ss listen and repeat.
- Pointing to each picture in turn, elicit anything Ss know about each holiday. Accept mimed and one-word answers. Restate or expand Ss' answers.
- Ask Ss about similar holidays in their country or countries. Write the names of their holidays on the board, and bring out the similarities to United States holidays.
- Ask the second and third questions, and elicit answers from Ss. If Ss are from more than one country, elicit answers about holidays one country at a time.

7 CONVERSATION

This conversation about Thanksgiving introduces Wh-questions with *be going to.*

(*Note:* Dennis's Thanksgiving dinner is traditional. Most Americans eat turkey on Thanksgiving.)

- Books open. Have Ss look at the illustration and the names in the conversation. Set the scene: Monica and Dennis are talking about their plans for the holiday. See if Ss can guess which holiday based on the illustration.
- Play the audio program while Ss read and listen.
- Play the audio program again. Ss read and listen. Try to elicit the meanings of *Any plans?* and *Sounds like fun.* Encourage guessing.
- Play the audio program again or model the conversation line by line. Ss listen and read, then look up and repeat. Make sure that Ss use the reduced form of *going to.*
- Ss practice the conversation in pairs using the Look Up and Say technique.
- **Optional:** Have a few Ss act out the conversation for the class.

8 GRAMMAR FOCUS *Wh-questions with* be going to

This grammar focus presents Wh-questions with *be going to.* It also introduces future time expressions.

(*Note:* The intonation of Wh-questions was practiced with the present continuous on page 32. All Wh-questions, including the ones in this exercise, have the same intonation: the voice goes up on the last stressed syllable, then down.)

- Play the audio program to present the questions and answers. Ss listen and read.
- Play the audio program again or model the sentences. Ss listen and repeat. Make sure they use the reduced form of *going to* and the correct intonation.
- Play the audio program to present the future time expressions. Ss listen and read.
- Play the audio program again or model the time expressions. Ss listen and repeat.
- Check comprehension of the time expressions. Ask, "Tonight. What's the date?" "Next week. What are the dates?" and so on.
- Use the example to demonstrate the task. Show Ss that they need to use *be going to* and the verb in parentheses.
- Ss complete the conversation individually.
- Elicit the answers from Ss. Write them on the board so that Ss can correct their work. Point out that *ask* in the last sentence means *invite.*
- **Optional:** To check answers, follow this procedure:

  Have Ss raise their hands when they finish the exercise. Go to the Ss one by one. Make an *X* next to any wrong answers. Ss raise their hands again when they have corrected the wrong answers.

  When a S's answers are all correct, have the S help correct other Ss' work. Have them walk around to check other Ss' papers. They do not have to explain anything or show their own answers – they just make *X*s.

Answers

A: What **are** you **going to do** for Halloween?
B: I don't know. I'**m not going to do** anything special.
A: Well, Pat and I **are going to have** a party.
Can you come?
B: Sure, I can come. Where **are** you **going to have** the party?
A: It's **going to be** at Pat's house.
B: What time **is** the party **going to start**?
A: At 6:00. And it's **going to end** around midnight.
B: Who **are** you **going to invite**?
A: We'**re going to ask** all our good friends.

- Ss practice the conversation in pairs using the Look Up and Say technique.

7 CONVERSATION

Listen and practice.

Monica: So, Dennis. What are you going to do for Thanksgiving?
Dennis: I'm going to have dinner at my parents' house. What about you? Any plans?
Monica: Yeah. I'm going to cook dinner with some friends. We're going to make fish soup.
Dennis: Hmm. That's unusual. We always have turkey, mashed potatoes . . . .
Monica: I know. Every year, my friends and I make something different.
Dennis: Sounds like fun. Well, have a happy Thanksgiving.
Monica: Thanks. You, too.

8 GRAMMAR FOCUS

Wh-questions with be going to

	Time expressions
Where are you going to go for the holiday?	tonight
We're going to go to my parents' house.	tomorrow
Who's going to be there?	tomorrow night
My whole family is going to be there.	next week
How are you going to get there?	next month
We're going to drive.	next summer

Complete this conversation with the correct verb forms. Then practice with a partner.

A: What *are* you *going to do* for Halloween? (do)
B: I don't know. I .... anything special. (not do)
A: Well, Pat and I .... a party. Can you come? (have)
B: Sure, I can come. Where .... you .... the party? (have)
A: It .... at Pat's house. (be)
B: What time .... the party .... ? (start)
A: At 6:00. And it .... around midnight. (end)
B: Who .... you .... ? (invite)
A: We .... all our good friends. (ask)

9 EVERYDAY EVENTS

Group work Ask and answer questions about your plans for . . . .

tomorrow night
Saturday night
next week
this/next summer

A: What are you going to do tomorrow night?
B: I'm going to stay home and watch television. What about you? What are you going to do?
C: I'm going to . . . .

10 HOLIDAYS

A ***Pair work*** Choose a holiday or celebration. Then ask and answer these questions with a partner. Use the activities in the box or your own ideas.

Some activities

see friends
have a party/picnic
make dinner
go to a parade
open presents

What holiday are you thinking about?
What are you going to do?
Where are you going to go?
Who's going to be there?
When are you going to go?
How are you going to get there?

A: What holiday are you thinking about?
B: I'm thinking about Lunar New Year.
A: What are you going to do for Lunar New Year?
B: I'm going to go to a parade with my brother. . . .

B ***Class activity*** Tell the class about your partner's plans for the holiday.

interchange 11

Celebrations

Talk about how people are celebrating special events. Turn to page IC-14.

9 EVERYDAY EVENTS

In this exercise, Ss talk about their own plans.

Group work

- Explain the task and model the time expressions. If it's late spring or early summer, Ss can ask about plans for "this summer." If it's fall, winter, or early spring, they can ask about plans for "next summer."
- Use the model conversation to demonstrate the task.
- Divide the class into groups of four to five Ss. Ss take turns asking and answering questions about their plans using the time expressions. Go around and listen to the groups. Help with vocabulary and pronunciation.
- **Optional:** After several minutes, have Ss make new groups, so that they get more practice with new information.

10 HOLIDAYS

In this activity, Ss practice Wh-questions and answers with *be going to* as they talk about holiday plans.

A Pair work

- Books open. Ask if Ss can identify the holiday in the photograph (Lunar New Year is celebrated in Chinese communities all over the world).
- Explain the task. Call on Ss to model the questions.
- Go over the activities in the box. These are things that people do on many different holidays. Some holidays the Ss choose may need other activities.
- Ask two Ss to read the model conversation for the class.
- Further demonstrate the task by answering questions yourself. Think of a holiday and have Ss ask the questions. Have one or two Ss make notes about your answers on the board. Leave the notes on the board for part B.
- Ss ask and answer questions in pairs, taking notes about their partners.
- Ss check their partner's notes to be sure the information is correct.

B Class activity

- Use the notes on the board to demonstrate the class activity. Elicit complete sentences about your plans from Ss, based on the notes.
- Give Ss time to prepare their reports. Then have them close their books and put their notes away while other Ss are speaking.
- Ss take turns describing their partner's holiday plans to the whole class. They can refer to their notes if necessary, but they should use the Look Up and Say technique.
- **Optional:** In a large class, Ss can report in small groups or new pairs to save time.

INTERCHANGE 11 Celebrations

See page T-118 of this Teacher's Edition for notes.

Optional activity: ***How much did you find out?***

- See page T-154.

 READING What are you going to do on your birthday?

In this article, Ss read about how four people in different countries are going to celebrate their birthdays. The exercises practice reading for main ideas and talking about birthdays.

- Books closed. Write these questions on the board and go over them:
  What's the question in the title?
  How many people are in the article?
  Where do they live?
- Tell Ss to open their books for 10–15 seconds, find as many answers as possible, and then close their books.
- Elicit the answers from Ss.
- Introduce the prereading task and elicit answers from Ss. If Ss are from different countries, try to elicit information about one country at a time.

A 

- Ss read the article. If you wish, play the audio program as Ss listen and read.
- **Optional:** Ss underline words they do not know. Encourage Ss to guess the meaning from the context of the paragraph. Ss will be able to do the exercise without understanding all the words.
- Use the example to demonstrate the task. Read the four statements aloud or have Ss read them. Explain that each statement has one mistake.
- Tell Ss to correct any sentences they can before rereading the article. Then they read the article silently to find the other mistakes.
- Ss work individually to complete the task.
- **Optional:** Let some Ss work in pairs if they prefer to.
- Have volunteers write the corrected statements on the board. Correct them with the class. Ss correct their own work from the board.

Possible answers

1. To celebrate her birthday, Elena**'s friends are going to pull on her ears**.
2. Yan-Ching**'s mother** is going to cook some noodles on her birthday.
3. On his birthday, Mr. Aoki is going to **get** something red.
4. Philippe **is going to take his friends** out to dinner on his birthday.

B Group work

- Read the questions. Write the possibilities on the board:
  Your next birthday
  Your friend's next birthday
  Your mother's, father's, grandmother's, grandfather's, brother's, or sister's next birthday
- Demonstrate the task. Make a statement. Give more information. Then elicit questions from Ss. Demonstrate and emphasize that Ss need to give additional information with their answers:

  T: My grandmother is going to be 90 next summer. We're going to have a party.
  S: Who's going to be there?
  T: The whole family. My sister is going to come from Ecuador, and my brother is going to come from South Africa.
- Before they get into groups, give Ss time to think about what they want to say, to make notes, or to write a sentence or two.
- In groups, Ss talk about their plans. Circulate to help them give additional information in their answers.
- **Optional:** Elicit a list of different things people are going to do to celebrate birthdays. Which is the most unusual plan? Which is the most fun?

 Workbook

Workbook Exercises 5–7 on pages 64–66 correspond to Cycle 2, Exercises 6–11, of the Student's Book. Answers to the Workbook exercises begin on page T-182 of this Teacher's Edition.

Optional activity: *Word associations*

- See page T-154.

11 READING

WHAT ARE YOU GOING TO DO ON YOUR BIRTHDAY?

How do people usually celebrate birthdays in your country?

Elena Buenaventura
Madrid

"My twenty-first birthday is on Saturday, and I'm going to go out with some friends. To wish me a happy birthday, they're going to pull on my ear 21 times, once for each year. It's an old custom. Some people pull on the ear just once, but my friends are very traditional!"

Yan-Ching Shi
Taipei

"Tomorrow is my sixteenth birthday. It's a special birthday, so we're going to have a family ceremony. I'm probably going to get some money in 'lucky' envelopes from my relatives. My mother is going to cook noodles – noodles are for a long life."

Mr. and Mrs. Aoki
Kyoto

"My husband is going to be 60 tomorrow. In Japan, the sixtieth birthday is called *kanreki* – it's the beginning of a new life. The color red represents a new life, so we always give something red for a sixtieth birthday. What am I going to give my husband? I can't say. It's a surprise!"

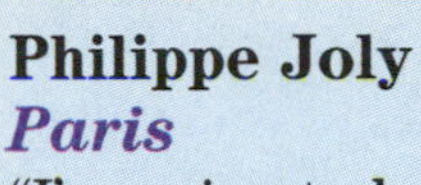

Philippe Joly
Paris

"I'm going to be 30 next week, so I'm going to invite three very good friends out to dinner. In France, when you have a birthday, you often invite people out. In some countries, I know it's the opposite – people take you out."

A Read the four paragraphs. Then correct these statements.

1. To celebrate her birthday, Elena is going to pull on her friends' ears.
2. Yan-Ching is going to cook some noodles on her birthday.
3. On his birthday, Mr. Aoki is going to buy something red.
4. Philippe's friends are going to take him out to dinner on his birthday.

B ***Group work*** What do you usually do on your birthday? Do you have plans for your next birthday, or for the birthday of a friend or family member? What are you going to do? Tell the group.

"I'm going to be 25 on March 15th. I'm going to . . . ."

12 What's the matter?

1 WORD POWER *Parts of the body*

A Listen and practice.

B ***Pair work*** Close your books. Point out the parts of the body named in the picture.

A: Point to your neck.
B: This is my neck.
Point to your feet.
A: These are my feet.

12 What's the matter?

This unit presents expressions for talking about health and health problems, including names for parts of the body, common illnesses, and medications. The unit also introduces have + *noun,* feel + *adjective, and imperatives.*

Cycle 1, Exercises 1–4

1 WORD POWER *Parts of the body*

This vocabulary exercise introduces and practices names for parts of the body.

A

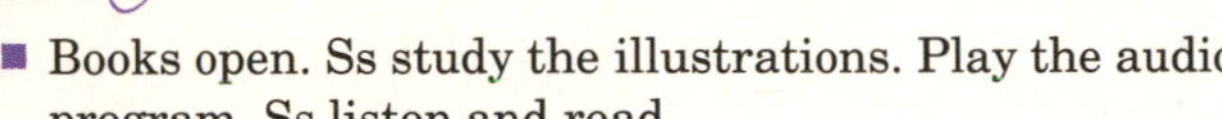

- Books open. Ss study the illustrations. Play the audio program. Ss listen and read.
- Point out the irregular plurals *teeth* and *feet,* the silent *b* in *thumb,* and the silent *k* in *knee.*
- Play the audio program or model the words one by one. Ss listen and repeat.
- **Optional:** Books closed. Say the parts of the body in random order. Have Ss point to their bodies as they repeat the words.

B ***Pair work***

- Demonstrate the task. Model the example conversation with a S. Tell Ss there are 24 body parts to name, not counting plurals.
- **Optional:** Have pairs close their books and make a list of the 24 words together before they begin to practice.
- In pairs and with books closed, Ss take turns giving and following instructions.

Optional activities

1. *Game – Spelling challenge*

- See page T-154.

2. *Game – Simon says*

- See page T-154.

2 CONVERSATION

This conversation introduces expressions for talking about health and feelings.

- Books open. Have Ss look at the illustration and the names in the conversation. Write these questions on the board:
  How is Ken? (Not so good.)
  What are Brian and Ken going to do? (They're going to have lunch at a Japanese restaurant.)
- Play the audio program while Ss read and listen for the answers. Elicit the answers.
- Play the audio program again. Ss read and listen. Try to elicit the meanings of *headache, backache, flu, homesick,* and *better.* Tell Ss it may be helpful to listen to the sound of Brian's and Ken's voices. Encourage guessing.
- Play the audio program again or model the conversation line by line. Ss listen and read, then look up and repeat.
- Ss practice the conversation in pairs using the Look Up and Say technique.
- **Optional:** Have a few Ss act out the conversation for the class.

3 GRAMMAR FOCUS Have + *noun;* feel + *adjective*

This exercise presents and practices *have* + noun and *feel* + adjective.

- Books open. Play the audio program to present the questions and answers. Ss read and listen.
- Point out the grammar in the two boxes. The first box shows the structure *have* + noun, which is often used when discussing physical problems. The second box shows the structure *feel* + adjective, which is often used when discussing a person's general state of being.
- Play the audio program again or model the sentences. Ss listen and repeat.
- Point out the adjectives in the third box. They provide additional vocabulary for sentences with *feel* + adjective. The adjectives under the minus sign (−) have a negative or "bad" meaning. The adjectives under the plus sign (+) have a positive or "good" meaning.
- Play the audio program again or model the adjectives. Ss listen and repeat.

A

(Note: Part A of this grammar focus functions similarly to a Word Power exercise. Make sure you give Ss sufficient time to familiarize themselves with the words presented here.)

- Books open. Have Ss study the illustrations. The illustrations provide additional vocabulary for sentences with *have* + noun. Play the audio program. Ss read and listen.
- Play the program again. Ss listen and repeat.
- To prepare for part B, Ss practice acting out the health problems. Ss stand. Act out one of the health problems yourself, and say, for example, "I have a backache." Ss imitate your actions and repeat the sentences. Have Ss come to the front of the room and do the same. (*Note:* The illustrations suggest actions for most of the problems.)

B *Pair work*

- Use the model conversation to demonstrate the task with a S. You read Student B's part. Act out B's earache.
- Lead two Ss through the conversation with another health problem.
- Ss work in pairs. They take turns acting out the health problems in part A. Have Ss change roles many times. Go around the room to give help.
- **Optional:** Do the activity as a class. Have one S come to the front of the room and act out a health problem. The other Ss raise their hands and guess the problem. The first Ss to guess correctly continue the game by going to the front of the room and acting out a health problem.

2 CONVERSATION

Listen and practice.

Brian: Hey, Ken. How are you?
Ken: Oh, I'm not so good, actually.
Brian: Why? What's the matter?
Ken: Well, I have a headache. And a backache.
Brian: Maybe you have the flu.
Ken: No, I think I just miss Japan – I feel a little homesick.
Brian: That's too bad. . . . But I think I can help. Let's have lunch at that new Japanese restaurant.
Ken: That's a great idea. Thanks, Brian. I feel better already!

3 GRAMMAR FOCUS

Have + *noun;* feel + *adjective*

What's the matter?	How do you feel?	*Adjectives*	–	+
What's wrong?	**I feel sick.**		sick	fine (well)
I have a headache.	**I feel sad.**		sad	happy
I have a sore throat.	**I feel better.**		bad	good (better)
I have the flu.	**I don't feel well.**		awful	great
			terrible	terrific

A Listen and practice. *"He has a backache."*

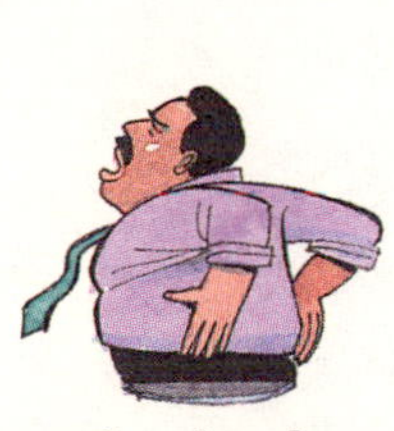
a backache

an earache

a headache

a stomachache

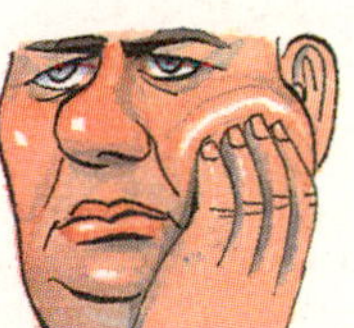
a toothache

a cold

a cough

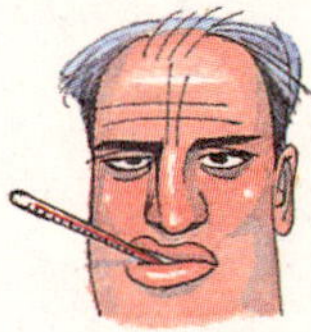
a fever

the flu

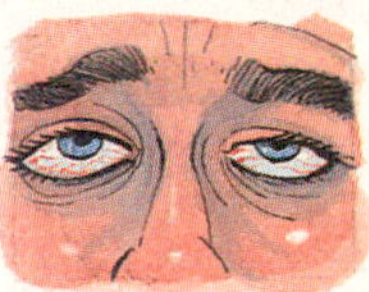
sore eyes

a sore throat

B ***Pair work*** Take turns acting out a health problem. Your partner guesses the problem and gives sympathy.

A: What's wrong? Do you have a headache?
B: No, I don't.
A: Do you have an earache?
B: Yes, I have an earache.
A: That's too bad.

C ***Group work*** Find out how your classmates feel today.

A: How do you feel today?
B: I feel fine, thanks. What about you?
A: I feel really terrible. I have a headache.
B: I'm sorry to hear that. How do you feel today, Sun-hee?
C: . . .

expressions
That's too bad.
I'm sorry to hear that.
I hope you feel better soon.

4 LISTENING *Health problems*

Listen to people talk about health problems. Where do they have problems? Write down the parts of the body. Then ask and answer questions.

1. Ben
head, throat

2. Alison
....

3. Jeffrey
....

4. Marta
....

A: What's wrong with Ben?
B: He has a headache and a sore throat.

5 SNAPSHOT

Listen and practice.

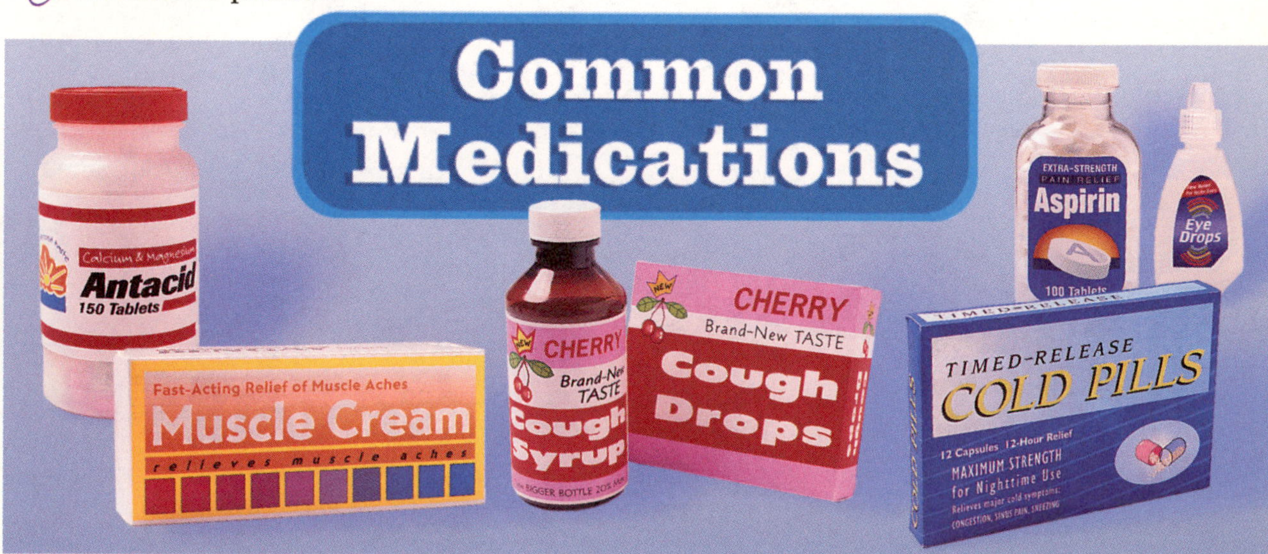

Sources: Adapted from *Almanac of the American People* and interviews with adults between 25 and 50

What can you use these medications for?
What medications do you have at home? Which do you use often?

C *Group work*

- Use the model conversation to demonstrate and explain the task.
- Refer Ss back to the grammar box. Show them they are practicing both structures: *have* + noun and *feel* + adjective. Review the adjectives in the grammar box.
- Point out the expressions box. Model the expressions one by one. Ss listen and repeat.
- Make statements. Choose S to respond appropriately with expressions from the box, for example:

  T: I feel terrible.
  S1: That's too bad.
  T: I have the flu.
  S2: I hope you feel better soon.

- Have three or four Ss demonstrate the task using their own names and information. Help them if necessary.
- Put Ss in groups of four or five. Ss ask about one another's health and offer sympathy if appropriate.
- **Optional:** Assign health problems for Ss to complain about. Write them down on slips of paper and have Ss pick them out.
- **Optional:** Do the activity as a class. Ss stand up and talk to as many people as possible.

4 LISTENING *Health problems*

This exercise presents information about health problems.

- Books open. Have Ss look at the illustrations. Explain the listening portion of the activity.
- Play the first part of the audio program, and use the example to demonstrate the task.
- Play the rest of the audio program as many times as necessary. Ss listen and write down the answers.

Audio script

1. BEN: I think I'm going to go home early. I don't feel well.
   WOMAN: What's the matter, Ben?
   BEN: I think I have a cold. I have a headache and I have a sore throat.
   WOMAN: Oh, that's too bad. Feel better.
2. ALISON: Ow!
   MAN: Oh, my gosh! Are you OK, Alison?
   ALISON: Uh, not really. My back and my elbow feel terrible. Ouch!
   MAN: Can you stand up?
   ALISON: I think so. Yeah. Thanks for your help.
3. WOMAN: Here. Have some ice cream, Jeffrey.
   JEFFREY: Oh, I love ice cream, but I can't eat any cold food.
   WOMAN: Why not?
   JEFFREY: I have a really bad toothache.
   WOMAN: Oh, I'm sorry.
4. MARTA: Ooh!
   MAN: What's wrong?
   MARTA: I have really sore eyes. And my wrists are sore, too.
   MAN: Well, take a break, Marta. Finish typing your homework later.

- Demonstrate the speaking portion of the activity. Show Ss that they are talking about the people in the illustrations and comparing their answers. Ss compare their answers in pairs.
- Play the audio program again so that Ss can verify their answers. Write the correct answers on the board.

Answers

1. head, throat	3. tooth
2. leg, elbow, back	4. eyes, back, wrists

Workbook

Workbook Exercises 1–5 on pages 67–70 correspond to Cycle 1, Exercises 1–4, of the Student's Book. Answers to the Workbook exercises begin on page T-182.

Cycle 2, Exercises 5–10

5 SNAPSHOT *Common Medications*

This graphic gives information about the names of medications used to treat common health problems.

- Books open. Have Ss study the illustrations. Play the audio program. Ss listen and read, then listen and repeat.
- Read the first question. Elicit answers from Ss.

Ask the second question. Elicit a list from the Ss and write it on the board. Ask the third question. Point to each medication on the list in turn. Ss raise their hands if they use it often. Write the number of Ss who use it next to each medication.

6 CONVERSATION

This conversation introduces expressions for asking and giving advice about health problems.

- Books open. Have Ss look at the illustration and the names in the conversation. Ask who the people are (a doctor and a patient) and where they are (in the doctor's office).
- Write these questions on the board:
  How does the woman feel? (terrible, exhausted)
  Why? (She can't sleep at night.)
  What is the doctor going to give her? (some pills)
- Play the audio program while Ss read and listen for the answers. Elicit the answers.
- Play the audio program again. Ss read and listen. Help Ss guess new vocabulary from the context. Encourage guessing. (*Note:* Doctors often say "let's" when they mean "I'm going to.")
- Play the audio program again or model the conversation line by line. Ss listen and read, then look up and repeat.
- Ss practice the conversation in pairs.
- **Optional:** Have a few Ss act out the conversation.

7 LISTENING

In this exercise, Ss listen for specific information.

- Books open. Ss are going to hear Dr. Young from Exercise 6 and the people from Exercise 4. Ss listen for the medication that Dr. Young gives each patient.
- Play the audio program. Ss check the correct boxes.

Audio script

1. DR. YOUNG: What's the matter, Ben?
   BEN: I think I have a cold. I feel awful. I have a sore throat and a headache.
   DR. YOUNG: OK. Let's take a look.
   DR. YOUNG: Yes, you have a cold. Let me give you some cold pills. Take one every four hours.
   BEN: Thanks, Dr. Young.
2. DR. YOUNG: How do you feel today, Alison?
   ALISON: A little better. But I have a sore elbow.
   DR. YOUNG: Hmm. Let me see. Yes. Well, I'm going to give you some muscle cream. Rub some on your elbow three times a day.
   ALISON: Three times a day. OK, Dr. Young. Thank you.
3. DR. YOUNG: That's it, Jeffrey. Everything's fine. Anything else?
   JEFFREY: Well, I have a really bad toothache.
   DR. YOUNG: Hmm. That's too bad. Well, go to a dentist soon. But here's some aspirin to take for the pain.
   JEFFREY: OK.
4. DR. YOUNG: What can I do for you, Marta?
   MARTA: I have really sore eyes. And my wrists are sore, too.
   DR. YOUNG: Well, let me look at you. Hmm. Do you use a computer a lot?
   MARTA: Well, yeah – for homework and other school things.
   DR. YOUNG: I see. Well, take breaks often. And use these eyedrops for your sore eyes.
   MARTA: OK. Thanks.
   DR. YOUNG: You're welcome. Feel better, Marta.

- In pairs, Ss compare and make changes if they wish.
- Play the audio program again so that Ss can verify their answers. Write the correct answers on the board.

Answers

1. Ben – cold pills	3. Jeffrey – aspirin
2. Alison – muscle cream	4. Marta – eyedrops

8 PRONUNCIATION Sentence stress

In this exercise, Ss further practice sentence stress.

A

- Write the six sentences on the board. Books closed. Play the audio program once or twice. Tell Ss to listen for the stressed words in each sentence. Mark the stress the Ss tell you. (It is not important for S to get the right answers, only to begin listening for the stress.)
- Books open. Play the audio program again. Ss listen and read to confirm their answers.
- Have Ss repeat chorally, first as a class, then in rows or sections, then individually. Give feedback on stress.

B

- Books open. Tell Ss to mark the part with the most stress. Play the audio program as many times as necessary. Ss listen and complete the task.

Answers

Take a hot **bath**.	Eat a lot of **veg**etables.
Don't drink **so**da.	Don't lift heavy **things**.
Stay in **bed**.	Don't go to **bed** late.

- Ss compare their answers in pairs. While they work, write the sentences on the board.
- Elicit answers from Ss. Underline them in the sentences on the board, or have a S underline them.

6 CONVERSATION

 Listen and practice.

Dr. Young: Hello, Ms. West. How are you today?
Ms. West: I feel terrible.
Dr. Young: So, what's wrong, exactly?
Ms. West: I'm exhausted.
Dr. Young: Hmm. Why are you so tired?
Ms. West: I just can't sleep at night.
Dr. Young: OK. Let's take a look at you.

Dr. Young: I'm going to give you some pills. Take one pill every night after dinner.
Ms. West: OK.
Dr. Young: And don't drink coffee, tea, or soda.
Ms. West: No soda?
Dr. Young: No. And don't work too hard.
Ms. West: All right. Thanks, Dr. Young.

7 LISTENING

Listen to Dr. Young talk to four other patients. What does she give them? Check (✓) the correct medication.

	Antacid	Aspirin	Cold pills	Eyedrops	Muscle cream
1. Ben	☐	☐	☐	☐	☐
2. Alison	☐	☐	☐	☐	☐
3. Jeffrey	☐	☐	☐	☐	☐
4. Marta	☐	☐	☐	☐	☐

8 PRONUNCIATION *Sentence stress*

A Listen and practice. Notice the main stress in these sentences.

Take some **áspirin**.
Go to **béd**.
Use some **múscle** cream.
Don't drink **cóffee**.
Don't go to **wórk**.
Don't **éxercise** this week.

B Listen and mark the main stress in these sentences.

Take a hot bath.
Don't drink soda.
Stay in bed.
Eat a lot of vegetables.
Don't lift heavy things.
Don't go to bed late.

9 GRAMMAR FOCUS

Imperatives

Take a pill every four hours.	**Don't work** too hard.
Drink lots of juice.	**Don't stay up** late.

A What are these people saying? Choose from the sentences in the box. Then compare with a partner.

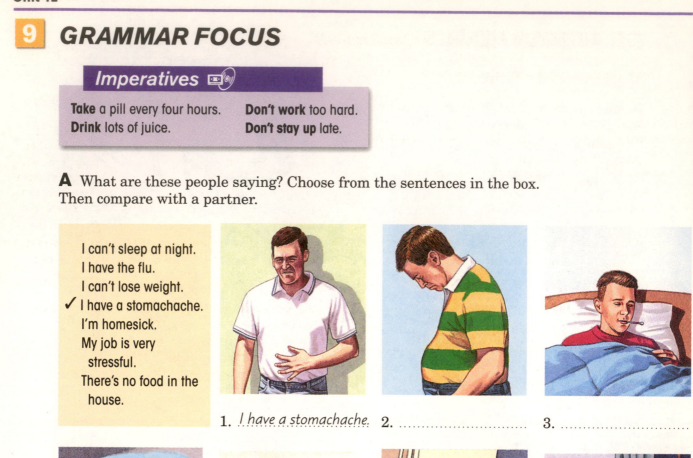

I can't sleep at night.
I have the flu.
I can't lose weight.
✓ I have a stomachache.
I'm homesick.
My job is very stressful.
There's no food in the house.

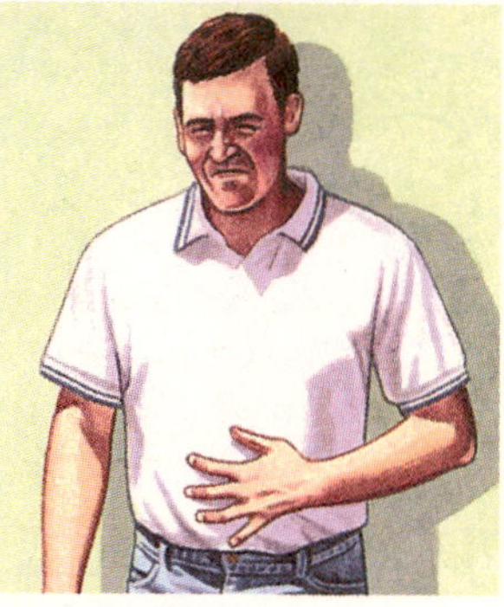

1. *I have a stomachache.*

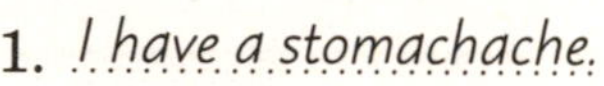

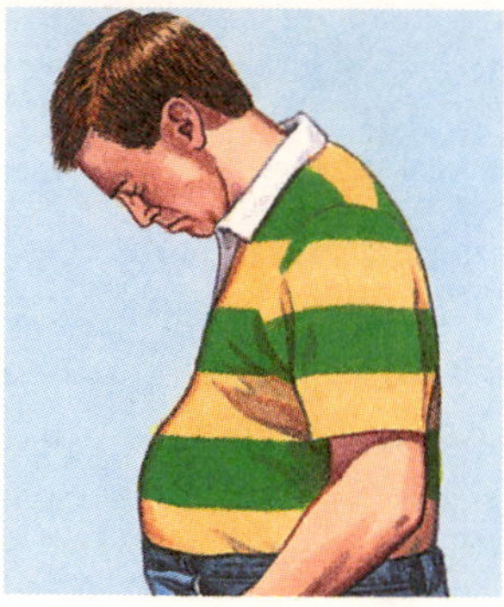

2. ....

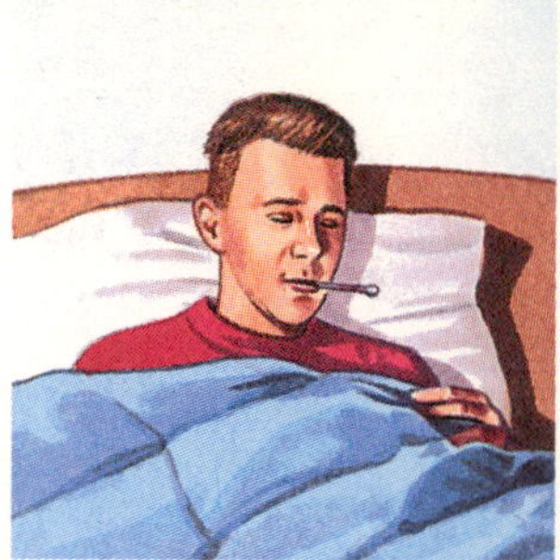

3. ....

4. ....

5. ....

6. ....

7. ....

B ***Pair work*** Act out the problems in part A and give advice. Use these or your own ideas.

Go to bed and sleep.
Go out to a restaurant.
Eat some toast and drink some tea.
Don't go to school this week.
Don't go outside.
Don't eat desserts.
Don't eat any heavy food today.
Take two aspirin.
Close your eyes for ten minutes.
Go home and relax.
Do something fun every evening.
Call your family on the phone.
Get some exercise every day.
Go to a store and buy some food.

A: I have a stomachache.
B: Don't eat any heavy food today.

9 GRAMMAR FOCUS *Imperatives*

This grammar focus presents and practices imperative sentences.

(*Note:* Part A is preparation for part B, where imperatives are practiced. You may prefer to present part A first, then the grammar box, then part B. The notes below follow the order in the book.)

- Books open. Play the audio program to present the information in the grammar box. Ss listen and read.
- Ask, "How are imperatives different from other sentences in English?" Accept any reasonable answer (e.g., There isn't a subject, They don't have the person first, The first word is the verb, They don't say "you"). If necessary, restate Ss' answers for clarity.
- Play the audio program again or model the sentences. Ss listen and repeat.

A

- Have S read the sentences in the box. (*Note:* Ss know enough vocabulary to match all of the sentences except "I can't lose weight." Ss can figure out "lose weight" by matching the other sentences first.)
- Use the example to demonstrate the task. Show Ss that they need to find a statement in the box for each illustration.
- Ss work individually to write the statements under the illustrations.
- Students compare their answers in pairs, making changes if they wish.
- Elicit answers from Ss. Confirm the correct answers, but this time don't write them on the board. Make sure that all the Ss hear the answers.

Answers

1. I have a stomachache.
2. I can't lose weight.
3. I have the flu.
4. I'm homesick.
5. My job is very stressful.
6. There's no food in the house.
7. I can't sleep at night.

B *Pair work*

- Books open. Use the example conversation to demonstrate the task. Act out A's problem when you read the sentence.
- Have Ss read the sentences in the speech bubbles. If necessary, answer questions about meaning. Let other Ss answer the questions if they can. (*Note: Aspirin* is a countable noun with an irregular plural – it is the same as the singular form. In recent years, *fun* has become an adjective. It is not necessary to give Ss this information unless they ask.)
- In pairs, Ss take turns acting out the problems in part A and giving the advice in part B. Encourage Ss to use their own ideas for problems and advice if they can. Walk around and help with vocabulary.
- Bring the class back together. Elicit the problems Ss talked about and the advice they gave.

Possible answers

1. Don't eat any heavy food today.
   Go home and relax.
2. Get some exercise every day.
   Don't eat desserts.
3. Go to bed and sleep.
   Don't go to school this week.
   Don't eat any heavy food today.
   Don't go outside.
   Take two aspirin.
   Eat some toast and drink some tea.
4. Do something fun every evening.
   Get some exercise every day.
   Call your family on the phone.
5. Go home and relax.
   Get some exercise every day.
   Do something fun every evening.
   Close your eyes for ten minutes.
6. Go out to a restaurant.
   Go to a store and buy some food.
7. Get some exercise every day.
   Do something fun every evening.
   Close your eyes for ten minutes.

10 READING 10 Simple Ways to Improve Your Health

In this article, Ss read about ten ways to improve one's health. The exercises practice reading for main ideas and talking about healthy habits.

- Introduce the prereading task. Ask, "How can you improve your health?" If necessary, clarify the questions with one or two examples. (Sleep eight hours every night. Don't smoke.)
- Elicit more ideas from Ss.
- Books open. Read the title aloud, and write it on the board.

A

- Ss read the article. If you wish, play the audio program as Ss listen and read.
- **Optional:** Ss underline words they do not know. Encourage Ss to guess the meaning from the context or the accompanying photo. Ss will be able to do the exercise without understanding all the words.
- Books open. Demonstrate the task. Read the incomplete sentences or have Ss read them.
- Ask Ss to identify the most important word in each sentence (*exercise, bones, muscles, gums, energy*, and *challenge* or *brain*). Ss circle the words. Do not explain vocabulary. Scanning the article for key words is an important part of the exercise.
- Tell Ss to find the circled words in the article, then complete the sentences.
- **Optional:** Set a time limit. This will encourage Ss to scan quickly for key words instead of reading slowly and carefully.
- Have volunteers write their completed sentences on the board. Correct them with the class.

Answers

1. To get exercise, **go for a walk**.
2. To help your bones, **get enough calcium**.
3. To help your muscles, **stretch for five minutes**.
4. To keep your gums healthy, **floss your teeth**.
5. To have enough energy for the morning, **eat breakfast**.
6. To challenge your brain, **do a crossword puzzle or read a new book**.

- **Optional:** Have Ss read the article again, with or without the audio program. Then let them choose three words for you to explain. Use the photos and the context if possible to explain the words they choose.

B *Group work*

- Read the instructions aloud. Have a S read the questions to the class. Elicit or explain the meaning of *regularly*.
- Put the Ss in groups of three to five. Ss answer the questions in groups.
- Write the numbers 1–10 on the board and record how many Ss do each of the ten things in the article.
- Elicit other ways Ss improve their health and write them on the board.

INTERCHANGE 12 Helpful advice

See page T-119 of this Teacher's Edition for notes.

Workbook

Workbook Exercises 6–8 on pages 71–72 correspond to Cycle 2, Exercises 5–10, of the Student's Book. Answers to the Workbook exercises begin on page T-182 of this Teacher's Edition.

Optional activities

1. *How to live dangerously*

- See page T-154.

2. *Game – Simon says*

- This game suggested on page T-154. This time, let Ss be the leaders.

10 READING

10 SIMPLE WAYS TO IMPROVE YOUR HEALTH

Cover the reading. Can you think of some ways to improve your health?

Believe it or not, you **can** greatly improve your health in these ten simple ways:

1 Eat breakfast. Breakfast gives you energy for the morning.

2 Go for a walk. Walking is good exercise, and exercise is necessary for good health.

3 Floss your teeth. Don't just brush them. Flossing keeps your gums healthy.

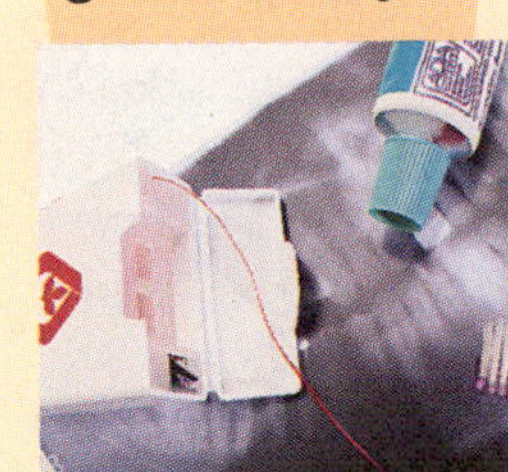

4 Drink eight cups of water every day. Water helps your body in many ways.

5 Stretch for five minutes. Stretching is important for your muscles.

6 Wear a seat belt. Every year, seat belts save thousands of lives.

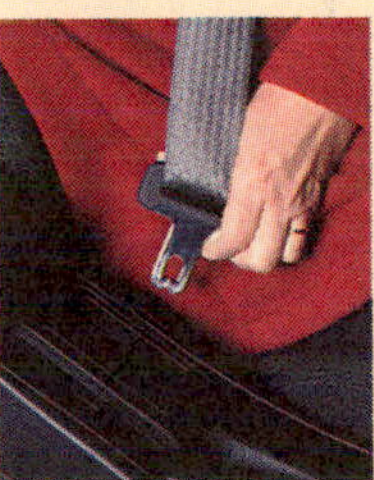

7 Do something to challenge your brain. For example, do a crossword puzzle or read a new book.

8 Moisturize your skin and use sunscreen.

9 Get enough calcium. Your bones need it. Yogurt and milk have calcium. Or drink orange juice with calcium added.

10 Take a "time-out" – a break of about 20 minutes. Do something different. For example, get up and walk. Or sit down and listen to music.

Source: *Cooking Light®* Magazine

A Read the article. Then complete the advice.

1. To get exercise, ...
2. To help your bones, ...
3. To help your muscles, ...
4. To keep your gums healthy, ...
5. To have enough energy for the morning, ...
6. To challenge your brain, ...

B ***Group work*** Talk about these questions.

1. Which of these ten things do you do regularly?
2. What else do you do for your health?

Helpful advice

Give advice for some common problems. Turn to page IC-15.

Review of Units 9–12

1 MEALTIME

A Complete the chart.

	Breakfast	Lunch	Dinner
1. What time do you usually eat?	....	....	....
2. Where do you usually eat?	....	....	....
3. What do you usually have?	....	....	....
	....	....	....

B ***Pair work*** Take turns. Ask and answer the questions.

2 LISTENING *What's the matter?*

Listen to these conversations. Match the conversations with the problems.

1. ...d... 2. .... 3. .... 4. .... 5. .... 6. ....

a. This person needs some ketchup.

b. This person has a backache.

c. This person can't dance very well.

d. This person feels sad.

e. This person is going to take a test tomorrow.

f. This person has the flu.

Review of Units 9–12

This unit reviews and practices the simple present and the future with be going to, *including countable and uncountable nouns, frequency adverbs, and* can. *It focuses on vocabulary and functions relating to food and eating habits, feelings and health problems, likes and dislikes, and plans.*

1 MEALTIME

This exercise reviews Wh-questions in the simple present, frequency adverbs, and vocabulary related to food.

A

- Books open. Go over the questions and headings in the chart.
- Tell Ss to answer in note form, not complete sentences. For vocabulary for question 3, Ss may refer to Unit Summary 9 at the back of the Student's Book.
- Ss complete the chart individually.

B *Pair work*

- Explain the task. Model a conversation with a S. For example:

T: What time do you usually eat breakfast?
S: I usually eat breakfast around 8 A.M.
T: Where do you usually eat breakfast?
S: I go to a restaurant.
T: What do you usually have?
S: I have coffee and toast.

- In pairs, Ss take turns asking and answering the questions.
- **Optional:** Bring the class back together. As a class activity, elicit Ss' answers to the questions.

2 LISTENING *What's the matter?*

This exercise practices listening and making inferences. It reviews the topics of health, food, and abilities.

- Books open. Give Ss a few minutes to work in pairs. Ss study the illustrations, read the sentences, and help each other understand them. Do not explain vocabulary.
- Play the first part of the audio program, and use the example to explain the task.
- Play the audio program as many times as necessary. Ss complete the matching task individually.

Audio script

1. MAN: Hi. How are you?
   WOMAN: Oh, not too good.
   MAN: What's the matter? Are you sick?
   WOMAN: No, I'm not sick. I just don't feel very happy.
2. MAN: This hamburger isn't very good.
   WOMAN: Really? What's wrong with it?
   MAN: I don't know. It needs something.
   WOMAN: Well, it has pickle and onion on it.
   MAN: Yeah, but something's wrong . . . . Oh, I know!
3. MAN: How do you feel?
   WOMAN: Terrible. I have a headache, and my whole body feels sore.
   MAN: Do you have a fever?
   WOMAN: I think so.
   MAN: Go home early and go to bed.
   WOMAN: Good idea.
4. WOMAN: Are you going to go to Angela's party?
   MAN: No, I don't think so.
   WOMAN: Why not? It's going to be fun.
   MAN: Well, there's going to be music, and everyone's going to dance. And I can't dance at all.
5. MAN: How do you feel today?
   WOMAN: Oh, about the same.
   MAN: Can I help you with your briefcase? It looks really heavy.
   WOMAN: Oh, yes. Thanks so much. I can't lift heavy things.
6. WOMAN: What are you doing? Are you getting up?
   MAN: Yeah, I am. I can't sleep.
   WOMAN: What are you going to do?
   MAN: I think I'm going to study again. I can't remember anything.

- Ss compare their answers in pairs. Then play the audio program again so that Ss can confirm their answers.
- Elicit the correct answers, and write them on the board.

Answers

1. d	2. a	3. f	4. c	5. b	6.e

3 LIKE IT OR NOT?

This exercise reviews expressing likes and dislikes and vocabulary related to the topics of food, sports, and music.

A

- Books open. Go over the verbs and headings in the chart.
- Ss complete the chart with information about themselves in note form. Refer them to Unit Summaries 9 and 10 at the back of the Student's Book. Allow Ss to ask you for additional vocabulary or to consult with each other as they fill in the chart.

B *Pair work*

- Use the model conversation to explain the task. Tell Ss to give additional information in their answers. Point out the answer "I hate bananas, but I love ice cream."
- In pairs, Ss ask and answer questions about their likes and dislikes. They should use all of the information in their charts. Have Ss practice again with new partners.
- **Optional:** As a class activity, elicit the food, sports, and/or music that Ss hate the most and list them on the board. Write the number of students after each thing.

4 PLANS, PLANS, PLANS

This exercise reviews the future with *be going to* in Wh-questions and answers.

A

- Books open. Ask for volunteers to read the seven questions aloud. Make sure they are using the reduced form of *going to* and correct intonation for Wh-questions.
- Ask seven Ss one of the questions each. Elicit complete sentences.
- Read the instructions. Have Ss work individually to write answers to the questions. Then have them write three similar questions on a separate piece of paper. (*Note:* They do not write answers to the questions they write themselves. These questions will be used in part B.)
- While they are working, go around and check their questions individually. Just mark them right or wrong. Let Ss find and correct their own mistakes. If there is time, go back to check their corrections.

B *Group work*

- Have Ss put away the answers they wrote in part A, but keep out the additional questions.
- Put Ss in groups of four or five. Ss ask and answer the questions from part A, including their additional questions. Ss will have prepared answers to the first seven questions, but will need to think of answers on the spot for the additional questions.
- Circulate while they practice to make sure that they are taking turns and to offer help and encouragement.

5 LISTENING

 In this exercise, Ss listen to statements and check the correct responses.

- Books open. Explain the task: Ss hear a question on the audio program and choose the right answer in the book.
- Play the first part of the audio program, and use the example to demonstrate the task.
- Play the audio program as many times as necessary. Ss choose the correct response to each question they hear.

Audio script

1. I think there are going to be twelve people at the barbecue. Oh, wait. Are Helen and Bob going to come?
2. I'm going to go shopping this afternoon. Can we make a shopping list?
3. What do we need for the barbecue? Do we need any soda?
4. Let's serve potato salad. Do you know how to make it?
5. By the way, we need ketchup for the hamburgers. Do we have any?
6. What's your favorite dessert? Do you like strawberries and ice cream?

- Play the audio program again. Stop it after each question and have Ss give the answer chorally.

Answers

1. No. They have the flu.	4. No, I don't.
2. Yes. Let's get some paper.	5. No. We need some.
3. Yes. Buy some.	6. No. I like chocolate cake.

Test 3

See page T-158 of this Teacher's Edition for general instructions on using the tests. Test 3 covers units 9–12. Photocopy the test (pages T-167–T-170) and give a copy to each S. Allow 45–60 minutes for the test. Listening material for the tests is at the end of the Class Audio Program. The Test Audio Scripts and Answer Key start on page T-175 of this book.

Optional activity: Vocabulary from Units 9–12 can be reviewed using the following exercise.

The other question

- See page T-155.

3 LIKE IT OR NOT?

A Complete the chart with one item in each category.

	Food	Sports	Music
Love	....	....	....
Like	....	....	....
Hate	....	....	....

B ***Pair work*** Compare your information.

A: What food do you love?
B: I love bananas. How about you?
What do you think of bananas?
A: I hate bananas, but I love ice cream.

4 PLANS, PLANS, PLANS

A Write answers to these questions. Then write three more questions.

1. Where are you going to go after class today?
2. How are you going to get home today?
3. Who's going to make your dinner this evening?
4. Who are you going to eat dinner with?
5. What are you going to do tonight?
6. What time are you going to go to bed tonight?
7. What are you going to do this weekend?
8. ....
9. ....
10. ....

B ***Group work*** Take turns. Ask and answer the questions.

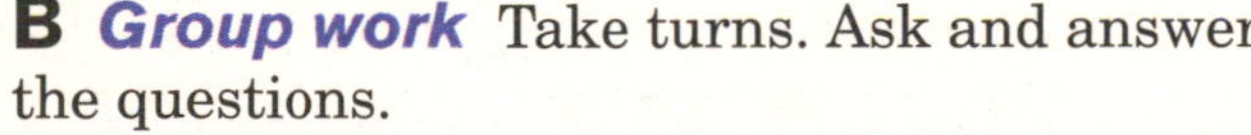

5 LISTENING

Some people are planning a barbecue. Listen to the questions. Check (✓) the correct response.

1. ☑ No. They have the flu.
   ☐ No, she isn't.
2. ☐ Yes, you can go.
   ☐ Yes. Let's get some paper.
3. ☐ Yes. Buy some.
   ☐ No, there aren't any.
4. ☐ No, I'm not.
   ☐ No, I don't.
5. ☐ No. We need some.
   ☐ No, we aren't.
6. ☐ No. I like chocolate cake.
   ☐ No, we don't have any.

13 You can't miss it.

1 WORD POWER *Places and things*

A Where can you buy these things? Match the items with the places. Then listen and practice.
"You can buy aspirin at a drugstore."

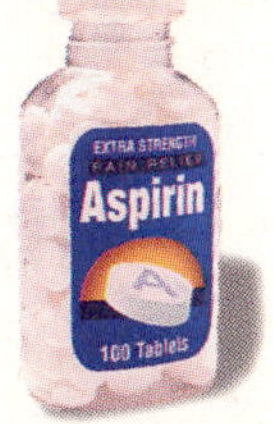

1. aspirin ..*b*..

2. traveler's checks ......

3. bread ......

4. a sandwich ......

5. a dictionary ......

6. stamps ......

7. gasoline ......

8. a sweatshirt ......

a. a bank

b. a drugstore

c. a bookstore

d. a gas station

e. a restaurant

f. a post office

g. a department store

h. a supermarket

B ***Pair work*** What else can you buy or do in these places? Make a list.

A: You can buy cough drops at a drugstore.
B: You can buy cold pills at a drugstore, too.

13 You can't miss it.

This unit introduces expressions for shopping and for asking and giving directions. It presents the names of stores and tourist attractions. It also introduces more prepositions of place and the imperative for giving directions.

Cycle 1, Exercises 1–6

1 WORD POWER *Places and things*

This exercise introduces and reviews the names of places around town and of things to buy.

A

- Books open. Ss study the photos. Read the words aloud. Ss listen and read. Then they listen and repeat.
- Demonstrate the task using the example. Show Ss the things on the left and places where they can buy them on the right.
- Ss work individually to complete the matching task. Walk around to check their work and to give help.
- Ss compare their answers in pairs, making changes if they wish.
- Play the audio program to check the answers. After each sentence, elicit the letter of the correct answer, and write it on the board.

Answers and audio script

1. (**b**) You can buy aspirin at a drugstore.
2. (**a**) You can buy traveler's checks at a bank.
3. (**h**) You can buy bread at a supermarket.
4. (**e**) You can buy a sandwich at a restaurant.
5. (**c**) You can buy a dictionary at a bookstore.
6. (**f**) You can buy stamps at a post office.
7. (**d**) You can buy gasoline at a gas station.
8. (**g**) You can buy a sweatshirt at a department store.

- Play the audio program again. Ss listen and repeat the sentences.
- **Optional:** Say the words in the left column in random order. Call on Ss to say about where you can buy the item.

B *Pair work*

- Explain the task. Give Ss a few minutes to think of other things to buy or do in the eight places in part A. Tell Ss that more than one answer may be possible.
- Model the example conversation with a S.
- Ss work in pairs. Have them make notes of their ideas. Circulate while they talk to hear their ideas.
- To check, elicit Ss' ideas. Make eight lists on the board.

(*Note: Rest room* is introduced in Exercise 3, where Ss can guess the meaning from the context. For now, if Ss ask, you can teach *rest room* (a public bathroom) or let them say "bathroom.")

Possible answers *(there are many other possibilities)*

a bank: deposit a check, get money
a drugstore: buy a newspaper, a card, candy, or a snack
a bookstore: read a magazine, buy a book or a map
a gas station: buy a soda or candy, use the rest room
a restaurant: eat breakfast, lunch, or dinner; have some coffee and a dessert
a post office: mail a letter, send a package
a department store: buy furniture, earrings, a calculator, or a briefcase; use the rest room; eat something
a supermarket: buy other groceries: aspirin, books, magazines, or tissues

- **Optional:** Have Ss spell their answers. Write the answers exactly as Ss spell them. If there is a mistake, Ss must tell you how to correct it in English.

Optional activity: *Where can you buy it?*

- See page T-155.

2 LISTENING

In this exercise, Ss listen for specific information about the things people need to buy and the places they are going to buy them.

A

- Books open. Explain the task. Use the examples in the chart to elicit from Ss that *What* in the chart means "What does the person need?" *Where* means "Where is the person going to buy it?"
- Play the audio program as many times as necessary while Ss fill in the chart.

Audio script

1. MOM: Sarah, are you going to go to the beach with us tomorrow?
   SARAH: Yes, but I want a new swimsuit. I'm going to go to a department store this afternoon. Maybe I can find one.
   MOM: Good. Can I come with you? I need to go downtown to get some things, too.
2. SARAH: Are you going to look for some clothes, Mom?
   MOM: Oh, no. I'm going to go to the supermarket.
   SARAH: What do you need?
   MOM: I just need some cookies for dessert tomorrow. We're going to take a picnic lunch to the beach.
   SARAH: Oh, good. Can you get chocolate cookies?
   MOM: *(laughs)* Sure.
3. MOM: What's wrong?
   DAD: I have a terrible headache.
   MOM: Oh, that's too bad.
   DAD: Do we have any aspirin? I can't find any in the house.
   MOM: No, we don't. Sorry.
   DAD: Hmm. I need some right now. I'm going to go to the drugstore and get some.
4. MIKE: Mom? Let's go to a movie tonight.
   MOM: Good idea, Mike, but which movie?
   MIKE: We need a newspaper to see which movies are playing.
   MOM: Well, your father is going to the drugstore right now. Go with him and get a newspaper.
   MIKE: Oh, great. . . . Dad? Dad!

- Ss compare their answers with a partner, making changes if they wish. Elicit answers and write them on the board. Play the audio program again to verify the answers.

Answers

	What	Where
1. Sarah	*a swimsuit*	*a department store*
2. Mom	*some cookies*	*the supermarket*
3. Dad	*aspirin*	*the drugstore*
4. Mike	*a newspaper*	*the drugstore*

B *Pair work*

- Use the example to demonstrate the task.
- In pairs, Ss talk about where they are going to go and what they need to buy. Encourage Ss to ask their partners questions about their shopping plans.
- Ask two or three Ss to share their shopping plans with the class.

3 CONVERSATION

This conversation introduces expressions for describing locations using prepositions of place.

- Books open. Have Ss look at the illustration. Write this question on the board:
  What's the little boy's problem? (He needs a bathroom.)
- Play the audio program while Ss read and listen for the answers. Elicit the answers.
- Play the audio program again. Ss read and listen. Try to elicit the meanings of *public rest room* (a bathroom in a public place, like a store or a restaurant), *I'm sorry, but I don't think so* (a polite way of saying "no"), and *You can't miss it* (you will see it). Encourage guessing.
- Play the audio program again or model the conversation line by line. Ss listen and read, then look up and repeat.
- Ss practice the conversation in pairs.

Optional activity: *Compound nouns*

- See page T-155.

4 PRONUNCIATION *Checking information*

In this exercise, Ss practice using rising intonation to check information.

- Write the two short conversations on the board. Books closed. Play the audio program. Draw the arrows that show rising intonation.
- Play the audio program again. Ss repeat the conversations.
- Books open. Ss say the conversations in pairs. Have them change partners several times. Walk around to help.
- Ask pairs of Ss to say the conversations for the class. Correct their intonation if necessary.

2 LISTENING

A Listen to the Andersons talk about shopping. What do they need? Where are they going to buy these things? Complete the chart.

	What	Where
1. Sarah	a swimsuit	
2. Mom		the supermarket
3. Dad		
4. Mike		

B ***Pair work*** What shopping plans do you have this week? Tell your partner.

"I'm going to go to a bookstore. I need to buy . . . ."

3 CONVERSATION

 Listen and practice.

Don: Excuse me. Can you help me? Is there a public rest room around here?
Woman: A public rest room? Hmm. I'm sorry. I don't think so.
Don: Oh, no. My son needs a bathroom.
Woman: Well, there's a department store on Main Street.
Don: Where on Main Street?
Woman: It's on the corner of Main and First Avenue.
Don: On the corner of Main and First?
Woman: Yes. It's across from the park. You can't miss it.
Don: Thanks a lot!

4 PRONUNCIATION *Checking information*

Listen and practice. To check information, repeat the information as a question. Use rising intonation.

1. A: The department store is on the corner of Main and First Avenue.
   B: **On the corner of Main and First?**
   A: Yes. It's across from the park.

2. A: There's a coffee shop next to the shoe store.
   B: **Next to the shoe store?**
   A: Yes. You can't miss it.

5 GRAMMAR FOCUS

Prepositions of place

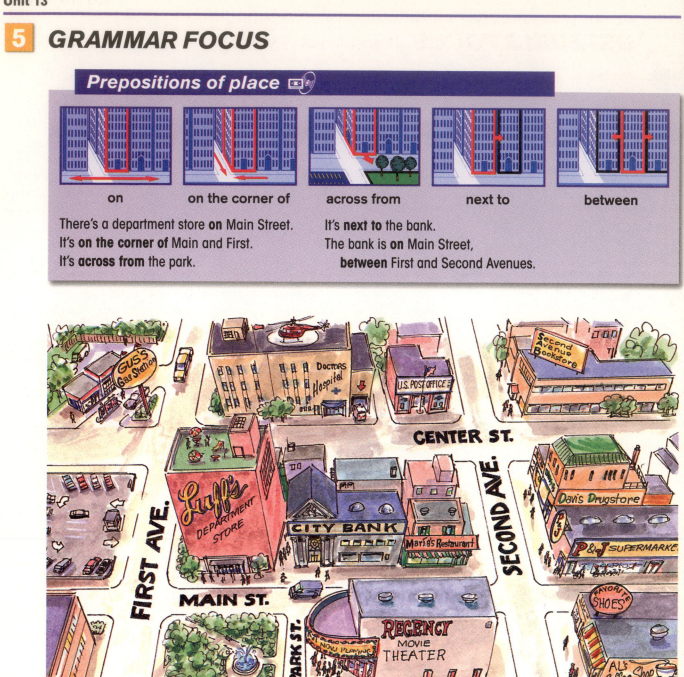

on | on the corner of | across from | next to | between

There's a department store **on** Main Street.
It's **on the corner of** Main and First.
It's **across from** the park.

It's **next to** the bank.
The bank is **on** Main Street,
between First and Second Avenues.

A Look at the map and complete these sentences. Then compare with a partner.

1. Al's Coffee Shop is ....on........ Second Avenue, ...next to........ the shoe store.
2. The Regency Movie Theater is .... Park Street, ... the park.
3. There's a bank .... the department store.
4. There's a drugstore .... Second Avenue. It's .... Main and Center.
5. There's a gas station .... First Avenue and Center Street.

B ***Pair work*** Write three sentences about other places on the map. Read your sentences to your partner. Your partner guesses the places.

A: It's on Main Street, across from the restaurant.
B: Is it the movie theater?
A: Yes, it is.

5 GRAMMAR FOCUS Prepositions of place

This grammar focus presents and practices expressions for giving locations using prepositions of place.

(*Note: Next to* and *on* were first introduced in Unit 2, Exercise 9. Here, the meaning of *next to* is the same. The meaning of *on* is expanded.)

- Books open. Have Ss study the illustrations. Play the audio program to present the information. Ss read and listen.
- Play the audio program, or model the information in the box. Ss listen and repeat.
- **Optional:** Books closed. Check understanding. Say the prepositions at random. Have volunteers go to the board and draw a simple picture to illustrate the preposition.

A

- Demonstrate the task using the example.
- Ss refer to the map and complete the sentences individually.
- Ss compare their answers in pairs, making changes if they wish.
- To check Ss' answers, follow this procedure:

  Have Ss raise their hands when they finish the exercise. Go to the Ss one by one. Make an *X* next to any wrong answers. Ss raise their hands again when they have corrected the wrong answers.

  When a S's answers are all correct, have the S help correct other Ss' work. Have them walk around to check other Ss' papers. They do not have to explain anything or show their own answers – they just make *X*s.

Answers

1. Al's Coffee Shop is **on** Second Avenue, **next to** the shoe store.
2. The Regency Movie Theater is **on** Park Street, **across from** the park.
3. There's a bank **next to** the department store.
4. There's a drugstore **on** Second Avenue. It's **between** Main and Center.
5. There's a gas station **on the corner of** First Avenue and Center Street.

- **Optional:** If Ss need further practice. Write these incomplete sentences on the board, and elicit the missing words from Ss:

  The drugstore is ________ *the supermarket.* (next to)

  The supermarket is ________ *Main and Second.* (on the corner of)

  María's Restaurant is ________ *Main Street.* (on)

  The bank is ________ *First and Second Avenues.* (between)

  The bookstore is ________ *the post office.* (across from)

B *Pair work*

- Use the instructions and the first line of the example conversation to demonstrate the writing task. Ss do not write the name of the place. They write "it" instead.
- Ss work individually to write three sentences. Walk around to give help and to quickly check papers.
- **Alternate presentation:** In pairs or groups of three, Ss work together to correct each paper, one at a time. Walk around to give help.
- Use the example conversation to demonstrate the speaking task.
- In pairs, Ss take turns reading their own sentences and guessing their partner's places. Have Ss change partners several times for additional practice.
- **Optional:** If Ss are familiar with the area around the school, have them write about places in the neighborhood. Then they have a partner guess the place.

Optional activity: *Say that again?*

- See page T-155.

6 LISTENING

In this exercise, Ss listen for information about the location of a place and make inferences about the place.

- Books open. Explain the task: Tell Ss that they are going to hear four conversations about places on the map on page 82. They have to guess the names of the places and write them down.
- Use the example and the first part of the audio program to demonstrate the task.
- Play the rest of the audio program. Ss listen, look at the map, and write down the place names.

Audio script

1. MAN: Hmm. I think it's on Main Street.
   WOMAN: Is it near the Regency Movie Theater?
   MAN: Yes, it is. It's right across from the movie theater.
   WOMAN: Oh, yeah, yeah. There's a restaurant there.
   MAN: Right. It's between the restaurant and Luff's Department Store.
2. WOMAN: Is it near María's Restaurant?
   MAN: Yes, it is. It's on Second Avenue, next to the supermarket.
   WOMAN: P & J Supermarket?
   MAN: Right. It's on Second Avenue, between Main and Center.
   WOMAN: OK. Thank you very much.
3. MAN: Where is it?
   WOMAN: Well, it's near the movie theater.
   MAN: So it's on Park Street?
   WOMAN: No, it's on Main Street, next to the bank.
   MAN: Is it on the corner of Main and Second?
   WOMAN: Yes it is. It's across from P & J.
   MAN: Thanks.
4. WOMAN: Is it near the bookstore?
   MAN: No, it isn't. It's on Second Avenue, across from the movie theater.
   WOMAN: On the corner of Main and Second Avenue?
   MAN: Yes, that's right. It's next to Al's Coffee Shop.
   WOMAN: OK. Thanks.

- In pairs, Ss compare their answers, making changes if they wish. Play the audio program again so that Ss can verify their answers. Write the correct answers on the board.

Answers

1. City Bank	3. María's Restaurant
2. Davis Drugstore	4. Favorite Shoes

Workbook

Workbook Exercises 1–3 on pages 73–75 correspond to Cycle 1, Exercises 1–6, of the Student's Book. Answers to the Workbook exercises begin on page T-182 of this Teacher's Edition.

Cycle 2, Exercises 7–11

7 SNAPSHOT Popular Tourist Attractions in the United States

These photographs give information about tourist attractions in four United States. cities.

- Books open. Have Ss study the information.
- Read the title and the captions aloud as Ss listen and repeat after you.
- Ask the first question, and elicit answers or guesses from Ss.
- Ss turn to the appendix in the back of the book to check their answers. Have Ss read the answers aloud.
- Ask the other questions one at a time. Elicit answers from Ss, and list them on the board.

8 CONVERSATION

This conversation introduces expressions for asking for and giving directions.

- Books open. Point to the illustration. Ask, "Who is the tourist – the man or the woman?" Elicit the answer (the man). Ask, "What city is it?" (New York City).
- Books closed. Write these questions on the board:

  Where does the tourist want to go?
  (To St. Patrick's Cathedral.)

  Where is St. Patrick's Cathedral?
  (On 50th Street/Across from Rockefeller Center.)

  Where is the Empire State Building?
  (Behind the tourist.)
- Play the audio program while Ss read and listen for the answers. Elicit the answers.
- Play the audio program again. Ss read and listen. Point out the two meanings of *right,* as in *on the right* and *right behind you. Right = directly* in the second case.
- Play the audio program again or model the conversation line by line. Ss listen and read, then look up and repeat.
- Ss practice the conversation in pairs using the Look Up and Say technique.
- **Optional:** Have Ss act out the conversation for the class.

6 LISTENING

ASS UDIO NLY

Look at the map in Exercise 5. Listen to four conversations. Where are the people going?

1. *City Bank* .... 2. .... 3. .... 4. ....

7 SNAPSHOT

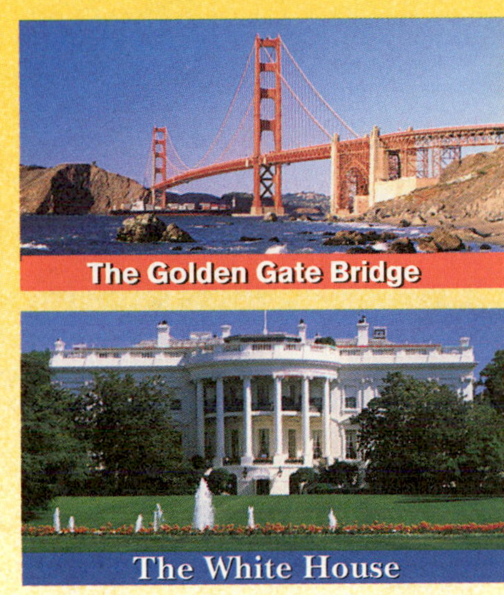

The Museum of Science and Industry
THE STATUE OF LIBERTY

Source: Adapted from *Fodor's USA*

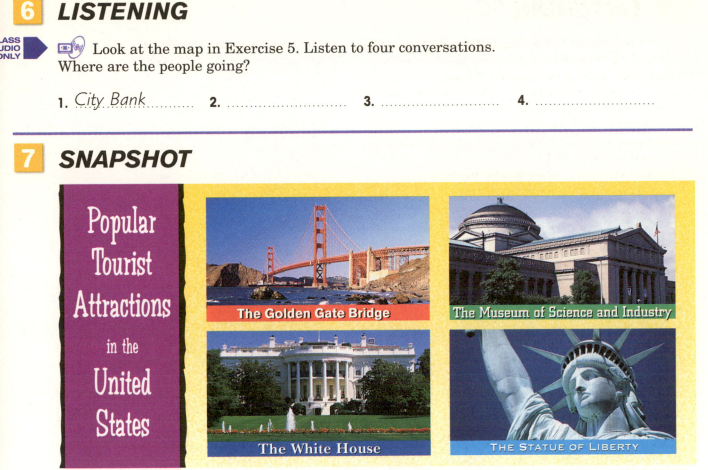

Do you know where these places are? (Check your answers in the appendix.)
Do you know any other tourist attractions in the United States?
What are some popular attractions in your country?

8 CONVERSATION

 Listen and practice.

Tourist: Excuse me, ma'am. Can you help me? How do I get to St. Patrick's Cathedral?
Woman: Just walk up Fifth Avenue to 50th Street. St. Patrick's is on the right.
Tourist: Is it near Rockefeller Center?
Woman: It's right across from Rockefeller Center.
Tourist: Thank you. And where is the Empire State Building? Is it far from here?
Woman: It's right behind you. Just turn around and look up!

9 GRAMMAR FOCUS

Giving directions

How do I get to Rockefeller Center?	How do I get to Bryant Park?
Walk up/Go up Fifth Avenue **to** 49th Street.	**Walk down/Go down** Fifth Avenue **for** eight blocks.
Turn left at 49th Street.	**Turn right** at 42nd Street.
It's **on the right**.	It's **on the left**.

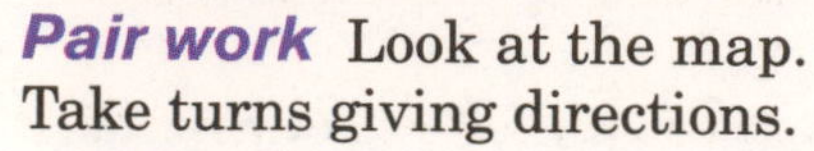

Pair work Look at the map. Take turns giving directions.

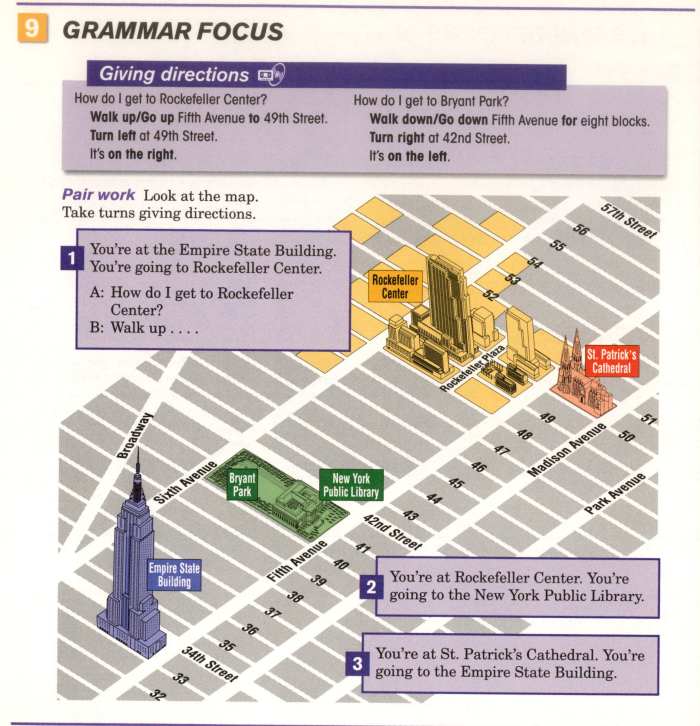

1 You're at the Empire State Building. You're going to Rockefeller Center.

A: How do I get to Rockefeller Center?
B: Walk up . . . .

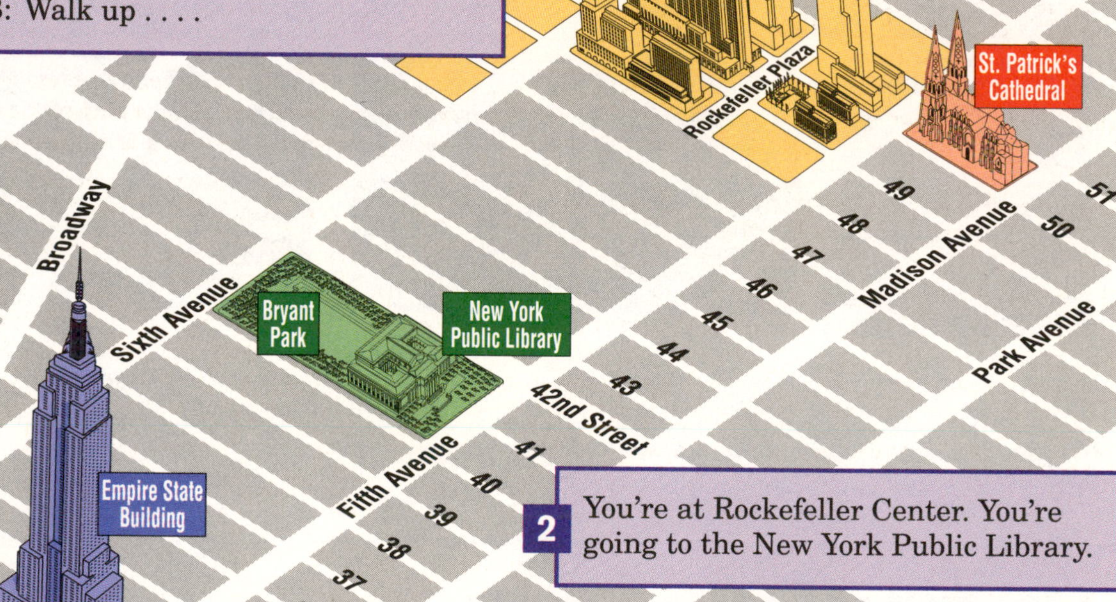

2 You're at Rockefeller Center. You're going to the New York Public Library.

3 You're at St. Patrick's Cathedral. You're going to the Empire State Building.

10 AROUND TOWN

Group work Choose an area of your city and draw a street map. Then take turns asking for and giving directions to places on your map.

A: Excuse me. Is there a bookstore near here?
B: Yes, there is. It's on California Avenue, across from Hannah's Restaurant.
A: How do I get there?
B: Walk . . . .

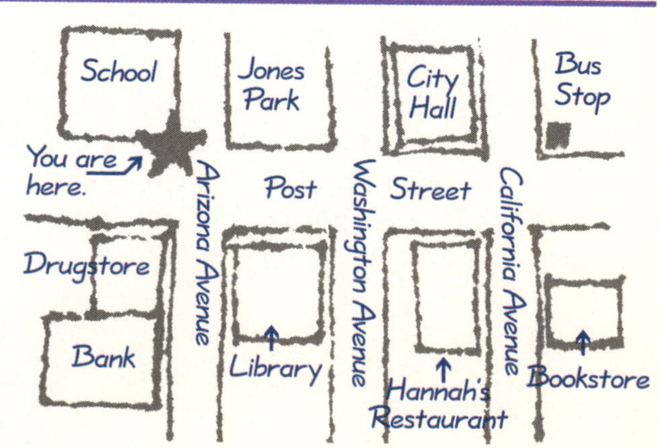

9 GRAMMAR FOCUS Giving directions

This grammar focus presents language for giving directions. Ss practice with a map of New York City.

(*Note:* In this part of New York City, the avenues run north and south. North is *up* and south is *down*. This is true in many other cities, too.)

- Play the audio program to present the questions and answers. Ss read and listen.
- If necessary, use the map to explain *up* and *down, right* and *left,* and *block*.
- Play the audio program again, or model the sentences. Ss listen and repeat.

Pair work

- Books open. Elicit the locations of the five places on the map, for example:

  T: Where's the Empire State Building?
  Ss: It's on Fifth Avenue.
  T: Between?
  Ss: Between 33rd and 34th Streets.
- Explain the task. If necessary, demonstrate the task with a S.
- Ss do the exercise in pairs, changing roles. When they finish, have them change partners and practice again.
- To check comprehension, call on a S to give the directions. If the answer is not complete, allow other Ss to help.

10 AROUND TOWN

This exercise gives more practice in asking for and giving directions.

Group work

- Explain that Ss are going to make maps of real places.
- To get Ss started, elicit names of different areas of the city that they are familiar with. Ask them about the main streets and some of the important places in each area. If necessary, draw a simple map on the board as an example.
- Assign Ss to groups based on the areas they want to map. Groups work to make a map of one area. As they work, go around to give help if necessary.
- When the groups have finished their maps, have two Ss read the model conversation aloud.
- In the same groups, Ss ask for and give locations and directions based on their maps.
- **Optional:** Each S in the group copies their map. Form new groups so that each person has a different map. Ss ask about places on one another's maps.

 READING A walk up Fifth Avenue

In this article, Ss read about a walking tour of New York City that includes some of the places that Ss talked about in Exercise 9. In part A, Ss practice reading for main ideas. In part B, Ss talk about their hometowns.

- Books open. Read the title aloud, and write it on the board.
- The completion of Exercise 9 prepared Ss for this reading, so this reading has a task for Ss to perform while they read rather than a prereading task.
- Ss read the article and follow the directions on the map. Give them enough time so that most of the Ss finish.
- **Optional:** To encourage faster reading, have Ss raise their hands when they finish paragraph 1. When about two-thirds of the Ss have raised their hands, tell everyone to go on to paragraph 2, and so on.
- **Optional:** To give slower readers a chance to finish, play the audio program while Ss read again. Pause after each paragraph to give Ss time to look at the map.

A

- Explain the task. Individually, Ss fill in all the answers they can without reading again.
- Ss read the article again to find the remaining answers. If you wish, play the tape as Ss listen and read.
- Ss check their answers in pairs, making changes if they wish. Elicit the correct answers, and write them on the board.

Answers

1. the Empire State Building
2. Rockefeller Center
3. Bryant Park
4. St. Patrick's Cathedral/the New York Public Library

- **Optional:** Elicit the key words in the questions and have Ss underline them: 1. view, 2. ice-skating, 3. music outdoors, 4. sit quietly indoors. Ask, "Which key words are in the article?" (1–3). For question 4, the key words are not in the article. Ss have to read more carefully and make inferences to find the answers. The cathedral is not "noisy" and it's probably OK to sit there. The library is probably quiet, and it's probably OK to sit there.

B *Group work*

- Read the instructions aloud, and go over the questions.
- Have three Ss read the example conversation aloud. Student C completes the last sentence.
- Ask several Ss questions about their hometowns. Try to elicit at least one negative answer:

  T: Where can you go ice-skating in your hometown, Juan?
  S1: You can't go ice-skating in my hometown.
  T: Where can you get a good view of your hometown, Min Ho?
  S2: There's a mountain near my hometown.
- Divide the class into groups. If possible, have different hometowns represented in each group. If most of the Ss are from the same large city, they can talk about their neighborhoods instead of their hometowns.
- Ss take turns asking and answering the questions in groups.
- Ask for volunteers to share what they found out about other Ss' hometowns.

INTERCHANGE 13 Directions

See page T-120 of this Teacher's Edition for notes.

Workbook

Workbook Exercises 4–7 on pages 76–78 correspond to Cycle 2, Exercises 7–11, of the Student's Book. Answers to the Workbook exercises begin on page T-182 of this Teacher's Edition.

Optional activity: *What's near Rita's house?*

- See page T-155.

11 READING

A walk up FIFTH Avenue

As you read, look at the map on page 84.

1 Start your tour at the **Empire State Building** on Fifth Avenue between 33rd and 34th Streets. This building has 102 floors. Take the elevator to the 102nd floor for a great view of New York City.

2 Now walk up Fifth Avenue seven blocks to the **New York Public Library**. The entrance is between 40th and 42nd Streets. This library holds over 10 million books. Behind the library is **Bryant Park**. In the summer, there's an outdoor café, and at lunch hour, there are free music concerts.

3 Walk up Sixth Avenue to 49th Street. You're standing in the middle of the 19 buildings of **Rockefeller Center**. Turn right on 49th Street, walk another block, and turn left. You're in Rockefeller Plaza. In the winter, you can ice-skate in the rink there.

4 Right across from Rockefeller Center on Fifth Avenue is **St. Patrick's Cathedral**. It's modeled after the cathedral in Cologne, Germany. Go inside St. Patrick's and leave the noisy city behind. Look at the beautiful blue windows. Many of these windows come from France.

A Read the article. Where can you . . . ?

1. have a view of the city ....
2. go ice-skating in the winter ....
3. listen to music outdoors ....
4. sit quietly indoors ....

B ***Group work*** Ask the questions in part A. Answer using information about your hometown.

A: Where can you listen to music outdoors?
B: You can listen to music in the park next to the river.
C: Or you can . . . .

interchange 13

Directions

Find your way around. Student A turns to page IC-16. Student B turns to page IC-18.

14 Did you have a good weekend?

1 SNAPSHOT

Which of these chores do you do on weekends?
What other chores do you do?
What else do you do on weekends?

2 CONVERSATION

 Listen and practice.

Michael: Did you have a good weekend?
Jennifer: Yes, I did. But I feel a little tired today.
Michael: Really? Why?
Jennifer: Well, on Saturday, I exercised in the morning. Then my roommate and I cleaned and shopped. And then I visited my parents.
Michael: So what did you do on Sunday?
Jennifer: I studied for the test all day.
Michael: Oh, no! Do we have a test today? I didn't study! I just watched TV all weekend!

14 Did you have a good weekend?

This unit presents expressions for talking about the weekend using the simple past. It includes statements and yes/no questions with regular and some irregular verbs.

Cycle 1, Exercises 1–5

1 SNAPSHOT Some Common Chores

This graphic gives information about common household chores. The questions relate the information to Ss' own lives.

(*Note:* In the majority of homes in the United States and Canada, all the adults in a household work and the children are busy during the week with school. They do many household chores on weekends.)

- Books open. Have Ss study the pictures. Read the title and the captions aloud one by one. Ss listen and repeat. (*Note: Clean the house* includes *vacuum and dust.* It can also include chores like *put things away, mop the floors,* and *clean the bathroom and kitchen.*)

Ask the questions one by one.
Other weekend chores might be *cook, take out the trash, wash the car, go to the gym,* and so on.
Other weekend activities might be *see friends, read, go to the movies, eat out, go dancing,* and so on.

(Note: One person's chore may be another person's leisure activity. Common examples are *cook, go to the gym,* and *work in the yard.)*

- **Optional:** List the chores on the board. Take a survey. Ask Ss which is their least favorite chore. Ss vote by raising their hands. Try to elicit reasons for their answers.
- **Optional:** List Ss' answers to each question on the board.

2 CONVERSATION

This conversation introduces expressions for talking about activities in the past.

- Books open. Have Ss look at the illustration and the names in the conversation. Ask, "What's Jennifer talking about?" (studying) "What's Michael talking about?" (watching TV).
- Play the audio program while Ss read and listen.
- Play the audio program again. Ss read and listen. If there are questions about vocabulary, see if other Ss can answer them.
- Play the audio program again or model the conversation line by line. Ss listen and read, then look up and repeat.
- Ss practice the conversation in pairs using the Look Up and Say technique.
- **Optional:** Have a few Ss act out the conversation for the class.

3 GRAMMAR FOCUS *Simple past statements: regular verbs*

This grammar focus presents and practices statements with regular verbs in the simple past tense.

(*Note:* The simple past tense is used for actions that began and ended in the past.)

- Books open. Play the audio program to present the information in the first grammar box. Ss read and listen.
- Point out the contraction *didn't. Didn't* is the contraction of the full forms *did not*. The auxiliary verb *did* (the past of *do*) is used to form negative statements and is followed by the base form of the main verb.
- **Optional:** Refer Ss back to Unit 6, page 35, Exercise 4. Point out that the construction of negative statements in the simple past is similar to the construction of negative statements in the simple present. In the simple past, there is only one auxiliary form (*didn't*) versus the two forms in the simple present (*don't/doesn't*).
- Go over the information in the spelling box. The examples illustrate these rules for spelling regular verbs in the simple past:
  1. For the past tense of most regular verbs, just add *-ed* (watch**ed**/stay**ed**),
  2. If the base form ends in *e*, just add *-d* (exercise**d**).
  3. If the base form ends in a consonant + *y*, in most cases change the *y* to *i* and add *-ed* (stud**ied**).
  4. If the base form ends in a vowel + a consonant, double the consonant and add *-ed* (shop**ped**).
- Play the audio program again, or model the sentences. Ss listen and repeat.
- Use the example to explain and demonstrate the task. Verbs with *not* (for example, *not call*) need *didn't.*
- **Optional:** Elicit verbs that are in the exercise but not in the grammar box (*wait, call, talk, listen, invite, cook, work, walk*). List them on the board. Elicit the past tense form of each one.
- Ss complete the exercise individually.
- To check answers, have Ss read their completed sentences, spelling each past tense verb. Write the correct answers on the board.

Answers

2. I **stayed** home and **watched** TV.
3. My friend Frank **visited** me. We **talked** and **listened** to music.
4. We **invited** some friends over, and we **cooked** a great meal.
5. I **studied** on Saturday, but I **didn't work** on Sunday. I **walked** to the mall and **shopped** all day.

Optional activity: *True or false?*

- See page T-148.

4 PRONUNCIATION *Regular simple past verbs*

In this exercise, Ss practice the three different pronunciations of the regular simple past ending.

(*Note:* These are the rules for pronouncing the regular simple past ending:

1. When the verb ends in a voiceless consonant (except /t/), use /t/ as in *worked* and *watched.*
2. When the verb ends in a vowel or a voiced consonant (except /d/), use /d/ as in *cleaned* and *stayed.*
3. When the verb ends in /d/ or /t/, add a whole syllable: /ɪd/ as in *invited* and *visited.*

For beginning Ss, it is most important to know when to add the extra syllable /ɪd/.)

A

- Books open. Point out the three pronunciation symbols at the top of the chart. They represent the pronunciation of *d* or *ed* in the verbs. Tell Ss to listen for the different pronunciations.
- Play the audio program. Ss listen and read.
- Play the audio program again. Ss listen and repeat.
- Say the simple forms of the verbs in the chart in random order. Ss say the past form. Practice until Ss are pronouncing the verbs correctly.

B

- Books closed. Play the audio program once. Ss listen only.
- Books open. Play the audio program as many times as necessary while Ss do the task. Ss listen and write the verbs in the correct column in the chart.
- Ss compare their answers in pairs, making changes if they wish.
- Play the audio program again. Ss check any answers they are unsure of.
- Elicit the correct answers, and write them on the board.

Answers

/t/	/d/	/ɪd/
worked	cleaned	invited
watched	stayed	visited
asked	called	needed
cooked	exercised	rented
shopped	listened	waited
walked	studied	wanted

Optional activity: *Role play*

- See page T-156.

3 GRAMMAR FOCUS

Simple past statements: regular verbs

I	**studied**	on Sunday.	I	**didn't study**	on Saturday.
You	**watched**	TV all weekend.	You	**didn't watch**	TV during the week.
She	**stayed**	home on Sunday.	She	**didn't stay**	home on Saturday.
We	**visited**	my parents.	We	**didn't visit**	any friends.
You	**shopped**	for groceries.	You	**didn't shop**	for clothes.
They	**exercised**	on Saturday.	They	**didn't exercise**	on Sunday.

didn't = did not

Spelling

watch → watch**ed**
exercise → exercise**d**
stud**y** → stud**ied**
stay → stay**ed**
shop → shop**ped**

Complete these sentences with the correct verb forms. Then compare with a partner.

What did you do this weekend?

1. I *waited* (wait) for a phone call, but my girlfriend *didn't call* (not call).
2. I .... (stay) home and .... (watch) TV.
3. My friend Frank .... (visit) me. We .... (talk) and .... (listen) to music.
4. We .... (invite) some friends over, and we .... (cook) a great meal.
5. I .... (study) on Saturday, but I .... (not work) on Sunday. I .... (walk) to the mall and .... (shop) all day.

4 PRONUNCIATION Regular simple past verbs

A Listen and practice. Notice the pronunciation of simple past endings.

/t/	/d/	/ɪd/
worked	cleaned	invited
watched	stayed	visited
....	....	....
....	....	....
....	....	....
....	....	....

B Listen and write these verbs under the correct sounds.

asked	cooked	listened	rented	studied	walked
called	exercised	needed	shopped	waited	wanted

5 DID YOU OR DIDN'T YOU?

Pair work Write about four things you did and four things you didn't do last weekend. Use these or other expressions. Then tell your partner about your weekend.

listen to music

work in the yard

wash my clothes

relax

rent a video

invite friends to my house

cook a meal

visit my family

Things I did last weekend	Things I didn't do last weekend
I listened to music.	I didn't work in the yard.

A: I listened to music last weekend.
B: I listened to music, too. I didn't work in the yard.
A: I didn't work in the yard, either.

6 WORD POWER *Irregular simple past verbs*

A Listen and practice. Notice the irregular simple past forms.

I **slept** late on Saturday. I **got up** at ten, **read** the newspaper, and **ate** breakfast.

We **saw** a movie. We **bought** popcorn, **drank** some soda, and **had** a lot of fun!

I **met** a friend at the park and **went** jogging. Then I **came** home and **felt** really tired.

B Complete the chart. Then compare with a partner.

Present	Past	Present	Past	Present	Past
buy	bought	....	felt	....	met
....	came	....	got up	....	read /rɛd/
....	drank	....	went	....	saw
....	ate	....	had	....	slept

For a list of more irregular past forms, see the appendix.

5 DID YOU OR DIDN'T YOU?

In this exercise, Ss practice the simple past of regular verbs while talking about what they did last weekend. They use *too* and *either*.

- Books open. Have Ss study the illustrations and captions. Call on Ss to model the phrases.
- Demonstrate the writing task using the two example sentences.
- Working individually, Ss write sentences about things they did and didn't do last weekend. As they write, go around the classroom to give help.
- **Alternate presentation:** Tell Ss to use verbs from Exercises 3, 4, and 5. Write two more examples on the board: "I called my family," "I didn't study."

  The verbs are:

asked	needed	visited
called	relaxed	waited
cleaned	rented	walked
cooked	shopped	wanted
exercised	stayed	washed
invited	studied	watched
listened	talked	worked

Pair work

- Introduce the speaking task. Have two Ss read the model conversation aloud, using the Look Up and Say technique.
- Help Ss figure out that *too* is for affirmative sentences and *either* is for negative sentences. Explain to Ss that they only use *too* and *either* when they did or didn't do the same things as their partners. Also model a conversation like this with a S:

  S: I listened to music last weekend.
  T: I didn't listen to music. I worked in the yard.
- In pairs, Ss talk about what they did and didn't do last weekend. If time permits, have Ss change partners once or twice to extend the practice.
- **Optional:** Take a quick survey of the things Ss did, and write the results on the board.

Workbook

Workbook Exercises 1–4 on pages 79–82 correspond to Cycle 1, Exercises 1–5, of the Student's Book. Answers to the Workbook Exercises begin on page T-182 of this Teacher's Edition.

Cycle 2, Exercises 6–11

6 WORD POWER *Irregular simple past verbs*

This exercise introduces and practices the simple past forms of some irregular verbs.

A

- Books open. Explain the task. Show Ss that the irregular simple past verb forms are in boldface type.
- Play the audio program. Ss listen and read.
- Play the audio program again or model the sentences line by line. Ss listen and repeat.

B

- Use the example to demonstrate the task
- Show Ss that the verbs in the chart are in the statements in part A. Ss know these verbs in the present tense. Ss use the context of the statements to figure out the verbs.
- Ss complete the chart individually.
- Ss compare their answers with a partner, making changes if they wish.
- Ss check their answers, individually or in pairs, referring to the list in the appendix.

Answers

buy	bought	**go**	went
come	came	**have**	had
drink	drank	**meet**	met
eat	ate	**read**	read
feel	felt	**see**	saw
get up	got up	**sleep**	slept

7 CONVERSATION

This conversation introduces expressions for talking about past activities using yes/no questions and short answers in the simple past.

- Books open. Have Ss look at the illustration. Set the scene: Laura and Erica are talking about last weekend. Write this question on the board:

  What did Erica and Sam do? (They saw the new Leonardo DiCaprio movie. They went to a dance club.)
- Play the audio program while Ss read and listen for the answers. Elicit the answers.
- Play the audio program again. Ss read and listen. It should not be necessary to explain vocabulary.
- Play the audio program again or model the conversation line by line. Ss listen and read, then look up and repeat.
- Ss practice the conversation in pairs using the Look Up and Say technique.
- **Optional:** Have a few Ss act out the conversation for the class.
- **Optional:** To prepare Ss for the Grammar Focus exercise, write the following on the board:

  What does Laura want to know?
  1. ?
  2. ?
  3. ?
  4. ?

  Books closed. Tell Ss that Laura asks four questions. Tell them to listen for the questions. Then play the audio program as many times as necessary. Elicit any words Ss can say after each listening. Write their correct words on the board with blanks for missing words, for example:

  1. Did you ___ ___ ___ Sam?

  Books open. Ss use their books to tell you the rest of the words.

8 GRAMMAR FOCUS *Simple past yes/no questions*

This grammar focus presents yes/no questions and short answers in the simple past. It practices the grammar with some of the irregular verbs presented in Exercise 6.

- Books open. Play the audio program to present the questions and answers. Ss read and listen.
- Point out the use of the auxiliary *did* (the past of *do*) in past tense questions and short answers. In questions, *did* is used as the past tense marker. The main verb is in the base form.
- **Optional:** Refer Ss back to Unit 6, page 38, Exercise 10. Point out that the construction of yes/no questions in the simple past is similar to the construction of yes/no questions in the simple present. In the simple past, there is only one auxiliary form (*did*) versus the two forms in the simple present (*do/does*).
- Play the audio program again or model the sentences. Ss listen and repeat.

A

- Use the example to explain and demonstrate the task.
- Ss complete the exercise individually.
- When Ss finish working, put them in pairs to compare their answers. They raise their hands so that you can check their papers.
- To check answers, follow this procedure:

  When a pair is sure their answers are correct, they raise their hands. Go to the Ss one by one. Make an *X* next to any wrong answers. Ss raise their hands again when they have corrected the wrong answers.

  When a S's answers are all correct, have the S help correct other Ss' work. Have them walk around to check other Ss' papers. They do not have to explain anything or show their own answers – they just make *X*s.

Answers

1. A: **Did** you **have** a good weekend?
   B: Yes, I **did**. I **had** a great weekend. I just relaxed.
2. A: **Did** you **eat out** on Friday night?
   B: No, I **didn't**. Some friends **came** over. We **ate** dinner at my apartment. Then we **went** to a movie.
3. A: **Did** you **read** the newspaper this morning?
   B: Yes, I **did**. I **read** it at work.
4. A: **Did** you **have** breakfast this morning?
   B: No, I **didn't**. I **got up** late. But I **bought** a cup of coffee and **drank** it on the bus.

- Ss practice the conversations in pairs. Walk around to help with pronunciation and expression.

B *Pair work*

- Write the four questions from part A on the board or have Ss write them.
- Books closed. Demonstrate the task. Have Ss ask you the questions one by one. Give answers that are different from the answers in part A.
- In pairs, and with books closed, Ss take turns asking and answering the questions. Have them change roles and then partners.

Optional activity: *Yesterday*

- See page T-156.

7 CONVERSATION

Listen and practice.

Laura: So, did you go out with Sam?
Erica: Yes, I did. We went out on Saturday night. We saw the new Leonardo DiCaprio movie.
Laura: Did you like it?
Erica: I liked it a lot, but Sam didn't.
Laura: Oh, well. Did you do anything else?
Erica: Yeah. We went to a dance club.
Laura: Did you have fun?
Erica: Yes, we did. We had a great time. And we're going to go out again next weekend.

8 GRAMMAR FOCUS

Simple past yes/no questions

Did you **go** out this weekend?
Yes, I **did**. I **went** to the movies.

Did you **have** a good time?
No, I **didn't**. I **had** a terrible time.

A Complete these conversations with the correct verb forms. Then practice with a partner.

1. A: ..Did... you ..have... (have) a good weekend?
   B: Yes, I .... I .... (have) a great weekend. I just relaxed.
2. A: .... you .... (eat out) on Friday night?
   B: No, I .... Some friends .... (come) over. We .... (eat) dinner at my apartment. Then we .... (go) to a movie.
3. A: .... you .... (read) the newspaper this morning?
   B: Yes, I .... I .... (read) it at work.
4. A: .... you .... (have) breakfast this morning?
   B: No, I .... I .... (get up) late. But I .... (buy) a cup of coffee and .... (drink) it on the bus.

B ***Pair work*** Take turns asking the questions in part A. Answer with your own information.

9 LISTENING

Listen to Andy, Mark, Patrick, and Matt talk about their weekends. What did they do on Saturday morning? Write their names under the pictures.

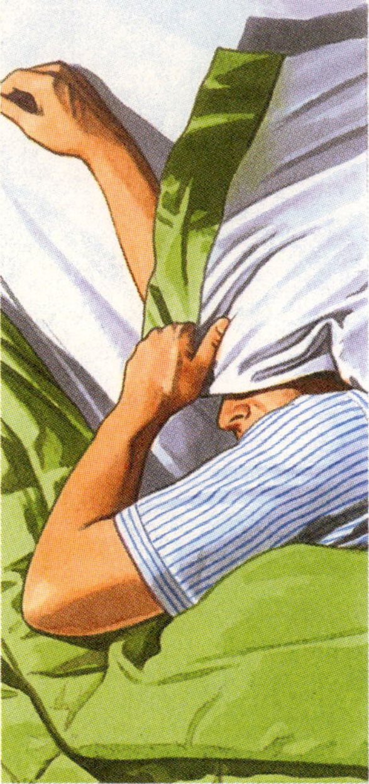

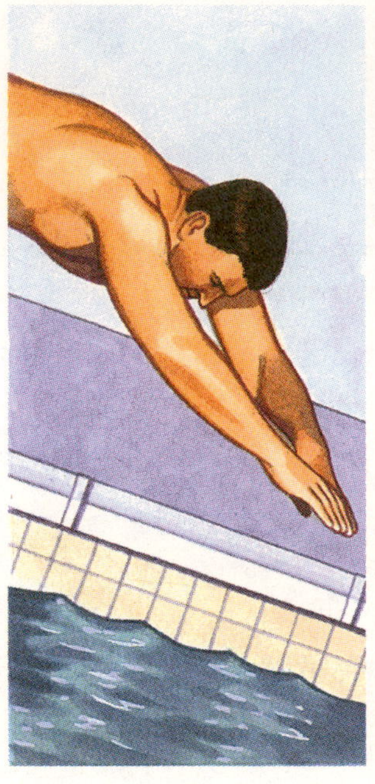

....

10 YOUR WEEKEND

A ***Pair work*** Check (✓) seven questions to ask your partner about last weekend. Then take turns asking and answering questions.

☐ Did you read any books last weekend?	☐ Did you have dinner at a restaurant?
☐ Did you write any letters?	☐ Did you see any movies?
☐ Did you work around the house?	☐ Did you go dancing?
☐ Did you exercise or play any sports?	☐ Did you meet any interesting people?
☐ Did you go shopping?	☐ Did you talk on the phone?
☐ Did you buy any clothes?	☐ Did you sleep late?
☐ Did you see any friends?	☐ Did you study?

A: Did you read any books last weekend?
B: Yes, I did. I finished John Grisham's new book. I loved it! Did you go shopping?
A: No, I didn't. I didn't have any money.

B ***Class activity*** Tell the class about your partner's weekend.

"Maria read John Grisham's new book. She loved it. . . ."

interchange 14

Past and present

Are you different now from when you were a child?
Turn to page IC-17.

9 LISTENING

In this exercise, Ss listen for specific information given about the past.

- Books open. Have Ss look at the illustration. Elicit key vocabulary. Ask, "What are they doing?" (shopping, sleeping, swimming, reading).
- Write the names Andy, Mark, Patrick, and Matt on the board. Explain the task: Ss listen to four short conversations. They listen for information about what each man did on Saturday morning. Show Ss that they need to write the names under the pictures.
- Play the audio program as many times as necessary while Ss listen and write the names.

Audio script

Conversation 1
WOMAN: Hey, Andy. Did you go to the beach on Saturday?
ANDY: No, I didn't. I got up too late. I slept until noon.

Conversation 2
WOMAN: Hi, Mark. How are you?
MARK: Fine, thanks.
WOMAN: Did you have a good weekend?
MARK: Yeah, I did. I stayed in bed all day Saturday.
WOMAN: Wow! All day?
MARK: Yeah. I read a really good book!

Conversation 3
WOMAN: So, Patrick, did you do anything interesting this weekend?
PATRICK: Well, I went shopping for clothes on Saturday morning.
WOMAN: Did you buy anything?
PATRICK: No, I didn't. Everything's so expensive these days.

Conversation 4
WOMAN: I called you on Saturday morning, Matt. But there was no answer.
MATT: Oh? Well, I left the house early. I went to the swimming pool.
WOMAN: Oh, so you got a little exercise.
MATT: Yeah, I did. And I really enjoyed it.

- Elicit the correct answers, and write them on the board.

Answers (in order from left to right)

Patrick, Andy, Matt, Mark

10 YOUR WEEKEND

This exercise practices asking and answering past tense questions.

A *Pair work*

- Have volunteers each read one of the questions aloud.
- Individually, Ss check seven questions they want to ask someone.
- Ask two Ss to read the model conversation aloud. Point out that the speakers don't just say "yes" or "no," they add information to their answers.
- Ask two more Ss to demonstrate with another question. Point out that the *first* question of their conversation needs to include ". . . last weekend?" For example, "Did you write any letters last weekend?"
- Ss take turns asking and answering questions in pairs. Walk around as Ss talk to help them add information to their answers.
- **Optional:** While Ss practice, have them take notes in preparation for part B. Put these notes on the board as a model:
  Saturday – saw a friend – went shopping – didn't buy anything
  Sunday – watched TV – studied

B *Class activity*

- Use the model to demonstrate the task. Add to the model in the book, for example:
  "Maria read John Grisham's book. She loved it. On Sunday, she saw a friend. They went shopping at the mall, buy she didn't buy anything. In the evening, she studied history and math."
- **Optional:** If you wrote notes on the board in part A, use them to demonstrate this task. Point to the notes on the board as you speak.
- Ask Ss to report to the class about their partners' weekends. In a large class, you may prefer to do this in groups.

INTERCHANGE 14 Past and present

See page T-122 of this Teacher's Edition for notes.

READING *The Changing Weekend*

In this article, Ss read a comparison of American weekend activities at the beginning of the twentieth century and today. The exercises practice reading for specific information, making inferences, and giving opinions.

- Books closed. Read the title aloud and write it on the board.
- Introduce the prereading task. Ask the questions one by one. Elicit ideas from Ss, and write them on the board.
- **Alternate presentation:** You may want to ask the second question first: "What do Americans do on weekends?" Then write the dates 1900–1925 on the board. Ask, "What did Americans do on weekends in the early twentieth century?"

A

- **Optional:** Books open. Help Ss preview the article. Ask questions to elicit these observations from Ss:
  1. The article has two parts: *Then* (= in the past) and *Now*.
  2. Each part has a photograph.
  3. The first paragraph in each part looks different (green print).
  4. The other paragraphs have red dots.

  Put these questions on the board. Tell Ss to answer the questions while they read. Elicit the answers after they have read it.
  Which paragraphs give general information? (The first paragraph in each part.)
  Which paragraphs give examples? (The paragraphs with the red dots.)
- Books open. Ss read the article. Let Ss read it at least twice. If you wish, play the audio program the second time they read.
- Introduce the diary, and read it aloud. Ss listen and read.
- Use the example to demonstrate the task. Point out the date of the diary. Then read the first sentence of the diary aloud. Ask, "Was this possible in 1925?" (No. There were no theme parks in 1925. There were only amusement parks.) Show Ss that the information is in the two second paragraphs in the article.
- Working individually or in pairs, Ss make the other corrections in the diary.
- While Ss are working, write the six sentences of the diary on the board, including the correction in the first sentence.
- When Ss are ready, send five Ss to the board to correct the other sentences. If the sentence is correct in the diary, they write *OK.*
- Go over the answers with the class, correcting the sentences on the board if necessary. Elicit where Ss found the information for each sentence.

Possible answers

1. Betty and I took a streetcar to the ~~theme~~ *amusement* park on Saturday.
2. We rode on the Ferris wheel and the roller coaster. **OK**
3. On Saturday night, I took Betty to a movie at the ~~multiplex~~ *movie theater*.
4. The movie ~~had really interesting sound effects~~ *was really interesting* or *was really good*
5. On Sunday afternoon, I bicycled with my sister. **OK**
6. By Sunday night, I felt pretty tired, so I stayed home and ~~watched TV~~ *listened to the radio*.

B *Group work*

- Ask, "In the United States, the weekend changed in the twentieth century. Did it change in your country, too?" Elicit answers from several Ss.
- Tell Ss that they need to give examples about the past and present. Give one or two examples, or elicit them from Ss.
- If Ss are all from the same country, they can form groups and begin talking right away. If they are from different countries, give them a few minutes to think before they form groups. They may want to write down a few ideas.
- While Ss discuss the question, go around to give help.
- **Optional:** Ss choose one person to be the group's secretary and take notes on the group's answers. After the discussion, the secretaries report their group's ideas to the class.

Workbook

Exercises 5–8 on pages 82–84 correspond to Cycle 2, Exercises 6–11, of the Student's Book. Answers to the Workbook exercises begin on page T-182 of this Teacher's Edition.

Optional activity: *Game – Tic-Tac-Toe*

- See page T-151. In this unit, Ss practice questions and statements in the simple past with regular and irregular verbs.

11 READING

THE CHANGING WEEKEND

What do you think Americans in the early twentieth century (1900–1925) did on weekends? What do they do on weekends now?

THEN

Once upon a time, people spent lots of time at home on weekends. Then, new inventions changed the weekend.

- People used electric streetcars to travel in cities. On weekends, they rode the streetcars to amusement parks. Young people liked roller coasters and the Ferris wheel.
- The first movies lasted only one minute. Soon, however, movies got longer. By the 1920s, movie theaters sold millions of tickets each week! In 1927, movies finally had sound. Sometimes, people stayed home instead, and listened to another new invention – the radio.
- People in cities worked indoors during the week, so they wanted to be outdoors on weekends. Bicycling became a popular activity.

NOW

With more time, money, and inventions, people have many more choices.

- They can visit huge "theme parks" like Disney World and ride modern roller coasters that go higher and faster than ever before.
- They can choose from lots of different movies at a multiplex (a building with many movie theaters) or watch a video at home.
- Many people jog, bicycle, work out at the gym, or play sports. Others turn on their TV and watch sports.

A Read the article. Then read a passage from a man's diary from 1925. Based on the article, some of the things he writes about are not possible. Rewrite the passage with information that is possible.

Monday, June 8, 1925

(1) Betty and I took a streetcar to the ~~theme~~ amusement park on Saturday. (2) We rode on the Ferris wheel and the roller coaster. (3) On Saturday night, I took Betty to a movie at the multiplex. (4) The movie had really interesting sound effects. (5) On Sunday afternoon, I bicycled with my sister. (6) By Sunday night, I felt pretty tired, so I stayed home and watched TV.

B ***Group work*** Talk about this question.

Do you think the weekend changed a lot from the early twentieth century to now in your country? Explain.

15 Where were you born?

1 SNAPSHOT

Famous Americans Born in Other Places

John Leguizamo

*Born in Colombia in 1964
*TV, theater, and film actor
*Playwright

Carolina Herrera

*Born in Venezuela in 1939
*Fashion designer
*Founder of an internationally known fashion-design house

Midori

*Born in Japan in 1971
*Concert violinist
*Founder of an organization to promote music education

Jerry Yang

*Born in Taiwan in 1968
*Co-founder of Yahoo! Inc., the first directory to the Internet's World Wide Web

Are there famous people in your country from other places? Who?
Do you have friends or relatives from other countries? Where are they from?

2 CONVERSATION

 Listen and practice.

Chuck: Where were you born, Melissa?
Melissa: I was born in Korea.
Chuck: Oh! So you weren't born in the U.S.
Melissa: No. I came here in 1995.
Chuck: Hmm. You were pretty young.
Melissa: Well, I was seventeen.
Chuck: Did you go to college right away?
Melissa: No. My English wasn't very good, so I took English classes for two years first.
Chuck: Your English is really fluent now.
Melissa: Thanks. Your English is pretty good, too!
Chuck: Yeah, but I was born here!

15 Where were you born?

This unit presents expressions for talking about personal history, school experiences, and the recent past. It presents the past of be *and* Wh-*questions in the simple past. It also introduces dates with years.*

Cycle 1, Exercises 1–5

1 SNAPSHOT *Famous Americans Born in Other Places*

These pictures give biographical information about four famous Americans.

- Books open. Have Ss study the pictures.
- Read the title and the four profiles aloud.
- Try to elicit the meaning of *founder of* (he/she began something). If necessary, answer questions about other vocabulary.
- Ask Ss if they are familiar with the people in the Snapshot. If Ss are familiar with any of the people, ask if they have any additional information to add.
- Ask the questions one by one. List Ss' answers about people and their countries on the board.
- **Optional:** Also ask, "Are there famous people *from* your country *in* other places? Who?"
- **Optional:** Have Ss answer the last question in groups. Encourage them to give as much information as they can about their friends and relatives from other countries.

2 CONVERSATION

This conversation introduces expressions for talking about personal histories. It introduces *was* and *were.*

- Books open. Have Ss look at the illustration and the names in the conversation. Ask, "Where is Melissa from?" Have Ss scan the conversation for the answer (Korea). (*Note:* Chuck is a nickname for Charles.)
- Play the audio program while Ss read and listen.
- Play the audio program again. Ss read and listen. Try to elicit the meanings of *pretty, right away,* and *fluent.* All of them can be guessed from the context.
- Play the audio program again or model the conversation line by line. Ss listen and read, then look up and repeat.
- Ss practice the conversation in pairs using the Look Up and Say technique.
- **Optional:** Have Ss change roles so that each S practices all the lines.
- **Optional:** Have Ss change partners for additional practice.
- **Optional:** Have Ss act out the conversation for the class.

3 GRAMMAR FOCUS Statements with the past of be

This grammar focus has two grammar boxes. This first box presents affirmative and negative statements with the past of *be.*

- Books open. Play the audio program to present the information in the grammar box. Ss read and listen.
- **Optional:** Point to yourself and say one affirmative and one negative sentence about your birthplace, for example, "I was born in the United States. I wasn't born in Japan." Then say, "What about you?" and elicit similar statements from several Ss.
- Play the audio program again or model the sentences. Ss listen and repeat.

A

- Use the example to explain and demonstrate the task.
- Ss complete the exercise individually.
- Ss compare their answers with a partner, making changes if they wish.
- Have Ss write the answers on the board. Finally, call on Ss to read the completed sentences.

Answers

My family and I **were** all born in Korea – we **weren't** born in the U.S. I **was** born in the city of Inchon, and my brother **was** born there, too. My parents **weren't** born in Inchon. They **were** born in the capital, Seoul.

Questions with the past of be

This grammar focus has two grammar boxes. This second box presents simple present Wh-questions and yes/no questions with the past of *be.*

(*Note:* The structure of questions with the past of *be* (*was/were*) is the same as with the present of *be* (*am/is/are*).)

- Play the audio program to present the language in the second grammar box and in the small box labeled *Years.*
- Play the audio program again or model the sentences. Ss listen and repeat.

B

- Use the example to explain and demonstrate the writing portion of the task.
- Ss work individually to complete the sentences with *was* or *were.*
- Write the numbers 1–10 on the board. Elicit answers, and send Ss with correct answers to the board to write them. Ss correct their own papers from the board.

Answers

1. **Were** you born in this city?
2. When **were** you born?
3. Where **were** your parents born?
4. When **was** your mother born?
5. When **was** your father born?
6. **Were** you and your family in this city last year?
7. **Were** you at this school last year?
8. Who **was** your first English teacher?
9. What nationality **was** your first English teacher?
10. What **was** he or she like?

- Introduce the speaking task. Ask two Ss to read the model conversation for the class.
- Elicit which questions need a "yes" or "no" answer (1, 6, and 7). Explain that these answers need additional information. If necessary, have volunteers demonstrate with questions 6 and 7.
- Ss take turns asking and answering the questions with a partner. Go around as they talk. Make sure they are giving additional information for 1, 6, and 7.
- When Ss finish, ask at least nine Ss questions about their partners, for example:

  T: Was Sun-hee born in this city?
  S: Yes, she was. She was born in 1983.
- **Alternate presentation:** Have Ss report about their partners in groups.

Optional activity: *Who is it?*

- See page T-156.

3 GRAMMAR FOCUS

Statements with the past of be

I	**was**	born in Korea.	I	**wasn't**	born in the U.S.	**wasn't** = **was not**
You	**were**	pretty young.	You	**weren't**	very old.	**weren't** = **were not**
She	**was**	seventeen.	She	**wasn't**	in college.	
We	**were**	born the same year.	We	**weren't**	born in the same country.	
They	**were**	in Korea in 1994.	They	**weren't**	in the U.S. in 1994.	

Seoul

A Melissa is talking about her family. Choose the correct verb form. Then compare with a partner.

My family and I ..*were*.. (was/were) all born
in Korea – we .... (wasn't/weren't) born in the U.S.
I .... (was/were) born in the city of Inchon,
and my brother .... (was/were) born there, too.
My parents .... (wasn't/weren't) born in Inchon.
They .... (was/were) born in the capital, Seoul.

Questions with the past of be

When	**were**	you born?	I **was** born in 1978.
	Were	you born in the U.S.?	No, I **wasn't**.
Where	**were**	you born?	I **was** born in Korea.
	Was	your brother born in Korea?	Yes, he **was**.
What city	**was**	he born in?	He **was** born in Inchon.
	Were	your parents born in Inchon?	No, they **weren't**.
Where	**were**	they born?	They **were** born in Seoul.

B Complete these questions with **was** or **were**. Then ask and answer the questions with a partner.

1. ..*Were*.. you born in this city?
2. When .... you born?
3. Where .... your parents born?
4. When .... your mother born?
5. When .... your father born?
6. .... you and your family in this city last year?
7. .... you at this school last year?
8. Who .... your first English teacher?
9. What nationality .... your first English teacher?
10. What .... he or she like?

A: Were you born in this city?
B: No, I wasn't. I was born in Istanbul.

Years

1906 (nineteen oh six)
1917 (nineteen seventeen)
1999 (nineteen ninety-nine)
2000 (two thousand)

4 LISTENING

Where were these people born? When were they born? Listen and complete the chart.

	Place of birth	Year of birth
1. Michelle Yeoh	....	....
2. Masahiko Harada	....	....
3. Helena Bonham Carter	....	....
4. Gustavo Kuerten	....	....

5 PRONUNCIATION *Negative contractions*

A Listen and practice.

one syllable	*two syllables*
aren't	isn't
weren't	wasn't
don't	doesn't
	didn't

B Listen and practice.

She **didn't** call because there **wasn't** time.
They **aren't** there, but she **doesn't** know.
They **don't** go out often, but they **aren't** home today.
he **isn't** going to wait because she **doesn't** have time.
ey **weren't** home yesterday, either.

4 LISTENING

In this exercise, Ss listen for specific information about four famous people.

- Books open. Have Ss look at the photographs. See if Ss know what each person does (Michelle Yeoh and Helena Bonham Carter are actors, Masahiko Harada is a skier, Gustavo Kuerten is a tennis player).
- Explain the task: Ss listen to conversations about the four famous people. Ss listen for their place of birth and year of birth. If necessary, explain that *Place of birth* answers "where," and *Year of birth* answers "when." Tell Ss to only listen for the country where the people were born.
- Play the audio program as many times as necessary while Ss fill in the information.

Audio script

1. MAN: Do you know who Michelle Yeoh is?
   WOMAN: Yeah. She was in that James Bond movie – *Tomorrow Never Dies.*
   MAN: I'm reading this great article about her. Did you know she was born in Malaysia?
   WOMAN: No, I didn't.
   MAN: Yeah. She was born in Malaysia in 1962.
2. MAN: Do you know anything about this guy, Masahiko Harada?
   WOMAN: Masahiko Harada? No, I don't think so. Who is he?
   MAN: He's a skier. He won third place in the 1998 Olympics, and he helped the Japanese team win the gold medal. He's a great person, too. People call him "Happy Harada."
   WOMAN: Where is he from?
   MAN: He was born in Japan.
   WOMAN: Is he young?
   MAN: Well . . . he was born in 1968.
3. MAN: Is Helena Bonham Carter English?
   WOMAN: I don't know. Let's check this book on movie stars. . . . It says here that, yes, she was born in England – in London.
   MAN: What else does that book say?
   WOMAN: Hey, I didn't know this. Her father is English, but her mother is French and Spanish.
   MAN: When was she born?
   WOMAN: Uh . . . she was born in 1966.
4. WOMAN: I just love Gustavo Kuerten. He's really terrific.
   MAN: Who's that?
   WOMAN: He's a Brazilian tennis player. He won the French Open in 1997.
   MAN: Hmm. How old is he?
   WOMAN: Well, he was born in 1976.
   MAN: Wow, he's really young! And he already won the French Open?
   WOMAN: Yep. He sure did.

- Ss compare answers in pairs, changing them if they wish.
- Play the audio program again so that Ss can verify their answers.
- Elicit answers, and have a S write the answers on the board. Ss correct their answers from the board.

Answers

Place of birth	*Year of birth*
1. Malaysia	1962
2. Japan	1968
3. England	1966
4. Brazil	1976

5 PRONUNCIATION Negative contractions

In this exercise, Ss practice the pronunciation of some negative contractions.

A 

- Books open. Play the audio program to model the contractions. Ss listen and read.
- **Optional:** Practice recognition. With books closed, say the contractions in random order. Ss hold up one finger if they hear one syllable, two fingers if they hear two syllables.
- Books open. Play the audio program again. Ss listen and repeat.
- **Optional:** Practice pronunciation. Say the affirmative forms of the verbs in random order (e.g., *is, do,* and so on). Ss say the negative contractions.

B 

- Play the audio program to model the sentences. Ss listen and read. (*Note:* In these sentences, boldface type calls attention to the contractions. It does not show stress.)
- Play the audio program again. Ss listen and repeat.
- Call on Ss to read the sentences aloud. Check their pronunciation of the contractions.
- **Alternate presentation:** Have Ss practice in pairs. Go around to listen to their pronunciation individually.

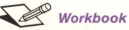

Workbook

Workbook Exercises 1–4 on pages 85–88 correspond to Cycle 1, Exercises 1–5, of the Student's Book. Answers to the Workbook exercises begin on page T-182 of this Teacher's Edition.

Cycle 2, Exercises 6–10

6 CONVERSATION

This conversation introduces expressions for talking about personal history. It introduces Wh-questions with *did* and *was,* questions with *why,* and answers with *because.*

- Books open. Have Ss look at the illustration. Remind Ss that Chuck and Melissa were in the conversation on page 92. Ask, "Where was Melissa born?" (Korea.)
- Say, "Now Melissa is asking Chuck some questions. What's her first question?" Ss scan the conversation to find it. ("Where did you grow up?")
- Play the audio program while Ss read and listen.
- Play the audio program again. Ss read and listen. Try to elicit the meaning of *What was your major?* and *drama.* If necessary, help Ss use the context to guess vocabulary.
- Play the audio program again or model the conversation line by line. Ss listen and read, then look up and repeat.
- Ss practice the conversation in pairs using the Look Up and Say technique.
- **Optional:** Have a few Ss act out the conversation for the class.
- **Optional:** To prepare Ss for the Grammar Focus exercise, write the following on the board:

  What does Laura want to know?
  1. Where did you grow up?
  2. And when _______________ ?
  3. What _______________ ?
  4. So why _______________ ?

  Books closed. Ask, "What other questions does Melissa ask?" Tell them to listen for the questions. Then play the audio program as many times as necessary. Elicit any words Ss can say after each listening. Write their correct words on the board with blanks for missing words.

  Books open. Ss use their books to tell you the rest of the words.

7 GRAMMAR FOCUS *Wh-questions with* did, was, *and* were

This grammar focus contrasts the structure of questions with *did* and questions with *was/were.*

1. In the simple past, the structure is:

Wh-word +	*did* +	subject +	main verb +	complement
When	did	you	come	to Los Angeles?

2. With the past of *be,* the structure is:

Wh-word +	*was/were* +	subject +	complement
What	was	your major	in college?

- Books open. Play the audio program to present the questions and answers. Ss read and listen. Encourage Ss to guess vocabulary, if necessary.
- Play the audio program again or model the sentences. Ss listen and repeat.
- **Optional:** Say the questions, and have the class give the answers. Then have half the class say the questions and the other half say the answers. Change roles for additional practice.

A

- Use the example to demonstrate the task.
- Ss work alone to match the answers to the questions.
- Ss compare their answers in pairs, making changes if they wish.
- To check, call on Ss to ask and answer the questions for the class.
- Elicit the answers, and write them on the board. Ss correct their own answers.

Answers

1. c	5. h
2. f	6. d
3. g	7. b
4. a	8. e

B *Pair work*

- To demonstrate the task, have a S ask you a few of the questions in part A. Answer with information about yourself.
- Ss take turns asking and answering the questions in pairs.
- **Optional:** Each pair shares some of their answers with the class. In a large class, you may prefer to do this in groups.

1. *Game – What's the question?*

- See page T-149. In this unit, Ss write statement that can be answered with Wh-questions with *did, was,* and *were.*

2. *When was that?*

- See page T-156.

6 CONVERSATION

Listen and practice.

Melissa: Where did you grow up, Chuck?
Chuck: I grew up in Texas. I was born there, too.
Melissa: And when did you come to Los Angeles?
Chuck: In 1985. I went to college here.
Melissa: Oh. What was your major?
Chuck: Drama. I was an actor for five years after college.
Melissa: That's interesting. So why did you become a hairstylist?
Chuck: Because I needed the money. And I love it. Look. What do you think?

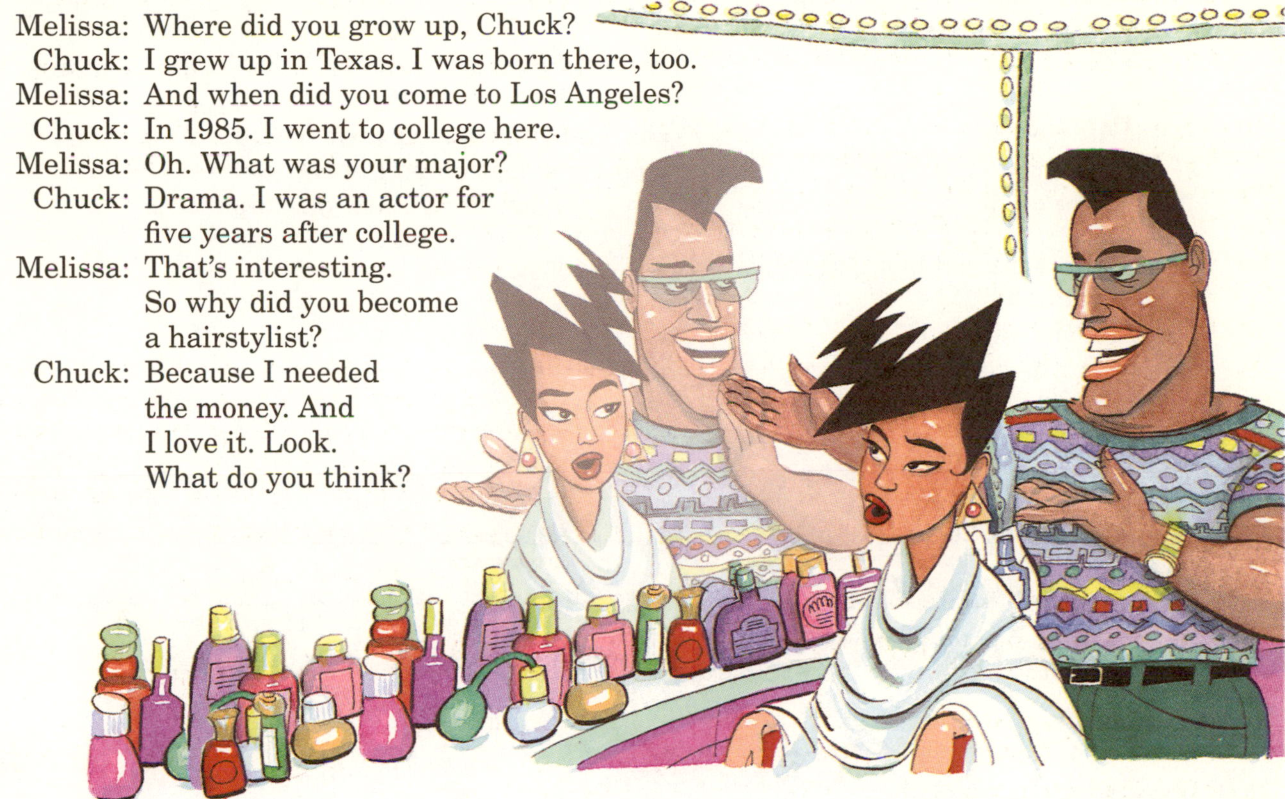

7 GRAMMAR FOCUS

Wh-questions with did, was, *and* were

Where did you grow up?	I **grew up** in Texas.	**How old were you** in 1985?	I **was** eighteen.
When did you come to L.A.?	I **came** to L.A. in 1985.	**What was your major** in college?	It **was** drama.
Why did you become a hairstylist?	Because I **needed** the money.	**How was college?**	It **was** great.

A Match the questions with the answers. Then compare with a partner.

1. When and where were you born? ....
2. Where did you grow up? ....
3. When did you start school? ....
4. How old were you then? ....
5. How was your first day of school? ....
6. Who was your first friend in school? ....
7. What was he/she like? ....
8. Why did you take this class? ....

a. I was six.
b. She was really shy.
c. I was born in 1978 in Puebla, Mexico.
d. Her name was Margarita.
e. My English wasn't very good.
f. I grew up in Mexico City.
g. I entered first grade in 1984.
h. It was a little scary.

B *Pair work* Take turns asking the questions in part A. Answer with your own information.

8 LAST SATURDAY

Group work Take turns. Ask and answer questions about last Saturday. Use these questions and your own ideas.

Where were you last Saturday?
Who was with you?
What did you do?
Where did you have lunch?
What did you do in the afternoon?

Where were you in the evening? Were you alone?
When did you have dinner?
What did you eat? Was the food good?
What time did you go to bed?
Were you very tired Saturday night?

A: Where were you last Saturday?
B: I was at home.
C: Who was with you?
B: My mother and brother were at home, too.
My father was at work.
D: What did you . . . ?

9 WORD POWER *School subjects*

A Complete the chart with words from the list. Then compare with a partner.

algebra ✓
art
biology
calculus
chemistry
Chinese
computer science
drama
French
geometry
history
journalism
music
physical education
physics
psychology
sociology
Spanish

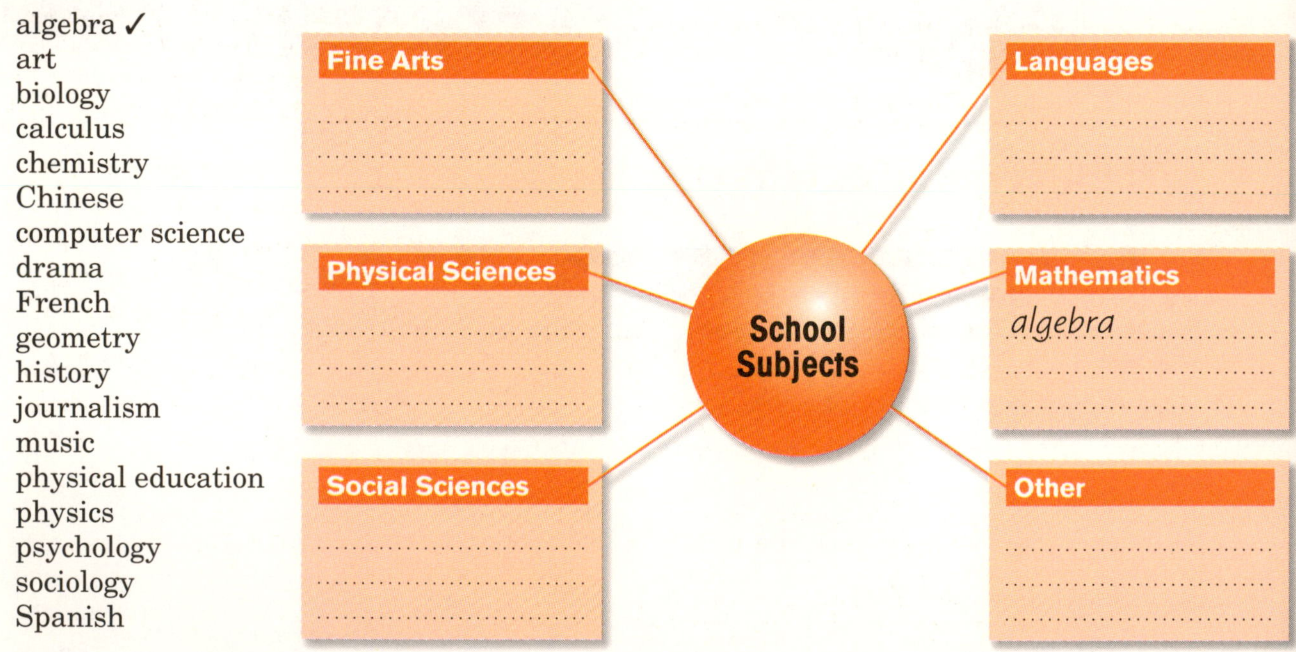

B ***Pair work*** Choose a column. Then take turns asking and answering the questions.

You're in high school now.	You're not in high school now.
What classes did you take last year?	What classes did you take in high school?
What was your favorite class?	What were your favorite subjects?
What classes didn't you like?	Which subjects didn't you like?
Who was your favorite teacher? Why?	Who was your favorite teacher? Why?

8 LAST SATURDAY

In this exercise, Ss practice talking about events in the past using simple past with regular and irregular verbs, and the past of *be*.

Group work

- Ask Ss to read the questions aloud one by one.
- Have three Ss read the model conversation. Have Student C complete the third question, and have someone answer it.
- Demonstrate to Ss how to use their own ideas. Ask one of the Ss some questions, changing the order and adding a question that is not on the list, for example:

  T: Where were you last Saturday?
  S: I was in the country.
  T: What did you do?
  S: I went swimming.
  T: Where did you go swimming?
- Ss have conversations in groups. Each S answers at least four questions.
- **Optional:** Have a few volunteers say conversations for the class without looking at their books.

9 WORD POWER School subjects

This exercise introduces and practices the names of school subjects.

(*Note:* In English, school subjects are not capitalized except for languages.)

A

- Books open. Model pronunciation of the six categories and the school subjects one by one. Ss listen and read.
- If necessary, answer questions about vocabulary. Let Ss answer one another's questions if they can.
- Use the example to demonstrate the matching task. If you feel more examples are needed, elicit one subject for each category.
- Individually, Ss complete the chart. Then they compare answers with a partner, making changes if they wish.
- **Optional:** Have Ss add other school subjects to the categories. Limit them to vocabulary Ss know. Let them ask you for vocabulary, or allow them to use dictionaries.
- Elicit answers, and have Ss write them on the board.

Answers

Fine Arts: art, drama, music
Physical Sciences: biology, chemistry, physics
Social Sciences: history, psychology, sociology
Languages: Chinese, Japanese, Spanish
Mathematics: algebra, calculus, geometry
Other: computer science, journalism, physical education

B Pair work

- Explain the task, and show Ss the two sets of questions.
- If some Ss are in high school and some are not, put this question on the board for Ss to ask at the beginning of their conversations:
  Are you in high school now?
- Demonstrate a conversation with a S.
- **Optional:** Demonstrate that Ss can add other questions they think of:

  T: What classes did you take last year?
  S: I took history, algebra, biology . . .
  T: Did you take music?
  S: No, I didn't.
  T: Why not?
- Ss have conversations about high school in pairs. Ss take turns asking the questions.
- Have Ss report some of their partners' answers to the class or to a small group.

10 READING Three Famous Artists

In this article, Ss read three short biographies of famous artists. In part A, Ss write questions about the artists' lives. In part B, Ss give opinions.

- Books open. Read the title aloud, and write it on the board.
- Introduce the prereading task. Tell Ss they only need to read the name, the years, and the first sentence about each artist. Then they can guess the artist for each work of art. (*Note:* Some Ss may know the artists already, but they should still read the information. Students will be able to guess the meanings of *printmaker, painter,* and *sculptor* when they read the article. It is not necessary to explain these words now.)
- Ss work individually to match the artists with the works of art. Then they compare answers with a partner, making changes if they wish.
- Elicit the answers, and write them on the board.

Answers

1. Alexander Calder
2. Frida Kahlo
3. Hiroshige

- Have Ss explain how they guessed. Ask that they use English, but accept ungrammatical answers if they are understandable.

A

- Ss read the article. If you wish, play the tape as Ss listen and read.
- **Optional:** Ss underline words they do not know. Encourage Ss to guess the meaning from the context of the paragraph of the accompanying photo. Ss will be able to do the exercise without understanding all the words.
- To prepare for the exercise, have Ss read the short answers in the exercise aloud. Elicit the key word in each answer and have Ss circle it (*landscapes, Philadelphia, 1797, Mexico City, 1898, self-portraits*).
- Tell Ss to scan the article to find the same key words in the article and circle them. Set a time limit.
- Read the instructions for part A aloud. Use the example to demonstrate the writing task.
- Ss write the question for each answer. Walk around to give help.
- Ss compare their questions in pairs, making changes if they wish.
- Elicit the correct questions from the class. Write them on the board or have a S write them.

Answers

1. What is Hiroshige famous for?
2. Where was Alexander Calder born?
3. When was Hiroshige born?
4. Where was Frida Kahlo born?
5. When was Alexander Calder born?
6. What is Frida Kahlo famous for?

B Group work

- Read the instructions aloud, and go over the questions. If necessary, demonstrate the task by answering Ss' questions yourself.
- Put the Ss in groups of three to five. Ss talk about which work of art each one wants to have. Encourage them to give at least two reasons.
- **Optional:** Elicit a list of Ss' reasons, and write them on the board.

INTERCHANGE 15 Time line

See page T-123 of this Teacher's Edition for notes.

Workbook

Workbook Exercises 5–7 on pages 88–90 correspond to Cycle 2, Exercises 6–10, of the Student's Book. Answers to the Workbook exercises begin on page T-182 of this Teacher's Edition.

10 READING

Three Famous Artists

The article is about a printmaker, a painter, and a sculptor. Look at the artists' names, when they lived, and where they were born. Can you match each work of art with the artist?

Hiroshige (1797–1858)
Hiroshige was born in Edo (now Tokyo). As a boy, he studied with a famous artist. Hiroshige traveled to many beautiful places in Japan. His woodblock prints are landscapes – mountains, fields, rivers – with small human figures. Hiroshige's prints suggest strong feelings about these places.

1. ....

2. ....

Frida Kahlo (1907–1954)
Frida Kahlo was born near Mexico City. At 15, she almost died in a bus accident. For the rest of her life, she was disabled and in pain. Soon after the accident, Kahlo taught herself how to paint. Kahlo is especially famous for her self-portraits. In these paintings, Kahlo used bright colors and strange symbols to show her feelings.

Alexander Calder (1898–1976)
Alexander Calder was born in Philadelphia. First, he studied engineering. At the age of 25, he went to art school. Calder developed a new kind of sculpture: the mobile. Mobiles hang from the ceiling and move in interesting patterns. In many of Calder's mobiles, wires connect flat, colorful metal shapes.

3. ....

A Read the article. Then write a question with **What**, **Where**, or **When**. Include the artist's name in the question.

1. *What is Hiroshige famous for?* .... For beautiful landscapes.
2. .... In Philadelphia.
3. .... In 1797.
4. .... Near Mexico City.
5. .... In 1898.
6. .... For self-portraits.

B ***Group work*** Imagine you can have one of the three works of art on this page. Which one are you going to choose? Why?

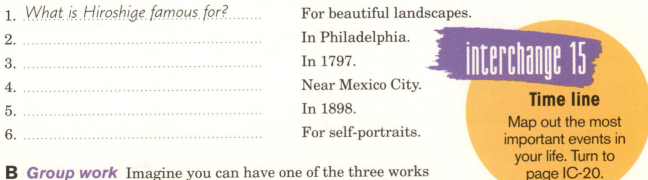

interchange 15

Time line

Map out the most important events in your life. Turn to page IC-20.

16 Please leave us a message.

1 CONVERSATION

 Listen and practice.

Answering
machine: Hi. This is Jennifer, and this is Nicole. We can't come to the phone right now. Please leave us a message, and . . . .
Nicole: Hello?
Michael: Hi. Nicole? It's Michael. Is Jennifer there?
Nicole: Oh, hi, Michael. She's here, but she's in bed – she's sleeping. Can she call you later?
Michael: Yeah, thanks. Please ask her to call me at my parents' house.
Nicole: Sure. Just give me the number.
Michael: It's 555-0367.
Nicole: 555-0367. OK.
Michael: Thanks a lot, Nicole.

2 WORD POWER *Places*

A  Listen and practice.

Jennifer can't come to the phone right now. . . .

She's **in** the shower.
in the yard.
in bed.

Jennifer isn't here right now. . . .

She's **at** the beach.
at her parents' house.
at the library.
at the mall.
at school.
at home.
at work.

She's **in** the hospital.
in South America.
in class.

She's **on** vacation.
on a trip.

B ***Pair work*** Make a list of friends and relatives and give it to your partner. Where are these people right now? Ask and answer questions.

A: Where's your brother right now?
B: He's on a trip. He's in Thailand.

16 Please leave us a message.

This unit presents expressions for leaving and for taking telephone messages, and for making plans with friends. The unit introduces object pronouns and the pattern verb + *to* + verb *with* want to, need to, have to, would like to, *and* would love to.

Cycle 1, Exercises 1–4

1 CONVERSATION

This conversation introduces expressions used to make telephone calls and leave messages. It includes a typical home answering machine message.

- Books open. Have Ss look at the illustration and the names in the conversation. Write these questions on the board:

  Who answers the phone? (the answering machine)
  Who does Michael speak to? (Nicole)
  Who is Michael calling? (Jennifer)
  Where is Jennifer? (in bed/sleeping)

- Play the audio program while Ss read and listen for the answers. Elicit the answers.
- Play the audio program again. Ss read and listen. If necessary, let Ss ask about key vocabulary. Encourage guessing.
- Play the audio program again or model the conversation line by line. Ss listen and read, then look up and repeat.
- Ss practice the conversation in pairs using the Look Up and Say technique. "Michael" reads the answering machine message. Ss change roles so that everyone practices both parts.
- **Optional:** Have a few Ss act out the conversation for the class.

2 WORD POWER *Places*

This exercise introduces and practices expressions with the prepositions of place *in, at,* and *on.*

A

- Books open. Play the audio program. Ss listen and read. Explain vocabulary if necessary, or let Ss explain it. Three new expressions are illustrated. *Vacation* and *trip* are also new.
- Play the audio program again. Ss listen and repeat.

B *Pair work*

- Model the first part of the task by listing some of your friends and relatives on the board, for example:

  my husband/wife
  my brother
  my parents
  my friend Roger

- Working individually, Ss make similar lists of people they know.
- Have two Ss read the model conversation aloud.
- Demonstrate the task. Elicit questions with *where* about the people on your list and answer them.
- In pairs, Ss exchange lists. Then they take turns asking and answering questions about the people on their partner's lists.

Optional activity: *Game – Who's where?*

- See page T-156.

3 LISTENING

In this exercise, Ss listen for names and places in telephone conversations.

A

- Explain the task. Have Ss look at the pictures and identify where the people are. List the names Ss need to write:
  Jeff, Kate, John, Chris, Lisa
- Play the audio program as many times as necessary.

Audio script

1. WOMAN: Hello?
   MAN: Hello. Is Jeff there, please?
   WOMAN: I'm sorry, he can't come to the phone right now. He's in the shower.
   MAN: OK. Thanks. Good-bye
2. MAN: Hello?
   WOMAN: Hello. Can I talk to Kate?
   MAN: Sorry. She's at work. Do you have her number at the office?
   WOMAN: Yes, I do. Thank you.
   MAN: You're welcome. Bye.
3. WOMAN: Hello?
   MAN: Uh, hello. Can I speak to John?
   WOMAN: Well, John's not here right now. He's on vacation . . . in France.
   MAN: Oh. When is he going to come home?
   WOMAN: He's going to come home Saturday.
   MAN: OK. Thanks. Bye.
   WOMAN: Good-bye.
4. MRS. JONES: Hello?
   BOY: Hi, Mrs. Jones. Is Chris there?
   MRS. JONES: No, I'm sorry. Chris isn't here right now. He's at the library.
   BOY: Oh, OK. I'm going to go to the library in a few minutes, too.
   MRS. JONES: You're welcome. Bye-bye.
5. MAN: Hello?
   SUE: Hello. Is Lisa there, please?
   MAN: Yes, but she can't come to the phone right now. She's working in the yard. Can I give her a message?
   SUE: Yes, this is Sue. Please ask her to call me.
   MAN: OK, sure.
   SUE: Thank you. Good-bye.

- Ss compare in pairs, making changes if they wish. Then have Ss write the answers on the board.

Answers

Chris, Lisa, Jeff, Kate, John

B *Pair work*

- Books open. Explain the task. Have two Ss read the model conversation for the class.
- In pairs, Ss take turns "calling" people in part A.

4 GRAMMAR FOCUS *Object pronouns*

This grammar focus presents and practices singular and plural object pronouns.

- Books open. Play the audio program while Ss listen and read.
- Write this sentence on the board:
  subject *object*
  Michael called Jennifer.
- Change the names to subject and object pronouns.
  subject pronoun *object pronoun*
  He called her.
- Write these rules on the board:
  1. Subject pronouns go before the verb.
  2. Object pronouns go after the verb.
- In the grammar box, point out that *it* and *you* are both subject pronouns and object pronouns.
- Use the example to demonstrate the task. Ss complete the conversations individually.
- Ss go to the board and write the completed sentences. Ss check the answers on the board and their own answers.

Answers

1. A: Is Sandra there, please?
   B: I'm sorry, she isn't here right now. Can I give **her** a message?
   A: Yes, this is David. Please ask **her** to call **me** at work.
   B: OK. Can you give **me** your phone number, please?
   A: Sure. It's 555-2981.
2. A: Can I speak with Mr. Ford, please?
   B: He isn't here today. But maybe I can help **you**.
   A: Thanks. Can you ask **him** to call **me**? This is John Rivers.
   B: John Rivers. Does he have your number, Mr. Rivers?
   A: Yes, he has it.
3. A: Hi. This is Carol and Mark. We can't come to the phone. Please leave **us** a message after the beep. *Beep.*
   B: Hi. It's Betsy and James. Carol, you left your sunglasses here. We can bring **them** to **you** tomorrow. Just give **us** a call.

- Ss practice the conversations in pairs.

Workbook

Workbook Exercises 1–4 on pages 91–94 correspond to Cycle 1, Exercises 1–4, of the Student's Book. Answers to the Workbook exercises begin on page T-182 of this Teacher's Edition.

3 LISTENING

A Listen to people making phone calls. Who are they calling? Write the names under the photos.

....Jeff.... ....

B ***Pair work*** Take turns calling the people in part A.

A: Hello?
B: Hello. Is Jeff there, please?
A: I'm sorry, he can't come to the phone right now. He's in the shower.
B: OK. Thanks.

4 GRAMMAR FOCUS

Object pronouns

		Subject pronouns		Object pronouns	Subject pronouns		Object pronouns
Just give **me** the number.	Can I give **him** a message?	I	→	me	it	→	it
I don't have **it**.	Please leave **us** a message.	you	→	you	we	→	us
Can she call **you** later?	Please call **them** at work.	he	→	him	you	→	you
Give **her** a call later.	Please ask **her** to call **me**.	she	→	her	they	→	them

Complete these phone conversations. Then practice with a partner.

1. A: Is Sandra there, please?
   B: I'm sorry, she isn't here right now. Can I give ...her... a message?
   A: Yes, this is David. Please ask .... to call .... at work.
   B: OK. Can you give .... your phone number, please?
   A: Sure. It's 555-2981.

2. A: Can I speak with Mr. Ford, please?
   B: He isn't here today. But maybe I can help ....
   A: Thanks. Can you ask .... to call .... ? This is John Rivers.
   B: John Rivers. Does he have your number, Mr. Rivers?
   A: Yes, he has ....

3. A: Hi. This is Carol and Mark. We can't come to the phone.
   Please leave .... a message after the beep. *Beep.*
   B: Hi. It's Betsy and James. Carol, you left your sunglasses here.
   We can bring .... to .... tomorrow. Just give .... a call.

5 SNAPSHOT

Are these dating activities popular in your country?
What other activities are popular?
What are your favorite dating activities?

6 CONVERSATION

 Listen and practice.

Michael: Hello?
Jennifer: Hi, Michael. It's Jennifer. I got your message.
Michael: Hi. Thanks for calling me back.
Jennifer: So, what's up?
Michael: Uh, well, do you want to have dinner with me tomorrow night?
Jennifer: Tomorrow night? I'm really sorry, but I can't. I have to stay home and study.
Michael: Oh, that's too bad. How about Friday night?
Jennifer: Uh . . . sure. I'd love to. What time do you want to meet?
Michael: How about around seven o'clock?
Jennifer: Terrific!

Cycle 2, Exercises 5–11

5 SNAPSHOT *Ideas for a First Date*

This graphic gives information about popular dating activities in North America. The questions relate the information to Ss' own lives.

- Books open. Read the title and the seven activities one by one. Ss listen and repeat. If necessary, help Ss guess the meaning of *date*.
- Ask the questions one by one. If necessary, explain *popular*. Give Ss time to think about their answers to the questions.
- Ss ask and answer the questions with partners or in a small group.
- **Optional:** Elicit several different answers to each question. Write them on the board as notes. If Ss are from different countries, list the notes by country.

6 CONVERSATION

This conversation introduces expressions for making, accepting, and declining invitations.

- Books open. Have Ss look at the illustration and the names in the conversation. Michael called Jennifer in Exercise 1. See if Ss remember what happened. (Jennifer was in bed. Nicole took a message.)
- Set the scene: Jennifer is calling Michael back. Write this question on the board:

  What does Michael want? (A date/dinner with Jennifer)
- Play the audio program while Ss read and listen for the answer. Elicit the answers.
- Play the audio program again. Ss read and listen. Ss should be able to guess vocabulary from the context and the sound of the speakers' voices.
- Play the audio program again or model the conversation line by line. Ss listen and read, then look up and repeat.
- Ss practice the conversation in pairs using the Look Up and Say technique.
- **Optional:** Have a few Ss act out the conversation for the class.

Optional activity: ***Game – What's your excuse?***

- See page T-157.

7 PRONUNCIATION Want to *and* have to

In this exercise, Ss practice the reduced pronunciation of *want to* and *have to.*

(*Note:* Reduced forms occur when English is spoken at normal speed – faster than most Ss can speak. It is important that Ss be aware of reductions and be able to understand them. It is less important for Ss to use them in their own speech.)

- Books open. Play the audio program to present the reduced forms. Ss listen and repeat several times.
- Play the audio program to model the sentences. Ss listen and read. (*Note:* In these sentences, boldface type calls attention to the pronunciation of the reduced forms. It does not show stress.)
- Play the audio program again. Ss listen and read, then look up and repeat.
- Ss practice the conversations in pairs. As they practice, go around the room to listen and to help with pronunciation.

8 GRAMMAR FOCUS *Verb* + to + *verb;* would

This grammar focus presents *want to* for making invitations and *have to, need to, would like to,* and *would love to* for accepting and refusing invitations and making excuses.

- Books open. Play the audio program to present *Accepting an invitation.* Ss listen and read.
- Explain that *accepting* means *saying yes.* Point out that the answer to "Do you want to . . . ?" is not "Yes, I do." Show Ss the contraction *I'd* (I would). Also mention *Sure* for accepting an invitation, as in Exercises 6 and 7.
- Play the audio program again or model the sentences. Ss listen and repeat.
- Play the audio program to present *Refusing an invitation and making an excuse.* Ss listen and read.
- Explain that *refusing* means *saying no,* but the answers do not use the word *no.* Go over the appropriate answers.
- Play the audio program again or model the sentences. Ss listen and repeat.

A

- Explain that Ss are going to work first on the responses (the right-hand side). Write the four possible answers on the board. Show Ss that they need to fill in the blanks in a–d.
- If necessary, answer questions about vocabulary. Ss should be able to guess *baby-sit* from the context. *Dentist* is also new here.
- Ss work individually to complete the responses.
- Call on four Ss to read the completed responses. Write their answers on the board, and correct them with the whole class. Accept all possible answers.

Possible answers

a. Tonight? I'm sorry, I can't. My parents are going to go out, and I **have to** baby-sit for my sister.
b. Sorry, I **have to**/**need to** talk to the teacher after school.
c. Gee, **I'd love to**/**I'd like to** see the game, but I **have to**/**need to** study for the exam on Thursday.
d. **I'd love to**/**I'd like to** go to the beach, but I can't. I **have to** go to the dentist on Saturday.

B

- Books open. Explain the task. Use the example to show how to match the responses to the invitations.
- Ss work individually to complete the task.
- Elicit answers, and write them on the board. Ss correct their own work.

Answers

1. c
2. a
3. d
4. b

- Ss practice the invitations and responses with a partner. As they practice, go around the room to check their pronunciation of the reduced forms of *have to* and *want to.*

7 PRONUNCIATION Want to *and* have to

Listen and practice. Notice the pronunciation of **want to** and **have to**.

/wanə/	/hæftə/
want to	**have to**

A: Do you **want to** see a movie with me tomorrow night?
B: I'm sorry, I can't. I **have to** stay home and study.
A: Do you **want to** go out on Friday night?
B: Sure. I really **want to** see the new James Bond movie.

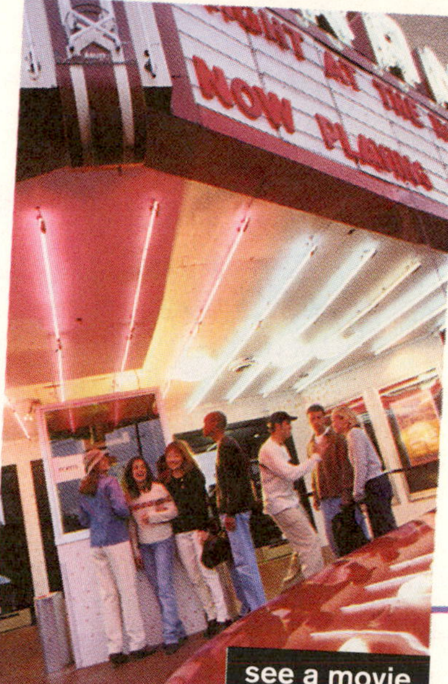

see a movie

8 GRAMMAR FOCUS

Verb + to + verb; would

Accepting an invitation

Do you **want to see** a movie with me tomorrow?
Yes, **I'd love to** (**see** a movie with you tomorrow).

I'd = I would

Refusing an invitation and making an excuse

Do you **want to have** dinner with me on Friday night?
I'm sorry, but I can't. I **have to study**.
Sorry, I **need to stay** home with my brother.
Gee, **I'd like to**, but I **want to go** to bed early.

A Complete these responses with **'d love to, 'd like to, have to**, or **need to**. (More than one answer is sometimes possible.)

Invitations

1. Do you want to go to the basketball game tomorrow night? ...c...
2. Do you want to see a movie with me tonight? ....
3. Do you want to go to the beach on Saturday? ....
4. Do you want to play volleyball after school today? ....

Responses

a. Tonight? I'm sorry, I can't. My parents are going to go out, and I .... baby-sit for my sister.
b. Sorry, I .... talk to the teacher after school.
c. Gee, I .... see the game, but I .... study for the exam on Thursday.
d. I .... go to the beach, but I can't. I .... go to the dentist on Saturday.

B Match the invitations with the responses in part A. Then practice with a partner.

9 EXCUSES

A Do you use these excuses? Check (✓) **often**, **sometimes**, or **never**. What are your three favorite excuses? Compare with a partner.

	Often	Sometimes	Never
I have to baby-sit.	☐	☐	☐
I need to study.	☐	☐	☐
I have to work late.	☐	☐	☐
I want to go to bed early.	☐	☐	☐
I want to visit my family.	☐	☐	☐
I have to go to class.	☐	☐	☐
I have a terrible headache.	☐	☐	☐
My back hurts.	☐	☐	☐
I need to stay home and clean.	☐	☐	☐
I have other plans.	☐	☐	☐

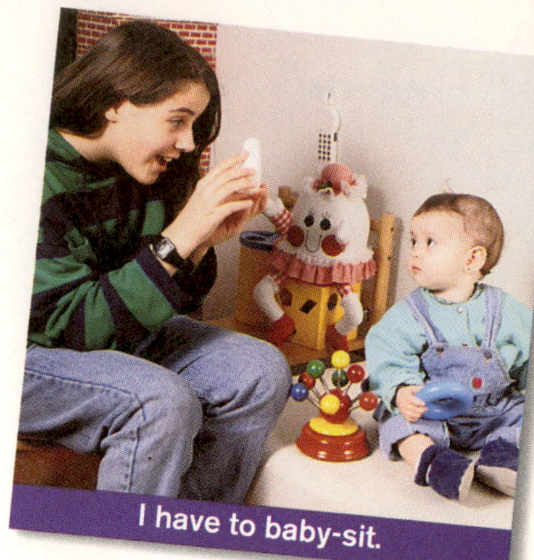
I have to baby-sit.

B Write down three things you want to do this weekend, with the day and time.

I want to go to the ball game on Saturday night.

C ***Class activity*** Use your ideas from part B. Invite your classmates to go with you.

A: Do you want to . . . on . . . ?
B: I'm sorry, but I can't. I have to . . . .
A: Do you want to . . . on . . . ?
C: I'd love to. What time do you want to meet?

10 LISTENING

A Jennifer and Nicole invited some friends to a party on Saturday. Listen to the messages on their answering machine. Who can come? Who can't come? Check (✓) the correct answers.

	Can come	Can't come	Excuse
Steven	☑	☐	....
Anna	☐	☐	....
David	☐	☐	....
Sarah	☐	☐	....
Michael	☐	☐	....

B Listen again. For the friends who can't come, what excuse do they give?

9 EXCUSES

This exercise provides further practice with *have to, need to,* and *want to* as excuses. Ss also write about things they want to do.

A

- Have volunteers read the ten excuses aloud. Vocabulary should be familiar. If Ss have questions about it, let other Ss answer.
- Explain the task. Ss choose their three favorite excuses from the chart.
- **Optional:** Ss can also write down favorite excuses that are not in the chart.
- Ss work individually to complete the task, then share their favorite excuses with a partner.
- **Optional:** Take a quick survey. Ss raise their hands to show their favorite excuses. Keep track on the board. Which one is the class favorite?

B

- Use the model to explain and demonstrate the task.
- Elicit several things that Ss want to do this weekend, with the day and time.
- Working individually, Ss write three sentences on a separate piece of paper.
- **Optional:** In pairs, Ss exchange papers with another pair. Working together, they correct the two papers they received.

C *Class activity*

- Demonstrate the task. Ask for three volunteers. Have them come to the front of the room with their sentences from part B.
- Ask S1 to write one sentence on the board. Show Ss how to form invitations using the sentence on the board and the model conversation.
- Lead the three Ss through the model conversation. S1 makes the invitation. S2 refuses and gives an excuse. S3 accepts. For example:

  S1: Do you want to go to the ball game on Saturday night?
  S2: I'm sorry, but I can't. I have to study.
  S1: Do you want to go to the ball game on Saturday night?
  S3: I'd love to. What time do you want to meet?

- Tell Ss they are free to decide whether to accept or refuse an invitation. Ss stand up and walk around the room making and responding to invitations.

Optional activity: *Silly excuses*

- See page T-157.

10 LISTENING

In this exercise, Ss listen for five people's responses to an invitation.

A

- Books open. Go over the names in the chart. Explain the task: Ss are going to hear five messages on Jennifer and Nicole's answering machine. Ss listen and check who can and can't come. Play the first part of the audio program, and use the example to demonstrate the task.
- Play the audio program once or twice.

Audio script

STEVEN: Hello, Jennifer and Nicole. This is Steven. Thanks for the invitation. I'd love to come. So . . . uhh . . . well, see you Saturday around eight o'clock.
ANNA: Hello, Jennifer. This is Anna. Thanks for inviting me to your party. I'm going to be a little late. I hope that's OK. Can I bring some food or soda? Call me: 555-2547.
DAVID: Hey, Jennifer and Nicole. This is David. Thanks for the invitation. I'd love to come, but I have to go out to dinner with my parents. It's my mother's fiftieth birthday, so it's kind of important. Sorry. Talk to you soon.
SARAH: Hi, Nicole. This is Sarah. I'm really sorry, but I can't come to your party on Saturday. I'm going to go to a concert with my friend Robert. Sorry I can't change my plans. He bought the tickets already. Again, I'm really sorry. Talk to you soon.
MICHAEL: Hi, Jennifer. This is Michael. Thanks for inviting me to your party on Saturday. I would love to come. I'm going to bring some chips and soda. I hope that's OK with you. If not, call me. You have my number.

- Check Ss' answers.

Answers *(for parts A and B)*

Steven	*can come*	
Anna	*can come*	
David	*can't come*	*having dinner with his parents*
Sarah	*can't come*	*going to a concert*
Michael	*can come*	

B

- Play the audio program a second time. This time, Ss listen for and write the two excuses.
- Have Ss write the excuses on the board. There may be some variation in the wording. Accept all reasonable answers.

11 READING *Free Activities This Weekend*

In this text, Ss read about five things that are going to happen on the weekend. They practice scanning for specific information, making inferences, and giving opinions.

- Books open. Read the title aloud, and write it on the board. If necessary, explain *free*.
- Introduce the prereading task. Elicit answers from the Ss. Help them with vocabulary, if necessary.

Possible answers

holiday parades, fireworks, church concerts, street musicians, street fairs, school plays, school sports, school dances

A

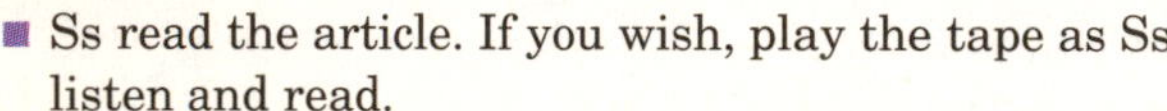

- Ss read the article. If you wish, play the tape as Ss listen and read.
- **Optional:** Ss underline words they do not know. Encourage Ss to guess the meaning from the context of the paragraph of the accompanying photo. Ss will be able to do the exercise without understanding all the words.
- Use the instructions and the chart to explain the task.
- Have Ss read the phrases in the chart aloud. If necessary, clarify the meaning of *jewelry*.
- Have Ss scan the article for key words and circle them. Set a time limit. At this time, Ss only need to find the phrases. They do not need to read the whole article.
- Tell Ss to use their circled phrases and read just enough to figure out the answers. They need two places for every item in the chart. If some Ss finish early, have them compare their answers in pairs. They may want to change some of their answers as a result.
- When Ss are ready, elicit answers and fill in the chart on the board.

Possible answers

1. *buy clothes or jewelry:* Craft Fair, Fall Fashion Show
2. *buy food:* Craft Fair, Library Lecture
3. *sit indoors:* City Museum, Library Lecture, Fall Fashion Show
4. *be outdoors:* Craft Fair, Rock Concert

- **Optional:** Ask Ss what words in the text helped them answer the questions. For example, *on sale* and *$50* mean that you can *buy clothes* at the fashion show. *Park* says that the rock concert was *outdoors*.
- Ss read the whole article again for general understanding. They do not need to understand every word.

B *Pair work*

- Explain the task. Tell Ss that they need to choose three activities from the article.
- Point out the words *First choice, Second choice,* and *Third choice.* Their *first choice* is the activity they like the most.
- Ss fill in the chart individually. Then compare their choices in pairs.
- Bring the class back together. Ask Ss about the activities they and their partners both chose. Ask them to give reasons why they chose the activities they did. List them on the board. Is there clearly a class favorite?

INTERCHANGE 16 Let s make a date

See page T-124 of this Teacher's Edition for notes.

Workbook

Workbook Exercises 5–8 on pages 94–96 correspond to Cycle 2, Exercises 5–11, of the Student's Book. Answers to the Workbook exercises begin on page T-182 of this Teacher's Edition.

Optional activity: ***Do you want to . . . ?***

- See page T-157.

11 READING

Free Activities This Weekend

What are some free activities in your city?

Craft Fair in Front of City Hall

Sunday from 9:00 A.M. to 5:00 P.M.

Need to buy a present? Find pottery, jewelry, paintings, sculpture, and more! Food from around the world, too!

Rock Concert at University Park

Saturday from 9:00 P.M. to midnight

Come hear some great music. Five terrific student bands are going to play. Bring your own food and drink.

City Museum Travel Movies

Saturday and Sunday at 2:30 P.M.

Do you want to travel, but don't have enough money? See movies on Japan, Indonesia, Brazil, Italy, and Australia. There are only 100 seats, so come early.

Library Lecture

City Library Auditorium
Saturday at 10:00 A.M.

How to find the job you really want! Two-hour lecture. Advice on choosing and getting the right job for you. Sandwiches and soda sold.

Fall Fashion Show

Golden Shopping Plaza
Sunday at 3:00 P.M.

Men's and women's fall clothes. See 25 fabulous models wearing the latest fashions. All clothing on sale after the show for under $100.

A Read the article. Then write two places where you can . . . .

1. buy clothes or jewelry ....
2. buy food ....
3. sit indoors ....
4. be outdoors ....

B ***Pair work*** List three things you want to do. Then compare with a partner. Is there one activity you both want to do?

First choice ....
Second choice ....
Third choice ....

interchange 16

Let's make a date!

Check your calendar and make a date. Student A turns to page IC-19. Student B turns to page IC-21.

Review of Units 13–16

1 NO, HE WASN'T!

Class activity Write three false statements about famous people using the simple past. Read your sentences to the class. Can anyone correct them?

Albert Einstein was a famous football player.
Marilyn Monroe . . . .

A: Albert Einstein was a famous football player.
B: No, he wasn't. He was a scientist.

2 LOCATIONS

A ***Pair work*** Take turns saying the location of these places. Say the location in two different ways.

1. parking lot
2. drugstore
3. dance club
4. bus stop
5. Japanese restaurant

A: The parking lot is on Second Avenue.
B: The parking lot is across from the Korean restaurant.

B ***Pair work*** Give directions to two places on the map. Your partner guesses the place.

A: Walk up First Avenue and turn left. It's on the right, on the corner of First and Lincoln.
B: It's the Japanese restaurant.
A: Right.

Review of Units 13–16

This unit reviews the simple past, the past of be, *prepositions of place, and* have to. *It focuses on vocabulary and functions relating to biographical information, locations and directions, obligations, and recent past activities.*

1 NO, HE WASN'T!

This exercise reviews making statements about biographical information using the simple past and the past of *be*.

Class activity

- Books open. Explain the task. Have a S read the first model aloud. Have a volunteer complete the false statement about Marilyn Monroe, for example, "Marilyn Monroe lived in Europe."
- Tell Ss to write about people who are deceased. If they write about people who are alive, they will often need to use the present tense, not the past.
- **Optional:** Elicit a few verbs for Ss to use: for example, *was, were, lived, worked, liked, had,* and so on. Make a list on the board.
- Ss work individually to write three false statements about famous people.
- Introduce the speaking task. Have two Ss read the model conversation aloud. If necessary, have two more Ss demonstrate with another statement and correction.
- Ss take turns reading their false statements to the class. Have them call on other Ss who can correct the statements.
- **Optional:** In a large class, you may need to limit each S to one statement. Alternatively, do the speaking activity in smaller groups.

Optional activities: Vocabulary from Units 13-16 can be reviewed using any of the following games or exercises.

1. *Spelling contest*

- See page T-148.

2. *Game – Hangman*

- See page T-148.

3. *Crossword puzzle*

- See page T-148.

4. *The other question*

- See page T-155.

2 LOCATIONS

This exercise reviews giving locations and directions.

A *Pair work*

- Books open. Explain the task. Use the model conversation to show two ways of saying locations.
- Remind Ss of the prepositions of place they have learned. Refer them to the Grammar Focus on page 82, or brainstorm with the class a list of prepositions on the board.
- In pairs, each S says the location of each place. The second S says it in a different way.

Possible answers *(Accept any reasonable answer.)*

1. The parking lot is **on** Second Avenue/**between** Washington and Jefferson/**across from** the Korean restaurant.
2. The drugstore is **on** Lincoln Street/**between** the coffee bar and Computer Wizards.
3. The dance club is **on** Second Avenue/**between** Lincoln Street and Jefferson Street/**across from** the movie theater.
4. The bus stop is **on the corner of** Lincoln Street and Third Avenue/**in front of** the coffee bar. The other bus stop is **on the corner of** Washington Street and Third Avenue/**behind** the parking lot.
5. The Japanese restaurant is **on the corner of** Lincoln Street and First Avenue/**next to** the Hair Salon.

- With the whole class, elicit all the possible ways to express the location of each place. Use the prepositions of place to cue Ss' responses, for example:

  T: The parking lot is on . . . ?
  S1: The parking lot is on Second Avenue.

B *Pair work*

- Explain the task.
- Point out the "You are here" location on the map. All directions start from there. Have two Ss read the model conversation aloud. The other Ss follow the directions on the map.
- Remind Ss of the expressions they have learned for giving directions. Refer them to the Grammar Focus on page 84, if necessary. Then with the class brainstorm a list of expressions on the board.
- In pairs, Ss take turns giving directions to places on the map and guessing the places.
- **Optional:** Ss draw maps of real or imaginary downtown areas. They use the maps for additional practice.

3 LISTENING

In this exercise, Ss listen to questions and check the correct responses.

- Books open. Explain the task: Ss hear a question on the audio program and choose the right answer in the book.
- Play the first part of the audio program, and use the example to demonstrate the task.
- Play the audio program as many times as necessary. Ss choose the correct response to each question they hear.

Audio script

1. Were Brian and Victor in class last night?
2. What time did you go to work this morning?
3. Who did you go to the beach with on Saturday?
4. How was the party at Jennifer and Nicole's?
5. We had a great barbecue on Sunday afternoon. Why didn't you go?
6. There's an interesting movie at Cinema City. Do you want to go tonight?
7. Hi. This is Sandra. Is David there, please?
8. Is there a public rest room near here?

- Play the audio program again. Stop it after each question and have Ss give the answer together.

Answers

1. No, they weren't.
2. At eleven o'clock.
3. Amy and Katherine.
4. It was great.
5. I had a terrible headache.
6. I'm sorry, but I can't go.
7. I'm sorry, he's not here right now.
8. No, there isn't. Sorry.

4 CLASSROOM RULES

This writing exercise reviews *have to* and *can't* in a new context.

- Books open. Explain the task, and go over the models.
- Ss work individually to write four classroom rules with *have to* and four with *can't.*
- In pairs, Ss work together to correct each of their papers, one at a time. In case of disagreement, they raise their hands and consult with you.
- Elicit rules from the class, and write them on the board.

Possible answers

You have to listen to the teacher.
You have to sit at your desk.
You have to do your homework.
You have to bring your book.
You can't eat.
You can't listen to music.
You can't sleep.
You can't talk all the time.

5 TELL US ABOUT IT

This exercise reviews statements and questions in the simple past and statements with *want to.*

A Group work

- Books open. Read the four sentences that begin "Tell them about . . . . " Show Ss that they need to tell about four different experiences. Give Ss a few minutes to prepare four statements.
- Use the model conversation to explain and demonstrate the task. With the class, complete the model conversation on the board. Elicit the movie, the actor, and the reaction from the Ss.
- Have four volunteers model the completed conversation for the class.
- Divide the class into groups of four. Ss take turns making statements and answering questions while the other members of the group ask questions. Circulate while they talk to make sure everyone asks a question.

B Group work

- With Ss in the same groups, use the example to explain the task. Elicit two or three more statements with *want to.* Ss then write their statements individually.
- **Optional:** Tell Ss that they can't read their statements to their group. They have to remember them. Give Ss a few minutes to study and practice.
- In groups, Ss practice as in part A, but with their new statements.
- To wrap up, have a S from each group report on what the people in their group want to do next week.
- **Optional:** Ss tell their group about things they *don't* want to do next week but have to do.

Test 4

See page T-158 of this Teacher's Edition for general instructions on using the tests. Test 4 covers Units 13–16. Photocopy the test (pages T-171–T-174) and give a copy to each S. Allow 45–60 minutes for the test. Listening material for the tests is at the end of the Class Audio Program. The Test Audio Scripts and Answer Key start on page T-182 of this book.

3 LISTENING

CLASS AUDIO ONLY

Listen and check (✓) the correct response.

1. ☑ No, they weren't.
   ☐ No, they aren't.
2. ☐ At eleven o'clock.
   ☐ No, I didn't.
3. ☐ We took the bus.
   ☐ Amy and Katherine.
4. ☐ It was great.
   ☐ Sue and Tom were.
5. ☐ I'm going to visit my parents on Sunday.
   ☐ I had a terrible headache.
6. ☐ I'm sorry, but I can't go.
   ☐ No, I didn't go. I was at work.
7. ☐ I'm sorry, he's not here right now.
   ☐ Sandra is at work right now.
8. ☐ There's a restaurant on Grant Street.
   ☐ No, there isn't. Sorry.

4 CLASSROOM RULES

Write down four things you **have to** do in class.
Write down four things you **can't** do in class.
Compare with a partner.

You have to listen to the teacher.
You can't eat. . . .

5 TELL US ABOUT IT

A ***Group work*** Tell your classmates some of the things you did last week. Each student then asks one question about it.

Tell them about . . . .
something you did last week that you liked
something you did last week that you didn't like
someone interesting you talked to last week
something interesting you bought last week

A: I saw a movie last week.
B: What was the name of the movie?
A: . . .
C: Who was in it?
A: . . .
D: How did you like it?
A: . . .

B ***Group work*** Make a list of four things you want to do next week. Tell the group about them.

I want to see the new James Bond movie.

Interchange Activities

Interchange Activities

interchange 1 DIRECTORY ASSISTANCE

Student A

A ***Pair work*** You are the customer. Student B is a telephone operator. Ask for the telephone numbers of these people.

Phone numbers	
Ms. Kumiko Sato	....
Ms. Ana Sanchez	....
Mr. Mark Saunders	....
Mr. Anan Songsawat	....

Operator: Directory Assistance.
Customer: Hello. What's the number for . . . ?
Operator: How do you spell the last name?
Customer: . . .
Operator: And the first name?
Customer: . . .
Operator: Thank you. The number is . . . .

B ***Pair work*** Change roles. You are a telephone operator. Student B asks for some telephone numbers. Find the numbers in the directory.

Directory

CAPUTO, Anthony	555-9873
CAPUTO, Frank	555-8614
CARDENA, Elena	555-8654
CARDENAS, Emilio	555-0396
CHANG, Min Li	555-0215
CHANG, Ming Li	555-4667
CHO, Dae-joong	555-9807
CHO, Hae-kyoung	555-7546
CUMMINGS, Andrea	555-4089
CUMMINS, Andrew	555-2390

IC-2

interchange 1

In this information-sharing role play, Ss ask for and give telephone numbers and the spelling of names. This task emphasizes communication.

A *Pair work*

- Divide the class into pairs – one S in each pair is Student A and the other is Student B. In part A, Student A is the customer and Student B is the telephone operator.
- Books open. Show Ss that Student A uses page IC-2 and Student B uses page IC-4. Ss do not look at their partner's pages.
- Explain the task: Student A needs telephone numbers. Student A calls the operator to find out the numbers. Student B is the operator and gives the numbers.
- **Optional:** Write the following on the board:

Student A

	Phone number
Ms. Kumiko Sato	________

Student B

Directory

Sato, Kumiko	*555-6734*

Model the conversation line by line using the information on the board.

Interchange Activities

interchange 1 DIRECTORY ASSISTANCE

Student B

A ***Pair work*** You are a telephone operator. Student A is the customer. Student A asks for some telephone numbers. Find the numbers in the directory.

Directory
SANCHES, Ada 555-2576
SANCHEZ, Ana 555-3519
SANDERS, Carl 555-8125
SATO, Hiroshi 555-9012
SATO, Kumiko 555-6734
SAUNDERS, Mark 555-1329
SILVA, Roberto 555-3418
SILVER, Roberta 555-0926
SONGSAWAT, Amara 555-6775
SONGSAWAT, Anan 555-2258

Operator: Directory Assistance.
Customer: Hello. What's the number for . . . ?
Operator: How do you spell the last name?
Customer: . . .
Operator: And the first name?
Customer: . . .
Operator: Thank you. The number is . . . .

B ***Pair work*** Change roles. You are the customer, and Student A is a telephone operator. Ask for the numbers of these people.

Phone numbers	
Ms. Min Li Chang	....
Mr. Frank Caputo	....
Miss Andrea Cummings	....
Mr. Dae-joong Cho	....

IC-4

Ss with the appropriate roles repeat. Student B – the operator – speaks first. Point to *Student A* when you say "Kumiko Sato," point to the *Directory* list when you say "555-6734" so that Ss see where to get the information to complete the conversation. Fill in the phone number on the board after Ss repeat it.

- Ss do the activity in pairs. Walk around to give help.
- Ss raise their hands when they have finished, but they continue practicing until you tell them to stop.
- **Optional:** Put some additional names and phone numbers on the board for the faster Ss to practice when they finish.
- Ss check answers in pairs. Student A reads the numbers he or she wrote. Student B checks them in his or her directory.

B *Pair work*

- Pairs change roles: Student A is the telephone operator. Student B is the customer. Ss practice and check answers in pairs as before.
- After all Ss have completed their charts, elicit correct answers as a class.

interchange 2

In this activity, Ss solve a visual puzzle while they review the names of common objects, prepositions of place, and *where* questions with *be.*

A *Pair work*

- Books open. Point out the two pictures on page IC-3.
- Have Ss name the things they see in the pictures. The same things are in both pictures, but they are sometimes in different places. Make a list on the board. Ss may use these words:

backpack	*floor*
bed	*lamp*
books	*notebook*
calculator	*pen*
camera	*sunglasses*
CD player	*table*
chair	*telephone*
clock	*TV*
desk	*wastebasket*
dictionary	

  Leave the list on the board.
- Model the conversation with a S to demonstrate and explain the task. If necessary, ask the class where another item is, and elicit the answer.
- In pairs, Ss take turns asking and answering questions about the locations of things in the two pictures. Walk around to give help as needed. (Part B checks the answers.)
- **Optional:** Ss take notes of the locations of the items in the two pictures.

B *Class activity*

- With the class, go over the list from part A. Elicit the eleven things that are in a different places in the two pictures. Write them on the board as follows:

	Picture 1	*Picture 2*
sunglasses		
TV		
wastebasket		
CD player		
dictionary		
telephone		
backpack		
books		
calculator		
chair		
camera		

Interchange Activities

interchange 2 ***FIND THE DIFFERENCES***

A ***Pair work*** How are the two pictures different? Ask questions to find the differences.

A: Where are the sunglasses?
B: In picture 1, they're on the television.
A: In picture 2, they're behind the television.

Picture 1

Picture 2

B ***Class activity*** Talk about the differences with your classmates.

"In picture 1, the sunglasses are on the television. In picture 2, they're behind the television."

IC-3

- Have a S read the model sentence and then write the location of the sunglasses for each picture on the board under the column heading.
- Volunteers make statements like the one in the example about the other items. Correct the statements if necessary. Then have another volunteer go to the board and write the two locations under each heading.
- Continue until the table on the board is complete.

Possible answers

	Picture 1	Picture 2
sunglasses	on the television	behind the television on the desk
TV	under the desk next to the desk	on the desk
wastebasket	under the desk in front of the desk	next to the desk
CD player	on the desk next to the dictionary	under the bed
dictionary	on the desk next to the telephone next to the CD player	on the chair

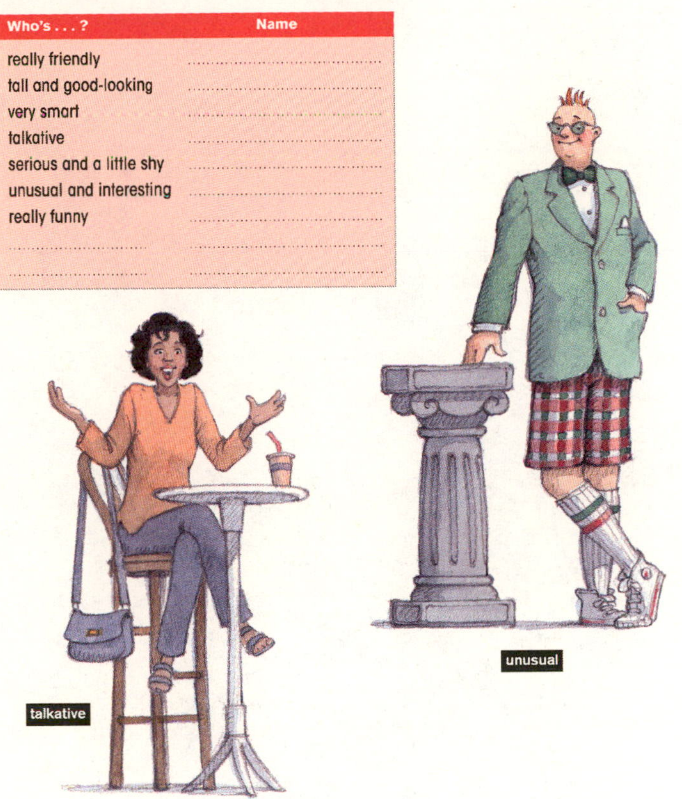

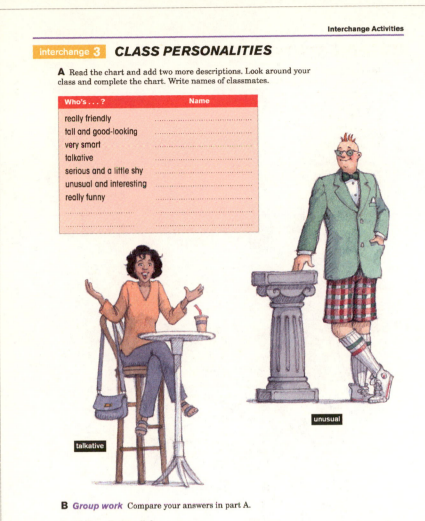

interchange 3 CLASS PERSONALITIES

A Read the chart and add two more descriptions. Look around your class and complete the chart. Write names of classmates.

Who's . . . ?	Name
really friendly	....
tall and good-looking	....
very smart	....
talkative	....
serious and a little shy	....
unusual and interesting	....
really funny	....
....	....
....	....

B ***Group work*** Compare your answers in part A.

A: Who's really friendly?
B: Sun-hee is really friendly.
C: Yes, and Yong-joon is friendly, too.

interchange 3

In this activity, Ss use adjectives and questions with *who* to describe people in their class.

A

- Books open. Use the illustrations and gestures to introduce the new vocabulary. Say each word. Ss listen and repeat. Ask Ss to explain the new vocabulary in their own words.
- Explain the task. Point out the chart, and have volunteers read the questions aloud.
- Give Ss a few minutes to write adjectives for two more questions. They may use the same adjectives in different combinations, or they may use other adjectives. Let them look at the Unit Summary in the back of the book for more adjectives.
- Elicit some of the questions using the new adjectives from Ss, and write them on the board.
- Ss work alone to complete their charts with the names of classmates who fit the descriptions.

B *Group work*

- Explain the task and model the conversation with two Ss.
- Put Ss in groups of four or five. Ss ask and answer the questions from part A, including their additional questions. Ss will have prepared answers to the first seven questions, but will need to think of answers on the spot for the additional questions.
- Circulate while they practice to make sure that they are taking turns and to offer help and encouragement.
- **Optional:** Have each group choose a secretary to ask the questions and write down the answers. Have the secretaries report back on their group's answers, for example, "We think Keiko and Kazuo are tall and good-looking."

telephone	on the desk next to the dictionary	on the table in front of the clock
backpack	on the chair	under the table
books	in the backpack	on the bed
calculator	in the backpack	on the floor under the chair
chair	in front of the desk	in front of the bed
camera	in front of the clock on the table	behind the clock

Optional: This activity provides for additional review of grammar and vocabulary from the unit.

- Look around the classroom and make some true and some false statements about the location of objects.
- If the statement is true, have Ss respond by saying, "Yes, it is" or "Yes, they are." If the statement is false, Ss say, "No, it's not" or "No, they're not," and correct the statement, for example:

  T: The eraser is in the wastebasket.
  Ss: No, it's not! It's on the desk.
- Continue the activity by having volunteers make true and false statements.

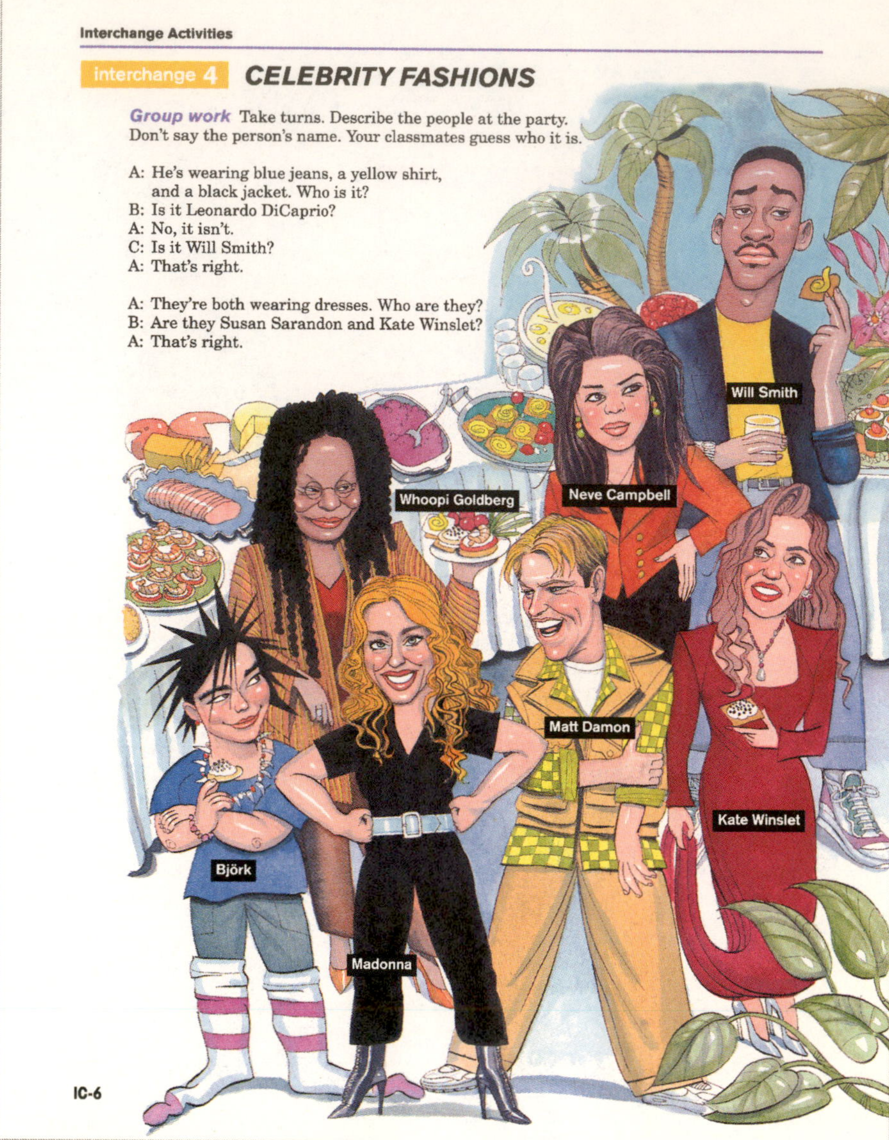

Interchange Activities
interchange 4 CELEBRITY FASHIONS
Group work Take turns. Describe the people at the party. Don't say the person's name. Your classmates guess who it is.
A: He's wearing blue jeans, a yellow shirt, and a black jacket. Who is it?
B: Is it Leonardo DiCaprio?
A: No, it isn't.
C: Is it Will Smith?
A: That's right.
A: They're both wearing dresses. Who are they?
B: Are they Susan Sarandon and Kate Winslet?
A: That's right.
Will Smith
Neve Campbell
Whoopi Goldberg
Matt Damon
Kate Winslet
Björk
Madonna
IC-6

interchange 4

In this activity, Ss play a guessing game and practice the present continuous and the names of colors and clothing.

Group work

- Books open. Read the names of the celebrities aloud one by one. Ss listen and repeat.
- **Optional:** If some Ss have information about some of the celebrities, let them share it with the other Ss.
- Give Ss a few minutes to look at the illustration. *(Note:* Ss may ask about the names of some of the other clothing in the illustration. Matt Damon is wearing *a vest.* Leonardo DiCaprio is wearing *a tuxedo.* Matt Damon is wearing *a checked* shirt. Whoopi Goldberg is wearing *a striped* jacket. Jennifer Lopez is wearing *a tube top.* Tom Cruise is wearing *a turtleneck.* It is not necessary to give this information unless Ss ask.)
- Have three volunteers read the first model conversation aloud. Emphasize that A gives only yes/no short answers. *(Note*: In guessing games, we guess and answer about one person with *it*, not *he* or *she*. In this conversation, the questions and answers are with *it*, although we know from the first sentence that the person is a man.)
- Have two other volunteers read the second model conversation aloud.
- **Optional:** To make the game more difficult, tell the first S to give very

little information. The other Ss have to ask more questions. Write this example conversation on the board:

A: He's wearing a T-shirt.
B: Is he wearing red pants?
A: No, he isn't.
C: Is the T-shirt blue?
A: Yes, it is.
C: Is it Chayanne?
A: Yes, it is.

- Put Ss in groups of four or five. Ss take turns giving information and guessing.
- **Optional:** Play a game. Make groups of six, with two teams of three Ss each.

  Both teams start with ten points. Tell one S on each team to keep score.

  Team A chooses a celebrity and writes the name on a piece of paper. They answer Team B's questions. Team A gets one point for every question that they answer. They show the name on the paper when the correct celebrity is named.

  Team B asks Team A questions to guess the name of the celebrity. If they guess a wrong name, they lose two points. They get two points for the right name.

  Team A's turn + Team B's turn = one round. The game can end after any round. The team with the most points wins.

Interchange Activities

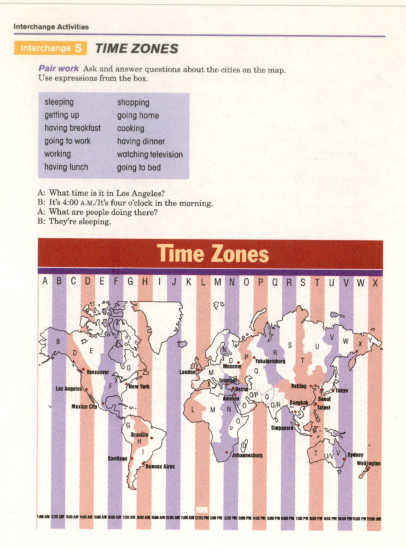

interchange 5 *TIME ZONES*

Pair work Ask and answer questions about the cities on the map. Use expressions from the box.

sleeping	shopping
getting up	going home
having breakfast	cooking
going to work	having dinner
working	watching television
having lunch	going to bed

A: What time is it in Los Angeles?
B: It's 4:00 A.M./It's four o'clock in the morning.
A: What are people doing there?
B: They're sleeping.

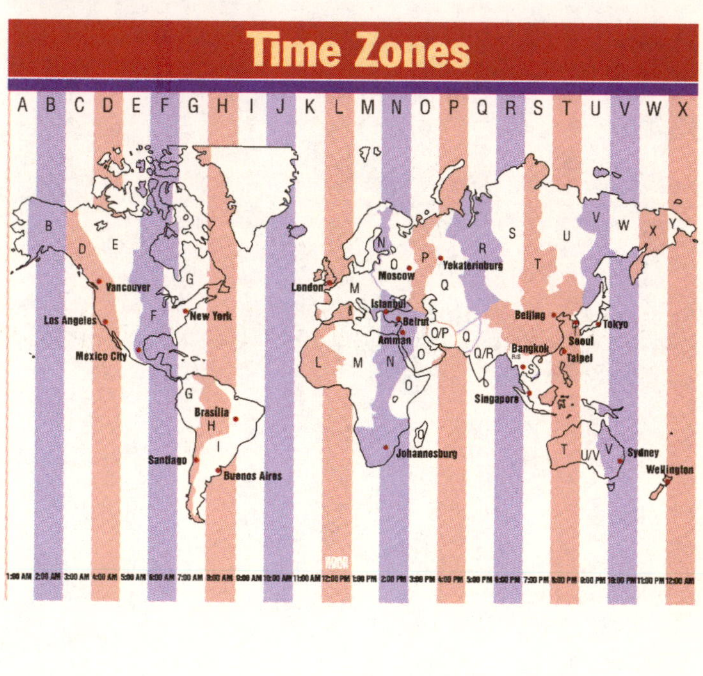

IC-8

interchange 5

In this activity, Ss practice the present continuous with expressions for discussing clock time and daily activities.

Pair work

- Books open. Go over the map as a class. Point out the times at the bottom. Check comprehension by asking "What time is it in Santiago?" (It's 7:00 A.M. / It's seven o'clock in the morning.)
- Go over the activities listed in the box. If there are questions, refer Ss to the Grammar Focus exercise on page 31 or the Word Power exercise on page 32.
- **Optional:** Have Ss suggest a few more daily activities.
- Explain the task: Student A chooses the city; Student B looks for the time at the bottom of the map and thinks of an appropriate activity.
- Have two Ss model the conversation aloud.
- Ss practice in pairs. Walk around to give help.
- When things begin to quiet down, bring the class back together. Elicit some answers from the class. Ask about four or five cities in widely separated time zones, such as Vancouver, London, Singapore, and Wellington.

Optional:
Time: 10 minutes. This activity provides additional practice with the present continuous and the vocabulary of the unit.

- With the Ss, calculate the actual time in the cities on the map based on the time where you are. Round the time to the nearest hour.
- If you wish, let Ss add other cities.
- With new partners, Ss do the activity again, this time using the actual time of day.

Interchange Activities

interchange 6 CLASS SURVEY

A ***Class activity*** Go around the class and find this information. If possible, write a classmate's name only once.

Find someone who . . . .

	Name		Name
gets up at 5:00 A.M. on weekdays	....	rides a bicycle to class	....
gets up at noon on Saturdays	....	rides a motorcycle to class	....
has breakfast in bed	....	walks to class	....
works at night	....	goes on the Internet every day	....
works on weekends	....	doesn't own a computer	....
lives downtown	....	wears blue jeans every day	....
lives in the country	....	speaks three languages	....
lives alone	....		

having breakfast in bed

riding a motorcycle to class

speaking three languages

A: Do you get up at 5:00 A.M.?
B: No, I get up at 7:00 A.M.
A: Do you get up at 5:00 A.M.?
C: Yes, I get up at 5:00 A.M. every day.

B ***Group work*** Compare your information.

A: Keiko gets up at 5:00 A.M.
B: Akira gets up at 5:00 A.M., too.

IC-9

interchange 6

In this activity, Ss find out about one another's daily lives and habits.

A *Class activity*

- Books open. Have Ss read the phrases in the chart. Use the illustrations to explain the new expressions.
- **Optional:** Let Ss add two or three more phrases to the list. Write them on the board for Ss to copy.
- Have three Ss read the model conversation aloud.
- Demonstrate the task by asking a few Ss the same question. Walk from one S to another until you find someone who says yes. Encourage Ss to give true answers:

  T: Jennifer, do you get up at 5 A.M. on weekdays?
  S1: No, I don't. I get up at 7:00.
  T: How about you, Akira? Do you get up at 5:00 A.M. on weekdays?
  S2: No, I get up at 8:30.
  T: Sun-hee, do you get up at 5:00 A.M. on weekdays?
  S3: Yes, I do.
  T: *(writing Sun-hee's name on the board)* OK, Sun-hee gets up at 5:00 A.M. on weekdays.

- Have the Ss walk around the room, ask and answer questions, and fill in names. Encourage Ss to change interview partners frequently.
- This is a noisy activity! Bring the class back together when things begin to quiet down.

B *Group work*

- Have two Ss read the exchange. Tell Ss they can also ask questions (e.g., "Who gets up at 5:00 A.M. on weekdays?") Insist that they answer in complete sentences.
- Put Ss in groups of four or five. Have them compare their information.
- **Optional:** Have Ss take notes of all the answers in their group. Bring the class back together, and elicit all the names that Ss found for each activity.

interchange 7

In this activity, Ss review *there is, there are,* and vocabulary for rooms and furnishings.

A

Books open. Ss study the illustrations and make two vocabulary lists on the board: the names of the rooms in the two apartments and the names of the things that are in the rooms. There are different things in the two apartments.

Rooms

bathroom	*kitchen*	*bedroom*
living room		

Things in rooms

bed	*desk*	*plants*
bookcase	*dresser*	*rug*
cat	*lamps*	*sofa*
chairs	*microwave*	*table*
coffee table	*mirror*	*TV*
curtains	*pictures*	

- Demonstrate and explain the task by reading the written models.
- **Optional:** Have Ss also talk about differences in colors.
- Ss work individually to write five sentences about the differences between the two apartments.

B *Pair work*

- Ss compare sentences in pairs. Ss take turns reading their sentences aloud.
- **Optional:** Show Ss how to stress the words that give different information, for example: "There are four chairs in Bill's kitchen. There are only **three** chairs in **Jane's** kitchen."

Possible answers

Kitchen
1. There are four chairs in Bill's kitchen. There are only three chairs in Jane's kitchen.
2. There are curtains in Jane's kitchen, but there aren't any curtains in Bill's kitchen.
3. There's a microwave in Bill's kitchen. There's no microwave in Jane's kitchen.

Bathroom
4. There are curtains in Jane's bathroom. There are no curtains in Bill's bathroom.
5. There's a rug in Jane's bathroom, but there's no rug in Bill's bathroom.

Bedroom
6. There's a dresser in Jane's bedroom, but there's no dresser in Bill's bedroom.
7. There's a mirror in Jane's bedroom. There isn't a mirror in Bill's bedroom.
8. There's a TV in Bill's bedroom, but there isn't a TV in Jane's bedroom.
9. There's a desk and a chair in Bill's bedroom, but there isn't a desk or chair in Jane's bedroom.
10. There are curtains in Jane's bedroom, but there aren't any curtains in Bill's bedroom.
11. There's a picture in Jane's bedroom. There's no picture in Bill's bedroom.

Living room
12. There's a sofa in Bill's living room, but there's no sofa in Jane's living room.
13. There are two blue chairs in Bill's living room. There are two orange chairs in Jane's living room.
14. There's one lamp in Bill's living room. There are two lamps in Jane's living room.
15. There's a coffee table in Jane's living room. There isn't a coffee table in Bill's living room.
16. There's a bookcase in Jane's living room, but there's no bookcase in Bill's living room.
17. There's a TV in Bill's living room. There isn't a TV in Jane's living room.
18. There are some plants in Jane's living room, but there are no plants in Bill's living room.
19. Jane has a cat, but Bill doesn't.

Interchange Activities

interchange 7 ***FIND THE DIFFERENCES***

Bill's apartment

Jane's apartment

A Write five differences between Bill's apartment and Jane's apartment.

There are four chairs in Bill's kitchen. There are only three chairs in Jane's kitchen.
There's a sofa in Bill's living room, but there's no sofa in Jane's living room.

B ***Pair work*** Compare your answers.

IC-10

Interchange Activities

interchange 8 THE PERFECT JOB

A ***Pair work*** You're looking for a job. Which of these things do you want in a job? First, answer the questions. Then ask your partner the same questions.

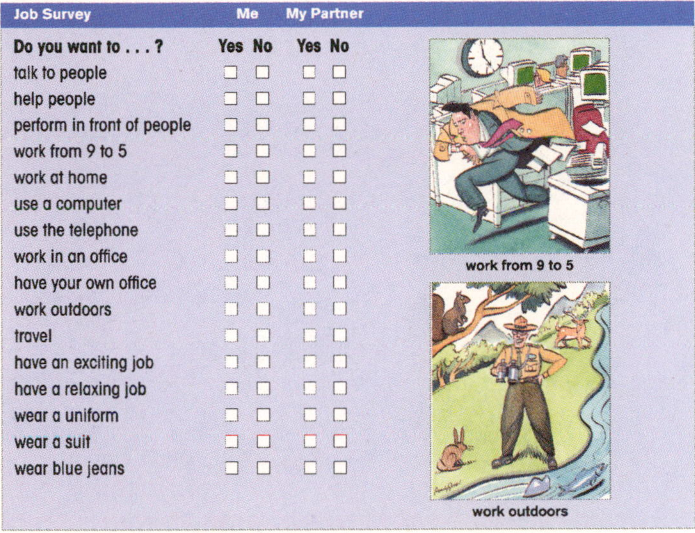

Job Survey	Me		My Partner	
Do you want to . . . ?	Yes	No	Yes	No
talk to people	☐	☐	☐	☐
help people	☐	☐	☐	☐
perform in front of people	☐	☐	☐	☐
work from 9 to 5	☐	☐	☐	☐
work at home	☐	☐	☐	☐
use a computer	☐	☐	☐	☐
use the telephone	☐	☐	☐	☐
work in an office	☐	☐	☐	☐
have your own office	☐	☐	☐	☐
work outdoors	☐	☐	☐	☐
travel	☐	☐	☐	☐
have an exciting job	☐	☐	☐	☐
have a relaxing job	☐	☐	☐	☐
wear a uniform	☐	☐	☐	☐
wear a suit	☐	☐	☐	☐
wear blue jeans	☐	☐	☐	☐

work from 9 to 5

work outdoors

B ***Class activity*** Think of a good job for yourself. Then tell the class.

"I want to be a musician because I want to work at home. . . ."

work at home

perform in front of people

travel

IC-11

- **Optional:** Bring the class together and elicit all the differences. How many differences did they find?
- **Optional:**
- Expand the list of *Things in rooms* on the board. Have Ss tell you things that are in their own kitchens, bedrooms, and living rooms that are not in the list.
- Put Ss in pairs. Each pair chooses one room in their own houses or apartments to compare.
- Ss take turns, for example:

  S1: I have a table and chairs in my kitchen.

  S2: There are a table and chairs in my kitchen, too. There isn't a window in my kitchen.

interchange 8

In this interesting exercise, Ss talk about their personal job preferences. *Note:* Ss use *want to* + verb in controlled expressions. *Want to* + verb is new here, but you don't need to teach it for this exercise. The structure is presented more fully in Unit 16.

A *Pair work*

- Books open. Explain the first part of the task. Have Ss read the survey questions aloud, one by one.
- Use the illustrations in parts A and B to explain the new expressions. If necessary, help Ss understand other new vocabulary.
- Ss work individually, checking *Yes* or *No* in the *Me* column.
- Explain the pair task. Have two Ss demonstrate asking each other the first question in the book and checking their partner's answer.
- Ss ask and answer the questions with a partner and check their partner's answers in the book.
- **Optional:** Take a class survey of the responses by asking for a show of hands for each question. Write the results on the board, and discuss them briefly.

B *Class activity*

- Refer Ss to the three illustrations at the bottom of the page. Ask a S to model the example sentence. The S completes the statement.
- Explain the task: "Think of a job for yourself. Think about the answers on your job survey." Give Ss a few minutes to think about their "perfect job" and their reasons.
- **Alternate presentation:** Have Ss look at their partner's responses and suggest a perfect job for them. Then have Ss tell the class the job and give the reasons.
- Go around the class and give each S a chance to talk about his or her perfect job and give the reasons.
- **Alternate presentation:** In larger classes, you may want to do this exercise in groups.

Interchange Activities

interchange 9 EATING HABITS

A Complete this survey about the foods you eat.
Use these foods and other foods you know.

Things I eat	every day	two/three times a week	about once a week
meat/fish			
dairy			
fruits			
vegetables			
snacks			
other foods			

B *Pair work* Compare your information.

A: I eat chicken once a week.
B: I never eat chicken. I eat steak once a week. . . .

C *Class activity* What are the class's favorite foods?

IC-12

interchange 9

In this extension activity, Ss practice the vocabulary of the unit while talking about their own eating habits and preferences. The exercise also illustrates some popular foods that Ss may want to talk about.

A

- Say the name of each food. Ss listen and repeat.
- Have Ss tell you other foods they like to eat. Refer Ss to the Unit Summary for more foods named in the unit. Let them consult with each other and refer to dictionaries if necessary. Write this additional vocabulary on the board for reference.
- Point out the chart heads: *Things I eat every day, two/three times a week,* and *about once a week.* Elicit two or three examples of foods in each category from Ss. (*Note:* A *snack* is any food you eat between meals.)
- Ss work individually to complete the chart. As they work, go around the class to give help and to check their work.

B *Pair work*

- Divide the class into pairs. To clarify the task, have two Ss model the example conversation.
- If necessary, have two other Ss compare answers using their own information.
- **Optional:** While comparing, tell Ss to give their opinions of their partner's food choices. How do they feel about the foods?
- Ss work in pairs to talk about the foods they eat.

C *Class activity*

- Write the six categories on the board. Have Ss look at the foods they put in the *every day* and *two/three times a week* columns. Ask Ss to call out the foods they wrote, and make a list of these foods on the board.
- Say the name of each food, and have Ss raise their hands to show how many eat each one. Write the number of people who raise their hands after each food. The foods with the most votes are the class's favorites.

interchange 10 **HIDDEN TALENTS**

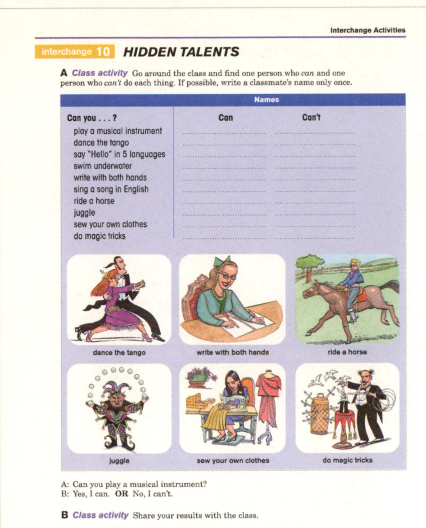

A ***Class activity*** Go around the class and find one person who *can* and one person who *can't* do each thing. If possible, write a classmate's name only once.

Can you . . . ?	Names: Can	Names: Can't
play a musical instrument	....	....
dance the tango	....	....
say "Hello" in 5 languages	....	....
swim underwater	....	....
write with both hands	....	....
sing a song in English	....	....
ride a horse	....	....
juggle	....	....
sew your own clothes	....	....
do magic tricks	....	....

dance the tango

write with both hands

ride a horse

juggle

sew your own clothes

do magic tricks

A: Can you play a musical instrument?
B: Yes, I can. **OR** No, I can't.

B ***Class activity*** Share your results with the class.

"Mei-Li can't play a musical instrument, but Wen Pin can."

IC-13

interchange 10

In this activity, Ss find out about their classmates' hidden talents while they practice *can* and *can't.*

A Class activity

- Books open. Have Ss read the questions in the chart. Use the illustrations in parts A and B to explain the new expressions. If necessary, help Ss understand other new vocabulary.
- **Optional:** Let Ss add two or three more phrases to the chart. Write the phrases on the board for Ss to copy.
- Have two Ss read the model conversation aloud.
- Demonstrate the task by asking a few Ss the same question. Walk from one S to another until you find someone who says yes. Encourage Ss to give true answers:

  T: Jennifer, can you play a musical instrument?
  S1: No, I can't.
  T: (*writing Jennifer's name on the board*) OK, Jennifer can't play a musical instrument. How about you, Akira? Can you play a musical instrument?
  S2: Yes, I can. I play the guitar.
  T: (*writing Akira's name on the board*) OK, Akira can play the guitar.
- Have the Ss walk around the room, ask and answer questions, and fill in names. Encourage Ss to change interview partners frequently.
- Participate in the activity yourself. End the activity when things begin to quiet down.

B Class activity

- Demonstrate the task. Use some of the information you collected while you did the activity, for example, "Kumiko can touch her toes, but Kenji can't."
- Have each S report about one "hidden talent" from the chart in part A. Several Ss may report on each talent. In large classes, have Ss report in groups.
- **Optional:** Copy the chart onto the board, leaving lots of space for names. Have one or two Ss write the names on the board as the other Ss report.

interchange 11

In this activity, Ss create stories and share them with a partner. They tell about things happening now and things that are going to happen.

A

- As a class, study each illustration and the sentence above it. Make sure that students understand each celebration.
- Many of the expressions are from Unit 11. Instead of explaining other vocabulary right away, have Ss work in pairs to match each expression to one or more of the pictures. In the process, most of the unfamiliar words will be explained.
- If necessary, help Ss with these few expressions: *listen to a speech* (*speech* comes from *speak*), *receive a diploma* (*receive* means *get*; Ss can see a *diploma* in the second illustration), and *fireworks* (explain using noises, gestures, and drawings on the board).
- Explain the task. Point out the first picture and say, "It's New Year's Eve. What are the people doing? What are they going to do?" Write Ss answers on the board.
- Working in pairs, Ss write four or five sentences about each picture. Encourage Ss to use their own ideas.
- **Optional:** If time is limited, have each pair choose just one of the pictures to write about. In this case, require at least one additional idea.

Possible stories *(Possible additional ideas are in boldface type.)*

1. It's New Year's Eve. They're having a party. They're going to shout "Happy New Year!" **and hug each other. Later, they are going to dance** and have a good time until morning.
2. It's Jessica's high school graduation. Jessica and her classmates are wearing special hats. They're going to listen to a speech and receive their diplomas. Later, they're going to open some presents **from their families** and **have a party**.
3. It's Jeremy's birthday. He's having a party. They're having a good time. His friends are singing "Happy Birthday" to him. He's going to **make a wish** and blow out the candles. Later, Jeremy is going to open his presents. They're all going to have a good time.
4. It's the Fourth of July in the United States. People are seeing their friends. Some people are having a picnic and barbecuing hamburgers. **At nine o'clock,** they are going to watch the fireworks. Everyone is having a good time.

interchange 11 ***CELEBRATIONS***

A *Pair work* What are these people doing? What are they going to do? Write a story for each picture. Use these expressions and your own ideas.

have a party	receive a diploma
shout "Happy New Year!"	get some presents
see friends	wear special hats
listen to a speech	have a good time
sing "Happy Birthday"	have a picnic
blow out the candles	barbecue hamburgers
open the presents	watch the fireworks

1. It's New Year's Eve. . . .

They're having a party. They're going to shout "Happy New Year!" . . .

2. It's Jessica's high school graduation. . . .

3. It's Jeremy's birthday. . . .

4. It's the Fourth of July in the U.S. . . .

B *Group work* Join another pair. Compare your stories.

IC-14

- **Optional:** Walk around to read what Ss are writing. When you see a good story, send the S to the board to write it there. You can correct mistakes before the S writes it, or correct it later with the whole class.

B *Group work*

- Ss read their stories to one another in groups.
- **Optional:** To shorten the time, have each S choose his or her best story to read to the whole class or to a group.
- **Optional:** Have pairs choose their best story, make a clean, corrected copy, and post it on the wall of the classroom for everyone to read.

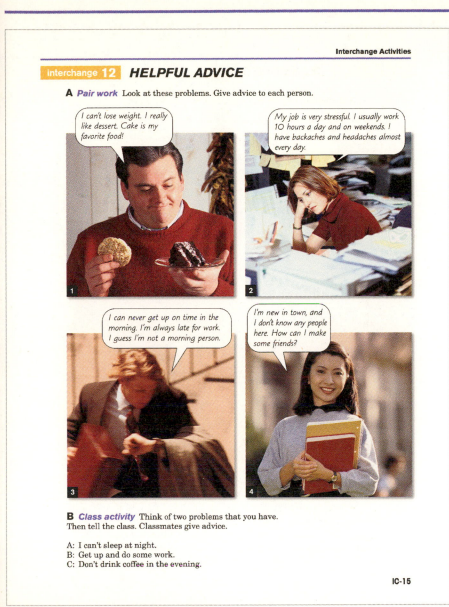

interchange 12 HELPFUL ADVICE

A ***Pair work*** Look at these problems. Give advice to each person.

I can't lose weight. I really like dessert. Cake is my favorite food!
1

My job is very stressful. I usually work 10 hours a day and on weekends. I have backaches and headaches almost every day.
2

I can never get up on time in the morning. I'm always late for work. I guess I'm not a morning person.
3

I'm new in town, and I don't know any people here. How can I make some friends?
4

B ***Class activity*** Think of two problems that you have. Then tell the class. Classmates give advice.

A: I can't sleep at night.
B: Get up and do some work.
C: Don't drink coffee in the evening.

interchange 12

In this communicative activity, Ss talk about some of their own problems, and they use imperatives to give advice.

A *Pair work*

- Books open. Explain the task: Ask four Ss to each read one of the speech bubbles aloud. It should not be necessary to explain vocabulary.
- Choose one of the problems as an example, and do it with the class. Read the speech bubble again, and elicit advice from the Ss.
- Ss work in pairs to give advice about the problems. Have Ss write their sentences on a piece of paper.

Possible advice

1. Don't eat ice cream every day.
   Eat it on weekends or once a week.
   Use a very small dish for your ice cream.
   Eat small bites.
   Don't eat fast.
   Exercise more.
   You look fine. Don't worry about it.
2. Get a new job.
   Don't work on weekends.
   Go to a gym or go swimming.
   See a doctor.
   Sit up straight at your desk.
   Try exercising.
3. Sleep for eight hours every night.
   Change your work hours.
   Change your job. Work at night.
4. Talk to people at work or at school.
   Go to a church.
   Join a club.
   Do volunteer work.
   Get a dog.

- To follow up, have pairs share their advice for each person with the class. Write the advice on the board.
- **Alternate presentation:** Have each pair write a piece of advice at random on the board. Ss guess which person the advice is for.

B *Class activity*

- Explain the task. Have three Ss read the model conversation aloud.
- Give Ss several minutes to write down two problems of their own. If Ss are not comfortable sharing their real problems, have them make up problems.
- Ss take turns telling the class their problems. Have the class give advice to each S.
- If time allows, do the same with the Ss' second problem, or put the Ss in groups to discuss the second problem.

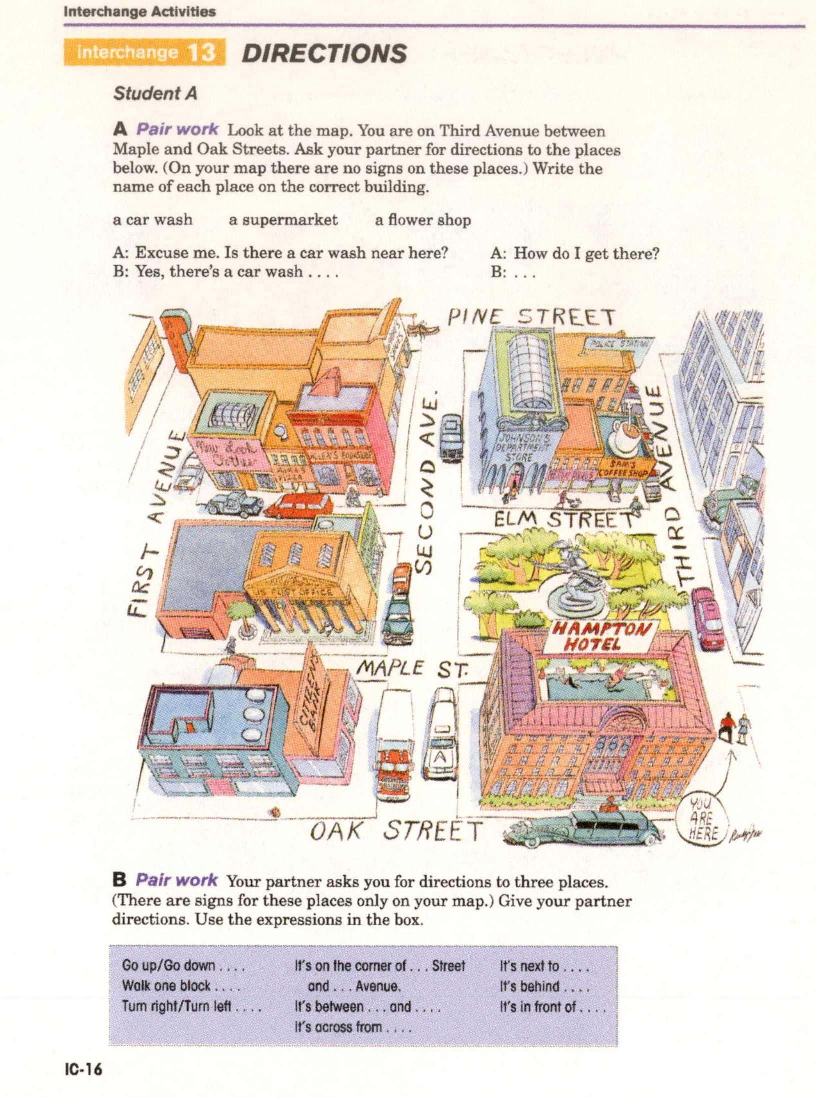

interchange 13 DIRECTIONS

Student A

A ***Pair work*** Look at the map. You are on Third Avenue between Maple and Oak Streets. Ask your partner for directions to the places below. (On your map there are no signs on these places.) Write the name of each place on the correct building.

a car wash   a supermarket   a flower shop

A: Excuse me. Is there a car wash near here?
B: Yes, there's a car wash . . . .

A: How do I get there?
B: . . .

B ***Pair work*** Your partner asks you for directions to three places. (There are signs for these places only on your map.) Give your partner directions. Use the expressions in the box.

Go up/Go down	It's on the corner of . . . Street and . . . Avenue.	It's next to . . . .
Walk one block	It's between . . . and	It's behind . . . .
Turn right/Turn left	It's across from	It's in front of . . . .

interchange 13

This information-sharing activity is a map-based puzzle. Ss ask for and give locations and directions.

A *Pair work*

- Divide the class into pairs and assign each student the role of Student A or Student B.
- Student As turn to page IC-16 and Student Bs turn to page IC-18. Tell partners that they should not look at each other's pages.
- Explain the task: Student A asks Student B how to find three places. Student B gives directions, and Student A follows them on the map. Student A writes the name of the store on the appropriate building.
- Have two Ss model the example conversation. Then Ss do the task in pairs.

B *Pair work*

- Ss change roles. Now Student B asks Student A how to find a coffee shop, a shoe store, and a bookstore.
- When talk begins to quiet down, bring the class back together. Ask several pairs to ask for and give directions to one of the places.
- **Optional:** Bring in a map of the city or town where your school is located. Ss ask for and give directions to places on the map.

interchange 13 DIRECTIONS

Student B

A ***Pair work*** Look at the map. You are on Third Avenue between Maple and Oak Streets. Your partner asks you for directions to three places. (There are signs for these places only on your map.) Answer using the expressions in the box.

A: Excuse me. Is there a car wash near here?
B: Yes, there's a car wash . . . .

A: How do I get there?
B: . . .

Go up/Go down	It's on the corner of . . . Street and . . . Avenue.	It's next to . . . .
Walk one block	It's between . . . and	It's behind . . . .
Turn right/Turn left	It's across from	It's in front of . . . .

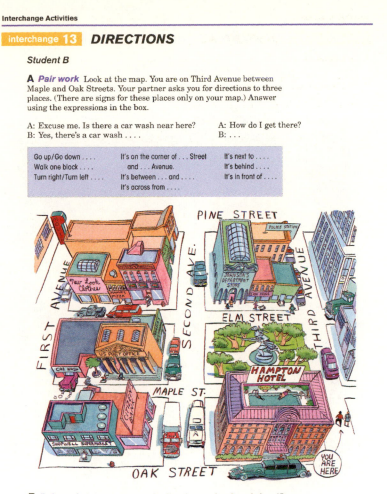

B ***Pair work*** Ask your partner for directions to the places below. (On your map there are no signs on these places.) Write the name of each place on the correct building.

coffee shop shoe store bookstore

Interchange Activities

interchange 14 PAST AND PRESENT

A ***Pair work*** Ask a partner questions about the past and about the present. Check (✓) the answers.

A: Did you clean your room as a child?
B: No, I didn't. (Yes, I did.)

A: Do you clean your room now?
B: Yes, I do. (No, I don't.)

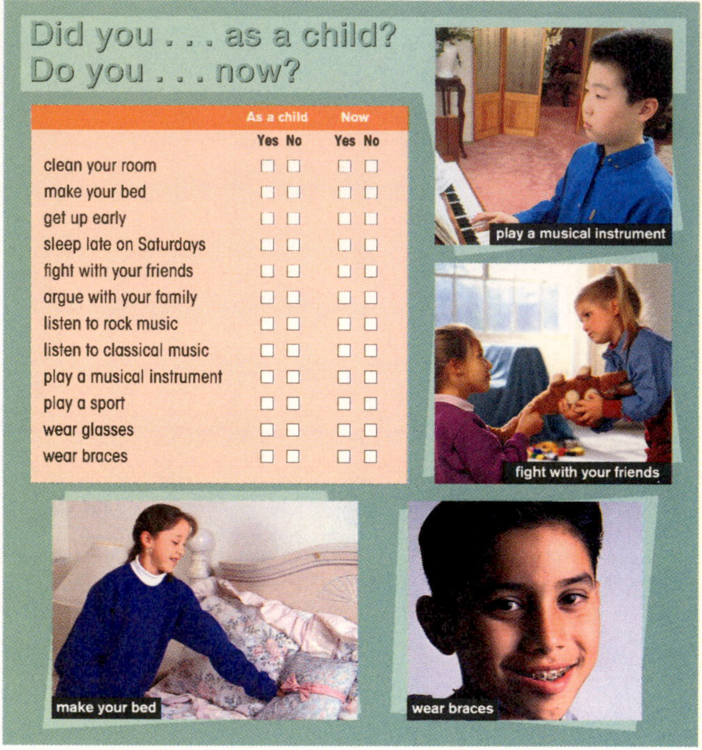

Did you . . . as a child?
Do you . . . now?

	As a child		Now	
	Yes	No	Yes	No
clean your room	☐	☐	☐	☐
make your bed	☐	☐	☐	☐
get up early	☐	☐	☐	☐
sleep late on Saturdays	☐	☐	☐	☐
fight with your friends	☐	☐	☐	☐
argue with your family	☐	☐	☐	☐
listen to rock music	☐	☐	☐	☐
listen to classical music	☐	☐	☐	☐
play a musical instrument	☐	☐	☐	☐
play a sport	☐	☐	☐	☐
wear glasses	☐	☐	☐	☐
wear braces	☐	☐	☐	☐

B ***Group work*** Join another pair. Tell them about your partner.

"Paulo didn't clean his room as a child, but he cleans his room now."

IC-17

interchange 14

This activity gives Ss an opportunity to compare their lives in the past and now. They practice questions and answers in the simple past and the simple present.

A *Pair work*

- Books open. Have S read the questions in the chart. Use the photos to explain the new expressions. If necessary, help Ss understand other new vocabulary.
- **Optional:** Let Ss add two or three more phrases to the chart. Write the phrases on the board for Ss to copy.
- Have two Ss read the model conversation aloud.
- Have the Ss walk around the room, ask and answer questions, and fill in names. Encourage Ss to change interview partners frequently.
- Participate in the activity yourself. End the activity when things begin to quiet down.

B *Group work*

- Explain the task and have a S read the model language.
- Two pairs join to form a small group. Then Ss take turns telling the group about their partners.
- Bring the class back together, and have several Ss tell the class one interesting thing about their partner as a child and now.

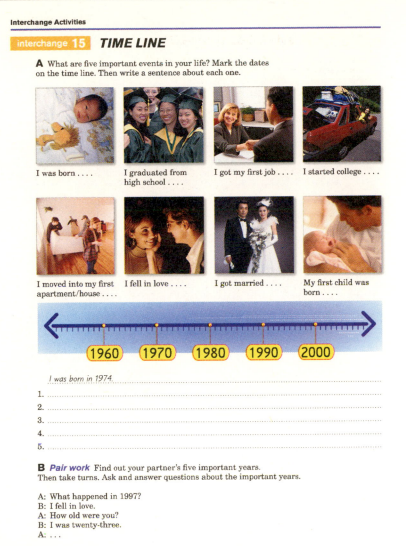

interchange 15 TIME LINE

A What are five important events in your life? Mark the dates on the time line. Then write a sentence about each one.

I was born . . . .

I graduated from high school . . . .

I got my first job . . . .

I started college . . . .

I moved into my first apartment/house . . . .

I fell in love . . . .

I got married . . . .

My first child was born . . . .

1960 1970 1980 1990 2000

I was born in 1974.

1. ....
2. ....
3. ....
4. ....
5. ....

B ***Pair work*** Find out your partner's five important years. Then take turns. Ask and answer questions about the important years.

A: What happened in 1997?
B: I fell in love.
A: How old were you?
B: I was twenty-three.
A: . . .

interchange 15

In this personalized activity, Ss practice the past tense as they talk about important events in their lives.

A

- Books open. Have Ss read the phrases under the photos. There should not be any questions about vocabulary since all the phrases are illustrated in the photographs.
- **Optional:** Let Ss add more events to choose from. Make a list on the board.

Other possible events

I started my own company . . . .
I adopted a child . . . .
My mother died . . . .
I lived in Hawaii . . . .
I finished graduate school . . . .

- Use the model to explain and demonstrate the task. Ss work individually to write five important events from their life and to mark the dates on the timeline. They can use the events in the photos or other important events in their lives.
- Go around while they work to check their progress and to help if necessary.

B *Pair work*

- Put Ss in pairs. Have Ss write down the dates they marked on their timelines on a separate piece of paper and exchange it with their partner.
- Use the model to explain and demonstrate the task: Ss ask each other what happened in each year and then ask further questions about the event.
- Books closed. Ss do the task in pairs, asking and answering questions about the five important years. They write down their partner's answers next to the years. The answers can be in note form.
- Bring the class back together, and have the Ss tell the class about one important event in their partner's life.
- **Alternate presentation:** In large classes, this step may be done in groups.

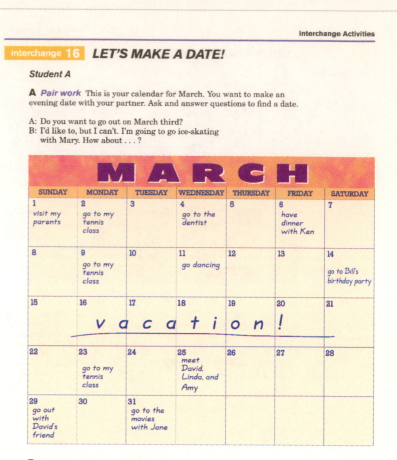

interchange 16 LET'S MAKE A DATE!

Student A

A ***Pair work*** This is your calendar for March. You want to make an evening date with your partner. Ask and answer questions to find a date.

A: Do you want to go out on March third?
B: I'd like to, but I can't. I'm going to go ice-skating with Mary. How about . . . ?

MARCH

SUNDAY	MONDAY	TUESDAY	WEDNESDAY	THURSDAY	FRIDAY	SATURDAY
1 visit my parents	2 go to my tennis class	3	4 go to the dentist	5	6 have dinner with Ken	7
8	9 go to my tennis class	10	11 go dancing	12	13	14 go to Bill's birthday party
15	16 vacation!	17	18	19	20	21
22	23 go to my tennis class	24	25 meet David, Linda, and Amy	26	27	28
29 go out with David's friend	30	31 go to the movies with Jane				

B ***Pair work*** Now you have a date. Discuss the possibilities. Decide what to do.

A: Do you want to play tennis?
B: No, I don't play tennis very well.
Do you want to go to a museum?
A: No, I don't like museums. . . .

C ***Class activity*** Tell the class your plan.

interchange 16

In this communicative activity, Ss practice invitations and excuses.

A *Pair work*

- Put Ss in pairs, and assign the roles of Student A or Student B.
- Student As turn to page IC-19 and Student Bs turn to page IC-21. They should not look at each other's pages.
- Explain the task: Student A invites B, B replies, giving an excuse if he or she is not available. Then B picks another date and asks A. Ss continue until they find a date when they are both free.
- Have two Ss read the model conversation. Then Ss do the activity in pairs.

B *Pair work*

- Explain the task: Pairs decide what they are going to do on their date.
- Have two Ss read the model conversation. Then Ss do the activity in pairs.

C *Class activity*

- Bring the class back together, and ask each pair to tell the class what they are going to do and when they are going to do it.

Interchange Activities

interchange 16 LET'S MAKE A DATE!

Student B

A ***Pair work*** This is your calendar for March. You want to make an evening date with your partner. Ask and answer questions to find a date.

A: Do you want to go out on March third?
B: I'd like to, but I can't. I'm going to go ice-skating with Mary. How about . . . ?

MARCH

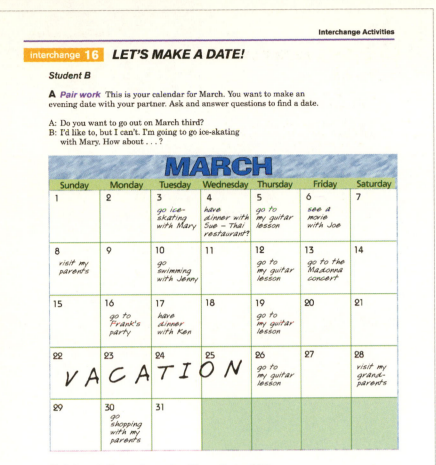

Sunday	Monday	Tuesday	Wednesday	Thursday	Friday	Saturday
1	2	3 go ice-skating with Mary	4 have dinner with Sue – Thai restaurant?	5 go to my guitar lesson	6 see a movie with Joe	7
8 visit my parents	9	10 go swimming with Jenny	11	12 go to my guitar lesson	13 go to the Madonna concert	14
15	16 go to Frank's party	17 have dinner with Ken	18	19 go to my guitar lesson	20	21
22 VA	23 CA	24 TI	25 ON	26 go to my guitar lesson	27	28 visit my grand-parents
29	30 go shopping with my parents	31				

B ***Pair work*** Now you have a date. Discuss the possibilities. Decide what to do.

A: Do you want to play tennis?
B: No, I don't play tennis very well.
Do you want to go to a museum?
A: No, I don't like museums. . . .

C ***Class activity*** Tell the class your plan.

IC-21

Unit Summaries

Unit Summaries contain lists of key vocabulary and functional expressions. Key vocabulary is listed in the unit in which a word first appears. For Grammar Focus models, please refer to the appropriate unit page.

IT'S NICE TO MEET YOU.

KEY VOCABULARY

Nouns
The alphabet
See Exercise 4 on page 3.

Numbers (1–10)
See Exercise 10 on page 6.

Titles
Miss
Mr.
Mrs.
Ms.

Parts of the day
morning
afternoon
evening
night

Other
book
(English/math) class
classmate
country
female
male
(first/last) name
(tele)phone number
teacher

Pronouns
Subject pronouns
I
you
he
she
it

Adjectives
Possessives
my
your
his
her

Other
favorite
first
last
popular

Verbs
am ('m)
are ('re)
is ('s)

Adverbs
Responses
no
yes

Other
again
(over) there
too

Preposition
in (my class)

Conjunction
and

Interjection
oh

EXPRESSIONS

Saying hello
Good morning/afternoon/evening.
Hello./Hi.
How are you?
(I'm) great. Thank you./Thanks.
(just) fine.
not bad.
OK.

Saying good-bye
Good-bye./Bye./Bye-bye.
Good night.
See you later/tomorrow.
Have a good evening/a nice day.
Thanks./You, too.

Introducing yourself
Hi. My name is . . . .
I'm . . . .
It's nice to meet you, ...
Nice to meet you, too.

Exchanging personal information
What's your name?
I'm . . . . / My name is . . . .
What's your phone number?
It's . . . .

Checking and confirming information
What's your last name again?
It's . . . .
How do you spell . . . ?
Is that . . . ?
Yes, that's right./No, it's . . . .
Are you . . . ?
No, I'm not./Yes, I am.

Introducing someone
. . . , this is . . . .
Hi, ... It's nice to meet you.

Apologizing
I'm sorry.

Getting someone's attention
Excuse me.

Giving an opinion
I think . . . .

2 WHAT'S THIS?

KEY VOCABULARY

Nouns
Classroom objects
board
book
book bag
calculator
cassette player
chair
clock
desk
(English) dictionary
encyclopedia
eraser
map
notebook
pen
pencil
table
wastebasket

Personal items
address
(electronic) address book
bag
briefcase
camera
CD player
cell phone
earring(s)
glasses
(car) keys
newspaper
pager
purse
stamp
sunglasses
(tele)phone
television
umbrella
wallet
watch

Other
box
chopsticks
classroom
door
exercise
location
pocket
restaurant
sentence
thing
wall
window

Pronouns
Demonstratives
that
these
this

Subject pronoun
they

Adjectives
gone
great
interesting
nice

Articles
a/an
the

Verbs
bet
open
relax
spell

Adverbs
still
very

Prepositions
behind
in
in front of
next to
on
under

Interjections
hmm
No problem.
Oh, cool!
Oh, no!
OK.
See?
uh
Wait!
Wow!

EXPRESSIONS

Identifying objects
What's this called in English?
  I don't know.
  It's a/an . . . .
What are these called in English?
  They're . . . .

Finding the owner of an item
Is this your . . . ?
  Yes, it is./No, it's not. It's . . . .
Are these his . . . ?
  Yes, they are./No, they're not. They're . . . .

Asking for and giving location
Where is . . . ?
  It's under/. . . the . . . .
Where are . . . ?
  They're under/. . . the . . . .

Checking information
How do you spell that?

Making a request
Let me . . . .

Thanking someone
Thank you.
  You're welcome.

Realizing something
Wait a minute!

3 WHERE ARE YOU FROM?

KEY VOCABULARY

Nouns
Countries, Nationalities, and Languages
See the appendix.

Regions of the world
Africa
Asia
Australia, New Zealand, and Pacific Islands
(the) Caribbean
Central America
Europe
North America
South America

People
best friend
brother
family
mother
parents
person (*plural* = people)
sister
student

Places
city (*plural* = cities)
world

Other
college
language

Pronouns
Subject pronouns
we
you *(plural)*

Adjectives
Describing people
cute
friendly
funny
good-looking
handsome
heavy
nice
pretty
serious
short
shy
smart
tall
thin

Numbers and ages (11–30; 40, 50, etc.)
See Exercise 6 on page 17.

Other
beautiful
fine
large
new
old

Verbs
call
know
think

Adverbs
a little
here
originally
really
so
this week
today

Prepositions
from (Seoul)
in (the United States)

EXPRESSIONS

Asking about countries, nationalities, and languages
Are you from Seoul/. . . ?
  Yes, I am./No, I'm not. I'm from . . . .
Where is he/she from?
  He's/She's from . . . .
Are you Japanese/. . . ?
  Yes, we are./No, we're not. We're . . . .
Is your first language English/. . . ?
  Yes, it is./No, it's not.

Asking about people
Who are they?/Who's that?/What are their names?
  He's . . . , and she's . . . .
Where are they from?
  They're from . . . .
What are they like?
  They're very/really . . . .

ANSWER KEY *Unit 3, Exercise 6, page 17*

Antonio Banderas: Born in 1960.
Yuka Honda: Doesn't tell her age. What is your guess?
Nelson Mandela: Born in 1918.
Celine Dion: Born in 1968.
Pelé: Born in 1940.
Se Ri Pak: Born in 1977.

4 I'M NOT WEARING BOOTS!

KEY VOCABULARY

Nouns
Clothes
belt
blouse
boot(s)
cap
coat
dress
glove(s)
hat
(high) heels
jacket
jeans
pajamas
pants
raincoat
running shoes
scarf
shirt
shoe(s)
shorts
skirt
sneakers
sock(s)
suit
sweater
sweatshirt
swimsuit
T-shirt
tie

Seasons of the year
spring
summer
fall
winter

Other
clothes
matter
problem
season
taxi
weather

Adjectives
Colors
beige
black
(dark/light) blue
(dark/light) brown
(dark/light) gray
(dark/light) green
orange
pink
purple
red
white
yellow

Weather
cloudy
cold
cool
hot
humid
sunny
warm
windy

Possessives
our
your *(plural)*
their

Other
dry
important
ruined

Verbs
rain
snow
take (a taxi)
wear

Adverbs
actually
probably

Conjunction
but

Interjections
Uh-oh!
Yeah.

EXPRESSIONS

Talking about preferences
What's your favorite color?
My favorite color is . . . .

Asking about and describing clothing
What color is/are . . . ?
It's/They're . . . .
Are you wearing . . . ?
Yes, I am./No, I'm not. I'm wearing . . . .

Showing opposition
I'm . . . , but I'm not . . . .

Talking about the weather
It's snowing/raining/. . . .
It's cloudy/cold/hot/sunny/. . . .

5 WHAT ARE YOU DOING?

KEY VOCABULARY

Nouns
Meals
breakfast
lunch
dinner

Form of address
Mom

Other
bike
conference
friend
hometown
movie
pizza
tennis
time zone
walk
work

Adjectives
awake
hungry
sorry

Verbs
cook
dance
do
drive
eat
get up
go (to work/to the movies)
have (breakfast/lunch/dinner)
make
play (tennis)
read
remember
ride (a bike)
run
shop
sleep
study
swim
take (a walk)
watch (television)
work

Adverbs
Times
at midnight/at noon
at night
in the afternoon
in the evening
in the morning

Clock times
A.M./P.M.
midnight
noon
o'clock

Other
(right) now

Prepositions
after (six)
at (six o'clock)
to (six)

Conjunction
so

Interjection
mmm

EXPRESSIONS

Asking for and telling time
What time is it?
It's . . . o'clock (in the morning/. . .).
It's . . . after . . . .
It's a quarter after . . . .
It's . . . -thirty.
It's a quarter to . . . .

Asking about and describing current activities
What are you doing?
I'm . . . .
Are you . . . ?
Yes, I am./No, I'm not. I'm . . . .

Giving a reason
What's he doing?
It's . . . , so he's . . . .

Making a suggestion
Let's . . . .

Checking information
. . . . Right?
Yes.

Responding to an apology
I'm really sorry.
That's OK.

Talking on the telephone
Hello?
Hi, ... This is . . . .

6 WE LIVE IN THE SUBURBS.

KEY VOCABULARY

Nouns
Hometown areas
country
downtown
suburbs

Modes of transportation
bus
bus station
car
ferry
ferry terminal
public transportation
subway
subway station
taxi
taxi stand
train
train station

Hometown places
apartment
house
office
park
restaurant
school
store

Family relationships
brother
children/kids
daughter
father/dad
husband
mother/mom
parents
sister
son
wife

Days of the week
Monday
Tuesday
Wednesday
Thursday
Friday
Saturday
Sunday

Other
computer
day
homework
Internet
paper
(flat) tire
weekday
weekend

Pronouns
Object pronouns
me
us

Determiners
all (day)
both
every (day)

Adjectives
busy
good
lucky
public
retired

Verbs
come
do (work)
go (to school/to bed)
go on (the Internet)
live
meet
need
say
serve
take (a bus/a train)
use
wait (for)
walk

Adverbs
Times
early
every day
late

Other
a lot of
alone
also
far
home
then
together
yet

Prepositions
at (home)
by (bus/car)
for (people like us)
like (us)
near (here)
on (Sundays/weekends)
with (my parents)

EXPRESSIONS

Talking about routines
What time do you . . . ?
At . . . .
When does he . . . ?
He . . . at . . . .
Does he . . . ?
Yes, he . . . every morning/. . . .
How do you go to . . . ?
I . . . .

Expressing an opinion
That's good.
You're lucky!

Expressing agreement
Yeah.
Sure.

Saying hello
Hey.

7 DOES THE APARTMENT HAVE A VIEW?

KEY VOCABULARY

Nouns
Houses and apartments
bathroom
bedroom
closet
dining room
elevator
(first/second) floor
garage
hall
kitchen
laundry room
living room
lobby
(swimming) pool
room
stairs
yard

Furniture
armchair
bed
bookcase
chair
clock
coffee table
curtain(s)
desk
dresser
lamp
mirror
picture
rug
sofa
table

Appliances
microwave oven
refrigerator
stove

Other
neighbor
river
view

Determiners
any
no
some

Adjectives
big
dream (house)
own (room)
super

Verbs
buy
go shopping
love

Prepositions
on (Lakeview Drive)
in (the country/the city)

EXPRESSIONS

Asking about and describing a home
What's the house/apartment like?
It's beautiful/. . . . / It has . . . .
Does it have . . . ?
Yes, it does./No, it doesn't.
Do you live/have . . . ?
Yes, I do./No, I don't.

Talking about quantity
How many rooms/. . . does it have?
It has . . . . / There's one . . . . / There are . . . .

Saying what there is and isn't
There's a/an . . . .
There isn't a/an . . . . / There's no . . . .
There are some . . . .
There aren't any . . . . / There are no . . . .

Asking for more information
What else does it have?

Telling someone surprising news
Guess what!

Responding to news
That's super.
That sounds nice.

Giving and responding to compliments
This . . . is great.
Thanks.
Oh, nice.

8 WHAT DO YOU DO?

KEY VOCABULARY

Nouns
Jobs / Occupations
accountant
actor
air traffic controller
artist
athlete
carpenter (carpentry)
cashier
cook/chef
DJ (disc jockey)
doctor
fashion designer
firefighter
flight attendant
florist
gardener
judge
lawyer
librarian
(rock) musician
nurse
photographer
pilot
police officer
receptionist
repairperson
salesperson
security guard
singer
waiter
waitress

Places
department store
electronics store
factory
hospital
hotel
office

Other
break
gun
money
opinion
relative
uniform
woman (*plural* = women)

Adjectives
boring
dangerous
difficult
easy
exciting
relaxing
safe
stressful
terrific

Verbs
agree
carry
disagree
finish
handle
hear
like
look for
repair
sell
sit
stand
start
take (a break)
talk (to)
teach

Adverbs
all day
exactly
hard

EXPRESSIONS

Exchanging information about work
Where do you work?
 I work in a/an . . . .
What do you do there?
 I'm a/an . . . .
When do you start/finish work?
 I start/finish work at . . . .
Do you take a break in the afternoon?
What do you do after work?
 I . . . .
Where does your brother work?
 He works . . . .
What does he do, exactly?
 He's a/an . . . .

Asking for and giving opinions about jobs
How do you like it?
 It's . . . .
A/An . . . has a/an boring/. . . job.
 I agree. A/An . . .'s job is very . . . .
 I disagree. A/An . . . doesn't have a/an . . . job. It's . . . .

Exchanging personal information
How are things with you?
 Not bad.

Expressing sympathy
That's too bad.

Expressing surprise
Really?

Giving more information
. . . , you know.

9 BROCCOLI IS GOOD FOR YOU.

KEY VOCABULARY

Nouns
Dairy foods
cheese
milk
yogurt

Desserts
cake
cookie(s)
ice cream
pie

Fat, Oil, Sugar
butter
candy
cream
oil
potato chips

Fruit
apple(s)
banana(s)
grape(s)
mango(es)
orange(s)
strawberry (-ies)
tangerine(s)

Meat / Protein
bacon
bean(s)
beef
chicken
egg(s)
fish
hamburger(s)
nut(s)

Grains
bread
cereal
cracker(s)
noodles
pasta
rice
rolls
toast

Salads
fruit salad
potato salad

Vegetables
broccoli
carrot(s)
celery
lettuce
onion(s)
potato(es)
tomato(es)

Beverages
lemonade
soda
(green) tea

Other
barbecue
freezer
grocery store
health
mayonnaise
snacks
soup

Pronouns
everyone
something

Determiners
any
some

Adjectives
awful
delicious
(Japanese)-style

Verbs
drink
get
hate
try
want

Adverbs
Adverbs of frequency
always
ever
never
often
seldom
sometimes
usually

Prepositions
at (my desk)
for (breakfast/the barbecue)
in (the salad)

EXPRESSIONS

Talking about likes and dislikes
I love oranges.
Everyone likes potato salad.
I hate onions.
I think . . . is/are delicious/awful.
. . . is/are my favorite . . . .

Talking about things you need
Do you need any . . . ?
Yes, we need some . . . .
No, we don't need any . . . .
What do you need?

Asking about eating habits
What time do you eat breakfast/lunch/dinner?
What do you usually have for breakfast/lunch/dinner?
Do you ever eat . . . for breakfast/lunch/dinner?
Do you ever go to a restaurant for breakfast/lunch/dinner?
Do you always drink the same thing in the morning/afternoon/evening?
What is something you never have for breakfast/lunch/dinner?

Determining what is healthy
For good health, eat a lot of . . . / eat some . . . /eat very little . . . .
. . . is/are very good for you.

Giving an opinion
I think . . . .

Making a suggestion
How about . . . ?

Hesitating
Hmm.

Expressing agreement
All right.
Good idea.
Oh, yeah.
OK.

10 YOU CAN PLAY BASEBALL REALLY WELL.

KEY VOCABULARY

Nouns
Sports
baseball
basketball
bike riding
football
golf
hiking
hockey
ice-skating
skiing
soccer
swimming
tennis
volleyball

Other
ability
beach
guitar
piano
poetry
talent
talent show
team
(free) time

Adjectives
artistic
athletic
great
mechanical
musical
technical

Verbs
draw
enjoy
enter
fix
play (a musical instrument)
play (a sport)
practice
sing
skate
speak
use (computers)
write

Adverbs
(not) at all
just
maybe
tomorrow
too
(not) very well
(really) well

Preposition
on (TV)

EXPRESSIONS

Talking about sports
What sports do you like/play . . . ?
  I love/play . . . .
  I don't like/play . . . .
  I like . . . , but I really love . . . .
Who do you play . . . with?
  With some friends from work.
When does your team practice?
  We practice on . . . .
What time do you practice?
  We start at . . . .
Where do you go skiing?
  I go skiing in Colorado.

Asking for and giving an opinion
What do you think of . . . ?
  I think it's dangerous/. . . .

Talking about abilities and talents
Can you . . . ?
  Yes, I can./No, I can't.
Can they . . . ?
  Yes, they can . . . very well.
  No, they can't . . . at all.
I can . . . , but I can't . . . very well.

Agreeing to do something
Sure. Why not?

Complimenting someone
You're a really good . . . !
You can . . . really well.
  Thanks.

11 WHAT ARE YOU GOING TO DO?

KEY VOCABULARY

Nouns
Months of the year
January
February
March
April
May
June
July
August
September
October
November
December

Other
birthday
gym
mashed potatoes
parade
party
picnic
plans
present
turkey

Pronoun
anything

Adjectives
Ordinal numbers (1–31)
See Exercise 1 on page 66.

Other
different
embarrassing
holiday
next
same
special
unusual

Verbs
ask (= invite)
celebrate
end
go out
have (a party/a picnic)
invite
order
see (a movie)
stay (home)
take (someone to a restaurant)
think about

Adverbs
around (midnight)
tonight

Preposition
for (Thanksgiving/your birthday)

EXPRESSIONS

Talking about future plans
Are you going to do anything exciting this/next . . . ?
  Yes, I am. I'm going to . . . .
  No, I'm not. I'm going to . . . .
What are your plans?/Any plans?
  I'm going to . . . .
What are you going to do?
  I'm going to . . . .
Where are you going to go?
  I'm going to go to . . . .
Who's going to be there?
  . . . is/are going to be there.
When are you going to go?
  We're going to . . . .
How are you going to get there?
  We're going to . . . .

Talking about dates
When is your birthday?
  It's August ninth.

Talking about holidays
What are you going to do for Thanksgiving?
  I'm going to have dinner at my parents' house.

Greeting someone on a special day
Happy birthday!
  Thanks.
Have a happy Thanksgiving/. . . .
  Thanks. You, too.

Asking for more information
What about you?

Expressing an opinion
Hmm. That's unusual.
(That) sounds like fun.

Giving a positive reaction
Fabulous!
Nice!

12 WHAT'S THE MATTER?

KEY VOCABULARY

Nouns
Parts of the body
ankle
arm
back
chest
chin
ear
elbow
eye
finger(s)
foot (*plural* = feet)
hand
head
knee
leg
mouth
neck
nose
shoulder
stomach
throat
thumb
toe(s)
tooth (*plural* = teeth)
wrist

Health problems
backache
cold
cough
earache
fever
the flu
headache
sore (eyes/throat)
stomachache
toothache

Medications
antacid
aspirin
cold pills
cough drops
cough syrup
eyedrops
muscle cream

Other
bath
coffee
fun
idea
juice
look
patient

Adjectives
Feelings
awful
bad
exhausted
fine (well)
good (better)
great
happy
homesick
sad
sick
terrible
terrific
tired

Other
sore
wrong

Verbs
feel
guess
help
hope
lift
lose (weight)
miss
point
stay (in bed)
stay up (late)
take (a bath)
take (a look at)
take (medicine)

Adverbs
already
soon
too

Prepositions
for (ten minutes)
in (bed/the house)
on (the phone)

EXPRESSIONS

Talking about health problems
How are you?
  I'm not so good, actually.
What's the matter?/What's wrong?
  I have . . . .
How do you feel?
  I feel sick/. . . .
  I don't feel well.
  I feel better already.

Expressing sympathy
That's too bad.
I'm sorry to hear that.
I hope you feel better soon.

Giving instructions/advice
Take/Don't take . . . .
Go to/Don't go to . . . .
Eat/Don't eat . . . .
Do/Don't do . . . .

13 YOU CAN'T MISS IT.

KEY VOCABULARY

Nouns
Places
bank
bookstore
bridge
cathedral
coffee shop
department store
drugstore
gas station
library
movie theater
museum
post office
restaurant
shoe store
statue
supermarket

Form of address
ma'am

Other
block
building
gasoline
rest room
sandwich
traveler's checks

Adjective
other

Verbs
get (to)
miss (something)
turn around

Adverbs
around
down
left
right
up

Prepositions
across from
behind
between
near
next to
on (Main Street)
on the corner of

EXPRESSIONS

Asking for and giving locations
Is there a/an . . . around here?
Yes, there is. It's next to/across from/. . . .
Where's the . . . ? Is it far from here?
It's right behind you.

Asking for and giving directions
How do I get to . . . ?
Walk up/Go up . . . (to . . .).
Walk down/Go down . . . for . . . block(s).
Turn right/Turn left at/on . . . .
It's on the right./It's on the left.
You can't miss it.

Saying where you can buy things
You can buy cough drops at a drugstore.

Asking for help
Excuse me, ma'am. Can you help me?

Checking information
The . . . is on the corner of . . . and . . . .
On the corner of . . . and . . . ?

14 DID YOU HAVE A GOOD WEEKEND?

KEY VOCABULARY

Nouns
bill
chore
cup
dance club
girlfriend
groceries
laundry
letter
mall
meal
popcorn
roommate
test
video

Verbs
clean
come over
do (the laundry)
dust
eat out
exercise
go jogging
listen (to music)
pay
rent
shop
vacuum
visit
wash

Adverbs
either
else
over

Prepositions
around (the house)
during (the week)
on (the bus)

Interjection
Oh, well.

EXPRESSIONS

Talking about past activities
Did you go out/. . . this weekend?
Yes, I did. I went to/. . . .
No, I didn't. I stayed home/. . . .
What did you do?
I . . . . I didn't . . . .

Giving opinions about past experiences
Did you like . . . ?
I liked it a lot.
I loved . . . .
Did you have fun?
We had a great time.

Asking for additional information
Did you do anything else?

15 WHERE WERE YOU BORN?

KEY VOCABULARY

Nouns
School subjects
algebra
art
biology
calculus
chemistry
Chinese
computer science
drama
fine arts
French
geometry
history
journalism
languages
mathematics
music
physical education
physical sciences
physics
psychology
social sciences
sociology
Spanish

Other
capital
founder
grade
hairstylist
high school
major
playwright
violinist

Adjectives
fluent
scary

Verbs
be born
become
grow up
promote

Adverb
pretty (young/good)

Preposition
in (college)

EXPRESSIONS

Exchanging personal information
When were you born?
  I was born in . . . .
Where were you born?
  I was born in . . . .
Were you born in . . . ?
  Yes, I was./No, I wasn't. I was born in . . . .
How old were you in . . . ?
  I was . . . .
What was your major in college?
  It was . . . .

Asking about someone
Who was . . . ?
  He was . . . .
What city was he born in?
  He was born in . . . .
What nationality was he?
  He was . . . .
What was he like?
  He was . . . . He wasn't . . . .

Asking for an opinion
What do you think?

16 PLEASE LEAVE US A MESSAGE.

KEY VOCABULARY

Nouns
art gallery
concert
date
dentist
exam
excuse
(basketball) game
invitation
message
picnic
play
shower
vacation

Pronouns
Object pronouns
me
you *(singular)*
him
her
it
us
you *(plural)*
them

Verbs
baby-sit
call back
give (someone a call)
have to
leave
need to
want to
would like to

Adverb
later

Prepositions
at (the beach)
on (vacation)

Interjection
gee

EXPRESSIONS

Making a phone call
Hello. Is . . . there, please?
No, I'm sorry, . . . isn't here right now.
Yes, but . . . can't come to the phone right now.

Recording an answering-machine message
Hi. This is . . . . I/We can't come to the phone right now. Please leave me/us a message after the beep.

Leaving a phone message
Please ask . . . to call me.
Sure, just give me the number.
Hi, it's . . . . Just give me/us a call.

Offering to help someone
Maybe I can help you.

Asking for a favor
Can you . . . ?
Please . . . .

Asking what is happening
What's up?

Inviting and accepting an invitation
Do you want to . . . with me?
Sure. I'd love to (. . . with you).
Yes, I'd like to.

Declining an invitation and making an excuse
Do you want to . . . with me?
I'm sorry, but I can't. I have to . . . .
Sorry, I need to . . . .
Gee, I'd like to, but I want to . . . .

Talking about an obligation
I can't . . . . I have to . . . .
Oh, that's too bad.

Suggesting something
How about . . . ?
Sure.

Expressing happy surprise
Terrific!

Appendix

ANSWER KEY *Unit 3, Exercise 1, page 14*

Tokyo	**Japan**	Shanghai	**China**
Mexico City	**Mexico**	Los Angeles	**The United States**
São Paulo	**Brazil**	Calcutta	**India**
New York	**The United States**	Buenos Aires	**Argentina**
Bombay	**India**	Seoul	**South Korea**

ANSWER KEY *Unit 3, Exercise 4, page 16* *Student B*

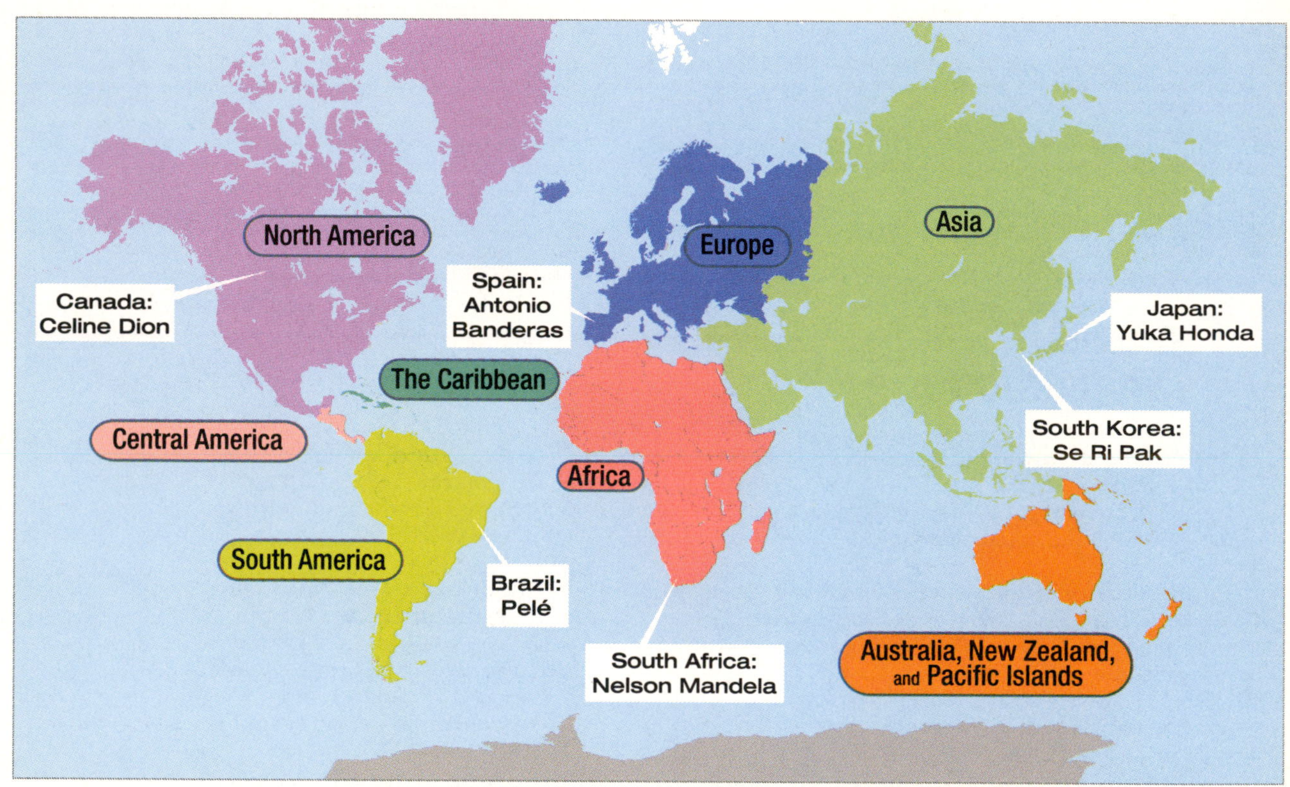

ANSWER KEY *Unit 13, Exercise 7, page 83*

The Golden Gate Bridge: San Francisco
The White House: Washington, D.C.
The Museum of Science and Industry: Chicago
The Statue of Liberty: New York City

COUNTRIES, NATIONALITIES, AND LANGUAGES

This is a partial list of countries, nationalities, and languages.

Countries	*Nationalities*
Argentina	Argentine
Australia	Australian
Austria	Austrian
Bolivia	Bolivian
Brazil	Brazilian
Cambodia	Cambodian
Canada	Canadian
Chile	Chilean
China	Chinese
Colombia	Colombian
Costa Rica	Costa Rican
Cuba	Cuban
the Dominican Republic	Dominican
Ecuador	Ecuadorian
Egypt	Egyptian
El Salvador	El Salvadoran
England	English
France	French
Germany	German
Ghana	Ghanian
Greece	Greek
Guatemala	Guatemalan
Haiti	Haitian
Honduras	Honduran
India	Indian
Indonesia	Indonesian
Ireland	Irish
Israel	Israeli
Italy	Italian
Japan	Japanese
Jordan	Jordanian
Laos	Laotian
Lebanon	Lebanese

Countries	*Nationalities*
Malaysia	Malaysian
Mexico	Mexican
Morocco	Moroccan
Nepal	Nepalese
the Netherlands	Dutch
New Zealand	New Zealander
Nicaragua	Nicaraguan
Nigeria	Nigerian
Panama	Panamanian
Paraguay	Paraguayan
Peru	Peruvian
the Philippines	Filipino
Poland	Polish
Portugal	Portuguese
Puerto Rico	Puerto Rican
Russia	Russian
Saudi Arabia	Saudi
Singapore	Singaporean
Somalia	Somalian
South Africa	South African
South Korea	South Korean
Spain	Spanish
Sudan	Sudanese
Sweden	Swedish
Switzerland	Swiss
Tanzania	Tanzanian
Thailand	Thai
Turkey	Turkish
the United Kingdom (the U.K.)	British
the United States (the U.S.)	American
Uruguay	Uruguayan
Venezuela	Venezuelan
Vietnam	Vietnamese

Languages

Afrikaans	German	Japanese	Spanish
Arabic	Greek	Korean	Swahili
Chinese	Hebrew	Malay	Swedish
Dutch	Hindi	Polish	Thai
English	Indonesian	Portuguese	Turkish
French	Italian	Russian	Vietnamese

IRREGULAR VERBS

Present	*Past*
(be) am/is, are	was, were
become	became
buy	bought
come	came
do	did
drink	drank
drive	drove
eat	ate
feel	felt
get	got
give	gave
go	went

Present	*Past*
have	had
know	knew
leave	left
make	made
meet	met
pay	paid
read	read /rɛd/
ride	rode
run	ran
say	said /sɛd/
see	saw
sell	sold

Present	*Past*
sing	sang
sit	sat
sleep	slept
speak	spoke
swim	swam
take	took
teach	taught
think	thought
wear	wore
write	wrote

Acknowledgments

ILLUSTRATIONS

Daisy de Puthod 42 *(top)*
Randy Jones 3 *(bottom)*, 9, 14 *(bottom)*, 20, 21 *(bottom)*, 22, 23 *(bottom)*, 26, 27, 29 *(bottom)*, 30 *(bottom)*, 31, 32, 40 *(bottom)*, 41, 42 *(bottom)*, 43, 46, 52, 53, 56, 68 *(top)*, 73 *(bottom)*, 74, 75, 88, 92, 95, 104 *(top)*, IC-3, IC-6, IC-7, IC-11, IC-13, IC-16, IC-18
Wally Neibart 28 *(bottom)*, 81, 82 *(bottom)*, 104 *(bottom)*, IC-10
Roger Roth 4, 7, 17, 24, 69, 73 *(top)*, 94, IC-5, IC-9
Bill Thomson 2 *(top)*, 3, 5, 28 *(top)*, 34 *(bottom)*, 35, 36, 47, 70, 76, 86 *(bottom)*, 90, 98, 100 *(bottom)*, 102
Daniel Vasconcellos 11, 13, 18, 23 *(top)*, 25, 61, 78, 89 *(bottom)*, 105, IC-14
Sam Viviano 37 *(bottom)*, 50, 62, 63, 66 *(bottom)*, 83, 89 *(top)*

PHOTOGRAPHIC CREDITS

6 *(top)* © Rob Gage/FPG International; *(bottom)* © Telegraph Colour Library/FPG International

8 *(Exercise 1)*: *(pager)* Courtesy of Motorola, Inc.; *(CD player and electronic address book)* © Steven Ogilvy; *(sunglasses, calculator, and cell phone)* © John Bessler; *(watch)* Courtesy of SWATCH Group U.S.; *(camera)* Courtesy of Canon USA, Inc.; *(Exercise 2)*: *(all)* © John Bessler

9 *(television)* © Steven Ogilvy; *(all others)* © John Bessler

10 *(Exercise 5)*: *(CD player)* © Steven Ogilvy; *(all others)* © John Bessler; *(Exercise 6)*: *(umbrella)* © John Bessler; *(chopsticks)* © Steven Ogilvy

12 *(television and CD player, newspaper and map, desk and chair)* © Steven Ogilvy; *(all others)* © John Bessler

15 *(top to bottom)* © Marcus Brooke/FPG International; © Joe Cornish/Tony Stone Images; © John Fuste Raga/The Stock Market

16 *(left to right)* © Benainous/Duclos/Liaison Agency; © Sonia Moscowitz/Globe Photos; © Mark Peters/Liaison Agency; © Evan Agostini/Liaison Agency; © Gamma/Liaison Agency; © AP/Wide World Photos

19 *(top to bottom)* © Adamsmith/FPG International; © James Davis/International Stock; © Gary Buss/FPG International

33 *(clockwise from top left)* © Telegraph Colour Library/FPG International; © Jose Pelaez Photography/The Stock Market; © Chip Simons/FPG International; © Arthur Tilley/FPG International

36 *(left to right)* © Telegraph Colour Library/FPG International; © Ken Reid/FPG International; © Jim Cummins/FPG International; © Jose Luis Banus-March/FPG International

37 © Telegraph Colour Library/FPG International

39 *(left to right)* © Sotographs/Liaison Agency; © VCG/FPG International; © Ken Chernus/FPG International

41 *(left to right)* © E. Alan McGee/FPG International; © Ping Amranand/SuperStock; © Erika Stone; © Chris Springmann/The Stock Market

44 *(top)* © Gerald French/FPG International; *(bottom)* © Robert Shafer/Tony Stone Images

45 *(left)* © Bryce Harper; *(right)* © Steve Northup/NYT Pictures

47 *(left to right)* © Pete Saloutos/The Stock Market; © Jose Pelaez Photography/The Stock Market; © Tom Prettyman/PhotoEdit; © Thomas H. Ives/The Stock Market

48 *(left to right)* © Jose L. Pelaez/The Stock Market; © Don Mason/The Stock Market; © Andy Sacks/Tony Stone Images

49 © Steven Ogilvy

50 *(top to bottom)* © Stephen Simpson/FPG International; © Gary Conner/PhotoEdit; © Bill Stormont/The Stock Market

51 *(top, left to right)* *(chef)* © Dick Luria/FPG International; *(guard)* © Mary Kate Denny/PhotoEdit; *(pilot)* © Tom McCarthy/PhotoEdit; *(bottom, left to right)* © Jose L. Pelaez/The Stock Market; © J. Barry O'Rourke/The Stock Market; © Jose L. Pelaez/The Stock Market

55 © Mark Segal/Tony Stone Images

56 *(all)* © Steven Ogilvy

57 *(both)* © Steven Ogilvy

58 © Jose L. Pelaez/The Stock Market

59 *(all)* © Steven Ogilvy

61 © DiMaggio/Kalish/The Stock Market

62 © Ed Bock/The Stock Market

65 *(all)* © AP/Wide World Photos

67 *(top row, left to right)* © Rob Lewine/The Stock Market; © Michael K. Daly/The Stock Market; © David Stoecklein/The Stock Market; © Jose L. Pelaez/The Stock Market; *(middle row, left)* © DiMaggio/Kalish/The Stock Market; *(middle row, right)* © Don Mason/The Stock Market; *(bottom row, left to right)* © Gary Landsman/The Stock Market; © Telegraph Colour Library/FPG International; © Klaus & Heide Benser/Zefa Germany/The Stock Market; © Michael Newman/PhotoEdit

70 © Steve Vidler/Leo de Wys

71 *(clockwise from top left)* © Roderick Chen/SuperStock; © Bill Walsh/The Stock Market; © Harvey Lloyd/The Stock Market; © David Young-Wolff/PhotoEdit

72 © Steven Ogilvy

74 *(all)* © Steven Ogilvy

77 *(number 3)* © Chris Rogers/The Stock Market; *(number 5)* © David Stoecklein/The Stock Market; *(number 6)* © Roy Morsch/The Stock Market; *(number 7)* © Michael A. Keller Studio/The Stock Market; *(number 8)* © David Raymer/The Stock Market; *(number 9)* © Steven Ogilvy

79 *(top, both)* © Steven Ogilvy; *(bottom)* © Ed Bock/The Stock Market

80 *(aspirin, bread, and sandwich)* © Steven Ogilvy; *(dictionary, stamps, gasoline, and sweatshirt)* © John Bessler; *(bank)* © Charles Orrico/SuperStock; *(drugstore)* © SuperStock; *(bookstore)* © Michael Newman/PhotoEdit; *(gas station)* © Charles Orrico/SuperStock; *(restaurant)* © Rick Rusing/Tony Stone Images; *(post office)* © James P. Dwyer/Stock Boston; *(department store)* © Robert Brenner/PhotoEdit; *(supermarket)* © Chuck Keeler/Tony Stone Images

83 *(clockwise from top left)* © Bruce Hands/Tony Stone Images; © International Stock; © Jean-Marc Truchet/Tony Stone Images; © Dennis O'Clair/Tony Stone Images

85 *(clockwise from top left)* © Fred George/Tony Stone Images; © Andreas Pollok/Tony Stone Images; © Dan Lecca/FPG International; © Thomas A. Kelly/CORBIS

87 © Steven Ogilvy

91 *(left)* © Bettmann/CORBIS; *(right)* © Doug Armand/Tony Stone Images

92 *(clockwise from top left)* © Photofest; © Walter Weissman/Globe Photos; © AFP/CORBIS; © Couponco Worldwide/Liaison Agency

93 © Paul Chesley/Tony Stone Images

94 *(left to right)* © Lisa Rose/Globe Photos; © AP/Wide World Photos; © PHM DeLuigi/M.P.A./Liaison Agency; © Ron Angle/Liaison Agency

97 *(clockwise from top left)* Alexander Calder, *Mobile on Two Planes*. Musée National d'Art Moderne Georges Pompidou Centre, Paris/SuperStock. © 1999 Estate of Alexander Calder/Artists Rights Society (ARS), New York; Frida Kahlo, *Self Portrait With Loose Hair* © Christie's Images/SuperStock. Reproduction authorized by Instituto Nacional de Bellas Artes y Literatura, Mexico; Hiroshigi, *Hida Province (Kago Watashi) Basket Ferry* © Culver Pictures/SuperStock

99 *(left to right)* © SuperStock; © Tony Freeman/PhotoEdit; © R.B. Studio/The Stock Market; © Chuck Savage/The Stock Market; © Philip & Karen Smith/Tony Stone Images

101 © Juan Silva Prod./The Image Bank

102 © Mary Kate Denny/PhotoEdit

103 *(top)* © Robert Brenner/PhotoEdit; *(bottom, left)* © David Young-Wolff/PhotoEdit; *(bottom, right)* © Vittoriano Rastelli/CORBIS

IC-2 and IC-4 © Jim Cummins/FPG International

IC-12 © Steven Ogilvy

IC-15 *(clockwise from top left)* © Gabe Palmer/Mug Shots/The Stock Market; © VCG/FPG International; © Mark Scott/FPG International; © John Terence Turner/FPG International

IC-17 *(clockwise from top right)* © Don Smetzer/Tony Stone Images; © Norbert Schäfer/The Stock Market; © Michael Newman/PhotoEdit; © Myrleen Ferguson Cate/PhotoEdit

IC-20 *(top row, left to right)* Courtesy of Natsu Ifill; © Jonathan Nourok/PhotoEdit; © Paul Barton/The Stock Market; © 100% Rag Productions/FPG International; *(bottom row, left to right)* © Steve Prezant/The Stock Market; © Mike Malyszko/FPG International; Courtesy of Natsu Ifill; © Jose L. Pelaez/The Stock Market

TEXT CREDITS

The authors and publishers are grateful for permission to reprint the following items.

14 *(Snapshot)* http://www.infoplease.com

54 *(Snapshot)* Adapted from the U.S. Department of Agriculture Food Guide Pyramid.

60 *(Snapshot)* Adapted from *1998 ESPN Information Please Sports Almanac*, Copyright © 1997 by Information Please LLC.

74 *(Snapshot)* Adapted from *Almanac of the American People*, Copyright © 1988 by Tom and Nancy Biracree.

77 *(Reading)* Copyright © 1996 *Cooking Light®* Magazine. For subscriptions, call 1-800-336-0125. Reprinted with permission.

83 *(Snapshot)* Adapted from *Fodor's USA*, Copyright © 1998 by Fodor's Travel Publications, Inc.

Thank you to the chef and management of Nadaman Hakubai restaurant at the hotel Kitano New York for their advice on the traditional Japanese breakfast on page 57.

Every effort has been made to trace the owners of copyright material in this book. We would be grateful to hear from anyone who recognizes his or her copyright material and who is unacknowledged. We will be pleased to make the necessary corrections in future editions of the book.

Optional Activities Index

The activities are listed according to the order in which they can first be used.

Title	*Function/Grammar*	*Unit/Exercise*	*Teacher's Page*
Comparing names	Learning native-language equivalents of English names	**1**/2	T-147
Classmate's names	Learning classmate's names and reviewing grammar	**1**/3	T-147
Game – Letter bingo	Capital and lowercase letters	**1**/4	T-147
Game – Number bingo	Reviewing numbers	**1**/9	T-147
Number rhythm	Reading numbers aloud	**1**/9	T-147
Scrambled letters **(G)**	Reviewing vocabulary and spelling	**1**/11	T-147
Spelling contest **(G)**	Reviewing classmate's names and spelling	**1**/11	T-148
Game – Hangman **(G)**	Reviewing vocabulary and spelling	**2**/6	T-148
Crossword puzzle **(G)**	Reviewing vocabulary and spelling	**2**/6	T-148
True or false? **(G)**	Statements and prepositions of place	**2**/9	T-148
Yes or no?	Yes/No questions and short answers	**3**/3	T-149
That's wrong!	Reviewing names of countries and regions	**3**/4	T-149
Game – Higher, lower	Reviewing numbers	**3**/6	T-149
Game – What's the question? **(G)**	Wh-questions	**3**/10	T-149
Game – Treasure hunt	Reviewing vocabulary of colors and objects	**4**/2	T-149
Sentence-making contest **(G)**	Writing statements and reviewing vocabulary	**4**/10	T-150
Game – Word bingo **(G)**	Reviewing vocabulary	**Rev. 1–4**/4	T-150
Telling time	Reviewing vocabulary related to telling time	**5**/2	T-150
Diary	Present continuous and *so*	**5**/7	T-150
Action verbs	Vocabulary development and present continuous statements	**5**/11	T-150
Complete the word **(G)**	Reviewing vocabulary and spelling	**5**/11	T-150
Thinking about grammar	Simple present and present continuous	**6**/4	T-151
Days of the week	Saying days of the week	**6**/9	T-151
Game – Tic-Tac-Toe **(G)**	Simple present questions and statements	**6**/10	T-151
My home	Reviewing names of rooms	**7**/4	T-151
I need some furniture!	Reviewing vocabulary of home furnishings and *there is/there are*	**7**/7	T-151
My favorite room	Reviewing vocabulary of housing and home furnishings	**7**/11	T-152

Note: **(G)** = a "generic" activity, i.e., it can be used in any *New Interchange* unit by using it as is or by slightly adapting it to other topics, grammar points, or vocabulary.

The activities are listed according to the order in which they can first be used.			
Title	***Function/Grammar***	***Unit/Exercise***	***Teacher's Page***
Game – Twenty questions **(G)**	Reviewing names of jobs and simple present yes/no questions	**8**/7	T-152
Opposites **(G)**	Reviewing vocabulary	**Rev. 5–8**/5	T-152
Shopping lists	Development of food vocabulary and spelling	**9**/5	T-152
Favorite snacks	Development of food vocabulary	**9**/5	T-153
Breakfast at my house	Exchanging personal information about meals	**9**/9	T-153
Olympic sports	Development of sports vocabulary	**10**/1	T-153
In my free time	Reviewing vocabulary and grammar	**10**/10	T-153
Birthday parties	Vocabulary development related to celebrations	**11**/2	T-153
How much did you find out?	Exchanging personal information about celebrations	**11**/10	T-154
Word associations	Vocabulary development related to celebrations	**11**/11	T-154
Game – Spelling challenge **(G)**	Spelling parts of the body	**12**/1	T-154
Game – Simon says	Reviewing vocabulary of parts of the body and previewing imperatives	**12**/1	T-154
How to live dangerously	Reviewing vocabulary and imperatives	**12**/10	T-154
The other question	Reviewing question forms	**Rev. 9–12**/5	T-155
Where can you buy it?	Reviewing vocabulary of things and places	**13**/1	T-155
Compound nouns	Previewing compound nouns	**13**/3	T-155
Say that again?	Reviewing vocabulary of place and rising intonation	**13**/5	T-155
What's near Rita's house?	Reviewing locations and directions	**13**/11	T-155
Role play	Pronunciation of past tense endings	**14**/4	T-156
Yesterday	Reviewing simple past tense	**14**/8	T-156
Who is it?	Reviewing questions and statements in the simple past tense	**15**/3	T-156
When was that?	Using world knowledge and reviewing simple past tense	**15**/7	T-156
Game – Who's where?	Reviewing prepositions of place	**16**/2	T-156
Game – What's your excuse?	Vocabulary development of invitations and excuses	**16**/6	T-157
Silly excuses	Making excuses	**16**/9	T-157
Do you want to . . .?	Reviewing vocabulary and grammar of invitations	**16**/11	T-157

Note: **(G)** = a "generic" activity, i.e., it can be used in any *New Interchange* unit by using it as is or by slightly adapting it to other topics, grammar points, or vocabulary.

Optional Activities

Comparing names

Time: 10–15 minutes. This activity allows Ss to talk about names that are more familiar.

- If appropriate, ask Ss to supply native-language equivalents for some of the English names in the Snapshot. Ask, for example, "What's the name John in your language?" (in Spanish-speaking countries, Juan /wân/; in French-speaking countries, Jean /ʒən/; in German-speaking countries, Johann /yowhan/).
- In a homogeneous class, Ss work in small groups to make a list of the first names from their native country. In a heterogeneous class, each S in the group can contribute two or three names from his or her country. Compare results as a class. Use a map to show where different names come from, if necessary.

Classmate's names

Time: 5–10 minutes. This activity provides additional controlled practice of grammar.

- Write this question and answer on the board:

  A: What's __________ name?
  B: __________ name is __________ .
- Ss work in pairs and take turns. Student A indicates another S in the class and asks the question. Student B supplies the name of the classmate Student A indicated.
- If Student B does not know the name of a S, Student B can say "I don't know" or shake his/her head. Student A can supply the name, if possible.
- Pairs should write down the names they ask about. If neither S knows the name of a classmate, they leave a blank on their paper.
- At the end of the activity, allow pairs of Ss to approach any classmates they did not know the names of and find out.

Game – Letter bingo

Time: 10–15 minutes. This activity reviews capital and lowercase letters.

- Show Ss how to make a Bingo card on an 8½ X 11-inch sheet of paper with 25 spaces on it, like this:

B	I	N	G	O
h	E	v	p	K
Q	R	y	W	b
g	t	FREE	C	D
M	u	x	N	i
s	A	F	j	L

- Ss write *free* in the center space. They fill in the other spaces at random with their choices of capital and lowercase letters, one to a space, without repetitions.
- Dictate letters at random, saying "capital" or "small." (You may repeat the letter several times, depending on your Ss abilities.) Ss find letters on their cards and circle them. Keep a list of the letters you call so that no letters are repeated. (You will need the list to check cards when Ss call "Bingo.")
- The first S to circle five letters in a row (or four letters plus the free space) in any direction shouts, "Bingo!"
- Ask the S to read the circled letters aloud. Check your list. If all the letters are correct, the S wins.

Game – Number bingo

- Preparation and procedures are the same as for *Letter bingo*, except that Ss fill in their bingo cards with numbers from 0 to 9.

Number rhythm

Time: 5–10 minutes. This game practices reading numbers aloud. You can do it as a whole-class activity, as it is here, or you can make it a team competition.

- Write many sets of three numbers on the board, for example:

  1 2 3 6 5 4 9 0 1
- Snap a rhythm with the Ss. Snap the fingers of your left hand, then your right hand, in a steady slow rhythm.
- While Ss keep the rhythm going by snapping, point to one of the three-digit numbers on the board and read it – one digit to a snap. Allow one extra snap at the end. For example, for 123 and 654, you read "one, two, three" (snap) "six, five, four" (snap).
- Have Ss read the numbers as you point. Start with the whole group, then have rows or individuals do each three-digit number. Increase the speed gradually until Ss cannot keep up.
- **Alternate presentation:** Do not write numbers on the board. Say any three numbers in rhythm and have the Ss repeat in rhythm. Have individual Ss also say three numbers for the class to repeat.

Scrambled letters (G)

Time: 5–10 minutes. **This type of activity can be used with any unit for a fun review.** This puzzle reviews vocabulary and spelling from Unit 1. All of the words in the puzzle come from Exercises 6 (Saying Hello) and 11 (Saying Good-bye).

- Copy this on the board:

nief	f___ ___ ___
realt	l___ ___ ___ ___
lohel	h___ ___ ___ ___
gtihn	n___ ___ ___ ___
skanth	t___ ___ ___ ___ ___
neeving	e___ ___ ___ ___ ___ ___
orgminn	m___ ___ ___ ___ ___ ___
rotormow	t___ ___ ___ ___ ___ ___ ___
gdoo-ybe	g___ ___ ___ ___ ___ ___ ___
foronanet	a___ ___ ___ ___ ___ ___ ___ ___

- Have Ss work in pairs to unscramble the words.
- Check answers on the board with the whole class. Make sure Ss have spelled the words correctly.

Answers

fine	thanks	good-bye
later	evening	afternoon
hello	morning	
night	tomorrow	

Spelling contest (G)

Time: 10–15 minutes. **This game is good for reviewing vocabulary in any unit and for practicing spelling.** Here, it also helps Ss learn each other's names.

Preparation: Give Ss a list of all the Ss' names to review beforehand, if necessary. Use first names alone. Cut up the list so that each name is on a separate slip of paper. Put the slips into an envelope.

- In class, divide the Ss into two teams and announce a time limit (10–15 minutes).

Draw a name from the envelope, and say the name to a S on the first team. If the S spells the name correctly, select a second name, and say it to the next person on the same team. When a S misspells a name, that S sits down and it becomes the turn of the other team.

- The winner is the team that spells the most names correctly (has the most people standing) within the time limit..

Game – Hangman (G)

Time: 20 minutes. **This popular game can be used to practice vocabulary and spelling in any unit.**

- Each S chooses a word from the unit.
- Ss take turns going to the board. The S at the board draws the hangman diagram and blanks – one blank for each letter of the word he or she has chosen:

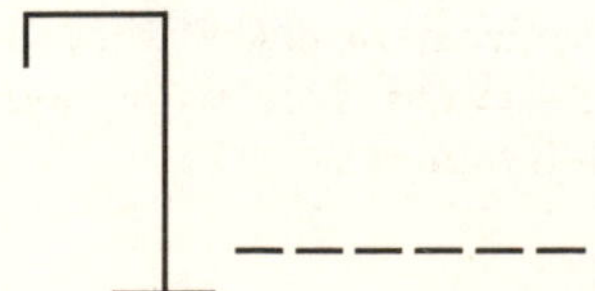

- The S at the board calls on other Ss take turns guessing the letters of the word. If someone guesses a correct letter, it is written in the appropriate blank. If the guess is wrong, the S at the board draws one part of the body on the gallows. There are nine body parts, which are drawn in this order: head, neck, left arm, right arm, body, left leg, right leg, left foot, and right foot.

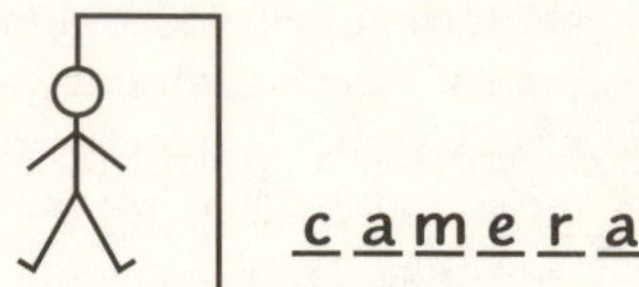

- The object of the game is for someone to guess the correct word before the picture of the hangman's body is completed. The S who guesses the word is the winner and gets to be the next S at the board. If the body is complete, the S at the board wins.

Crossword puzzle (G)

Time: 15 minutes. **This activity is good for reviewing vocabulary in any unit and for practicing spelling.**

- Ss form pairs or groups and then make crossword puzzle grids of 12 squares by 12.
- Ss can refer to the Unit Summary at the back of the Student's Book. Using words from the list, Ss try to fit in as many words as possible onto their grids. Words can go across or down. Every word must include at least one letter that is in another word. Letters that are next to each other must be part of a complete word.
- This example uses names of objects from Unit 2.

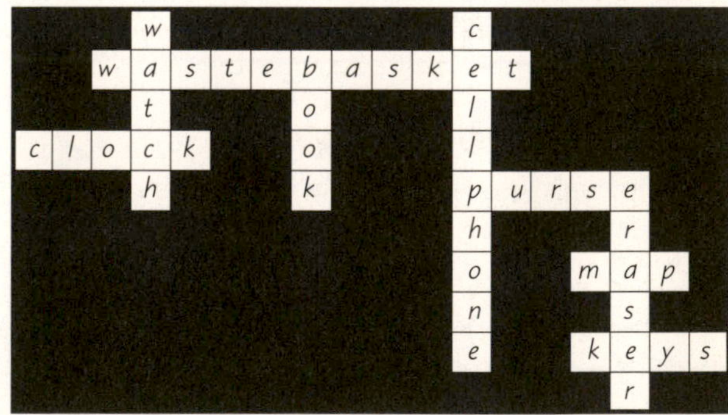

- After ten minutes, stop the activity and find out who has the most words on the grid.

True or false? (G)

Time: 10–15 minutes. **This activity can be used in any unit to practice writing descriptive statements.** In this unit, the activity practices prepositions of place.

- Explain the activity: Ss write six statements about the positions of objects in the classroom. Four should be true and two should be false.

- Ss form groups and take turns reading their statements while others look around the classroom to verify the statements. If a statement is true, Ss should say, "True." If a statement is false, they say, "False," and then correct the statement.

Yes or no?

Time: 5 minutes. This activity provides controlled practice of yes/no questions and short answers.

- Ask Ss about their city, country, or first language using yes/no questions. If they answer no, have them give the correct information. For example:

  T: Are you from Tokyo, Kenji?
  Kenji: Yes, I am.
  T: Sonia, is Kenji from Osaka?
  Sonia: No, he isn't. He's from Tokyo.

- After a few questions and answers, let volunteers ask the questions.

That's wrong!

Time: 20 minutes. This activity practices the names of countries and regions.

- Explain the task: Each S writes five to ten statements about the location of countries (in regions). Some of the statements should be false and some true, for example: "Mexico is in South America," "The United States is in North America."
- In groups of four, each S reads his or her statements aloud. The other Ss try to identify the false statements and to correct the false information in them.
- In case of disagreements, you can supply the answer yourself, or have Ss find out the answer for the next class.

Game – Higher, lower

Time: 10–15 minutes. This game reviews numbers from 1 to 100.

- Ss work in two groups. Each group writes down five numbers between 11 and 100, but does not let the other group see.
- Explain the game and the idea of *higher* and *lower.* Demonstrate the task with a S:

  T: I'm thinking of a number between 30 and 40.
  S: Is it 35?
  T: No. Higher. *(point up)*
  S: Is it 39?
  T: No. Lower. *(point down)*
  S: Is it 37?
  T: Yes, it is.

- The S who is up first tells the range of ten that the number is between. The S then calls on Ss in the other group to take turns guessing the number. Keep track on the board of how many guesses each group makes. The S who guesses the number gets to be the next S up.
- The winner is the group that has the fewest number of guesses at the end of the game.

Game – What's the question? (G)

Time: 10–15 minutes. **This activity can be used to practice the formation of questions in any unit.** In this unit, it reinforces the meaning of Wh-words related to personal information.

Preparation: Each S needs three index cards, or a sheet of paper torn into thirds.

- Divide the class into two teams. Make sure each S has three cards or slips of paper.
- Write these examples on the board:

  That's Jill.
  He's tall and thin.
  She's from Mexico.

- Elicit the question for each statement (Who's that? What's he like? Where's she from?)
- Explain that each S needs to think of three similar statements that can answer Wh-questions. Ss write one statement on each card. Walk around the class and give help as needed. Allow Ss to consult and help their teammates. It's all right if some answers will elicit the same question.
- Collect all the cards and put them in a pile facedown.
- Team A starts: One S picks up a card and reads it aloud to a S from Team B. That S then tries to make a suitable Wh-question for it.
- Ss on both teams decide whether the question is correct or not. If it is, Team B wins a point. If it isn't, a S from Team A tries to correct it. If the correction is acceptable, Team A gets the point instead.
- Keep a tally of the scores on the board. The team with the most points wins.
- To make the contest more exciting, set a time limit. Ss must begin to respond before the time is up.

Game – Treasure hunt

Time: 10–15 minutes. This game practices names of colors and objects.

- Divide the class into groups and choose a secretary for each group.
- Books closed. Have Ss tell you the names of the colors, and write them on the board for reference. The game will be easier to score if you do not use "light" and "dark."
- Explain the "treasure hunt." When you say "Go," Ss look around the classroom or among their own personal belongings to find one object of each color. The secretary collects the objects they find and/or writes down the names of classroom objects. Set a time limit of 4–5 minutes.

- When the time is up, stop all activity. Each group holds up or points to the things they found and says the color. The group with the most things wins.

Sentence-making contest (G)

Time: 5–10 minutes. **This activity can be used in any unit to practice writing descriptions.** In this unit, it synthesizes and reviews language related to clothing and descriptions of people.

Preparation: Collect some large photographs of people (famous or not) who illustrate the descriptive adjectives presented in Unit 3 and the clothes in Unit 4. Assign names to the people.

- Put Ss in groups. If necessary, review the vocabulary.
- Give each group a picture and explain the game: Ss try to make as many different sentences as they can about the people in the picture using clothing words or descriptive adjectives. Give Ss three minutes for each picture. On a separate piece of paper, the group secretary writes down the name on the picture and every sentence the group can think up.
- When the first three minutes is up, groups exchange pictures clockwise around the class. Groups do the task again with the next picture. Continue the activity until every group has written sentences for each picture.
- Bring the class back together. Find out which groups have written the most sentences for each picture. That group holds up the picture while the secretary reads their sentences aloud to the class.

Game – Word bingo

- See page 115. Preparation and procedures are the same as for *Letter bingo,* except that Ss fill in their bingo cards with words from Units 1–4. Make up a list of twenty-four words. This list could include names of objects, clothing, colors, countries and regions, descriptive adjectives, seasons and weather, or prepositions of place.
- Write the words on the board, and have Ss write them down in random order on their bingo cards.

Telling time

Time: 10–15 minutes. This activity provides extra practice in telling time.

- Draw a clock on the board, or bring in a clock with movable hands. Set the hands to various times and write A.M. or P.M. on the board. Ask, "What time is it?" Ss answer chorally, using "in the morning," "in the afternoon," "in the evening," or "at night" in their answers.
- Ask each S to draw five clocks on a piece of paper showing different times. They should be careful to draw the minute hand longer than the hour hand. Have them write A.M. or P.M. under each clock.
- Ss work in pairs to ask and answer about the time on each other's clocks.
- To follow up, ask several Ss to draw one of their clocks on the board and to ask another S the time.

Diary

This activity provides additional controlled practice of the present continuous and *so.*

- As a homework activity, ask Ss to keep a diary of one day in their lives. Explain that a diary is a notebook; people write their actions and thoughts in it.
- Tell Ss to keep a diary of what they are doing throughout the day, like this:

  It's 8:00 a.m., so I'm getting up.
  It's 8:15 a.m., so I'm having breakfast.
- Ss bring their diaries to class and share their activities with a partner or with the class.

Action verbs

Time: 10–15 minutes. This activity introduces more action verbs and practices present continuous statements.

- Bring in pictures from newspapers and magazines showing people engaged in different actions (photos from sports magazines can be especially useful for this activity).
- As you show each picture, ask, "What's he/she doing?" and allow Ss to answer if they can. If not, supply the answer. Write each verb on the board, model it, and have Ss repeat.
- Have Ss act out the new verbs.

Complete the word (G)

Time: 10–15 minutes. **This activity can be used to practice vocabulary and spelling in any unit.** Here Ss review verbs from Unit 5, Exercises 7 and 9.

- Copy the following on the board:

  1. _ a _
  2. _ w _ _
  3. _ _ d _
  4. _ r _ _ _
  5. _ _ _ _ p
  6. _ _ _ c _
  7. _ _ n _ _
  8. _ _ l _
  9. _ h _ _
  10. _ o _ _
- Tell Ss the answers are in Unit 5, Exercises 7 and 9. Have Ss work in pairs to find the words and fill in the missing letters.
- Check answers on the board with the class.

Answers

1. eat
2. swim
3. ride
4. drive
5. sleep
6. watch
7. dance
8. walk
9. shop
10. work

Thinking about grammar

Time: 5 minutes. This activity focuses on contrasting the meanings of the simple present and the present continuous.

- Have Ss look at the conversation in Unit 6, Exercise 2. Ask them to underline two statements that give information about "right now" and to circle two statements that tell about things that happen every day or often.

  Sentences about right now
  What are you doing?
  I'm waiting for my mom.
  Is she coming right now?
  I'm going home.
  Sentences about every day
  She works near here.
  I don't live far from here . . . .
  . . . I walk to school.

- Statements about "right now" are in the present continuous. Statements about "every day" are in the simple present. Elicit these observations from the Ss. (*Note:* The sentence, "My bike has a flat tire" is an exception. It means "right now," although it is in the simple present. *Have* belongs to a group of verbs that is not usually used with the continuous. They are taught in Student's Book 1.)

Days of the week

Time: 15 minutes. This activity gives extra practice in saying the days of the week.

- Divide the class into groups, with each group sitting in a circle. Have each group write the days of the week on seven slips of paper. Ss place the slips face up within easy reach of the entire group.
- Designate a leader for each group. Call out any day of the week. The leader quickly picks up the slip of paper with the *next* day of the week written on it and says this day. Moving to the left, the next S does the same with the day that follows. Ss continue around the group until they have picked up all the slips and said all the days of the week. The group that finishes first is the winner of this round.
- Play several times. The group that wins the most rounds is class champion.

Game – Tic-Tac-Toe (G)

Time: 10 minutes. **This activity can be used in any unit to practice forming questions and statements.** Here Ss practice questions and statements in the simple present with regular and irregular verbs.

- Draw a grid with nine squares on the board (i.e., three rows and three columns). Ask Ss to call out present tense verbs, some in the first-person form and some in the third-person singular form, with *–s* (e.g., *go, dances, play*). Write one verb on each square of the grid.
- Divide the class into two teams – Team X and Team O. Team X starts by choosing a verb and making either a question or a statement with it. If it is correct, Team X writes an X on the grid and takes another turn. If it is incorrect, Team O gets a chance with the same word. If Team O is correct, they write an O on the grid. Then it is Team O's turn.
- The game continues until one team gets Tic-Tac-Toe: three Xs or Os in a line; up, down, or diagonally across the grid.
- **Optional:** This game can also be played in pairs or groups, which gives each S more practice.

My home

Time: 15–20 minutes. This activity gives additional practice with the names of rooms.

- Ss work individually to make a floor plan of their house or apartment similar to those in the illustration in Unit 7, Exercise 1. Ask them to label each room (kitchen, dining room, living room, etc.)
- Write these sentences with blanks on the board:

  My house/apartment has _____ rooms.
  It has _____ , _____ , and _____ .
  _____ is next to _____ .

- Have Ss make several sentences using information from their plans.
- Ss compare plans with a partner or in small groups.
- Ask volunteers to copy their plans on the board and to describe their house or apartment to the class.

I need some furniture!

Time: 10 minutes. This activity provides extra practice with vocabulary about home furnishings and *there is/there are.*

- Draw a floor plan of a large house on the board. Label the rooms and include one or two pieces of furniture in the plan. Say, "This is my new house. There's a . . . in the . . . . I need some furniture."

- Ask Ss to call out the things they think you need and where these things should go (e.g., "You need a desk in the living room.") Draw the furnishings that Ss suggest, or draw boxes and write the words in them. Make sure there are a few plural nouns.
- When you have enough furniture in the house, Ss work in pairs to make lists of the furniture in each room. They ask one another questions to elicit sentences, for example, "What's in the living room?"

My favorite room

Time: 15–20 minutes. This exercise reviews vocabulary for housing and home furnishings.

Preparation: Choose a favorite room in your house or apartment. Make some notes to describe the room. Take to class a watch or clock that will show 30 seconds.

- Write your notes on the board, for example:

  My favorite room: living room
  Activities: relax, read, listen to music
  Favorite things: beautiful pictures, comfortable sofa, stereo
- Following your notes, talk about your favorite room for 30 seconds. (Check your time on the watch or clock.) Say what you do there and describe the features that make the room special for you, for example:

  "The living room is my favorite room. I relax in my living room at night. There are some beautiful pictures on the wall. There's a comfortable sofa. I sit on the sofa and read every evening. Sometimes I listen to music on the stereo."
- Ss work individually to make notes about their favorite room. Have them follow this outline:

  Name of room
  Activities
  Favorite things
- Ss tell a partner about their favorite room. They should speak for about 30 seconds each. Keep time. Ss change partners and talk again.
- Ask volunteers to describe their favorite room to the class.

Game – Twenty questions (G)

Time: 10–15 minutes. **This popular game can be used in other units to practice forming questions to elicit personal information.** Here, Ss practice asking yes/no questions in the simple present while trying to guess the name of a job from Unit 8.

- Ss form groups. Explain the game: One S thinks of a job that Ss are familiar with from the unit and then answers the group's questions with "Yes" or "No" about the job. The winner is either the S who correctly guesses the name of the job or the S who answers twenty questions before anyone in the group correctly guesses the name.
- If necessary, demonstrate the game. Tell Ss that you are thinking of a job. Ask them to guess what the job is. Model several yes/no questions that they could ask:

  "Do you work in a hospital?"
  "Is your job dangerous?"
  "Are you a policeman?"

Opposites (G)

Time: 10–15 minutes. **This activity can be adapted for use with later units.** Here, it provides a cumulative review of the vocabulary introduced in Units 1–8.

- Write *Opposites* on the board. Demonstrate the meaning by writing *yes* and *no* under it. Elicit a few more pairs of opposites from the Ss. Write the following lists of words on the board or give to Ss in a handout. Demonstrate the task by drawing a line between *yes* in the list on the left and *no* in the list on the right. Ss work in pairs to match the words on the left with their opposites on the right.

Words:

yes	*relaxing*
new	*boring*
day	*midnight*
exciting	*winter*
stressful	*good-bye*
dark	*old*
easy	*behind*
noon	*white*
A.M.	*last*
tall	*difficult*
first	*P.M.*
thin	*light*
hello	*night*
in front of	*heavy*
summer	*short*
black	*no*

Answers

yes/no	A.M./P.M.
new/old	tall/short
day/night	first/last
exciting/boring	thin/heavy
stressful/relaxing	hello/good-bye
dark/light	in front of/behind
easy/difficult	summer/winter
noon/midnight	black/white

Shopping lists

Time: 10–15 minutes. This activity practices the spelling of food words and teaches additional vocabulary related to food.

- Write the names of two simple dishes that Ss are likely to be familiar with on the board.

- Point to the name of the first dish and ask, "What do you need for ___ ?" Ss brainstorm the ingredients for the first dish and you write them on the board. Ss need to agree on the ingredients; use ingredients that a majority of Ss agree on.
- Practice the names of the ingredients.
- Have Ss work in pairs or small groups to list the ingredients of the other dish. As they work, go around the class to check on their progress and help them.
- Have individuals come to the board to write the names of the ingredients for the second dish. Each S writes one ingredient. Continue until Ss agree that all the necessary ingredients have been listed.
- Practice the names of the ingredients for the second dish.

Favorite snacks

Time: 10–15 minutes. This activity provides freer practice with food vocabulary.

- Write these questions on the board:

  What is the name of your favorite snack?
  What do you need to make it?

- Ask Ss to think of their favorite snack. (*Note:* A *snack* is any food you eat between meals.) Have them write down the name of the snack on a piece of paper and list what they need to make it. Walk around to give help.
- In pairs, Ss take turns asking the questions on the board and responding with the information they wrote.
- **Optional:** Bring the class back together. Ss take turns reading the ingredients they need to make their favorite snack – without mentioning the name of the food. The class guesses the name of the food.

Breakfast at my house

Time: 20–30 minutes.

- Have Ss write conversations like the one in Unit 9, Exercise 6 using information about what their own families have for breakfast, lunch, or dinner on Sundays.
- Ss role play their conversations in pairs. A few pairs can perform for the whole class.

Olympic sports

Time: 10–15 minutes. This whole-class activity provides additional practice with vocabulary for sports.

- Write the following chart on the board:

Olympic sports

Winter sports	*Summer sports*

- Have Ss come up with as many sports as possible for each category. If necessary, help Ss with the English names of Olympic sports.

Possible answers

Winter sports	*Summer sports*
Bobsled	Diving
Figure skating	Swimming
Hockey	Baseball
Luge	Cycling
Skiing	Gymnastics
Ski jumping	Sailing
Skating	Soccer
	Tennis
	Volleyball

- Ask Ss, "What is your favorite winter sport? What is your favorite summer sport?" Take a survey using the sports on the board.

In my free time

Time: 20–25 minutes. This activity provides additional practice with simple present questions and *can* and *can't*.

- Set a time limit of 10 minutes. Write the cues on the board:

  What I like to do in my free time
  I like . . . (sports/activities/music/etc.)
  I usually/often/sometimes . . . in the evening.
  I . . . on Saturdays/Sundays.
  I can . . . .
  I can't . . . .

- Ask Ss to use the cues to write five true statements about themselves – each on a separate piece of paper or index card. They should try to think of things that are unusual or even unique. As they write, go around the class to help and to check their work.
- Collect the papers, mix them up, and give one to each S. A S who gets his or her own paper should immediately trade it for another one.
- Explain the activity: Ss ask one another questions based on the information they have in the statements on the papers. When they find the person who fits a statement, they write the S's name on it. Then they get another statement.
- Set a time limit of about ten minutes. Ss walk around asking questions and matching Ss with statements. Whoever finds the most people is the winner.

Birthday parties

Time: 10–15 minutes. This group activity provides a framework for expanding on the vocabulary in Unit 11, Exercise 2.

- Put Ss in groups of four to six Ss. Ss work together to plan the perfect birthday celebration.
- Write these questions on the board to guide Ss' discussions:

  Who comes to the celebration?

Where does it take place?
What do people do?
What do people eat and drink?

Note: Ss can have this discussion using the simple present. It is not necessary at this point for Ss to use the future with *be going to*.

- Groups share their plans with the class. The class votes on the best celebration.

How much did you find out?

Time: about 20 minutes of class time. This activity reviews asking questions and describing customs. It gives Ss the opportunity to find out more about the customs in English-speaking countries.

- Choose one holiday for this activity or ask Ss to suggest one.
- Write a set of questions about the holiday on the board. Ss should copy these questions and include additional questions of their own. Here are some example questions about Christmas:

  Do you celebrate Christmas?
  How do you celebrate it? What do you do?
  Do you give presents?
  Do you have special dinner on Christmas day?
  Do you have Christmas parties?
  Is it your favorite holiday? Why or why not?
- Ss should try to find a native-English speaker and interview him or her using the questions. Alternatively, Ss could go to the library and get the information from a book, magazine, or the Internet.
- In class, Ss take turns sharing their information with the class. Encourage Ss to ask follow-up questions to find out about one another's research experiences during this task.

Word associations

Time: 15 minutes. This activity reviews vocabulary used to describe holidays.

- Write six holidays or celebrations on the board. Explain the task: Ss brainstorm and try to think of as many word associations as they can for each one.
- Model the task by eliciting word associations for the word *Christmas* and writing them on the board under it:

  Christmas
  presents *snow*
  December 25 *Santa Claus*
- Ss work in groups. Set a time limit of about ten minutes for groups to finish brainstorming for all six holidays. Walk around the class and give help as needed.
- Groups take turns sharing the word associations they made. Find out which group made the most word associations for each holiday.

Game – Spelling challenge (G)

Time: 10–15 minutes. **This game can be adapted for use with later units.** Here, Ss practice the spelling of the parts of the body. This is a noisy activity.

- Books closed. Divide the class into two teams and set a time limit. One S from Team A calls out the name of a part of the body. One S from Team B spells the word.
- You write each letter on the board as the S spells it. Write exactly what the S says. If the S says *e* when he or she means *i*, write *e*. If the S wants you to erase or start over, he must tell you that, understandably, in English. Otherwise, just write each letter as the S says it.
- **Optional:** To add more challenge, set a time limit (30 or 45 seconds) in which the S must spell the word. If you wish, you may also let other Ss on the team help, but write only what the S spelling the word says.
- Teams take turns giving a word and spelling. The winner is the team with the most right answers at the end of the game.

Game – Simon says

Time: 5–10 minutes. Ss will enjoy this active game, which reviews the parts of the body and previews imperatives.

- Explain or demonstrate the game. Ss are standing. The leader gives commands beginning with "Simon says" (for example, "Simon says, 'Point to your feet' "). Ss must follow the commands. When the leader does *not* include "Simon says" in the command (for example, "Point to your feet"), Ss must *not* follow the command. Ss who do follow the command that does not include "Simon says" are "out" and must sit down. The last S standing is the winner.
- Play the game, taking the role of leader yourself. To increase the challenge and to finish the game more quickly, give the commands more quickly. Ss make more mistakes when they have less time to think.

How to live dangerously

Time: 10–15 minutes. This activity practices imperatives and the vocabulary introduced in Unit 12.

- Tell Ss that they're going to give "advice" about how to live dangerously. (Many of the suggestions can be the opposites of the "good advice" in the article.) Write one or two examples on the board:

  Don't wear a seat belt.
  Always go to bed late.
- Divide the class into groups of four to five. Ask each group to come up with 10 suggestions for "living dangerously."
- Elicit the suggestions from the groups. Write them on the board.
- As a class, decide which suggestions are the most dangerous.

The other question

Time: 15 minutes. This activity reviews question forms and practices fluency and memory.

- Refer Ss to the wrong answers in Review of Units 9–12, Exercise 5. Work with the class to write a question for the first wrong answer (No, she isn't), for example, "Is Allison going to come to the party?"
- Ss work individually to write questions for the six wrong answers. Let them consult with each other if you wish.
- Circulate as they work. When you see a good question for one of the answers, have the S write it on the board.
- Correct the questions on the board with the class.
- Ss practice their questions and answers in pairs. Ask volunteers to act out their conversations in front of the class.

Where can you buy it?

Time: 15 minutes. This activity practices the names of things and places.

- Write these questions on the board. Use the name of your town or area:

  Where can you buy aspirin in (your town)?
  What else can you buy there?

- Elicit answers to the two questions. Ss answer with the name of a real place, for example: "You can buy aspirin at the Super Save Drugstore on Grant Street. You can buy newspapers there too."
- In small groups, Ss ask and answer questions about the eight things to buy in Unit 13, Exercise 1.
- Have groups share their answers with the class.

Compound nouns

Time: 20–25 minutes. This activity previews the idea of compound nouns using words from Unit 13, Exercise 3, and from earlier units in the book.

- Write these words and expressions on the board:

  rest room
  bathroom
  bookstore
  department store

- Show Ss that each word or expression contains a pair of words that go together. Some pairs are spelled as one word.
- Have Ss find other "word pairs" (compound nouns) in Unit 13, Exercise 1 (e.g., *traveler's checks, sweatshirt, drugstore, gas station, post office, supermarket*). Write them on the board.
- Write these two lists on the board:

A	*B*
drug	*basket*
swim	*station*
coffee	*end*
eye	*suit*
home	*glasses*
sales	*store*
sun	*person*
train	*drops*
waste	*table*
week	*work*

- Ss match the words in column A with the words in column B and write them as one word or two. Refer Ss to the Unit Summaries in the back of the book for ideas and spelling.
- Elicit answers from around the class. Have Ss write the answers on the board. Check that Ss have written the answers correctly as one or two words.

Answers *(Stress is shown in boldface type.)*

1. **drug**store
2. **swim**suit
3. **cof**fee table
4. **eye**drops
5. **home**work
6. **sales**person
7. **sun**glasses
8. **train** station
9. **waste**basket
10. **week**end

- Go over pronunciation. Compounds are always stressed on the first word.
- **Optional:** Have Ss work in groups to make similar puzzles for other groups. They can refer to the Unit Summaries to write and solve their puzzles.

Say that again?

Time: 5 minutes. This activity provides quick additional practice in describing locations and using rising intonation to check information.

- Have Ss look at the map in Unit 13, Exercise 5, on page 82. Demonstrate the activity using this example conversation with a S:

  T: Where's the gas station?
  S: It's on the corner of First and Center.
  T: First and Center?
  S: Right!

- Ss ask and answer the question in a chain, with each S calling on the next S at random.
- **Optional:** To make the activity more challenging, set a time limit (perhaps 10 seconds) for questions and answers. If a S does not speak in time, call on another S.

What's near Rita's house?

Time: 20 minutes. This activity gives additional practice with locations and directions.

- Ss draw simple maps of their neighborhoods. They include the names of three or four streets and five or six of the most important or interesting places. They write their names on the papers.
- Collect the maps and pass them out at random. Be sure that no one gets his or her own map.
- In pairs, Ss ask and answer questions about the maps they received, for example:

  S1: Where's Rita's house?
  S2: It's on Fourth Street, near Jackson Avenue.
  S1: Where's the Pyramid Restaurant?
  S2: It's on the corner of Fourth and Colorado.
  S1: How do you get to the restaurant from her house?

Role play

Time: 10–15 minutes. This activity provides further pronunciation practice of the regular past tense ending.

- Ss look back at Unit 14, Exercise 2. Have Ss circle the past tense verbs.
- Elicit the pronunciation of each past tense verb in the conversation. Play the audio program once or twice while Ss listen. Tell Ss to pay special attention to the pronunciation of the verbs.
- In pairs, Ss practice the conversation again. Encourage them to focus on the pronunciation of the past tense verbs and to use expression in their voices.
- Follow up by asking volunteers to say the conversation for the class without reading. If they forget parts, encourage them to improvise, or let other Ss prompt them.

Yesterday

Time: 15–20 minutes. This activity provides additional controlled practice of grammar.

- Write this question and answers on the board:

  _____ *you* _____ *yesterday?*
  Yes, I _____ *./No, I* _____ *.*

- Have Ss ask and answer questions about their own activities by completing the blanks in the sentences. Encourage Ss to add further information after answering yes or no, for example:

  S1: Did you watch TV yesterday?
  S2: No, I didn't. I studied.
  S3: Did you exercise yesterday?
  S4: Yes, I did. I went swimming.

Who is it?

Time: 15 minutes. This exercise provides additional practice with questions and statements in the simple past.

- Ask Ss to write three statements about their partner from Unit 15, Exercise 3, part B. As they write, go around the classroom to help and to check for accuracy.
- Collect all of the papers and redistribute them in random order, but be sure that no S gets his or her own paper.
- One at a time, have Ss read the answers on their papers. The other Ss say the question for each answer. Then everyone guesses who the S is.

When was that?

Time: 15 minutes. This fun activity tests Ss' world knowledge.

- Write on the board five questions about past events that Ss are likely to know about. For example:

  When did World War II start? (1939)
  When did it end? (1945)
  When was (famous person) born?
  When did (country) win the World Cup soccer tournament (or other popular sport)?
  When did (name) become prime minister (president, etc.) of (country)?

- Ss write answers and then compare them in pairs or small groups. Then elicit answers from the class.

Game – Who's where?

Time: 10 minutes. This game practices expressions with prepositions of place.

- Write these questions on the board. Set a time limit of five minutes. Ss complete the three incomplete questions. Tell Ss to think about people they know that are doing these things right now.

  Do you know someone . . .
  in the United States right now?
  in bed right now?
  in _______*?*
  on a trip?
  on a picnic?
  on _______*?*
  at the beach?
  at the library?
  at _______*?*

- Demonstrate the task by asking a few Ss the first question. Walk from one S to another until you find someone who says yes. Encourage Ss to give true answers:

  T: Sonia, do you know someone in the United States right now?
  S1: No, I don't.
  T: How about you, Juan? Do you know someone in the United States right now?
  S2: Yes, I do. My brother is in the United States.
  T: (*writing Juan's name on the board*) OK, Juan knows someone in the United States.

- Have the Ss walk around the room, asking and answering questions. When someone gives them a yes answer, they write down the S's name.

- The winner is the first person to have answers to all of the questions. If no one has answers to all the questions, the person with the most answers after five minutes is the winner.
- Check the names the winner wrote down. Just be sure the Ss gave a yes answer. (You don't have to be sure the answer was true.)

Game – What's your excuse?

Time: 15–20 minutes. This activity gives additional practice with invitations and excuses.

- Ss work in pairs to rewrite the conversation in Unit 16, Exercise 6 with a new invitation and a new excuse. As they write, go around the classroom to give help and to check for accuracy.
- Ss practice their new conversations in pairs.
- Have some of the Ss say their conversations for the class, or do this in small groups.

Silly excuses

Time: 10–15 minutes. This activity gives additional practice with making excuses.

- Write one or two "silly" excuses on the board, for example:

  I have to wash my dog.
  I have to shine my shoes.
- Ss work in pairs to write three silly excuses.
- Ss read their excuses aloud. As they read their excuses, write them on the board.
- The class votes on the silliest excuse.

Do you want to . . . ?

Time: 20 minutes. This activity practices invitations and the vocabulary of the unit.

- From a local English-language newspaper, cut out several announcements or advertisements for weekend activities. If no newspaper is available, you can write your own announcements based on things that are happening in your town. Copy the announcements so that each S has them.
- Ss read and discuss the activities in pairs or groups, helping each other with vocabulary. Each S chooses the activity he or she wants to do.
- Ss stand up and move around the room, inviting others to join them. Try to circulate at the same time to encourage Ss to make, refuse, and accept invitations using language from the unit.
- When a S finds someone who wants to do the same thing, they join together and invite more people.
- At the end, the largest group shows the most popular activity.

Tests

The following set of four tests may be used to assess students' mastery of the material presented in *New Interchange* Intro Student's Book. Each test covers four units. Not only will these criterion reference tests allow the teacher to determine how successfully students have mastered the material, but the tests will also give students a sense of accomplishment. For information about these tests – and about testing in general – see "Testing Students' Progress" on page x in the Introduction to this Teacher's Edition.

When to give a test

- Give the appropriate test after the class has completed each quarter of Intro Student's Book, i.e., four units and the accompanying review unit.

Before giving a test

- Photocopy, collate, and staple the test – one for each student in the class.
- Schedule a class period of about 45–60 minutes for the test.
- Locate and set the recorded Part A for the test listening section on the Class Audio Cassette or Audio CD. The tests are at the end of the cassettes (cassette 3, side 6) or CDs (CD 3, tracks 37–40).
- Tell the students that they are going to have a "pencil and paper" test (i.e., oral production will not be tested). Suggest that they prepare for the test by reviewing the appropriate units and unit summaries. In studying for the test, students should pay particular attention to the Conversations, Grammar Focus points, and Word Power Vocabulary exercises. Tell Ss that the test will also contain a short listening section.

How to give a test

- Explain that the point of the test is not to have students compete with each other for the highest grade; rather, the test will inform each student (and the teacher) about how well the material was learned and what material, if any, may need extra review and practice.
- On the day of the test, hand out one photocopy of the test to each student.
- Encourage Ss to take about five minutes to look through the test, without answering any of the test items. Make sure students understand the instructions, e.g., "Check (✓) the correct answers." "Fill in the blank." "Circle **T** for true or **F** for false."
- Tell Ss that about five minutes of the test time will be used for the listening section, part A, which is the first item on the test. However, it is up to the teacher to decide whether to give the listening section near the beginning or the end of the test-taking time.
- Tell Ss that they are not allowed to use their Student's Books or dictionaries during the test.
- To help Ss use their time efficiently and to finish on time, write the total time for the test on the board before beginning the test:

  Total time: 45 minutes

- After the test begins, revise the time shown on the board every ten minutes or so to tell the class how much time is left.
- When giving the listening section of the test, direct the class to part A, and go over the instructions. Advise Ss just to listen the first time they hear the audio recording, and then to listen and mark their answers during the second playing. Afterward, play the audio recording twice, straight through without stopping or pausing.

Alternate presentation

- If the teacher does not wish to use the class time for the test, tell Ss to complete the whole test at home except for part A, the listening test item. Advise the Ss to complete the test at home in 40 minutes and not to use their Student's Books or dictionaries. During the following class, take five minutes to play the audio recording and to complete part A of the test.

How to score a test

- Either collect the test and use the Test Answer Key to score it, or go over the test with the class while allowing each student to correct his or her own test. Alternatively, tell the students to exchange tests with a partner and correct each other's answers as the teacher elicits or reads the answers aloud.
- Each test has a total score of 100 points (50 correct answers are possible at 2 points each). If a letter grade is useful to the teacher and the Ss, this scoring system can be used:

90–100 points	=	A or Excellent
80–89 points	=	B or Very good
70–79 points	=	C or Fair
69 or below	=	Need to review the unit(s)

Test 1 Units 1–4

Name: ____________
Date: ____________
Score: ____________

A Listen to people talking. Check (✓) the correct answer.

1. Mr. Young's first name is ____.
   ☐ Z-A-C-H-A-R-Y
   ☐ Z-A-C-K-A-R-Y
   ☐ S-A-C-H-A-R-Y
2. Sue's phone number is ____.
   ☐ 555–8781
   ☐ 555–8871
   ☐ 555–8771
3. Brandon's ____ is in his bag.
   ☐ CD player
   ☐ cellular phone
   ☐ pager
4. Justine is ____.
   ☐ French
   ☐ Italian
   ☐ Canadian
5. Michelle's favorite pants are ____.
   ☐ ruined
   ☐ good-looking
   ☐ blue

B Complete these sentences. Use the correct pronoun.

1. Kenji and I are in the same English class. He is in ________ English class.
2. This is my teacher. ________ name is Ms. Brown.
3. This is Tom's book. This is ________ book.
4. You have an interesting name. How do you spell ________ name?

C Complete these conversations. Use the correct form of *be*.

1. A: Hi. My name ________ María Rivera.
   B: It's nice to meet you.
2. A: This is Mark Taylor.
   B: I think you ________ in my math class.
3. A: What ________ your name?
   B: It's Yumiko.
4. A: Hi. I ________ Bill Smith.
   B: It's nice to meet you.

D Check (✓) the correct response.

1. Good-bye. Have a nice day.
   - ☐ I'm sorry.
   - ☐ It's nice to meet you.
   - ☐ Thanks, you too.
2. See you later.
   - ☐ I'm OK. Thank you.
   - ☐ OK. Good-bye.
   - ☐ Not bad. How are you?
3. Hi, how are you?
   - ☐ Not bad, thanks.
   - ☐ Good night.
   - ☐ Nice to meet you, too.

E Complete these conversations.

1. A: What are **(it / this / these)**?

   B: **(They / They're / It's)** chopsticks.
2. A: What's this?

   B: **(It / It's / This)** my wallet.
3. A: **(Is this / This is / Are these)** your sunglasses?

   B: No, **(is / it's / they're)** not.
4. A: Is **(the / this / they)** a cell phone?

   B: No, it isn't. It's **(a / an / the)** electronic address book.
5. A: **(Where are / What's / Is it)** my keys?

   B: On the table.
6. A: **(Is your / What's this / Is it)** dictionary in your book bag?

   B: Yes, **(it's / it is / it's this)**.

F Look at the picture and answer these questions. Circle the correct word.

1. Where's the newspaper? It's **(under / on / next to)** the briefcase.
2. Is the telephone behind the briefcase? No, it's **(in front of / next to / in)** the briefcase.
3. Are the papers **(in / under / behind)** the briefcase? Yes, they are.
4. Where are the books? They are **(in front of / behind / under)** the telephone.
5. Where's the lamp? It's **(in front of / next to / behind)** the briefcase.

G Write the missing questions. Use the key words in parentheses.

Example: A: **(name)** What's your name?

B: My name is Sandy.

1. A: **(England)** ______________________________

   B: No, I'm not. I'm from Australia.
2. A: **(from)** ______________________________

   B: We're from New York.
3. A: **(Spanish)** ______________________________

   B: No, it's not. My first language is Portuguese.
4. A: **(today)** ______________________________

   B: I'm fine.
5. A: **(Brazil)** ______________________________

   B: Yes, they are. My parents are from Brazil.
6. A: **(short)** ______________________________

   B: No, she's not. She's really tall.
7. A: **(like)** ______________________________

   B: He's very serious.

H Circle the correct word.

1. Larry always tells jokes. He is (**heavy** / **cute** / **funny**).
2. Jean is a good student. She is (**friendly** / **smart** / **thin**).
3. Tom always smiles. He is (**friendly** / **interesting** / **serious**).
4. My girlfriend is good-looking. She is (**nice** / **short** / **pretty**).
5. My teacher is very kind. She is (**interesting** / **nice** / **handsome**).

I Complete this chart.

I	
you	your
he	his
she	her
we	
they	

J Join these sentences with *and* or *but*.

Example: I have a purple sweatshirt. I am wearing a green one now.
I have a purple sweatshirt, but I'm wearing a green one now.

1. It's very cold today. David is not wearing a coat.
____
2. Myra is very pretty. She's wearing a blue dress.
____
3. Frank is wearing a suit. He's not wearing a tie.
____

K Complete these sentences.

1. A: __________ you __________ black pants?
   B: Yes, I __________ . I'm wearing black pants.
2. It's sunny. It __________ raining.
3. They're wearing jackets. __________ wearing coats.
4. We're wearing sneakers. __________ wearing boots.
5. A: __________ he __________ a hat?
   B: No, he __________ . He's wearing a cap.

Test **2**

Units 5–8

Name: ______________________
Date: ______________________
Score: ______________________

A Listen to people talking. Check (✓) the correct answer.

1. It is ____ in Los Angeles.
   - ☐ 6:30
   - ☐ 7:30
   - ☐ 10:30
2. Andrew studies ____ .
   - ☐ at 12:00
   - ☐ in the afternoon
   - ☐ on Saturdays and Sundays
3. Julia's apartment doesn't have a ____ .
   - ☐ view
   - ☐ yard
   - ☐ balcony
4. Robert works as a ____ .
   - ☐ chef
   - ☐ waiter
   - ☐ singer

B Look at these clocks. Complete these sentences.

1. It's a quarter __________ twelve.
2. It's __________ after __________ .
3. It's twenty __________ five.
4. It's seven __________ .

C Make sentences with *What* + *doing* and *so*. Use the words in the box.

What's	eat dinner
What are	get up
	have lunch
	sleep
	~~watch TV~~

Example: What's she doing?
It's 8:00 P.M., so she's watching TV .

1. ________________ you doing?
   It's 2:00 A.M., ______________________________ .
2. ________________ Mr. and Mrs. Park doing?
   It's 7:30 A.M., ______________________________ .
3. ________________ James doing?
   It's noon, ______________________________ .

4. ________________ they doing?

   It's 6:30 P.M., ______________________________ .

D Complete these sentences. Use the correct form of the verb in parentheses.

1. My brother __________ **(work)** and __________ **(live)** downtown.
2. He __________ **(walk)** to work. He ________________ **(need, not)** a car.
3. My parents and I __________ **(live)** in the suburbs. We __________ **(have)** a big house.
4. My parents __________ **(drive)** to work. They ________________ **(use, not)** public transportation.
5. My brother ________________ **(live, not)** near here. He __________ **(take)** a train to come here.
6. I'm 13 years old. I ________________ **(drive, not)**. I __________ **(take)** a bus to school.
7. I ________________ **(do, not)** my homework after school. I __________ **(do)** it after dinner.

E Write the missing questions in each conversation.

1. A: ____ ?

   B: No, I don't have a computer.
2. A: ____ at 3:00 ?

   B: No, he doesn't. He finishes school at 3:30.
3. A: ____ ?

   B: Yes, they do. They study English together.
4. A: ____ ?

   B: She reads the newspaper after breakfast.
5. A: ____ ?

   B: I have dinner at seven o'clock.

F Complete these sentences with *at, in,* or *on*.

1. I get up late ______ weekends.
2. I exercise ______ the morning.
3. I go to bed ______ midnight.
4. School starts ______ 9:00.

G Complete these conversations. Use the words in the box.
(You will not use all the words.)

do	does	have	has
don't	doesn't	haven't	hasn't
	how many		

1. A: ________ rooms does your apartment ________ ?

   B: It ________ three rooms.
2. A: ________ your bedroom ________ a view?

   B: Yes, it ________ .
3. A: ________ you live alone?

   B: No, I ________ .

4: A: ________ your house ________ a big garage?

   B: No, it ________ .

H Make sentences with *There is (There's)* or *There are*. Use the words in parentheses.

Example: **(is, bookcase, bedroom)**

There's a bookcase in the bedroom.

1. **(isn't, mirror, bedroom)**

   ____
2. **(no, pictures, hall)**

   ____
3. **(some, chairs, dining room)**

   ____
4. **(no, microwave oven, kitchen)**

   ____
5. **(any, armchairs, living room)**

   ____

I Write the missing questions in each conversation.

1. A: ____?

   B: I work at the airport.

2. A: ____?

   B: I'm an air traffic controller.

3. A: ____?

   B: I start work at 9:00 A.M.

4. A: ____?

   B: After work, I go home and cook dinner.

J Circle the correct word(s).

1. A **(security guard / cashier / florist)** wears a uniform.
2. A **(pilot / nurse / salesperson)** works in a hospital.
3. A **(receptionist / gardener / police officer)** has a dangerous job.
4. A **(flight attendant / judge / chef)** sits all day.
5. A **(fashion designer / photographer / salesperson)** works in a department store.

K Write sentences about jobs. Use the words in parentheses. The verb should be in the correct form.

1. **(air traffic controller / have / stressful / job)**

An air traffic controller ______________________________________.

2. **(firefighter / job / be / dangerous)**

A firefighter's job ______________________________________.

3. **(photographer / have / interesting / job)**

____.

4. **(librarian / job / be / safe)**

____.

Test 3 Units 9–12

Name: ______________________

Date: ______________________

Score: ______________________

A Listen to people talking. Check (✓) the correct answer.

1. Steve ____ eats a salad and some fruit.
   - ☐ always
   - ☐ usually
   - ☐ never
2. Linda doesn't play ____ .
   - ☐ baseball
   - ☐ soccer
   - ☐ skiing
3. Hilary and Mark are going to ____ .
   - ☐ buy a cake
   - ☐ cook dinner
   - ☐ go to a movie
4. Tim's mother tells Tim to ____ .
   - ☐ relax
   - ☐ walk around
   - ☐ call the doctor

B Complete this conversation with *a/an, some,* or *any*.

A: What do we need at the supermarket?

B: Well, let's see. We need __________ (1) cereal and __________ (2) bread.

A: Do we have __________ (3) eggs?

B: Yes, we have __________ (4) . But we don't have __________ (5) vegetables. We need to buy __________ (6) onion and __________ (7) potato.

A: And we should buy __________ (8) yogurt.

C Look at the chart. How often do these people have orange juice for breakfast? Complete these sentences with *always, sometimes, seldom,* or *never.*

✓ = has orange juice for breakfast

	Monday	Tuesday	Wednesday	Thursday	Friday	Saturday	Sunday
Marta	✓		✓		✓	✓	
Frank	✓	✓	✓	✓	✓	✓	✓
Tom							
Louisa					✓		

1. Marta ________________ has orange juice for breakfast.
2. Frank ________________ has orange juice for breakfast.
3. Tom ________________ has orange juice for breakfast.
4. Louisa ________________ has orange juice for breakfast.

D Write the missing questions. Use the words in parentheses.

1. A: ____? (sports, play)
   B: I play soccer and tennis.
2. A: ____? (play, soccer)
   B: I play soccer at school.
3. A: ____? (play, soccer)
   B: I play soccer with my friends.
4. A: ____? (your team, practice)
   B: We practice on weekends.
5. A: ____? (your team, practice)
   B: We start at eleven o'clock in the morning.

E Complete these sentences. Use the correct form of *can*.

1. A: __________ you speak a foreign language?
   B: Yes, I __________ .
2. Toshi __________ play volleyball at all, but Tomoko __________ .
3. A: __________ you play the guitar?
   B: No, I __________ .
4. Marcos and Paulo __________ sing really well, so they __________ enter the talent show.

F Match A and B to make questions and answers with *be going to*. An example is given.

A	B	C
Example: Are you going to do anything this weekend?	Yes, I am.	He's going to study all weekend.
1. Are we going to work this weekend?	Yes, they are.	I'm going to relax.
2. Is Mary going to celebrate her birthday?	No, I'm not.	She's going to have a party.
3. Are you going to stay at home?	Yes, I am.	I'm going to stay at home and read a book.
4. Are you going to do anything on Monday after work?	No, we're not.	They're going to cook pasta.
5. Is Bill going to study this weekend?	Yes, he is.	We're going to see a movie.
6. Are they going to cook dinner?	Yes, she is.	I'm going to go to the gym.

G Complete these sentences. Use the expressions in the box.

go	going to go
get	where
how	take
who	

A: ________(1) are you going to ________(2) next summer?

B: Alaska.

A: Alaska! ________(3) are you going to ________(4) there?

B: We're going to ________(5) a ship.

A: That sounds exciting! ________(6) are you ________(7) with?

B: My family.

H Complete these sentences with *feel, get, go, have,* or *take.*

A: I __________ (1) a headache. I __________ (2) terrible.

B: __________ (3) some aspirin.

A: I __________ (4) a fever and a cough. What should I do?

B: __________ (5) to bed. I'm going to call the doctor.

A: I'm tired. I __________ (6) awful.

B: Stop working! __________ (7) some exercise – __________ (8) for a walk.

I Complete these sentences.

1. My teeth feel fine. I don't have a ________________ .
2. My throat feels bad. I have a ________________ .
3. My back feels terrible. I have a ________________ .
4. My eyes feel good. I don't have ________________ .

Test 4

Units 13–16

A Listen to people talking. Check (✓) the correct answer.

1. The supermarket is ____.
   - ☐ next to the drugstore
   - ☐ at the next corner
   - ☐ on the left
2. Last weekend Ted didn't ____.
   - ☐ study
   - ☐ go hiking
   - ☐ rent a video
3. Alex was born in ____.
   - ☐ Mexico
   - ☐ Miami
   - ☐ New York
4. Sam and Megan are going to ____.
   - ☐ baby-sit
   - ☐ see a movie
   - ☐ go to a fashion show

B Read Paul's shopping list on the left. Where did he buy these things? Match the places and things.

1. stamps ____ — **a.** a gas station
2. cough drops ____ — **b.** a bank
3. a raincoat ____ — **c.** a drugstore
4. gasoline ____ — **d.** a department store
5. traveler's checks ____ — **e.** a post office

C Look at the map. Then use the expressions in the box to complete the sentences.

across from	on
between	on the corner of
next to	

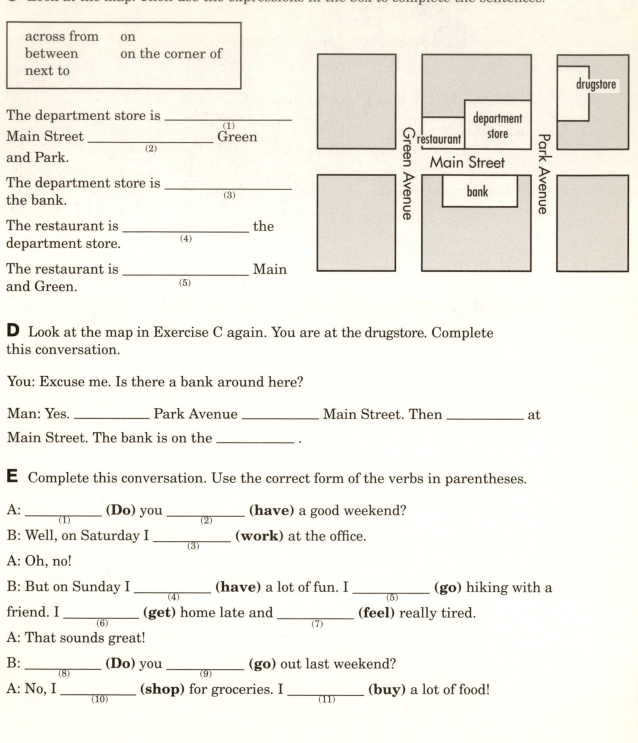

The department store is ________ (1) Main Street ________ (2) Green and Park.

The department store is ________ (3) the bank.

The restaurant is ________ (4) the department store.

The restaurant is ________ (5) Main and Green.

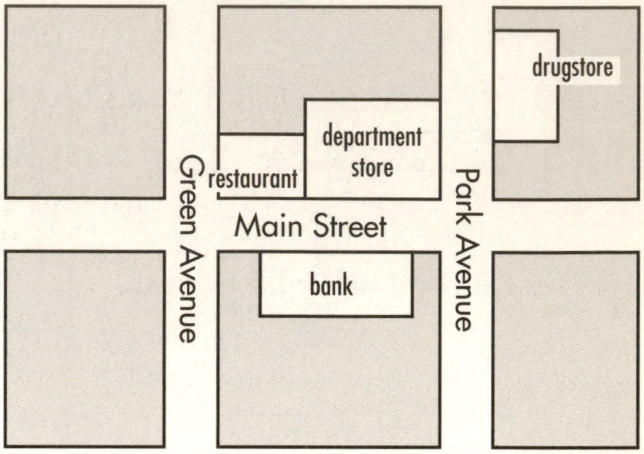

drugstore
department store
restaurant
Green Avenue
Main Street
Park Avenue
bank

D Look at the map in Exercise C again. You are at the drugstore. Complete this conversation.

You: Excuse me. Is there a bank around here?

Man: Yes. ________ Park Avenue ________ Main Street. Then ________ at Main Street. The bank is on the ________ .

E Complete this conversation. Use the correct form of the verbs in parentheses.

A: ________ (1) **(Do)** you ________ (2) **(have)** a good weekend?

B: Well, on Saturday I ________ (3) **(work)** at the office.

A: Oh, no!

B: But on Sunday I ________ (4) **(have)** a lot of fun. I ________ (5) **(go)** hiking with a friend. I ________ (6) **(get)** home late and ________ (7) **(feel)** really tired.

A: That sounds great!

B: ________ (8) **(Do)** you ________ (9) **(go)** out last weekend?

A: No, I ________ (10) **(shop)** for groceries. I ________ (11) **(buy)** a lot of food!

F Look at the illustration. Complete the sentences. Use the correct past form of *be*.

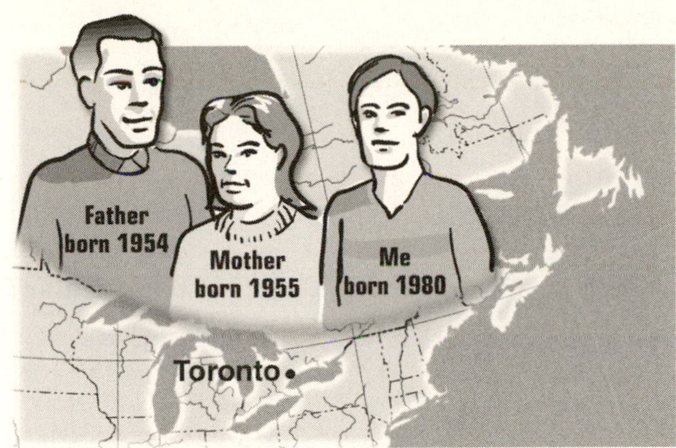

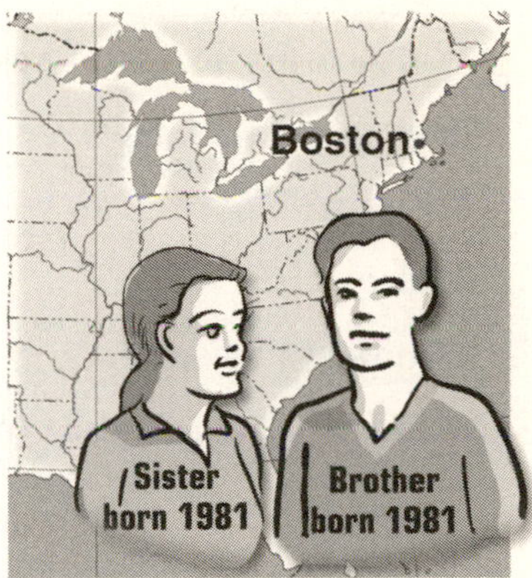

My parents __________ born in Toronto. I __________ born in Toronto, too.

My brother and sister __________ born in Toronto – they __________ born in Boston in 1981.

I __________ very old in 1981.

G Write the missing questions.

1. ____
   I grew up in Tokyo.
2. ____
   Yes, they were. My parents were born in Japan.
3. ____
   My life in Tokyo was very busy.
4. ____
   I came to New York in 1998.
5. ____
   My first English teacher was Mr. Sato.
6. ____
   My favorite subject in college was English literature.

H Complete this telephone conversation. Use the correct pronoun forms.

Man: Hello?

Woman: Hello. Can I speak with Mr. Morris, please?

Man: I'm sorry. He's not here. Can I help _______?

Woman: Maybe. Can you give _______ a message?

Man: Sure.

Woman: Please ask _______ to call _______ tonight at home. My name is Carol Evans.

Man: OK. What's your telephone number?

Woman: He already has _______.

I Circle the correct word(s).

1. There's no food in the refrigerator. I **('d like to / have to / 'd love to)** go shopping.
2. I have a test tomorrow. I **(need to / 'd love to)** study.
3. A: Let's see a movie.
   B: I **('d like to / need to / have to)**, but I can't.
4. A: Do you **(have to / want to / need to)** come to my house for a party?
5. B: Thanks. I **(have to / need to / 'd love to)**!

Test Audio Scripts

Test 1: Units 1–4

A Listen to people talking. Check the correct answer.

1.
ANNA: Hi. My name is Anna Chang.
ZACHARY: Hi, Anna. I'm Zachary Young.
ANNA: Zachary . . . Hmm . . . How do you spell your first name?
ZACHARY: Z-A-C-H-A-R-Y.
ANNA: Oh, thanks.

2.
CHRIS: What's your phone number, Sue?
SUE: It's 555-8871.
CHRIS: Thanks.

3.
MARTA: Brandon, what's on your desk?
BRANDON: Oh, it's my CD player.
MARTA: It's cool! . . . And what's in your bag? Is it a pager?
BRANDON: No, it's not. It's a cellular phone.

4.
JASON: Justine, your name is interesting. Are you French?
JUSTINE: No, I'm not.
JASON: Are you Italian?
JUSTINE: No, I'm Canadian. My family is originally from Canada, from Montreal.

5.
TONY: Are you ready to go to the party, Michelle?
MICHELLE: No, I'm not. My favorite pants are ruined!
TONY: Oh, that's too bad. What color are they?
MICHELLE: Black.
TONY: But, you're wearing black pants now!
MICHELLE: I know, but these are old and not very good-looking.

Test 2: Units 5–8

A Listen to people talking. Check the correct answer.

1.
NICK: Hello?
LAURA: Hi, Nick. This is Laura. I'm calling from New York.
NICK: Hi, Laura. How are you?
LAURA: Fine, thanks. What are you doing?
NICK: I'm having breakfast.
LAURA: Breakfast? At ten-thirty in the morning?
NICK: But it's *seven-thirty* in the morning here in Los Angeles.
LAURA: Oh, I'm sorry! It's ten-thirty here . . .

2.
DAD: So, Andrew, what's your new roommate like?
ANDREW: He's great, Dad. He's really friendly.
DAD: And how about your classes? What's your schedule like?
ANDREW: Well, I get up and go for a run. At 12:00 I eat lunch. I practice with my rock band in the afternoon.
DAD: Andrew . . . ?
ANDREW: Yes, Father.
DAD: When do you *study?*
ANDREW: Oh . . . um . . . I study on Saturdays and Sundays. Sometimes I study all night!

3.
DAN: What's your new house like, Julia?
JULIA: Well, it has three bedrooms and two bathrooms. The bedrooms all have big closets.
DAN: That sounds nice. Does it have a yard?
JULIA: No, but it has a balcony. There's a great view of downtown.
DAN: Super!
JULIA: I really love it. It's my dream house.

4.
ROBERT: I have a new job.
SAMANTHA: Congratulations, Robert! Where do you work?
ROBERT: I work at the French restaurant on Center Street.
SAMANTHA: Oh, yes, I know it. There's a singer at that restaurant on weekends. . . . So, you're a waiter?
ROBERT: No, I'm a chef!
SAMANTHA: Oh. What time do you finish work?
ROBERT: Ten p.m. But sometimes I finish at midnight. It's a very busy place!

Test 3: Units 9–12

A Listen to people talking. Check the correct answer.

1.

STEVE: So, what do you want for lunch, Teresa?
TERESA: How about a hamburger . . . and some potato chips.
STEVE: Hmm. I don't usually eat hamburgers. And I never eat potato chips. They're not good for you.
TERESA: Well, what do *you* want?
STEVE: I want a salad and some fruit.
TERESA: You always eat the same thing!
STEVE: I know, but I can't help it. I like it!

2.

LINDA: Tom, you're a really good soccer player!
TOM: Thanks, Linda. I practice a lot.
LINDA: I can't play soccer at all.
TOM: Really? What sports do you like?
LINDA: My favorite is skiing.
TOM: What sports do you play in the summer?
LINDA: Baseball. We play every weekend.

3.

KATHY: Are you going to do anything special this weekend, Hilary?
HILARY: Well, it's Mark's birthday . . .
KATHY: Oh? How old is he?
HILARY: I don't know. He won't tell me.
KATHY: What are you going to do?
HILARY: He's coming to my house after work and I'm going to cook dinner.
KATHY: How nice!
HILARY: Then . . . Mark and I are going to go to a movie.
KATHY: Well, have fun!

4.

MOM: Tim, what's wrong?
TIM: I hurt my ankle in a basketball game.
MOM: Oh, no! Can you walk?
TIM: I can walk a little, but it really hurts.
MOM: Well, sit down and relax. And don't walk around anymore!
TIM: Yes, Mother.
MOM: I'm going to call Dr. Brown.
TIM: Thanks, Mom.

Test 4: Units 13–16

A Listen to people talking. Check the correct answer.

1.

WOMAN: Excuse me . . .
MAN: Yes?
WOMAN: Is there a drugstore around here?
MAN: Let's see . . . No, I don't think so.
WOMAN: Hmmm. I need to buy some aspirin. I have a terrible headache.
MAN: Well, you can buy aspirin at the supermarket, too.
WOMAN: Where is it?
MAN: Walk two blocks up the street. It's on the left.
WOMAN: Thank you.

2.

MARY: Hi, Ted. Did you have a good weekend?
TED: Yes. It was great! On Saturday we went hiking.
MARY: You did?
TED: Yes. And last night we rented a video and stayed home.
MARY: Very relaxing . . .
TED: Yes, it was. What did you do?
MARY: I did chores Friday night and then I studied all weekend.
TED: Why did you study so much?
MARY: I have a big exam tomorrow. I have to be ready for it.

3.

BARBARA: Where are you going to go for vacation, Alex?
ALEX: I'm going to visit my grandparents. They live in Mexico City.
BARBARA: Mexico City? Are you from Mexico?
ALEX: Yes, I am.
BARBARA: Alex, I didn't know that!
ALEX: Well, I grew up in Miami, but I was born in Mexico.
BARBARA: Really?
ALEX: It's true. Everyone calls me "Alex" in English, but my real name is Alejandro.

4.

MEGAN: Hello?
SAM: Hi, Megan. It's Sam.
MEGAN: Hi, Sam. How are you?
SAM: Good, good. Listen . . . I have two tickets for a fashion show tonight. Do you want to go?
MEGAN: I'd love to, but I can't. I have to baby-sit.
SAM: Oh, I see . . .
MEGAN: But I'm free tomorrow night. Let's see a movie.
SAM: Terrific!

Test Answer Keys

Note: Each test has 50 possible answers at 2 points each.

Test 1: Units 1–4

A. [5 × 2 = 10]

1. Z-A-C-H-A-R-Y
2. 555–8871
3. cellular phone
4. Canadian
5. ruined

B. [4 × 2 = 8]

1. my 2. Her 3. his 4. your

C. [4 × 2 = 8]

1. is 2. 're / are 3. 's / is 4. 'm / am

D. [3 × 2 = 6]

1. Thanks, you too.
2. OK. Good-bye.
3. Not bad, thanks.

E. [6 × 2 = 12]

1. A: What are these?
   B: They're chopsticks.
2. A: What's this?
   B: It's my wallet.
3. A: Are these your sunglasses?
   B: No, they're not.
4. A: Is this a cell phone?
   B: No, it isn't. It's an electronic address book.
5. A: Where are my keys?
   B: On the table.
6. A: Is your dictionary in your book bag?
   B: Yes, it is.

F. [5 × 2 = 10]

1. on
2. next to
3. in
4. under
5. behind

G. [7 × 2 = 14]

1. Are you from England?
2. Where are you from?
3. Is your first language Spanish?
4. How are you today?
5. Are your parents from Brazil?
6. Is she short?
7. What's / What is he like?

H. [5 × 2 = 10]

1. funny
2. smart
3. friendly
4. pretty
5. nice

I. [3 × 2 = 6]

I	my	she	her
you	your	we	our
he	his	they	their

J. [3 × 2 = 6]

1. It's very cold today, but David is not wearing a coat.
2. Myra is very pretty and she's wearing a blue dress.
3. Frank is wearing a suit, but he's not wearing a tie.

K. [5 × 2 = 10]

1. A: Are you wearing black pants?
   B: Yes, I am. I'm wearing / black pants.
2. It's sunny. It isn't / 's not raining.
3. They're wearing jackets. They're not / They aren't wearing coats.
4. We're wearing sneakers. We're not / We aren't wearing boots.
5. A: Is he wearing a hat?
   B: No, he isn't / 's not. He's wearing a cap.

Test 2: Units 5–8

A. [4 × 2 = 8]

1. 7:30
2. on Saturdays and Sundays
3. yard
4. chef

B. [4 × 2 = 8]

1. It's a quarter to twelve.
2. It's ten after three.
3. It's twenty to five.
4. It's seven fifty.

C. [4 × 2 = 8]

1. What are you doing?
   It's 2:00 A.M., so I'm sleeping.
2. What are Mr. and Mrs. Park doing?
   It's 7:30 A.M., so they're getting up.
3. What's James doing?
   It's noon, so he's having lunch.
4. What are they doing?
   It's 6:30 P.M., so they're eating dinner.

D. [7 × 2 = 14]

1. My brother works and lives downtown.
2. He walks to work. He doesn't need a car.
3. My parents and I live in the suburbs. We have a big house.
4. My parents drive to work. They don't use public transportation.
5. My brother doesn't live near here. He takes a train to come here.
6. I'm 13 years old. I don't drive. I take a bus to school.
7. I don't do my homework after school. I do it after dinner.

E. [5 × 2 = 10]

1. Do you have a computer?
2. Does he finish school (at 3:00)?
3. Do they study (English) together?
4. When does she read the newspaper?
5. What time do you have dinner?

F. [4 × 2 = 8]
1. on
2. in
3. at
4. at

G. [4 × 2 = 8]
1. A: How many rooms does your apartment have?
   B: It has three rooms.
2. A: Does your bedroom have a view?
   B: Yes, it does.
3. A: Do you live alone?
   B: No, I don't.
4. A: Does your house have a big garage?
   B: No, it doesn't.

H. [5 × 2 = 10]
1. There isn't a mirror in the bedroom.
2. There are no pictures in the hall.
3. There are some chairs in the dining room.
4. There is no microwave oven in the kitchen.
5. There aren't any armchairs in the living room.

I. [4 × 2 = 8]
1. Where do you work?
2. What do you do?
3. What time/When do you start (work)?
4. What do you do after work?

J. [5 × 2 = 10]
1. security guard
2. nurse
3. police officer
4. judge
5. salesperson

K. [4 × 2 = 8]
1. An air traffic controller has a stressful job.
2. A firefighter's job is dangerous.
3. A photographer has an interesting job.
4. A librarian's job is safe.

Test 3: Units 9–12

A. [4 × 2 = 8]
1. always
2. soccer
3. go to a movie
4. relax

B. [8 × 2 = 16]
1. some
2. some
3. any
4. some
5. any
6. an
7. a
8. some

C. [4 × 2 = 8]
1. sometimes
2. always
3. never
4. seldom

D. [5 × 2 = 10]
1. What sports do you play?
2. Where do you play soccer?
3. Who do you play soccer with?
4. When does your team practice?
5. What time does your team practice (on weekends)?

E. [4 × 2 = 8]
1. A: Can you speak a foreign language?
   B: Yes, I can.
2. Toshi can't play volleyball at all, but Tomoko can.
3. A: Can you play the guitar?
   B: No, I can't.
4. Marcos and Paulo can sing really well, so they can enter the talent show.

F. [6 × 2 = 12]
1. Are we going to work this weekend? No, we're not. We're going to see a movie.
2. Is Mary going to celebrate her birthday? Yes, she is. She's going to have a party.
3. Are you going to stay at home? Yes, I am. I'm going to stay at home and read a book.
4. Are you going to do anything Monday after work? Yes, I am. I'm going to go to the gym.
5. Is Bill going to study this weekend? Yes, he is. He's going to study all weekend.
6. Are they going to cook dinner? Yes, they are. They're going to cook pasta.

G. [7 × 2 = 14]
1. Where
2. go
3. How
4. get
5. take
6. who
7. going to go

H. [8 × 2 = 16]
1. have
2. feel
3. Take
4. have
5. Go
6. feel
7. Get
8. go

I. [4 × 2 = 8]
1. toothache
2. sore throat
3. backache
4. sore eyes

Test 4: Units 13–16

A. [4 × 2 = 8]
1. on the left
2. study
3. Mexico
4. see a movie

B. [5 × 2 = 10]
1. e
2. c
3. d
4. a
5. b

C. [5 × 2 = 10]
1. on
2. between
3. across from
4. next to
5. on the corner of

D. [4 × 2 = 8]
You: Excuse me. Is there a bank around here?
Man: Yes. Walk down/Go down Park Avenue to Main Street. Then turn right at Main Street. The bank is on the left.

E. **[11 × 2 = 22]**

1. Did
2. have
3. worked
4. had
5. went
6. got
7. felt
8. Did
9. go
10. shopped
11. bought

F **[5 × 2 = 10]**

My parents were born in Toronto. I was born in Toronto, too.
My brother and sister weren't born in Toronto – they were born in Boston in 1981.
I wasn't very old in 1981.

G **[6 × 2 = 12]**

1. Where did you grow up?
2. Were your parents born in Japan?
3. How was your life in Tokyo? / What was your life in Tokyo like?
4. When did you come to New York?
5. Who was your first English teacher?
6. What was your favorite subject in college?

H **[5 × 2 = 10]**

1. you
2. him
3. him
4. me
5. it

I **[5 × 2 = 10]**

1. have to
2. need to
3. 'd like to
4. want to
5. 'd love to

Test Cross-Reference Indexes

Test 1 Cross-reference Index: Units and Areas Tested

Part	*Items*	*Unit*	*Areas tested*
A	1 2 3 4 5	1 1 2 3 4	**Listening:** Spelling of names **Listening:** Telephone numbers **Listening:** Personal items **Listening:** Giving information about nationality **Listening:** Talking about and describing clothing
B	1–4	1	**Grammar:** *My, yours, his, hers*
C	1–4	1	**Grammar:** The verb *be* **Function:** Introducing yourself and friends
D	1–3	1	**Function:** Saying hello and good-bye
E	1–6	2	**Grammar:** Articles *a, an,* and *the, this/It, these/they;* plurals Yes/No and *where* questions with *be* **Function:** Naming objects Asking for and giving the location of an object
F	1–5	2	**Grammar:** Prepositions of place **Function:** Asking for and giving the location of an object
G	1–7	3	**Grammar:** Statements and yes/no questions with *be* Wh-questions with *be* **Function:** Asking for and giving information about places of origin, native language and descriptions of people
H	1–5	3	**Vocabulary:** Describing people
I	1–3	4	**Grammar:** Possessives
J	1–3	4	**Grammar:** Conjunctions *and* and *but* **Function:** Describing what people are wearing
K	1–5	4	**Grammar:** Present continuous statements; *isn't* and *aren't* Present continuous yes/no questions **Function:** Asking about and describing what people are wearing

Test 2 Cross-reference Index: Units and Areas Tested

Part	*Items*	*Unit*	*Areas tested*
A	1 2 3 4	5 6 7 8	**Listening:** Listening for the time **Listening:** Daily routines **Listening:** Descriptions of houses **Listening:** Descriptions of jobs
B	1–4	5	**Function:** Telling time
C	1–4	5	**Grammar:** *What* + doing; conjunction *so* **Function:** Asking about and describing current activities
D	1–7	6	**Grammar:** Simple present statements with regular and irregular verbs **Function:** Asking for and giving information about where people live and how they go to work or school
E	1–5	6	**Grammar:** Simple present questions
F	1–4	6	**Grammar:** Time Expressions **Function:** Talking about daily routines
G	1–4		**Grammar:** Simple present short answers; *how many* **Function:** Asking about and describing homes
H	1–5	7	**Grammar:** There is / There are **Function:** Saying what furniture is in a room
I	1–4	8	**Grammar:** Simple present Wh-questions with *do* **Function:** Asking for and giving information about work
J	1–5	8	**Vocabulary:** Jobs
K	1–4	8	**Grammar:** Adjectives before nouns **Function:** Giving opinions about jobs

Test 3 Cross-reference Index: Units and Areas Tested

Part	*Items*	*Unit*	*Areas tested*
A	1 2 3 4	9 10 11 12	**Listening:** Food preferences **Listening:** Favorite sports **Listening:** Weekend plans **Listening:** Health problems and advice
B	1–8	9	**Grammar:** Countable and uncountable nouns; *some* and *any* **Function:** Talking about food items you need
C	1–4	9	**Grammar:** Adverbs of frequency **Function:** Talking about eating habits
D	1–5	10	**Grammar:** Simple present Wh-questions **Function:** Talking about sports you like and dislike
E	1–4	10	**Grammar:** *Can* for ability **Function:** Talking about talents and abilities
F	1–6	11	**Grammar:** The future with *be going to* **Function:** Asking for and giving information about future plans
G	1–7	11	**Grammar:** Wh-questions with *be going to* **Function:** Asking for and giving information about future holidays
H	1–8	12	**Grammar:** *Have* + noun; *feel* + adjective; imperatives **Function:** Talking about health problems; giving advice

Test 4 Cross-reference Index: Units and Areas Tested

Part	*Items*	*Unit*	*Areas tested*
A	1 2 3 4	13 14 15 16	**Listening:** Directions **Listening:** Past weekend activities **Listening:** Place and date of birth **Listening:** Inviting people
B	1–5	13	**Vocabulary:** Places and things
C	1–5	13	**Grammar:** Prepositions of place **Function:** Giving locations
D	1–4	13	**Function:** Giving directions
E	1–11	14	**Grammar:** Simple past statements with regular and irregular verbs **Grammar:** Simple past yes/no questions **Function:** Asking for and giving information about activities in the recent past
F	1–5	15	**Grammar:** Statements with the past of *be* **Function:** Giving information about date and place of birth
G	1–6	15	**Grammar:** Questions with the past of *be* **Grammar:** Wh-questions with *did, was,* and *were* **Function:** Asking for and giving information about school experiences and the recent past
H	1–5	16	**Grammar:** Object pronouns **Function:** Leaving phone messages
I	1–5	16	**Grammar:** Verb + *to* + verb; *would* **Function:** Talking about what you need/want to do; inviting people and accepting and declining invitations

Workbook Answer Key

1 It's nice to meet you.

Exercise 1

1. Hi, Stephanie.
   Hello, Mr. Valencia.
2. It's nice to meet you, Ms. Landon.
   Nice to meet you, too, John.

Exercise 2

1. A: your
   B: My
2. A: his
   B: His
3. A: her
   B: Her
4. A: your
   B: My

Exercise 3

1. good
   How
   Mr.
2. you
   fine
   you
   Mr.
3. evening
   are
   thank

Exercise 4

1. Hello.
2. I'm Jake Williams.
3. Fine, thanks.
4. R-O-G-E-R-S.
5. It's nice to meet you.

Exercise 5

Across	*Down*
a. two	a. three
c. eight	b. one
e. seven	d. ten
g. five	e. six
h. zero	f. nine
	g. four

Exercise 6

1. 555-6115
2. 555-9304
3. 555-4731
4. 555-3802
5. 555-5686
6. 555-1779

Exercise 7

A: 's	B: 's
B: 'm	A: 's
A: 's	B: 's
B: 're	A: 're
A: 'm	

Exercise 8

Debra: *me, you*
Kevin: *I'm not, He's*
Debra: *I'm*
Debra: *Are*
James: *am*
Debra: *is*
James: *you're*
Debra: *It's*

Exercise 9

1. Are you Ashley Nevins?
2. Oh, I'm sorry. What's your name?
3. How do you spell your first name?
4. And how do you spell your last name?
5. What's your phone number?

Exercise 10

A

a. Hi.
b. Excuse me.
c. Good night.
d. Good evening.

B

1. b 2. a 3. d 4. c

2 What's this?

Exercise 1

A

1. calculator
2. address book
3. pen
4. encyclopedia
5. camera
6. pencil
7. wastebasket
8. watch

B

1. This is a calculator.
2. This is an address book.
3. This is a pen.
4. This is an encyclopedia.
5. This is a camera.
6. This is a pencil.
7. This is a wastebasket.
8. This is a watch.

Exercise 2

/z/	/s/	/ɪz/
keys	*books*	*watches*
book bags	clocks	addresses
telephones	desks	briefcases
calculators	wallets	
cameras		

Exercise 3

1. this
   It's a wastebasket.
2. this
   It's a purse.
3. these
   They're earrings.
4. this
   It's a CD player.
5. these
   They're sunglasses.
6. these
   They're stamps.

Exercise 4

Megan: Wow! What's this?
Christopher: It's a pager.
Megan: you
Christopher: You're, this
Megan: is
Christopher: a
Megan: these
Christopher: they
Megan: are
Megan: an

Exercise 5

1. B: Yes, it is.
2. B: No, it's not.
3. B: Yes, they are.
4. B: Yes, I am.
5. B: No, they're not.
6. B: No, I'm not.

Exercise 6

1. A: is
   B: it
   A: not
   B: Is
   A: it
2. A: Is
   B: it's
   A: Where
   B: It's
   A: It
3. A: are
   B: they
   A: not
   B: Are
   A: they
4. A: Are
   B: they're
   A: Where
   B: Are
   A: are

Exercise 7

Answers will vary. Possible answers:

1. No, I'm not. I'm a student.
2. No, it's not. My name is . . . *or* It's . . .
3. Yes, it is. *or* Yes, my workbook is on my desk. *or* No, it is not on my desk. *or* No, it isn't.
4. No, it isn't. My telephone number is . . . *or* It's . . .
5. No, I'm not. *or* No, I'm not. I'm in English class.

Exercise 8

1. The glasses are on the chair.
2. The wallet is in the purse.
3. The clock is behind the desk.
4. The phone is under the table.
5. The newspaper is in front of the books.
6. The key is next to the pager.

Exercise 9

A

1. Where is the briefcase? The briefcase is next to the television.
2. Where is the umbrella? The umbrella is behind the chair.
3. Where are the keys? The keys are on the table.
4. Where are the pens? The pens are on the desk *or* next to the earrings.
5. Where is the cell phone? The cell phone is in the purse.
6. Where are the books? The books are in front of the desk *or* wastebasket *or* next to the wastebasket.

B

Answers will vary. Possible answers:

1. The wastebasket is under the desk.
2. The glasses are on the chair.
3. The chair/table is next to the table/chair.
4. The wallet is on the television.

3 Where are you from?

Exercise 1

A

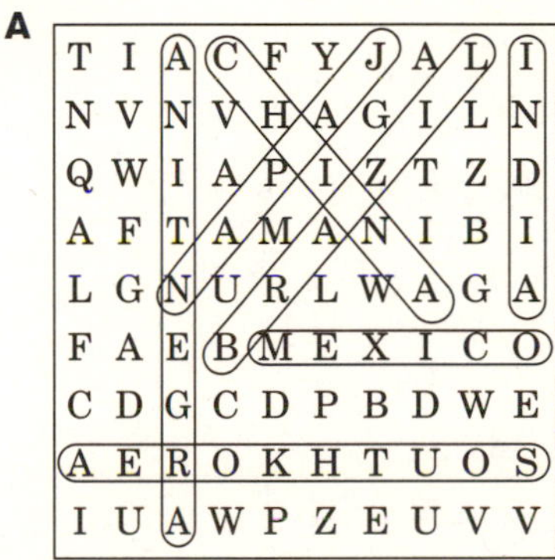

B

1. Bombay and Calcutta are in India.
2. Shanghai is in China.
3. Tokyo and Osaka are in Japan.
4. São Paulo and Rio de Janeiro are in Brazil.
5. Mexico City is in Mexico.
6. Buenos Aires is in Argentina.

Exercise 2

1. A: Is
   B: are *or* 're,
   are *or* 're
   A: are *or* 're
   B: am,
   am *or* 'm
2. A: Is
   B: is *or* 's, is *or* 's
   A: Are
   B: are, are *or* 're, are *or* 're
   B: are, are *or* 're
3. A: Is
   B: is
   A: are
   B: are, are *or* 're
4. A: Is
   B: is, is *or* 's
   A: Is
   B: is, is

Exercise 3

1. No, he is not. He's from Ireland.
2. Yes, they are. They're/They are from Bombay and Calcutta.
3. No, she is not. She's/She is from the United States.
4. No, she is not. She's/She is in Japan.
5. No, they are not. They're/They are in New York.
6. Yes, they are. They're/They are in Sydney.

Exercise 4

1. eleven
2. fifteen
3. fifty
4. one hundred and one
5. twenty-four
6. thirteen
7. seventy
8. thirty
9. nineteen
10. ninety

Exercise 5

Possible adjectives:
Jessica: short, pretty, a little heavy, serious
Victor: tall, thin, good-looking, funny
Susan: shy, smart, pretty, short
Jeff: nice, friendly, good-looking, thin
Jessica and Susan: short, pretty
Victor and Jeff: good-looking, thin

Exercise 6

1. He's from the U.S., and she's from Australia.
2. I'm fine.
3. They're very nice.
4. He's the new math teacher.
5. They're in the U.S. now.
6. He's very smart.
7. She's Soo Mi, and he's Akio.
8. He's twenty-eight.

Exercise 7

1. B: we, We're
   A: What's
   B: My, her, are
2. A: what's
   B: He's, His
   A: Where, Is
   B: not

Exercise 8

Answers will vary.
1. I'm from . . . .
2. My first language is . . . *or* . . . is my first language.
3. I'm . . .
4. My teacher is from . . . . *or* He's/She's from . . . . *or* He/She is from . . . .
5. My teacher is . . . . *or* He's/She's . . . . *or* He/She is . . . .
6. I'm . . . .

4 I'm not wearing boots!

Exercise 1

Woman: belt, jacket, high heels, raincoat, scarf, skirt
Man: hat, shorts, sneakers, socks, swimsuit, T-shirt

Exercise 2

Clothes
For leisure: suit
For cold weather: shorts
For warm weather: boots

Exercise 3

Answers will vary.

Exercise 4

Answers will vary.

Exercise 5

Answers will vary. Possible answers:
1. It's winter. It's very cold.
2. It's spring. It's raining. *or* It's cool/warm.
3. It's summer. It's warm and sunny. *or* It's hot and sunny.
4. It's fall. It's windy and cool.
5. It's summer. It's very hot and humid.
6. It's winter. It's cold and windy.

Exercise 6

A
1. Susan and Oscar are wearing hats.
2. Laurie is wearing jeans.
3. Oscar is wearing pants.
4. Susan is wearing a skirt.
5. Jessica is wearing a swimsuit. *or* Michael, Andy, and Jessica are wearing swimsuits.
6. Oscar and Laurie are wearing T-shirts.
7. Michael and Andy are wearing running shoes.

B
1. No, she isn't/she's not. She's wearing a skirt.
2. No, they aren't/they're not. They're wearing running shoes.
3. No, she isn't/she's not. She's wearing jeans.
4. No, she isn't/she's not. She's wearing a swimsuit.
5. No, they aren't/they're not. They're wearing swimsuits.
6. No, they aren't/they're not They're wearing hats.

Exercise 7

1. *I'm wearing*
   I'm wearing
   I'm not wearing
2. It's
   isn't *or* is not
   's wearing
   isn't wearing *or* is not wearing
   isn't wearing *or* is not wearing
3. and
   aren't wearing *or* are not wearing
   're wearing
   's wearing
   's wearing
4. 's wearing
   isn't wearing *or* is not wearing
   's wearing
   's wearing
   It's

Exercise 8

Answers will vary.

What are you doing?

Exercise 1

1. It's twelve o'clock at night.
2. It's four o'clock in the afternoon.
3. It's nine-fifteen in the morning.
4. It's eight o'clock at night.
5. It's ten forty-five at night.
6. It's three-thirty in the afternoon.
7. It's six o'clock in the evening.

Exercise 2

Suggested answers:

1. It's 10:00 A.M. in Los Angeles.
   It's ten o'clock in the morning.
2. It's 11:00 A.M. in Denver.
   It's eleven o'clock in the morning.
3. It's 12:00 P.M. in Mexico City.
   It's noon.
4. It's 1:00 P.M. in Lima.
   It's one o'clock in the afternoon.
5. It's 2:00 P.M. in Santiago.
   It's two o'clock in the afternoon.
6. It's 3:00 P.M. in Rio de Janeiro.
   It's three o'clock in the afternoon.

Exercise 3

1. It's twenty after nine.
2. It's ten to eight.
3. It's a quarter after one.
4. It's five-oh-five.
5. It's a quarter to three.
6. It's eight after six.

Exercise 4

Across	*Down*
1. A.M.	2. morning
4. after	3. thirty
6. midnight	4. afternoon
8. evening	5. fifteen
9. noon	7. time
	10. night

Exercise 5

1. He's sleeping.
2. He's getting up.
3. He's having breakfast.
4. He's going to work.
5. He's working.
6. He's cooking (dinner).
7. He's eating dinner.
8. He's watching television.
9. He's going to bed.

Exercise 6

1. What are you and Ricky doing? We're eating pizza.
2. What are you and Paul doing? We're cooking dinner.
3. What are you doing? I'm watching television.
4. What are Lisa and Beth doing? They're reading the newspaper.
5. What is James doing? He's studying math.
6. What are you doing? I'm learning/studying English.

Exercise 7

1. They're in English, <u>so</u> they're reading English books.
2. My first name is Kevin, <u>and</u> my last name is Mason.
3. We're hungry, <u>so</u> we're eating dinner.
4. My family and I are from Korea originally, <u>but</u> we're here in the U.S. now.
5. I'm studying, <u>so</u> I'm not watching television.
6. Harold is very good-looking, <u>but</u> he isn't very nice.

Exercise 8

1. No, she isn't. She's sleeping.
2. Yes, they are.
3. No, they aren't. They're dancing.
4. No, she isn't. She's riding a bike.
5. Yes, he is.
6. No, she isn't. She's watching television.
7. Yes, she is.
8. No, I'm not. I'm studying/reading/writing.

Exercise 9

1. Is Terry wearing shorts?
   No, he isn't. He's wearing jeans.
2. Are Pedro and Sonia watching television?
   No, they aren't. They're talking.
3. Is Tai-lin wearing a raincoat?
   Yes, he is.
4. Is Brandon eating pizza?
   Yes, he is.
5. Is Maria dancing?
   No, she's not. She's sleeping.
6. Is Carlos reading the newspaper?
   No, he isn't. He's reading a book.
7. Are Terry and Helen eating?
   No, they aren't. They're dancing.
8. Is Maria wearing boots?
   No, she isn't. She's wearing high heels.

We live in the suburbs.

Exercise 1

A

parents
mother
father
husband
wife
children
daughters
son
sister
brother

B

Answers will vary.

Exercise 2

David: live, has
Sue: walk
David: don't, take, walk
Sue: have, drive, work, works, goes

Exercise 3

s = /s/	s = /z/	(e)s = /ɪz/	irregular
sits	lives	dances	has
takes	goes	uses	does
walks	studies	watches	says

Exercise 4

A

Answers will vary.

B

Answers will vary.

Exercise 5

1. He gets up at 8:00 every day.
2. He goes to work at 9:00 every day.
3. He has lunch at noon every day.
4. He takes a break at 3:00 every day.
5. He finishes work at 5:00 every day.
6. He goes to school at 6:00 on Mondays and Wednesdays.
7. He plays tennis at 6:00 on Tuesdays and Thursdays.
8. He has dinner with friends at 6:00 on Fridays.

Exercise 6

Answers will vary.

Exercise 7

1. A: in, on
   B: at
2. A: in
   B: at, in, on, On, at
3. A: on
   B: at
4. A: in
   B: in, on, in, on

Exercise 8

1. A: Do you live alone?
   B: No, I don't live alone. I live with my family.
2. A: Do you get up late on Sundays?
   B: Yes, I get up late on Sundays. I get up at 11:00.
3. A: Does your sister drive to work?
   B: No, my sister doesn't drive to work. She takes the bus.
4. A: Do you and your family watch television in the evening?
   B: Yes, my family and I watch television in the evening.
5. A: Does your mother have a job?
   B: Yes, my mother has a job.
6. A: Does your mother use public transportation?
   B: No, my mother doesn't use public transportation. She drives to work.
7. A: Does your father work on Saturdays?
   B: No, my father doesn't work on Saturdays.
8. A: Do you have a big dinner on Sundays?
   B: Yes, we have a big dinner on Sundays.

Exercise 9

1. Sam is Sarah's husband.
   Sarah is Sam's wife.
2. We have an apartment in the city.
   We don't live in the suburbs.
3. We use public transportation.
   We take the bus, the train, or the subway.
4. He goes to work in the morning.
   He goes to work before noon.
5. My office is near here.
   I don't work far from here.
6. She sleeps late on Sundays.
   She doesn't get up early on Sundays.

Exercise 10

Answers will vary.

7 Does the apartment have a view?

Exercise 1

1. bedroom
2. bathroom
3. kitchen
4. dining room
5. living room
6. yard
7. closet
8. garage

Exercise 2

1. No, I don't. I have a small apartment on Spring Street.
2. It has three rooms.
3. Yes, it does. It has a beautiful view of the city.
4. Yes, I do. I love it!

Exercise 3

BETSY: Do, live
LAUREN: do, live
BETSY: live
LAUREN: don't, have
BETSY: Do, have
LAUREN: don't, lives
LAUREN: is, cooks
BETSY: live, cook

Exercise 4

Answers will vary.

Exercise 5

1. Does she have a television?
   Yes, she does.
2. Does she need curtains?
   No, she doesn't.
3. Does she need a sofa?
   Yes, she does.
4. Does she have an armchair?
   No, she doesn't.
5. Does she have a rug?
   Yes, she does.
6. Do they have a lamp?
   Yes, they do.
7. Do they need a table?
   Yes, they do.

8. Do they have chairs?
   No, they don't.
9. Do they have a clock?
   Yes, they do.
10. Do they have a mirror?
    No, they don't.

Exercise 6

In Roger's house, there's a big living room. There are two bedrooms and two bathrooms. There's no yard, but there's a balcony. He has a lot of books, so there are bookcases in the living room and bedrooms. There aren't any chairs in the kitchen, but there's a big table with chairs in the dining room. There isn't a stove in the kitchen, but there's a microwave oven. There are two televisions in Roger's house – there's one television in the living room, and there's one television in the bedroom.

Exercise 7

Answers will vary. Possible answers:

1. Yes, there's a window in my kitchen. *or* No, there isn't a window in my kitchen./No, there's no window in my kitchen.
2. Yes, there's a dishwasher in my kitchen. *or* No, there isn't a dishwasher in my kitchen./No, there's no dishwasher in my kitchen.
3. Yes, there's a television in my living room. *or* No, there's no television in my living room./No, there isn't a television in my living room.
4. Yes, there's a mirror in the bathroom. *or* No, there isn't a mirror in the bathroom./No, there isn't a mirror in the bathroom.
5. Yes, there are some pictures in my bedroom. *or* No, there aren't any pictures in my bedroom./No, there are no pictures in my bedroom.
6. Yes, there's a closet in my bedroom. *or* No, there's no closet in my bedroom./No, there isn't a closet in my bedroom.

Exercise 8

A

1. There's no stove in the kitchen./There isn't a stove in the kitchen.
2. There are no chairs in the dining room./There aren't any chairs in the dining room.
3. There's a stove in the living room.
4. There's a refrigerator in the bedroom.
5. There's no bed in the bedroom./There isn't a bed in the bedroom.
6. There are some armchairs in the bathroom.

B

Answers will vary. Possible answers:
There's a bed in the kitchen.
There's no refrigerator in the kitchen./There isn't a refrigerator in the kitchen.

Exercise 9

1. You're lucky.
2. Yes, I do. I need a dresser and a lamp.
3. So let's go shopping on Saturday.
4. There are six.

Exercise 10

Answers will vary.

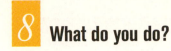

8 What do you do?

Exercise 1

Across	*Down*
1. cashier	1. cook
5. teacher	2. singer
6. nurse	3. receptionist
7. doctor	4. salesperson
8. pilot	

Exercise 2

Answers will vary. Possible answers:

1. She's a doctor. She works in a hospital. She talks to people.
2. He's a waiter. He stands all day/night. He talks to people. He works hard.
3. He's a singer. He works at night. He stands all night. He works hard.
4. She's a police officer. She wears a uniform. She stands all day. She talks to people. She carries a gun.
5. She's a chef. She works at night. She stands all night. She wears a uniform.
6. They are pilots. They sit all day. They wear a uniforms.

Exercise 3

Suggested answers:

1. A: Where does your brother work? What does he do there?
2. A: What do Kelly and Pam do? Where do they work?
3. A: Where does your son work? What does he do there?
4. A: Where do you and Joe work? What do you do there?

Exercise 4

1. A: Do, have
   B: do
   A: do, do
   B: 'm *or* am
   A: do, work
   B: work
   A: Do, like
   B: do
   A: do
   B: start, finish
2. A: has
   B: does, work
   A: works
   B: does, do
   A: 's *or* is
   B: Does, like
   A: does, likes
   B: does, start
   A: starts, finishes

Exercise 5

A

1. exciting d (boring)
2. easy b (difficult)
3. relaxing a (stressful)
4. safe c (dangerous)

B

1. A flight attendant has an exciting job.
2. A security guard's job is boring.
3. Steven has a dangerous job.
4. Ms. Redman has nice students.
5. Linda's apartment is very small.
6. Chris has a very big house.
7. A cashier has a stressful job.
8. Sarah's friend is Italian.

Exercise 6

Answers will vary.

Exercise 7

Answers will vary.

Broccoli is good for you.

Exercise 1

1. mangoes 2. oranges 3. strawberries 4. bananas
5. lettuce 6. tomatoes 7. potatoes 8. carrots
9. rice 10. bread 11. cereal 12. potato chips
13. butter 14. candy 15. milk 16. cheese
17. chicken 18. beans 19. nuts 20. fish

Exercise 2

Answers will vary. (Use *is, are*.)

Exercise 3

Answers will vary.

1. Strawberries are delicious.
2. Cheese is . . . .
3. Broccoli is . . . .
4. Fish is . . . .
5. Potato chips are . . . .
6. Noodles are . . . .
7. Mangoes are . . . .
8. Yogurt is . . . .

Exercise 4

1. B: some
   A: any
   B: some, any, some
   A: any
   B: some, some
   A: any, some
   B: some, some
2. B: some
   A: any
   B: any
   B: some, any
   B: some, any, some

Exercise 5

Suggested answers:

1. You need some bread, some chicken, lettuce, and mayonnaise. You don't need any cheese.
2. You need a (hamburger) roll, some beef, some cheese, an onion, and some ketchup. You don't need any apples.
3. You need some chicken, noodles (or pasta), some carrots, and onions. You don't need any bread.
4. You need some lettuce, broccoli, some tomatoes, carrots, and onions. You don't need any chicken.
5. You need apples, bananas, some mangoes, and strawberries. You don't need any candy.
6. Answer will vary

Exercise 6

1. Americans often put cream in their coffee.
2. Some people in Korea always eat pickled vegetables for breakfast.
3. In China, people seldom use sugar in their tea.
4. In England, people usually have milk in their tea.
5. In Japan, people sometimes have fish for breakfast.
6. Brazilians often make drinks with fruit.
7. People in Canada seldom have salad for breakfast.
8. Some Mexicans never eat pasta.

Exercise 7

Answers will vary.

Exercise 8

Answers will vary.

Exercise 9

Answers will vary.

You can play baseball really well.

Exercise 1

A

Across	*Down*
1. swimming	2. golf
3. baseball	3. bike riding
6. hockey	4. basketball
7. skiing	5. volleyball
8. tennis	9. soccer

B

play:
golf, basketball, volleyball, soccer, baseball, hockey, tennis

go:
bike riding, swimming, skiing

Exercise 2

1. Do you like sports?
2. What do you think of basketball?
3. What sports do you like?
4. Do you play tennis?
5. Does your sister play, too?

Exercise 3

1. Do you like baseball?
2. What sports do you like?
3. What sports do you play?
4. Do you like golf?
5. What do you think of soccer?

Exercise 4

1. Can Andrew fix a car? No, he can't.
2. Can Chris and Nick swim? Yes, they can.
3. Can Rebecca play the piano? Yes, she can.
4. Can Jennifer cook? No, she can't.
5. Can Sue and Lisa draw? Yes, they can. *or* No, they can't.
6. Can Alan ice-skate? Yes, he can.

Exercise 5

1. She can't play the piano, but she can play the guitar.
2. He can use a computer, but he can't repair the TV.
3. She can play soccer, but she can't sing.
4. He can ride a bike, but he can't drive a car.

Exercise 6

1. No, I don't.
2. My sister.
3. It's very exciting.
4. In Colorado.

Exercise 7

A

Answers will vary.

B

Answers will vary.

Exercise 8

1. Yes, I can./No, I can't.
2. Yes, I can./No, I can't.
3. Yes, I can./No, I can't.
4. Yes, I do./No, I don't.
5. Yes, I am./No, I'm not.
6. Yes, I do./No, I don't.
7. Yes, I can./No, I can't.
8. Yes, I do./No, I don't.
9. Yes, I do./No, I don't.
10. Yes, I can./No, I can't.

Exercise 9

1. I hate it.
2. What do you think of it?
3. I like it a lot.
4. He can't sing at all.
5. It's OK.
6. He can play sports very well.

11 What are you going to do?

Exercise 1

A

1. January 2. February 3. March 4. April 5. May 6. June 7. July 8. August 9. September 10. October 11. November 12. December

B

Answers will vary.

C

1. March twelfth
2. September eleventh
3. January sixteenth
4. February ninth
5. October twelfth
6. May tenth
7. July twentieth
8. August twenty-third

Exercise 2

1. Alex is going to be seventy-six on March thirtieth.
2. Anita is going to be twenty-six on July twenty-seventh.
3. Toshi is going to be fifty-one on May fifteenth.
4. Peggy and Patty are going to be nineteen on September thirteenth.
5. Mei is going to be forty-five on August twenty-second.
6. I'm going to be . . . on. . . . .

Exercise 3

1. On February second, she's gong to play golf after work.
2. On February third, she's gong to have lunch with Tony.
3. On February seventh, she's going to go shopping with Julie.
4. On February eighth, she's going to meet John for dinner.
5. On February eleventh, she's going to work late.
6. On February thirteenth, she's gong to go to Sam's party.
7. On February sixteenth, she's going to see a movie with Tony.
8. On February twenty-first, she's going to sleep until noon.
9. On February twenty-fourth, she's going to buy Paula's birthday present.
10. On February twenty-fifth, she's going to go to Paula's birthday dinner.

Exercise 4

1. is going to be
2. are going to see, are going to eat
3. are going to visit, are going to drive, are going to go, is going to love, is not going to like, are going to watch, are going to go
4. am going to sleep, am going to read, am going to take, are going to study

Exercise 5

1. What are you going to do this weekend?
   Where are you going to stay?
   What are you going to do?
   Is your friend going to go with you?
2. Where is it going to be?
   And when is the party going to start?
   Is Bob going to be there?
   Are you going to make a cake?

Exercise 6

Answers will vary.

Exercise 7

Answers will vary.

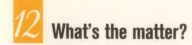

What's the matter?

Exercise 1

1. head 2. eye 3. mouth 4. neck 5. arm
6. stomach 7. leg 8. foot 9. feet 10. hand
11. shoulder 12. teeth 13. nose 14. ear 15. hair

Exercise 2

1. He has an earache.
2. She has a sore throat.
3. She has a stomachache.
4. She has a headache.
5. He has a toothache.
6. She has a cold.

Exercise 3

1.
I'm fine, thanks. How about you?
What's the matter?
Oh, that's too bad.
I hope you feel better soon.

2.
How do you feel tonight?
I'm glad to hear that.
So, are you going to go to school tomorrow?
Great. See you tomorrow.

Exercise 4

1. eyedrops
2. cough drops *or* cough syrup
3. aspirin
4. muscle cream
5. antacid
6. cold pills

Exercise 5

1. What's wrong?
2. I have a sore throat.
3. I'm not happy.
4. I'm sorry to hear that.
5. I miss my family.
6. My head feels terrible.
7. I'm glad to hear that.
8. I'm very tired.

Exercise 6

1. Don't work too hard.
2. Take a hot bath.
3. Don't go outside.
4. Don't lift heavy things.
5. Go home early.
6. Don't go to bed late.
7. Go to the grocery store.
8. Drink some water.

Exercise 7

Answers will vary.

Exercise 8

Answers will vary.

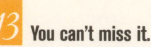

You can't miss it.

Exercise 1

A

1. drugstore 2. hotel 3. supermarket 4. bookstore
5. post office 6. restaurant 7. bank 8. gas station

Z	P	H	K	T	Y	W	X	D	C	H	B	S	S	R
N	D	O	A	W	O	J	R	P	T	O	O	Y	R	E
E	F	M	S	J	D	R	U	G	S	T	O	R	E	S
W	S	C	K	T	F	U	Z	V	N	E	K	T	M	T
S	N	P	W	O	O	H	Y	P	R	L	S	E	L	A
S	S	P	P	U	K	F	N	S	A	Q	T	N	X	U
B	K	O	I	B	Y	S	F	U	Y	W	O	M	I	R
A	G	A	S	S	T	A	T	I	O	N	R	V	G	A
N	E	C	L	F	W	G	P	C	C	M	E	A	O	N
K	S	U	P	E	R	M	A	R	K	E	T	K	G	T

B

1. drugstore 2. bank 3. bookstore 4. post office
5. supermarket 6. hotel 7. gas station 8. restaurant

Exercise 2

1. on
2. behind
3. on the corner of
4. between
5. next to
6. across from

Exercise 3

Answers will vary. Suggested answers:

1. There's a bookstore on the corner of Catherine Street and Fifth Avenue. It's next to the English school.
2. There's a supermarket on Diane Street. It's between Fourth and Fifth Avenues.
3. There's a department store on Beatrice Street. It's between Fourth and Fifth Avenues. It's next to the drugstore.
4. There's a gas station on Fourth Avenue. It's behind the Mexican restaurant.
5. There's a Chinese restaurant on Catherine Street. It's between Sixth and Seventh Avenues.
6. There's a hotel on Catherine Street. It's between Fifth and Sixth Avenues. It's across from the park.
7. There's a post office on Diane Street. It's between Sixth and Seventh Avenues. It's next to the coffee shop.
8. There's a drugstore on Beatrice Street. It's between Fourth and Fifth Avenues. It's between the Mexican restaurant and the department store.

Exercise 4

Excuse me. Can you help me?
Is there a post office around here?
Where on Center Avenue?
Next to the bank?
Thanks a lot.

Exercise 5

1. left
2. behind
3. up
4. near

Exercise 6

Answers will vary.

1. Go up Fifth Avenue for two blocks to Beatrice Street. Turn left. Walk for one block. It's on the right.
2. Walk down Fourth Avenue to Diane Street. Turn left. Walk for three blocks. It's on the left.
3. Go down Sixth Avenue to Catherine Street. Turn right. It's on the right.
4. Walk down Seventh Avenue for two blocks to Diane Street. Turn right. Walk for three blocks. It's on the right.
5. Walk for one block on Ann Street to Sixth Avenue. Turn right. Walk for one block to Barbara Street. Turn left. It's on the left.

Exercise 7

Answers will vary.

14 Did you have a good weekend?

Exercise 1

1. Mrs. Harrison paid bills.
2. Mr. Harrison vacuumed.
3. Janet washed the clothes.
4. John exercised.
5. Andy dusted.
6. Henry worked in the yard.
7. Sarah shopped for groceries.
8. Will cooked dinner.

Exercise 2

Friday: invited, stopped, didn't rent, played, listened, cooked, watched
Saturday: called, invited, needed, walked, started, ended, danced, talked
Sunday: studied, shopped, helped, cleaned, called, didn't talk

Exercise 3

1. Carol studied last weekend. Max didn't study last weekend.
2. Carol cleaned last weekend. Max didn't clean last weekend.
3. Carol didn't play golf last weekend. Max played golf last weekend.
4. Carol and Max cooked last weekend.
5. Carol listened to music last weekend. Max didn't listen to music last weekend.
6. Carol didn't walk in the park last weekend. Max walked in the park last weekend.
7. Carol didn't watch television last weekend. Max watched television last weekend.

Exercise 4

bought, came, drank, eat, felt, get up, went, had, meet, read, see, slept

Exercise 5

KEVIN: did, have
MEGAN: had, visited
KEVIN:
MEGAN: didn't feel, went, slept
KEVIN: Did, have
MEGAN: played, had, ate
KEVIN: Did, get up
MEGAN: got up
KEVIN: Did, feel
MEGAN: felt, stayed, went
KEVIN: Did, see
MEGAN: saw, loved

Exercise 6

Questions below. Answers will vary.

1. A: Did you sleep well last night?
2. A: Did you read the newspaper yesterday?
3. A: Did you have a good breakfast this morning?
4. A: Did you drink any tea this morning?
5. A: Did you play any sports yesterday?
6. A: Did you meet any interesting people?
7. A: Did you buy anything yesterday?
8. A: Did you see a movie last weekend?

Answers will vary.

Exercise 7

1. On Friday night, she read a book.
2. On Saturday morning, she exercised.
3. On Saturday afternoon, she played the piano.
4. On Saturday night, she ate/had dinner at a restaurant.
5. On Sunday morning, she got up at 11:30 A.M./slept late.
6. On Sunday afternoon, she read the newspaper.
7. On Sunday afternoon, she slept.
8. On Sunday night, she went to the movies /saw a movie.

Exercise 8

Answers will vary.

15 Where were you born?

Exercise 1

1. No, I wasn't. I was born in the Caribbean.
2. No, I'm from the Dominican Republic.
3. I was born in Puerto Plata.
4. Yes, they were. We were all born there.
5. I came to the U.S. to study English.
6. It was in San Diego.
7. I moved here in 1998.
8. No, it wasn't. I loved it.

Exercise 2

1. PETER: weren't
   DAVID: wasn't, was
   PETER: was
   DAVID: was
   PETER: Were
   DAVID: weren't, was, was
2. SUE: Were
   KIM: was, were
   SUE: was, Were
   KIM: wasn't, was, was
   SUE: were
3. NANCY: Were
   CHUCK: wasn't
   NANCY: were
   CHUCK: was
   NANCY: Were

CHUCK: wasn't, was
NANCY: was
CHUCK: was

Exercise 3

1. Bruce Lee was an actor. He was born in 1940 in the United States. He was in the movie *Enter the Dragon* in 1973. He died in 1973.
2. Roberto Clemente was a baseball player. He was born in 1934 in Puerto Rico. He became a member of the Baseball Hall of Fame in 1973. He died in 1972.
3. Marie Curie was a scientist. She was born in 1867 in Poland. She won the Nobel Prize for Chemistry in 1911. She died in 1934.
4. Audrey Hepburn was an actress. She was born in 1929 in Belgium. She was in the movie *Breakfast at Tiffany's* in 1961. She died in 1993.
5. Georgia O'Keeffe was a painter. She was born in 1887 in the United States. She painted *White Flower* in 1929. She died in 1986.
6. Ernest Hemingway was a novelist. He was born in 1899 in the United States. He wrote *The Old Man and the Sea* in 1952. He died in 1961.

Exercise 4

Answers will vary.

Exercise 5

1. What
2. Who
3. When
4. Where
5. What
6. Why
7. How
8. How old

Exercise 6

1. A: Where were you at midnight last night?
2. A: How was your weekend?
3. A: What did you do on the weekend?
4. A: How old were you on your last birthday?
5. A: When was your last vacation?
6. A: Where did you go on your vacation?

Answers will vary.

Exercise 7

1. Were you born in the United States?
2. Was your first English teacher born in the United States?
3. Did you grow up in a big city?
4. Do you have any brothers and sisters?
5. Do you live with your family now?
6. Did you live with your family last year?
7. Were you in high school last year?
8. Did you take an English class last year?
9. Are you going to take an English class next year?

Answers will vary.

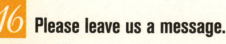

16 Please leave us a message.

Exercise 1

BILLY: Hello?
CLAIRE: Hi, Billy. It's Claire.
BILLY: Oh, hi, Claire.
CLAIRE: Can I speak to Linda, please?
BILLY: I'm sorry, she's not here right now.
CLAIRE: Oh. Can you give her a message?
BILLY: Sure. What's the message?
CLAIRE: Please ask her to call me.
BILLY: OK. Give me your number.
CLAIRE: It's 555-0662.
BILLY: 555-0662. Got it.
CLAIRE: Thanks, Billy.
BILLY: No problem. Bye.
CLAIRE: Bye-bye.

Exercise 2

1. Is Jorge there, please?
   . . . he isn't here. He's at the library.
2. Is Diane there, please?
   . . . she's not here. She's at the beach.
3. Are Brian and Jane there, please?
   . . . they're not here. They're at the mall.
4. Is Pravit there, please?
   . . . he's not. He's in the hospital.
5. Is Laurie there, please?
   . . . but she's in the shower.
6. Are Ross and Dan there, please?
   . . . No, I'm sorry, they're not. They're in class.

Exercise 3

A

me, you, him, her, it, us, you, they

B

BOB: me, it, us, me
JIM: you, you, her, her, me, them, me, him

Exercise 4

RAY: Can, please
SAM: but, in, her
RAY: This, give, at
SAM: have
RAY: it

Exercise 5

Answers will vary.

Exercise 6

Answers will vary. Suggested answers:

1. Hi, this is Amy.
2. Can I talk to Barbara?
3. I'd like to go to the movies tonight.
4. Does he have my number?
5. I'm hungry.
6. I'm busy.

Exercise 7

Answers will vary.

Exercise 8

Answers will vary.

1. I like to . . . .
2. I want to visit . . . .
3. I want to meet . . . .
4. I need to . . . .
5. I like to go . . . .
6. I need to . . . .
7. I like to . . . .
8. I want to . . . .